# A REAL MIND

Law and Philosophy Library

VOLUME 87



For further volumes:
http://www.springer.com/series/6210

# A REAL MIND

## THE LIFE AND WORK OF AXEL HÄGERSTRÖM

by

PATRICIA MINDUS

Springer

Dr. Patricia Mindus
Dipartimento Studi Politici
Universitè degli Studi di Torino
Via Giolitti 33
10124 Turin
Italy
patricia.mindus@unito.it

ISBN 978-90-481-2894-5 e-ISBN 978-90-481-2895-2
DOI 10.1007/978-90-481-2895-2
Springer Dordrecht Heidelberg London New York

Library of Congress Control Number: 2009933681



Printed on acid-free paper

Springer is part of Springer Science+Business Media (www.springer.com)

# Contents

# Introduction: The Rare Renown of a Swedish Scholar

Axel Hägerström (1868–1939) is the most eminent name in modern Swedish philosophy. He co-founded the Uppsala School and is considered to be the inspirational source of Scandinavian legal realism. Notwithstanding his relevance and even popularity in some parts of the world – notably Scandinavia and the Latin speaking world – what his English translator, Robert Sandin, claimed in 1959 is still true: «The study of the philosophy of Hägerström in American and British circles is really long overdue.»[1] Based on his complete work, including unpublished material and personal correspondence, this book aims to fill the void. It offers a comprehensive picture of Hägerström's life and work within the framework of the philosophy of his day, by summarising the main arguments and issues so as to enable further critical assessment.

From a theoretical standpoint, it is often claimed that Scandinavian realism survives «only in the museums of jurisprudential archeology.»[2] The present work intends to show why this is not so. «The recurrent "obituaries" are themselves in fact proof of Hägerström's confirmed presence and the virulence of his thought, which is not yet fully incorporated into the body of social thought, despite the fact that he addresses precisely the central topics on the postmodernist agenda.»[3]

For the legal and political scholar with some interest in philosophy, Hägerström is a classic author for three reasons: An extraordinary interpreter of his own time, he left his mark on his contemporaries; his thought continues to suggest interesting and contrasting readings, which is proved by the fact that he is repeatedly studied by each new generation of scholars; finally, he developed general categories that we still use today to understand the world we now live in. But, like all classic authors, Hägerström is by no means the object of any simple interpretation.

Here, the complex web of issues he addressed is located within the broader context of twentieth century philosophy, stretching from epistemology to theory of

[1] R. Sandin, *Axel Hägerström's Philosophy of Religion, with Special Reference to His Philosophy of Knowledge and His Concept of Reality*, Ann Arbor University Microfilm, Michigan 1959, p. 1.

[2] F. Schauer, V. J. Wise, *Legal Positivism as Legal Information*, in «Cornell Law Review», 1996–1997, p. 1081.

[3] S. Eliaeson, *Axel Hägerström and Modern Social Thought*, in «Nordeuropaforum», 2000:1, p. 21.

law. This account follows the chronological progression of his intellectual career. The starting chapter reflects his background and the cultural milieu that influenced him. Originally educated in nineteenth-century-idealism, and later converting to early twentieth-century neo-Kantianism, Hägerström developed theories in parallel with – yet independently from – some of the major philosophical currents in Europe, namely neo-empiricism and logical positivism. Like the Cambridge and Vienna schools, Hägerström firmly believed in Hume's thesis, the need to distinguish between *is* and *ought*, facts and values. But unlike these philosophical movements, his analysis of language, at least in his earlier writings, is less central than his attention to psychology (as developed mainly by Franz Brentano and Alexius Meinong).

Focus then switches to Hägerström's theory of reality and its genesis (Chapter 2). It is this thesis that brought many scholars to accredit him with being the *real mind* behind the epistemological realism which later inspired legal realism. Hägerström, who was very knowledgeable about the neo-Kantian movement, quite popular among German scholars at that time, moved towards ontological monism by criticising the Marburg school's credo: «Nothing is given to thought except thought itself» (*Nichts ist dem Denkens gegeben außer dem Denken selbst*). In his *Kants Ethik im Verhältnis zu seinen erkenntnistheoretischen Grundgedanken systematisch darstellt* (1902), he offered an uncompromising anti-psychologistic reading of Kant. He stressed that the object of knowledge, for Kant, is not psychological in its nature, but rather a timeless logical principle. In slight opposition to this position, Hägerström later developed a form of radical anti-metaphysical objectivism by arguing that the fundamental error of modern philosophy consists in the idea of consciousness as the only self-evident datum. All in all this is the core of Hägerström's *Copernican revolution*: Consciousness refers to something else than itself and, therefore, the objectivity of knowledge has to relate to the nature of the object.

Some years later, in his treatise *Das Prinzip der Wissenschaft. Eine logisch-erkenntnistheoretische Untersuchung* (1908), Hägerström aimed to demonstrate three further theses. First, he considers the fundamental assumption of subjectivism (consciousness is the only self-evident datum) to be wrong, because the knowledge we think we have concerning our own consciousness presupposes time and space. If consciousness was not inserted into the all-encompassing spatio-temporal world of experience, knowledge would be impossible. Secondly, Hägerström argued that the classical postulation of philosophy, according to which the world we perceive is defined by logical form and non-logical matter, is misleading since the apparent world as such is perfectly logical. This stance later brought him to argue, broadly speaking, that "the space-and-time context" coincides with the only real world. Finally, metaphysics – i.e., the search for an absolute entity upon which the world is founded or the attribution of existence to an indeterminate property – must be considered fallacious because it tends to identify reality with a single part of it; e.g., matter for materialism or spirit for spiritualism. Thus metaphysics would hold other parts of reality as "less real." On the contrary, for Hägerström, every determination of reality by something else presupposes the reality of the latter. Therefore, reality cannot be defined or determined by something else because what determines reality must then be considered reality as such.

The greater part of Hägerström's later writings left aside the theoretical problems he dealt with in the earlier stages of his scholarship, but his third thesis concerning metaphysics actually formed the thread of Ariadne in his teachings. In his account of his own philosophy in *Die Philosophie der Gegenwart in Selbstdarstellungen* (1929), Hägerström adopted as motto a modified version of Cato's aphorism, *praeterea censeo metaphysicam esse delendam*: Metaphysics is nothing but a compilation of words which happen to be connected with emotions. What distinguishes this assumption from other anti-metaphysical positions – quite recurrent in the history of ideas since nineteenth-century positivism – is that the "superstitious" web of metaphysical beliefs spreads its mantle not only over the humanities or *Geisteswissenschaften*, but over natural science as well.

Hägerström's scholarship focused mainly on the epistemological nature of norms that are, in his words, «neither true, nor false.» This very approach came to be called *axiological nihilism*, but it does not share much with nihilism as a philosophical movement. Chapter 3 is dedicated to this "value nihilism" that Hägerström developed in ethics. He was appointed professor of practical philosophy in 1911 and he thus spent much of his time dealing with moral, political, and legal aspects of philosophy. Whereas his early theoretical writings received attention only in academic circles and for a limited time, his practical philosophy, especially his axiological nihilism, was widely discussed and harshly criticised for decades in the public debate. This is the specific point that later jurists found attractive and which makes him the "father" of Scandinavian legal realism. Since truth, according to Hägerström, is defined by logical determination (absence of contradiction) and corresponds to the reality of the object, there can be no knowledge of values. He argued that values are expressions of feelings, and not judgments about reality.[4] His argument is that if values were judgments about reality, their emotional content could be separated from the feeling itself, which is not the case. Hence, in our judgments about values we are not really judging anything. Rather we are expressing, in the linguistic form of a judgment or assertion, an emotion connected by association to a representation or conception. The belief in the objectivity of values arises from the habit of associating emotions with specific ideas. In turn, this habit is grounded in education and depends on two factors. The command needs to be

[4]A. Hägerström, *Kritiska punkter i värdepsykologien*, in *Festskrift tillägnad E.O. Burman*, Appelgrens boktr., Uppsala 1910, pp. 17–75; *Om moraliska föreställningars sanning*, Bonniers, Stockholm 1911 [translated in A. Hägerström, *Philosophy and Religion*, Allen & Unwin, London 1964; by T. Mautner, *On the Truth of Moral Ideas*, ANU, Canberra, 1971; German translation by D. Lang, *Über die Wahrheit moralischer Vorstellungen* in «Perspektiven der Philosophie», 1979, pp. 219–242]; *Till frågan on den objektiva rättens begrepp*, I: *Viljeteorien*, Almqvist & Wiksell, Uppsala 1917 [translated by C.D. Broad in *Inquiries into the Nature of Law and Morals* (ed. Karl Olivecrona), Almqvist & Wiksell, Stockholm 1953]; *Socialfilosofiska uppsatser*, Bonniers, Stockholm 1939, 2nd ed. 1961.

derived from some kind of authority (parents, teachers, public authorities or statesmen) which has, in some fashion, a symbolic grip on the individual. Furthermore, the different commands have to overlap to some extent in society. The idea that a certain action is good, for instance, is accentuated in individuals by the fact that they find similar ideas about the rightness of that specific action in the social environment. All in all, the belief in the objectivity of values derives from the so-called "suggestive effect" which authority has upon the individual due to its symbolic dimension. Predicates of value (good, evil...) are therefore connected to expressions of emotions. Hägerström's emphasis on the importance of the symbolic dimension of power can be considered one of the motives that brought Ernst Cassirer to study Hägerström's thought.[5]

Hägerström's philosophy of law is examined in the core chapters of the book (Chapters 4 and 5), with emphasis on the will-theory and the relationship between law and power, foremost political. In general terms, we can say that his non-cognitivist approach, combined with some elements taken from error-theory implies that no knowledge is really possible about rights and duties. So, to be conscious of your duty actually means that you are experiencing the emotion of being bound by a psychological association with an action considered to be the right one. Since Hägerström endorsed the idea that no social system can survive by grounding obedience to the law only on fear of punishment and hence on the mere use of power, the feeling of duty played a significant role in his legal and political thought. Moreover, by "legal system" Hägerström meant the normative system that effectively coordinates the State's action. This way of considering law is quite similar to legal positivism, but the recurrent emphasis on efficiency and the actual functioning of the legal system is not too far from an institutional theory of law. The nature of the normative system does not depend on formalism, rather it is grounded in a system of interest among social classes.

As far as alternative philosophical answers are concerned, Hägerström has two different rivals: Legal positivism and natural law theories. On one side, legal positivism claims that (civil) law is an expression of the will of the Sovereign, and so the legal dilemma is ultimately a question of deriving the validity of law from entitlement. Hägerström's critique of this position, which seems a little rudimentary compared to the work of other contemporary jurists, like Maurice Hauriou and Santi Romano for instance, does not truly hit the core of the issue. In opposition to Hans Kelsen,[6] Hägerström claimed that the State has really no will at all, since only

[5] E. Cassirer, *Axel Hägerström. Eine Studie zur schwedischen Philosophie der Gegenwart*, Göteborgs högskolas årskrift, Göteborg 1939; now in *Gesammelte Werke. Nachgelassene Manuskripte und Texte* (eds. K. Ch. Köhnke, J. M. Krois, O. Schwemmer), Bd. 21, Meiner, Hamburg 2005.

[6] As far as philosophy is concerned, Hägerström insisted against pragmatism and *Wertphilosophie* that facts cannot be reduced to values, and against positivism that values cannot be reduced to facts. Kelsen also stressed this conceptual dualism. However, Hägerström and Kelsen did not share the same ontology. While Kelsen treated *Sein* and *Sollen* as given distinct statuses, Hägerström criticised Kelsen for his preposterous two-world metaphysics (see Hägerström's review of *Hans*

human beings, and not collective associations, are able to form a will in psychological terms. In this way, however, Hägerström's problem is no longer of strictly jurisprudential nature. Rather, what is interesting in Hägerström's criticism of legal positivism is that he clearly stresses the feedback effect of the legal system on the individual's beliefs and actions (and vice versa), a point that legal positivism hardly ever makes.[7]

On the other hand, natural law theories, which are nothing but primitive metaphysical beliefs in Hägerström's view, seem to begin where Hägerström left the problem open. Just like the more classical theories of natural law, Hägerström presupposed some kind of "common sense of justice" although he maintained that legal norms certainly do not derive their binding force from such a "common feeling." On the contrary, the binding force depends on the effectiveness of law and, more generally, on social institutions. This produces, however, a vicious circle: What Hägerström called the "consciousness of justice," caused by the overlapping moral claims of authorities in a society, is nothing but a common sense of justice. So, the main difference between natural law theories and Hägerström's idea of such a common sense depends on its basis. For Hägerström, there is no need to refer to any supreme being, to the ontological structure of the Universe, to any phenomenological necessity, etc. since the common sense of justice can be adequately explained in genealogical terms. Once the genesis and historical evolution of a given set of norms is clarified, the common sense of justice should appear as self-evident to whoever realises that norms, and thus rights and duties are, by no means objective, yet they are necessary. The question then becomes political in nature: What rights and duties can plausibly be considered necessary for peaceful living? Would the very same sense of justice be adopted in a traditional society characterised by metaphysical thinking and in a society in which the veil of Maya, i.e., the belief in the objectivity of values, has fallen?

---

*Kelsen. Allgemeine Staatslehre* [Springer, Berlin 1925] in «Litteris. An International Critical Review of the Humanities», 1928, 5, pp. 81–99; English translation by C.D. Broad, entitled *Kelsen's Theory of Law and the State* in *Inquiries*, cit., pp. 257–298). See Åke Frändberg, *Die skandinavische Reaktion auf Hans Kelsens Reine Rechtslehre*, in *Einfluss der Reinen Rechtslehre auf die Rechtstheorie in verschiedenen Ländern*, Manz, Wien 1978, pp. 69–97. As far as personal relations are concerned, Kelsen came into contact with the school of Uppsala through Anders Wedberg, who also translated *General Theory of Law and State* into English. In 1933, the Swedish translation of *Die Reine Rechtslehre* was published (*Den rena rättsläran. Dess metod och grundbegrepp*, in «Statsvetenskaplig Tidskrift», 36, 1933, pp. 193–244) and this is why Kelsen journeyed to Sweden in March to lecture in Lund, Uppsala and Stockholm (see R.A. Métall, *Hans Kelsen. Leben und Werk*, Franz Deuticke, Wien 1969, p. 61). While the Uppsala philosophers well remembered Kelsen, the latter did not: His *Vortragsreise* in Scandinavia happened in the same period as his Köln days came to an abrupt end. With the rise of Nazism to power, Kelsen, as a filo-liberal-socialist, had to leave Germany under unpleasant circumstances (see R.A. Métall, *Hans Kelsen. Leben und Werk*, cit., pp. 68 ff.).

[7]For a framing of the interactions between the legal field and the sphere of conviction, foremost political, in relation to the major current schools of legal theory, see M. Zamboni, *The Policy of Law. A Legal-Theoretical Framework*, Hart, Oxford 2007.

The key issue upon which Hägerström's scholarship sheds light, and that has also been the focal point of the philosophical controversies concerning his thought, is whether axiological nihilism and the belief in the unscientific nature of norms necessarily lead to forms of scepticism or nihilism in moral, political and legal action. The problem is whether the assumption that norms are *neither true, nor false* (i.e., that legal norms can neither be derived from a "common sense of justice" nor from the positive will of the Sovereign State) entails moral and legal relativism that, ultimately, ends up in sheer nihilism. Here I show why Hägerström believed this was not the case. Legal norms need to be considered as a stratification of inter-subjective and effective symbolic forms of language which underpins both obligation (especially political obligation) and its counterpart, authority. By considering norms from such a viewpoint, Hägerström believed he had found a way to avoid the idea of Thrasymachus in Plato's *Republic* (Rep. I, 338 c), namely the reduction of law to the mere use of power.

One of the most recurring false ideas among scholars concerning Hägerström's theory of law and his political philosophy, is therefore that it leaves no room for «substantial normative inquiries into the law and its application.»[8] There are various levels of argumentation in objecting to this thesis. For Hägerström, non-cognitivism does not mean that norms cannot be issued. It does imply, however, that, in moral reasoning, its basic assumption – value – is only posited as an axiom that cannot be justified as such. Hence, we reason and argue *from* a certain starting point, not *on* the value as such. If this were not so, non-cognitivism would imply a ban on reasoning in ethics as purely irrational. This ambiguity had led some to embrace the counterintuitive conclusion that the critical fury of Hägerström was actually not at all what it seemed: «The moral implication of the lack of moral knowledge is that there can be no moral criticism of the positive law. This in turn has political implications concerning the "bitter strife between capital and labour" (. . .) [since] the strife cannot be solved by the appeal to moral reasoning grounded on universal principles to arrive at political solutions that aim to create a just society.»[9] This reading of Hägerström's moral teachings has on many occasions led to its bleeding over on the political side. Hägerström is thus depicted as the father of Scandinavian state absolutism, or accused of being the mascot of social-democracy, or generally attributed all kinds of twentieth century evils, including – at the extremes of the journalistic debate – that of Nazism.

This brings us to Hägerström's views on politics which I address in Chapter 6. In his own view, mankind would fall back into despotism and ultimately anarchy without the "suggestive effect" of authority. Through symbolic means, this is what allows the psychological association that makes us act according to what we consider to be

[8] For a recent account see J. Bjarup, *Ought and Reality. Hägerström's Inaugural Lecture Reconsidered* in P. Wahlgren (ed.), «Scandinavian Studies in Law», vol. 40, Almqvist & Wiksell, Stockholm 2000, p. 72.

[9] J. Bjarup, *The Philosophy of Scandinavian Legal Realism*, in «Ratio Juris», 2005, vol. 18, n. 1, p. 5.

our moral duty. This view, however, is not grounded in authoritarianism and heteronomy, but rather in a call for autonomous ethical reasoning and tolerance, combined with a strong faith in the democratic form of government and an enlightenment-inspired view of history. The strength of Hägerström's position depends on the fact that it stresses some social factors that need to be considered as necessary preconditions for a well functioning society. In particular, Hägerström pointed to the central function of education and social cohesion. This is why he claims that axiological nihilism does not lead to practical nihilism, but rather entails a new (and, according to him, more scientific and thus nobler) way of thinking about norms. Obedience therefore will no longer depend on the fear of punishment, or on "superstition" (in his own vocabulary, "metaphysical beliefs"), but rather on a shared comprehension of why norms are necessary for social life and a deeper understanding of how society really works. Consensus thus plays an important role in the Hägerströmian conception of law, even though its origin is often unclear and buried in past times. However, the very fact that the definition of duty – as a crucial element for ensuring consensus – may vary considerably from person to person does not seem to bother Hägerström as he presupposed large overlaps among the commands of different authorities. This idea points to a conformist vision of society, and this has to be considered a weak point in Hägerström's theory since it rests on a fundamentally static view of society, hardly comparable to what usually goes under the name of globalisation or, *a fortiori*, multiculturalism.

Given that Hägerström dedicated his last years to the study of law from an historical viewpoint and to the critical assessment of epistemology, the final chapter of the book focuses on these two topics (Chapter 7). Since he argued as early as the first two decades of the twentieth century that there can be no teaching *in* morals, but only *about* morals, the moral phenomenon in human life can only be studied from a historical, genealogical (in Nietzsche's sense) and/or sociological perspective. Such studies aim to highlight how the values of a specific morality came to be shaped, rather than a theoretical standpoint wanting to compare different sets of values. Hägerström embarked on such a journey in his quite controversial studies on the history of legal thought,[10] that seem to provide a kind of case study for his more general theoretical theses found in other essays.[11] The thread of Ariadne in *Der römische Obligationsbegriff* is that the model of civil rights in Roman law which still influences modern legal systems, originated in a specifically juridical form of magic, rooted in animistic beliefs. Obligation, both political and strictly legal, derives from the archaic conception whereby the person owing the obligation was literally under the potential power of the person to whom he owed allegiance or obligation, a power that could be activated through specific ceremonies in the case of

[10]See foremost A. Hägerström, *Der römische Obligationsbegriff im Lichte der allgemeinen römischen Rechtsanschauung*, vols. 1–2, Almqvist & Wiksell, Uppsala-Leipzig 1927–1941; *Das magistratische Ius in seinem Zusammenhang mit dem römischen Sakralrechte*, in *Minnesskrift utgiven av Juridiska fakulteten i Uppsala 1929 till hågkomst av dess första doktorspromotion 1629*, Lundequistska bokh., Uppsala 1929.

[11]For instance, A. Hägerström, *Socialfilosofiska uppsatser*, cit.

disobedience. In order to demonstrate this and other fundamental ideas, Hägerström used a quite eclectic pattern of sources, including philosophers like Kant, Hegel, Marx, Nietzsche and Kierkegaard, psychologists like Franz Brentano and Wilhelm Wundt, sociologists like Émile Durkheim and James Frazer, anthropologists like Edward Westermarck, and many more. This bring us to the *vexata quaestio* of the sources.

While writing this book, I often hesitated on whether to complete the formidable task of bringing to unity such a complex network of sources and ideas. One reason for accomplishing it was that I so often found sheer misconceptions of this quite obscure twentieth century Swede and it is not hard to understand why:

Notwithstanding that Axel Hägerström was unquestionably the most notable among Swedish philosophers and the father of Scandinavian Legal Realism, and despite the fact that generations of scholars have studied his thought, no critical or complete edition of his work has ever been published. This makes an accurate reconstruction of his real thought just as needed as it is impervious. A few texts have been translated into English, but the greater part of these were translated by Robert Sandin, an American who learnt Swedish very swiftly and who translated just as fast, making flaws inevitable. Moreover, in the original language, some of his writings are virtually impossible to come across. Other books of his can be found in unopened and totally intact exemplars in Swedish libraries, saying a lot on how many actually read them. Hägerström also left a significant amount of manuscripts after his death; this material has been subjected to classification, re-ordering and editing of varying quality. The appendix provides a bibliography, cataloguing various types of literature and adding extra information. The appendix also includes a chronology with a brief synopsis of the major events in his life, both private and intellectual. All this material serves the purpose of a map.[12]

In addition to this, the secondary literature on Hägerström is of extremely variable quality: It stretches from old-school literary analysis to short papers that require a wide range of technical skills; it includes voluminous and broadly circulating academic material of the regular kind and narrow biographical sketches, not to mention

[12]Some scholars have pointed out that it would not be truthful to use Hägerström's lectures and unpublished work. The argument goes: If all this material meant so much to him, he would have published it. There are several counterarguments: During his life he published material that he recognized as less significant (he participated in *liber amicorum* for friends, he responded to other friends who asked him to write papers. See for instance *Per Persson. En Biografi*, in *Kungliga Svenska Vetenskapsakademiens årsbok för år 1931*, Almqvist and Wiksell, Uppsala 1931, pp. 350–352; *Sydney Alrutz in memoriam; Tab. III, 1–3 des Zwölftafelgesetzes*, in *Symbolae philologicae. O.A. Danielson octogenario dicatae*, A. Nelson (ed.), Lundequistska Bokhandeln, Uppsala 1932, pp. 113–121) while he never managed to publish some of the work he spent most of his time on, like the second volume of *Obligationsbegriff*, that came out 3 years after his death and that he worried about so much during his last weeks. It should also be remembered that scholars usually use all the material they can find, because the date of death is not a good watermark. Otherwise, we would not study John Austin's *Lectures on Jurisprudence*, Alexandre Kojève's *Phénoménologie du droit*, or a great part of Hegel's production. Western thought would be drastically reduced if we were to read only material published in life.

that the inexperienced reader is unlikely to stumble upon the best studies. Moreover, the secondary sources are written in a variety of languages, including Swedish, English, German, French, Italian, and Spanish, and cover many scientific fields, from legal science to the history of physics. Svante Nordin, a specialist on history of Scandinavian philosophy who is very knowledgeable on Hägerström, believes that «the scholar who wants to write on Hägerström has to struggle with a quite vast secondary literature. It varies in quality and leaves, notwithstanding its width, many problems unsolved.»[13] I agree.

As far as the *status quaestionis* is concerned, the different readings can be ordered into two major currents. On one hand, there are those who developed an interest in Hägerström primarily as the founder of the Uppsala school, and specifically as the *founder of modern non-cognitivism* in ethics; therefore these scholars directed their attention to his role in the history of twentieth century philosophy, concerning foremost practical but also theoretical philosophy. In this group, prominent names such as Alfred Ayer, Charles L. Stevenson, R.M. Hare, Steven Satris should be listed, along with the translators and editors Robert Sandin, Martin Fries, C.D. Broad and Thomas Mautner; and more broadly the Swedish intellectuals Ingmar Hedenius, Konrad Marc-Wogau, Anders Wedberg, Herbert Tingsten, Gunnar Myrdal, Manfred Moritz, Svante Nordin, Sven Danielsson, Bo Petersson, and Hans Ruin. Many of these authors were themselves ethical thinkers, analytical philosophers or historians of philosophy. They focused on Hägerström because he was held to be the first thinker to have developed an elaborate version of what was to become one of the most important – and criticized – currents in contemporary meta-ethical theory. This aspect was also the feature that aroused the interest of the greater public: There was a time when journalists as well as the (educated) public opinion made both the fame and the notoriety of his name.

On the other hand, there are those interpreters that discovered a "third way" in Hägerström; a position different from both natural law theories and legal positivism. This position of Hägerström naturally led both to criticisms and to further the interest for his controversial insertion into the great dichotomy separating the two traditional schools of thought in jurisprudence and philosophy of law. The alternative that he came to represent as the *spiritual father of Scandinavian legal realism*, in legal and political theory, may be mentioned as motivation behind the interest of scholars such as Vilhelm Lundstedt, Karl Olivecrona, Alf Ross, Herbert Hart, Silvana Castignone, Enrico Pattaro, Liborio Hierro, Carla Faralli, John Rawls, N.E. Simmonds, Åke Frändberg, Jes Bjarup, Jacob Sundberg, Folke Schmidt, Stig Strömholm, and lately, Claes Peterson, Marie Sandström, and Max Lyles. If Scandinavian realism represented a live option and was often called on to offer new perspectives on some fundamental issues in philosophy of law, Hägerström was seen as the key unlocking the door to an innovative jurisprudential debate.

---

[13]S. Nordin, *Från Hägerström till Hedenius. Den moderna svenska filosofin*, Doxa, Lund 1984, p. 25: «den som skiver om Hägerström har att kämpa med en tämligen omfattande sekundärlitteratur. Denna är av skiftande kvalitet och lämnar trots sitt omfång många problem olösta.»

I have faced both of these types of interpretation that have proven useful for me to confront and to come to terms with.[14] Perhaps, I should add another course to the mainstream readings: Special mention should be made of Ernst Cassirer whose analysis is different from the abovementioned outlooks since his interpretation is both a methodological criticism and a philosophical dialogue against the background of his own thought.

In the same way we lack a critical edition of Hägerström's work, the secondary literature offers no general outline or critical review of the studies made. Presenting such a report would therefore constitute another key undertaking that I will nonetheless leave to another.

In addition to this, Hägerström enjoyed for a very long time the reputation of being a "free thinker."[15] This means that scholarly work on Hägerström's sources is rather scarce.[16] He was usually depicted as the great pioneer whose sources and influences need not be mapped. To make matters worse, there are not many great works on the history of Swedish philosophy in general.[17]

Now, a word on purpose and choice of material is needed. The intention is to offer a comprehensive presentation, in the tradition of *Leben und Lehre*, based on a transdisciplinary approach that reflects Hägerström's various interests, against the background of the contemporary streaming of ideas. The method stems from the understanding that it is just as vain to appreciate concepts without context as vice versa. I have chosen to disregard no primary material, which often implies a choice between various formulations of the same idea. Hence, I systematically selected the material through two criteria: The clearest account and the lesser known source. Only in cases where the quotation is fairly well-known do I use the standard formula. In translating, I rely on the existing English versions, but disregard them in the event of inaccuracy. For the benefit of the reader, I translate all foreign quotes in the main body of the text, leaving the original version in the footnotes as well as all

---

[14] See bibliography at the end for references to these works.

[15] Hägerström famously claimed «I have not been significantly influenced by contemporary philosophy, on account of what is, in my opinion, its uncritical point of departure.» (*Philosophy and Religion*, Allen & Unwin, London 1964, p. 38). This observation, as we shall see in Chapter 2, was probably ungenerous and directed against the diatribe on the "paternity" of the Uppsala school; see also *Moralfilosofins grundläggning*, Almqvist & Wiksell International, Stockholm 1987, pp. 16 ff.

[16] One rare example of such a study can be found in S. Nordin, *Från Hägerström till Hedenius*, cit., pp. 27 ff.

[17] Mention has to be made of Svante Nordin's trilogy (*Den Boströmska skolan och den svenska idealismens fall*, Doxa, Lund 1981; *Från Hägerström till Hedenius*, cit.; *Den svenska liberalismens historia*, Timbro, Stockholm 1999) and his *Filosofins historia: det västerländska förnuftets äventyr*, Studlitt., Lund 2005; T. T:son Segerstedt, *Boströms betydelse i svenskt kulturliv*, in «Ord och bild», 1947, vol. 56; *Den Boströmska filosofin och det svenska samhället*, in «Lychnos», 1977/1978, pp. 1–9. The "classic" study of A. Nyblaeus, *Den filosofiska forskningen i Sverige från slutet av adertonde århundradet*, vols. I-IV, Gleerup, Lund 1873–1897; and Svenbjörn Kilander's PhD thesis *Den nya staten och den gamla. En studie i ideologisk förändring*, Studia historica upsaliensia 164, Acta universitatis upsaliensis, Uppsala 1991.

disquisitions on vocabulary and translations, especially from German, the mother tongue of philosophy in Hägerström's days.

Furthermore, this rich material of primary and secondary sources on Hägerström in its present, confusing condition has brought about what we might call a certain freedom of interpretation in the scholarly readings. As it is often the case in the history of thought, this state of affairs has prompted a series of "philosophical myths" or travesties, i.e., plainly misconceived and uninformed ideas about an author leading to far-fetched assertions being repeated uncritically, such as that of Plato longing for tyranny, that of Montesquieu as a forerunner of contemporary theories of fundamental rights, or that of Leibniz believing in the best of all worlds. Similar philosophical travesties find explanations as far as how they came to be, but will never find any justification as to why they should live on. In the case of Hägerström, the mist of the North engendered as many of these misunderstandings as there are chapters in this book: Hägerström was a systematic thinker (Chapter 1), his epistemology was related to the Vienna Circle (Chapter 2), he upheld a relativistic view in morals (Chapter 3), he believed that might is right (Chapter 4), he considered the individual as a mere cog in the social machinery (Chapter 5), he supported nihilism (Chapter 6), his methodology was empiricist and he favored sound contemporary science (Chapter 7).

None of these assertions are true. And this book attempts to provide the historical background and the theoretical reasons why. I hope to suggest a different portrait of this very grave thinker whose legacy is still vivid. Hopefully, in a more enjoyable fashion than the way these ideas were originally exposed. I trust eventual solecisms, due to the moving between languages, will only arouse mild misgivings. Needless to add that I often sat on the shoulders of giants, all errors are mine as well as every distortion of perspective.

This book is the development and deepening of what was once my first dissertation, discussed at the Department of Philosophy at the University of Rome III, under the direction of Giacomo Marramao in 2000. During the revision and drafting of this extended study, invaluable support and advice was offered to me by Michelangelo Bovero from the Department of Political Studies, University of Turin. My gratitude and appreciation also goes to those who kindly offered guidance and comments on the manuscript, particularly to those who, because of great competence in this specific field of study, contributed with constructive criticism and interesting remarks.

I am deeply grateful to the *Luisa Guzzo* Foundation for the award of the publication prize "Domenica Borello" which provided the financial means necessary for the completion of the project.

Last but not least, a dedication: To Lillis.

# Chapter 1
# An Obscure Man of Thought

*I was old when I was young, so I may take leave to be young when I am growing old*[1]

Axel Hägerström had more than one thing in common with Kant, but the most striking parallel is the lack of action in their lives.[2] Hägerström was born in mid-southern Sweden, at the parsonage of Vireda, in a time when history was taking a leap forward. He soon moved to Uppsala, to the famous university founded in 1477, which was a natural gravitation pole for youngsters like him. It was close to Stockholm, yet far away from the noise and business. He stayed there until he died at the age of 71, after a long career as professor in practical philosophy. As soon as he obtained an academic post, he married the love of his youth, Esther Nyander (1872–1957), and they then lived quietly with their two daughters. Immanuel himself would have envied his routines. He got up early in the morning to study and prepare his eleven o'clock lecture. He seldom left home, just a few summer sojourns in the peaceful forests up north and some quick visits to Stockholm to see his daughter and grandson in the autumn of his life.[3] Yet he is said to have «lived more adventures in books than all the knights of the Round Table.»[4]

---

[1] Hägerström on himself. Information from M. Waller, *Människan som få kände*, Natur & Kultur, Stockholm 1961; quote from C.D. Broad, *Memoir of Axel Hägerström*, in R.T. Sandin (ed.), *Philosophy and Religion*, Allen & Unwin, London 1964, p. 28.

[2] See S. Eliaeson, *Axel Hägerström and Modern Social Thought*, in «Nordeuropaforum», 2000:1, p. 20.

[3] Yet he dreamt of Rome and ... Köningsberg! For this information see M. Waller, *Människan som få kände*, cit., p. 199. In the early 30s, he was invited to participate in an International Congress on Roman Law and to hold a lecture on any subject he wished: He never went there.

[4] The brilliant description of his character can be found in Franco Cordero, *Riti e sapienza del diritto*, Laterza, Bari 1981, pp. 56–57. For a more detailed account (in English), see Jes Bjarup, *Reason, Emotion and the Law. Studies in the Philosophy of Axel Hägerström*, Press of the Faculty of Law, Aarhus 1982, pp. 1–27 and C.D. Broad, *Memoir of Axel Hägerström*, in *Philosophy and Religion*, cit., pp. 15–29.

P. Mindus, *A Real Mind*, Law and Philosophy Library 87,
DOI 10.1007/978-90-481-2895-2_1, 

His reputation was that of a great man, with «a charismatic personality (...) at the same time frightening and attracting.»[5] The Swedish novelist and poetess Karin Boye, who studied in Uppsala and depicted the roaring twenties, wrote that «even his appearance inspired curiosity; he looked just like a philosopher should. Moreover he seemed to be present in a strange way, not only in the discussions in the student rooms, but in the very air.»[6] Another witness, the philosopher Ingmar Hedenius, described him as showing «a bizarre appearance, totally different from the other professors in this university, so individualistic and provincial, for good or bad. He dressed somewhat awkwardly, sometimes wearing trousers with facings of the kind that was used only by so-called jazzboys. And he wore his hair a little long, which was unprecedented in those times and it could only be seen on the pictures of Einstein.»[7]

He was certainly not a mainstream man and still a figure Uppsala had become used to. In his old age, the students who never attended his classes would recognize him and mumble «there he goes, the old heron!»[8] The opinions by scholars on his thought are controversial, as well as the statements and memories of the people who met him. Even something as "objective" as teaching habits seem to polarize the recollections of those who knew him. Many insist he was a marvelous lecturer, a grand orator and «his only weakness as a teacher was that of a sectarian leader»[9] since many of his followers literally adored him.[10] Others, maybe not so close, gave a quite less romantic portrayal. Anders Wedberg, who later became a prominent

---

[5]S. Nordin, *Ingmar Hedenius. En filosof och hans tid*, Natur & Kultur, Stockholm 2004, p. 45. Svante Nordin offers detailed information on Hägerström, the Uppsala School and the cultural environment of his time.

[6]K. Boye, *Studentska på 20-talet*, in S. Thulin (ed.), *Bland professorer och studenter. Hågkomster och livsintryck XIX*, Lindblad, Uppsala 1938, 19, p. 402: «Redan hans yttre var ju ägnat att väcka intresse, så måste en filosof se ut. Men dessutom tycktes han på något märkligt sätt vara närvarande, som det tycktes, inte bara i samtalen på studentkulorna utan i själva luften.»

[7]I. Hedenius, *Om stora män och små*, Rabén och Sjögren, Stockholm 1980, p. 180: «en egendomlig framtoning, helt olik andra professorers i detta på gott och ont så individualistiska och provinsiella universitet. Han var en smula konstigt klädd, ibland iförd byxor med revärer, sådana som annars bara så kallade jazzgossar nyttjade, och han hade halvlångt hår, vilket var någonting oerhört i hans samtid och annars bara kunde ses på fotografierna av Einstein.» Hägerström has also been described as a «Mexican bandit (...) demoniacal» (E.H. Linder, *Mitt levande förflutna*, translation in J. Sundberg, *The Swedish Philosopher Axel Haegerstroem and his Relationship to Finland's Struggle to Preserve her Legal Order 1899–1917*, Rothman, Littleton, Co, 1983, p. 13).

[8]M. Waller, *Människan som få kände*, cit., p. 211: «Där går han, gamle Häger!» In Swedish, "häger" means heron, and the philosopher's name hence means "heron river."

[9]I. Hedenius, *I Egen Sak – och andras*, Rabén och Sjögren, Stockholm 1976, p. 113: «hans enda svaghet som lärare var sektledarens.»

[10]For some pejorative portrayals, see F. Schmidt, *The Uppsala School of Legal Thinking*, «Scandinavian Studies in Law», vol. 22, Almqvist & Wiksell International 1978, p. 160; J. Bjarup, *Reason, Emotion and the Law*, Press of the Faculty of Law, Aarhus 1982, p. 94. For positive memories, T. Fogelqvist, *Filosofie kandidaten*, in S. Thulin (ed.), *Bland professorer och studenter. Hågkomster och livsintryck*, Lindblad, Uppsala 1938, pp. 131–153.

name in analytical philosophy in Sweden (apart from being the English translator of Hans Kelsen's *General Theory of Law and State*), claimed that "the old heron" entered the classroom soundlessly and started his lectures before the students had filled up the rows: «There he sat, with his grizzled hair highly combed backwards from his forehead and with his pince-nez squeezed on to his nose, reading from a thick bunch of manuscripts, word by word.»[11]

What puzzles mostly is that for some, he was the last of his kind, and for others a new breed. He is remembered as a "radical" (Eliaeson), a nit-picker, "an unglamorous man of science" (Sandström), a sub-Hegelian scholar (Carlsson), an "irk" (Cordero), a pre-anthropologist, a rationalist (Cassirer), a Nietzschean (Ruin), a legal positivist (Lyles), an amateur of jurisprudence (Betti), a subversive pro-Marxian (Sundberg). Most labels have been used. There is only one opinion scholars are likely to beware of and that is the judgment of Hägerström's friend and follower Vilhelm Lundstedt (1882–1955) who had a certain tendency to exaggerate (otherwise, he was, according to C.D. Broad's elegant understatement, a "fertile writer"[12]). When it came to his guru, Lundstedt once exclaimed: «Just mention one pioneering achievement carried out by *one* single man of the same level that we now have before the very eyes!»[13]

Regardless of the accuracy of these fairly divergent opinions on Hägerström, there is one feature that all seem to agree upon: The obscurity of his language. Broad uses yet another graceful euphemism by calling this defect the «Germanized version of his native tongue.»[14] On another occasion, Broad states more explicitly that Hägerström's writing style is like «glue thickened with saw-dust.»[15] However, the real problem was never really the German-tinged phrasing of Hägerström's Swedish: A German mother tongue philosopher like Ernst Cassirer once claimed that «I shall not hide that this study has not been easy (...). I had to slowly work myself through in order to get access to Hägerström's doctrine, and the shape Hägerström has given some of his fundamental ideas did not facilitate the task. In his self-presentation Hägerström holds his most important work to be *Das Prinzip der Wissenschaft*. But this book, that I therefore started with, is also one of his most difficult works. According to me, it belongs to the most obscure and challenging

[11] A. Wedberg, *Axel Hägerström. Några minnesbilder och intryck*, in L. Bergström (ed.), *Ditt och datt. Festskrift till Harald Ofstad*, SthlmUnivers., Stockholm 1970, p. 1: «Där satt han då, med det gråsprängda håret högt uppkammat över pannan och med pincenén fastklämd kring näsroten, och läste innantill ur en tjock manuskriptbunt.»

[12] C.D. Broad, *Memoir*, cit., p. 27.

[13] Quote from S. Nordin, *Från Hägerström till Hedenius*, Doxa, Lund 1984, p. 70: «Nämn mig en banbrytande insats, som utförts av *en* människa och som kan ställas i jämnbredd med det vi nu har för ögonen!»

[14] C.D. Broad, *Memoir*, cit., p. 28. Laments on Hägerström's use of language can be found in most interpreters: See for instance E. Pattaro, *Il realismo giuridico scandinavo*, CLUEB, Bologna 1974, p. 243.

[15] C.D. Broad, *Hägerström's Account of Sense of Duty and Certain Allied Experiences*, in «Philosophy», XXVI, 1951, p. 99.

pieces in modern philosophical literature.»[16] Basically, Hägerström is no author just to skim through. Probably the clearest picture of what it is like to read this obscure Swede is given by Franco Cordero, an Italian scholar who must have spent far too much energy on this senior northern colleague: «Those books of his require huge concentration, a cry to the moon (...). The effort is neurotic, it is clear from the way he writes; he avoids all ellipses; under his pen every idea evokes another one; the material he had read rises to the surface by footnote-monstres. As if it were not enough, his prose dribbles of polemical tones. His labyrinth-like German-wise writing style contributes to the negative outcome, but the contents are the real knot: Even in crystal-clear English, this huge work of thought makes great demands on the reader.»[17]

Before getting into these abstruse doctrines, we should remember, however, some of Hägerström's own methodological advice. In the essay *Jesus*, written in 1907 but published only in the late sixties, Hägerström exposed his own methodology about how the telling of history must proceed. Let us follow his advice. «In order to understand the spirit of a bygone age it is necessary to start from the emotional life of the modern mind (...). Real knowledge can be attained only as far as we can use our own emotional devices for understanding. Where we cannot comprehend how certain situations and beliefs arise from emotions (which are still familiar to us) under the circumstances, exterior conditions and levels of knowledge of that time, there is a necessary limit to our knowledge.»[18] According to this methodological suggestion, help in grasping the thought of someone from another time in history comes from «knowledge of the spirit of the time, the emotional milieu in which the person lived.»[19] So what was his own milieu like?

---

[16]E. Cassirer, *Axel Hägerström. Eine Studie zur schwedischen Philosophie der Gegenwart*, Göteborgs högskolas årskrift, Göteborg 1939; now in *Gesammelte Werke*, Bd. 21, Meiner, Hamburg 2005, p. 5: «Daß mir dieses Studium nicht leicht gefallen ist, will ich nicht verschweigen. (...) die Form, in die Hägerström manche seiner Grundgedanken gekleidet hat, trug nicht dazu bei, diese Arbeit zu erleichtern. Hägerström hat in seiner Selbstdarstellung seine Schrift über das »Prinzip der Wissenschaft« als seine wichtigste gemäß begann, ist auch eine seiner schwierigsten Schriften; ja es gehört meines Erachtens zu den dunkelsten und am schwersten zugänglichen Werken der modernen philosophischen Literatur.»

[17]F. Cordero, *Riti e sapienza del diritto*, Laterza, Bari 1981, p. 56: «quei suoi libri chiedono un'attenzione tesa ossia la luna (...). Evidente da come scrive, lo sforzo nevrotico; evita ogni ellissi, in mano sua ogni idea ne evoca altre, le cose lette vengono a galla dettandogli note-monstre. Come se non bastasse, la sua prosa trasuda umore polemico. Contribuisce all'esito negativo uno stile labirintico-tedesco, ma il groviglio sta nei contenuti: anche tradotto in nitido inglese, quest'enorme lavoro pensante esige molto da chi lo visita.»

[18]A. Hägerström, *Jesus. En karaktärsanalys*, Natur & Kultur, Stockholm 1968, p. 14: «[för att förstå en gången tids anda] är det nödvändigt att gripa in i det moderna medvetandets eget känsloliv (...). Endast i den grad det är oss möjligt att använda vår egen känsloapparat som förklaringsgrund, endast så långt kunna vi komma till ett verkligt vetande. Där vi icke kunna (...) förstå, hur under dåtida yttre förhållanden och med den dåtida graden av kunskap just dessa handlingar och dessa föreställningssätt kunnat uppstå ur känslor, som även för oss är förtroliga, där är en nödvändig gräns för vårt vetande satt.»

[19]A. Hägerström, *Jesus. En karaktärsanalys*, cit., p. 13: «icke minst kunskap om tidsandan, om den emotionella miljö i vilken individen lever.» That the original environment (*ursprungsmiljön*) was

## 1.1 Background and Youth

Axel Anders Theodor Hägerström was born in 1868, "the year of hunger." Nevertheless, the late Sixties also happened to be the dawning of a new era for Sweden. Starting in the mid-nineteenth century, the industrialisation of Sweden had produced some significant effects by the time he developed his philosophy. The timber industry flourished along the northern coastline, along with the mass production of paper-manufacturing. The famous iron ore from the mines in the North was increasingly being exported to Germany. After 1862, railways ended rural isolation and made terrestrial transportation possible, while steamboats by 1900 were replacing sailingvessels.

The industrialisation was strictly linked to the massive demographical growth that had occurred after 1820 and that determined both the rural exodus and emigration. Hägerström belonged to this baby boom. The population of Sweden increased from 2.3 to 3.5 million during the first half of the nineteenth century,[20] and during Axel's youth it increased by another 2 million, reaching 6 million inhabitants by 1920. The demographic curve was partly due to new farming techniques and the introduction of the potato. Since Swedes traditionally divided their land in equal parts among their sons, the boom soon led to increasing poverty and by 1850, 40 percent of the population were landless peasants.

As the agricultural world changed into an industrial society, many moved into the urbanised areas, which harbored the industries, or made their way to the emigrant ships leaving for the New World. When Axel Hägerström, on the 1st of January 1900, obtained his first salary as a lecturer, a modest sum of 1500 crowns per year, he was definitely to be congratulated. In 1900 one in three wages were paid to an industrial worker.

The New World had of course witnessed a few arrivals from Sweden before the end of the nineteenth century: Some Swedes left because of religious reasons (baptism was hardly tolerated) or personal beliefs (teetotalism, among others). But the "land of milk and honey" really started to attract the landless masses by the middle of the century: 40 000 people emigrated only in 1869. By the year Hägerström succeeded on the chair of practical philosophy, previously held by his professor Erik Olof Burman (1845–1929), one in five Swedes was now living in America.[21] The years from 1850 to 1920 were also the golden age for the popular movements in Sweden. Population growth and urbanisation made new forms of socialisation possible. It involved teetotalism, the revivalist and Pentecostal movements as well as the labour movement. This context came to play an important role in the development of Axel Hägerström.

---

of great importance for the "context of explanation" is repeated by Hägerström's younger daughter Margit Waller in the biography *Människan som få kände*, cit., p. 7.

[20] The highest increase was in the countryside, especially in the counties of Norrland, followed by Scania and the central provinces of Sweden, i.e. the homeland of Axel.

[21] The calculation is based on the fact that between 1820 and 1930, over one million people emigrated from Sweden. Most of them settled in Chicago or Minnesota.

### *1.1.1 The Family, Childhood and Adolescence*

Axel was the son of a cleric, an old fashioned minister born in the small city of Norrköping in 1834: Karl Fredrik Theodor Hägerström. Karl Hägerström had followed in his own father's footsteps, a man of God himself. North-East from the town of Jönköping lies the small community of Vireda. This settlement, flanked by hills and woods, found a new spiritual leader in Karl Fredrik who took up service in 1861. As he arrived in Småland – a central region of Sweden where lakes engrave the productive lands known for its "spirit of undertaking" (*gnosjöandan*) – Karl Fredrik followed local custom and married the reverend's daughter, Ida Embring, mother of Axel Hägerström's two elder brothers, Reinhold and Gustaf. Like many other women, Ida died in childbirth. And after the customary year of mourning, the priest and his cherished friend, Nils Johan Nyander, sleigh-rode all the way to the nearby town of Gränna – today mostly known for its traditional striped sweets – where Karl Fredrik proposed to a woman whose wit is said to have been extraordinary, Augusta Maria Skarin. So was her health: Of the five children, four survived. The first-born was Axel.

In 1880, when Axel turned twelve, the family moved to Örberga, a village next to Vadstena, home for the only catholic Saint of Sweden, Brigitte. The family house in Östergötland, which eventually would shelter Prince Eugen in 1915, offers the view of *Vättern*, the second largest lake of Sweden at the west and the medieval towers of Vadstena at the east. The young Axel, however, remained a guest in this house. The year before, when he was only eleven years old, he was sent to school in Jönköping, where he stayed at his grandmother's for a few years, before gaining independence.[22]

This «vividly tempered»[23] grandmother Charlotte Skarin was most certainly the stimulating factor in Axel's upbringing, putting a twist to this composed countryside life. Even her youth was adventurous: She was born in Finland in 1814 of Swedish parents who decided to move back to Sweden in 1823, but, while crossing the Baltic in a three-week long journey, the family was shipwrecked and lost all their belongings.[24] Later, Charlotte Skarin came to play a significant role in Axel's life: She did not only provide lodgings to him and his brothers between 1879 and 1883, even though she had already turned 65; she also took care of every aspect of their daily life. She was a woman of conviction more than faith. She never left home without her hat and during summer she would never fail to bring her parasol. Her interest in politics and international relations was authentic and deep. She claimed she would never get too old for politics. She frequently discussed the state of the world with her grandson. Even though no research has been done on the sources or development of

---

[22]On the family background and for personal correspondence, see M. Waller, *Människan som få kände,* cit., pp. 9–12.

[23]M. Waller, *Människan som få kände*, cit., p. 17.

[24]The anecdote of the shipwreck is actually the plot of the poem *Sjöresan* written by Charlotte Skarin and published at her own expense in the brief poetry booklet, *Björkqvistarne: dikter*, förf:s förlag, Jönköping 1897.

Hägerström's interest in politics, surely Charlotte Skarin's profound concern should be listed. She often thanked him for his opinions and considerations on political matters. In her letters to him from 1899, for instance, she discussed the problems in the Balkans and the hostilities in the Far-East: «We shall see where all this leads. The Europeans have occupied fortresses and land in China and the Chinese will retaliate in an awful way.»[25] She died in 1903 at the age of 88. As a warning sign she wrote to her grandson: «We should fear what the future holds for the world as we know it: When all is ready, a world war will break out.»[26]

Hägerström's previous schooling had been taken care of by his father. He learnt to read at the age of five. His education has been depicted as "Spartan"[27] with focus on sports, nature and strict morality. But it was during adolescence that he laid the foundation for almost all his later interests. He did well in the Jönköping school and was particularly interested in the Latin and Greek classics.[28] Under the vigilance of the principle of the school and teacher of classical languages C.P. Velin (1820–1889), Axel fostered his love for the classical age, a life-long affection. «Over almost three decades, when Hägerström deepened his research for *Der römischen Obligationsbegriff*, he always sought the primary sources. While preparing this work, he revisited practically all classical literature in its original languages.»[29] Nevertheless, his main interest and his favorite pastime were mathematics. As a teenager he started to instruct his less gifted classmates. For his first degree (*fil.*

[25]M. Waller, *Människan som få kände*, cit., p. 19: «Nu får man se, vart detta bär, att européerna tagit fästen och land från Kina. Kineserna kommer att hämnas väldigt.»

[26]M. Waller, *Människan som få kände*, cit., p. 20: «en människa kan bäva för den framtid som väntar hela den kända världen – ett världskrig kommer när allt är i ordning.»

[27]M. Waller, *Människan som få kände*, cit., p. 24.

[28]The end of Hägerström's diary, from the autumn 1884 to the end of April 1885, is in fact scribbled with miniature transcriptions, horizontal and vertical, of Greek and Latin classics. He continued the transcriptions all his life. See the manuscript *Excerpter ur grekiska författare* from 1933. Moreover, he kept his habit of using the same piece of paper for more than one use. He gained the habit as a child when he worked hard to get a single arc of paper, the precious "papier en continue" that Louis Piette had invented just a few years before.

[29]M. Waller, *Människan som få kände*, cit., p. 29: «När Hägerström under nära tre decennier var fördjupad i undersökningar för sitt stora verk *Der römische Obligationsbegriff*, eftersträvade han alltid kontakten med primärmaterialet. För detta arbete har han således genomplöjt praktiskt taget hela den klassiska litteraturen på originalspråken.» Hägerström's knowledge and familiarity with the great writers of the classical age, but also of the minor details of this gone era, gives us a clue to why the Hägerström committee – which, after the philosopher's death, handled the unpublished material and was responsible for the editing – included Björn Collinder. He was specialized in linguistics and member of the Science Academy, as well as the Swedish translator of Sophocles' satyricon *Ichneutai*. Erudite and conversant in Greek, Björn Collinder lacked interest in such worldly things as ordinary Swedish or English. This might explain why the English translation of Hägerström in *Philosophy and Religion* from 1964, made by Robert Sandin is so lacunose. For some criticisms see E. Pattaro, *Il realismo giuridico scandinavo*, cit., pp. 51–52. Sandin, an American of Swedish descent, had English as mother tongue, but learnt Swedish very quickly (M. Waller, *Människan som få kände*, cit., p. 215). In the preface of the translation (p. 12), Sandin claims the translations were accepted by the committee after an accurate review by Martin Fries and Björn Collinder. Thomas Mautner, who classified Hägerström's *Nachlaß* and who knows the

*kand.*) he opted for mathematics as a specialty, and for his second degree (*lic.*) he obtained a "derogation from the King" in order to major in the subject.[30] In 1884, he taught mathematics at a high-school in Uppsala. All his life he continued resolving equations. The quantity of mathematical calculations included in the unpublished material in Uppsala is impressive: This ability proved important for his understanding of Einstein's theory of relativity to which he dedicated a lengthy critique.

Much like other adolescents, Axel did not find pleasure in philosophy. In a letter written on February 17th, 1885 to his older brother Gustaf – who was then studying in Uppsala – Hägerström wondered: «Can I, please, eliminate history, philosophy and physics from the admission exams?»[31] This interest was not aroused until his religious faith began to shake and he encountered Erik Olof Burman in the autumn 1886.

Consequently, Axel's theoretical interest awoke in tender years. His curiosity brought him to deepen several other subject matters on his own. He learnt English by himself. At seventeen he decided to present himself in order to pass the final high-school exams (*studentexamen*) a year in advance and independently. The same day as he was received by the principle to set the minor formalities the case required, he was given a letter from his elder brother Reinhold, which immediately dissuaded him from the bold move. The letter has not been kept, but from the subsequent correspondence it is clear that the young boy renounced the enterprise due to ethical and religious considerations. Reinhold, in a letter from the end of March 1885, makes clear that «there is a sort of *hubris* that should not be sought for, the one guided by the desire to outshine all the others only to appear *great* in the eyes of the world. Hence the heart becomes superb and proud and Christian humility is pushed aside.»[32] The fact that such arguments bit so hard on the boy shows the family's firm attachment to the Protestant tradition of self-scrutiny.

On this occasion Axel bowed to the family's will. But to Gustaf – the brother he seems to have been mostly attached to – he described his state of mind in rather dramatic words: «You want to climb a tree, and every day and night you struggle to clamber upwards, concentrating all your efforts on this endeavor. Reaching out for the last branch, a hurricane sucks you up and throws you to the ground far from the tree. Such a tough chock cannot be overlooked, can it?»[33] And indeed it could not.

story well, quite convincingly claims that especially «Björn Collinder (...) must be held responsible for the errors that where not corrected» (Thomas Mautner, *Vägledning till Hägerströmstudiet*, SKHVSU, Almqvist & Wiksell, Uppsala 1994, p. 221).

[30] M. Waller, *Människan som få kände*, cit., p. 29.

[31] M. Waller, *Människan som få kände*, cit., p. 40: «om det är möjligt att kunna slippa att för examen läsa *historia, fysik* och *filosofi*.»

[32] Quoting from M. Waller, *Människan som få kände*, cit., p. 34: «det finns dock ett slags ärelystnad, som icke är att eftersträva, och det är den, som förestavas av begäret att vilja överglänsa alla andra, blott för att synas stor i världens ögon. Därav bliver hjärtat högmodigt och stolt, den kristliga ödmjukheten, som borde ha sin plats i ett människohjärta undantränges allt mer och mer.»

[33] Quoting from M. Waller, *Människan som få kände*, cit., p. 38: «Du vill klättra upp i ett träd, du klättrar dag ut och dag in och dina strävanden gå blott ut på att komma upp i toppen. Du är på den

His youth may be viewed as a time of emotional turmoil and disaffiliation which prompted his later philosophical "conversion." These were the hard years in which he disentangled himself and broke with the intent of his family meaning to make him follow the path of his father and become a priest.

### *1.1.2 The Religious Scenery Behind an Emotivist*

For the Hägerströms there was no doubt: Axel had to become a minister of the Church and possibly inherit the parsonage. The study of theology would pave the way that his father, and his grandfather, the reverend Carl Peter Hägerström (1798–1863) had followed. His paternal ancestors were all men of God since the days of the Reform or at least since the time of his forefather Olavus Claravensius, an important clergy member linked to the Crown in the sixteenth century.

Until his late teens, Axel obediently pursued the course. By the time he was fifteen he had already held Sunday sermons in his father's place with the bishop's blessing. Later he recalled how he «wagged his pow» in the paternal pulpit.[34] The years of adolescence were not only those of his intellectual dawning, but also of his religious awakening, which occurred in Jönköping. The town was the center of a renewed religiosity, the revivalist and Pentecostal movements, to which Axel's mother felt rather close.[35] It was also the heart of the neo-evangelical movement of Carl Olof Rosenius, according to which the sins of the born-again were forgiven. In 1853 the movement had established its headquarters in the town. Here Hägerström frequented J.A.E. Sundelin, a famed clerical representative, and he also met Carl Axel Hägglund (1852–1938) who was initially his teacher in religious and theological matters, but soon became one of his most reliable friends. After retirement Hägglund moved to Uppsala and was a regular guest in Hägerström's home.[36]

Another interesting detail is that during the second half of the nineteenth century a movement within protestant theology grew, which seems to hold quite a few ideas later shared by Hägerström. For instance, Albrecht Ritschl (1822–1889) developed an unconventional standpoint according to which the distinction between science and theology corresponds to the difference between judgments on existence and

nedersta delen av den översta grenen, en orkan kommer och kastar dig ner, långt från trädet. Månne det inte skulle kännas, en sådan stöt?» Gustaf helpfully advised him to prepare the admission exams for university so as to focus on the future.

[34] M. Waller, *Människan som få kände*, cit., p. 31: «dundrade väldeligen som gymnasist.»

[35] The revivalist movement was founded after the English methodist, George Scott came to Sweden in 1830. Since the methodists did not want to break with the Swedish state church, they did not become a free church, but a revivalist church. Scott also established the newspaper *Pietisten*. During the 1860s the revivalist movement spread across the country. It should also be mentioned that the year 1910 was the break-through for the Pentecostal movement and many baptists became Pentecostalists.

[36] M. Waller, *Människan som få kände*, cit., p. 50.

judgments on values. It is not clear whether Hägerström was acquainted with this particular distinction, but it is probable that something was, so to say, in the air.[37]

According to Margit Waller, «from the letters it seems that Axel had experienced the sense of peace that he later describes in his lectures on the philosophy of religion (. . .). Surely behind the understanding of the importance of Christ for the believer, lies a personal experience»: The confidence a child feels when holding his father's hand.[38] Whether or not he experienced a religious epiphany before loosing his childhood faith may be debated, but surely his frequentation of the traditional paternal church and the neo-evangelical environments left a distinctive writing-style that he kept during his first years in Uppsala.

It seems undisputable that this period coincided with the break with his father's protestant dogmatism. Karl Hägerström was a conservative who, according to his granddaughter, «was not particularly interested in theological debate (. . .), he preferred spending his free time doing woodwork.»[39] Everything about him reflected traditional, orthodox "Church-and-State" Lutheranism. «For Karl Hägerström, the faith of the forefathers was self-evident and secure. His theological thought was determined by his unshakable conviction in the absolute truth of the Christian dogmas, the sacred character of spiritual values and the inviolability of God's word. In his sermons (. . .) it seemed that the commanding word was protagonist, especially when it came to sin and damnation after death.»[40] His son Axel, as we shall see, became almost obsessed with "command" and "duty."[41] There is no understatement in claiming that «at home, his father represented meticulous order and rigid discipline (. . .). Through his own example and the strict ethical requirements that shaped his educational methods, his father seems to have strongly influenced the formation of Axel's character.»[42]

---

[37] Albrecht Ritschl had one source in common with Hägerström: «Lotze's view that value judgements express something over and above the mere holding of this or that proposition to be true or false» (S. Satris, *Ethical Emotivism*, Martinus Nijhoff/Kluwer, Dordrecht 1987, p. 9).

[38] M. Waller, *Människan som få kände*, cit., p. 41: «Av breven synes dock som om Axel själv erfarit något av den lyckokänslan han sedemera skildrat i sina religionsfilosofiska föreläsningar (. . .). Säkerligen finns det en personlig upplevelse bakom denna tolkning av Kristi betydelse för den troende.» On the figure of Christ, see *Jesus. En karaktärsanalys*, edited 1968 by Martin Fries.

[39] M. Waller, *Människan som få kände*, cit., pp. 15 and 21: «Karl Hägerström ägde inte något intresse för teologiska debatter (. . .) han helst tillbragte sin lediga tid i snickarboden.»

[40] M. Waller, *Människan som få kände*, cit., p. 13: «För Karl Hägerström var den tro han ärvt av sina fäder något självklart och tryggt. Hans teologiska tänkesätt präglades av en orubblig övertygelse om de kristna dogmernas absoluta sanning, de andliga värdenas helighet och gudsordets oantastlighet?»

[41] See infra, Chapters 4 and 5.

[42] M. Waller, *Människan som få kände*, cit., p. 14: «Inom hemmet representerade fadern den minutiösa ordningen och den stränga disciplinen (. . .). Genom sitt eget föredöme och de stränga etiska krav, som kom till uttryck i hans uppfostringsmetoder, synes fadern starkt ha påverkat Axels karaktärsdaning.» It happened that he would ask his mother to hide letters from him out of fear for his father's raging against his imperfect calligraphy.

In a nutshell, this influence is best resumed in the German word *Angst*. «Through the paternal homilies Axel became familiar with the revengeful God who punishes sinners with eternal damnation. The threat of the eternal fire became so real for the boy that it engendered anxiety and torment.»[43] Axel was just a few years old when, sitting before the fireplace in the drawing room he determinedly thrust his little hand into the flames, severely burning himself. Solicited to give an explanation the boy just answered that he «wanted to know what suffering might be awaiting him.»[44] No wonder scholars claim that Hägerström abandoned theology for philosophy as an attempt at emancipation from his tyrannical father.[45]

Consequently, not long after the awakening in Jönköping his faith was shaken by doubts. Axel soon confessed to his brother Gustaf that he felt like a "leaf in the wind": «Perhaps you are wondering why I do not want to join the theology course straight away. The fact is that I cannot decide wholeheartedly if I am summoned by God to become his minister.»[46] After his freshman's year in Uppsala when he studied the propedeutic course of theology, he did in fact make up his mind and, in May 1887, he wrote a polite, yet determined letter to his father Karl informing him of his choice to become a philosopher: «I do not want to be subject to other people's opinions on the outer aspects of my life and consequently I do not want to become a priest, especially since I am not gifted with the skill to be representative, an ability required for the clerical task.»[47] He signed the letter "your *philosophical* son." Not only did he refuse to follow the path of his forefathers, but he chose a career that was not exactly lucrative. This was an inconceivable decision for a not too well-off family from the countryside. His father was furious.[48]

These very personal experiences seem to have reverberated on Hägerström's intellectual comprehension of religion as well. He wrote extensively on spiritual phenomena, but he rarely published it.[49] Once he lost his childhood faith, he never

---

[43] M. Waller, *Människan som få kände*, cit., p. 25: «genom faderns predikningar [fick han] stifta bekantskap med den stränge Guden, vilken bestraffar syndarna med evig fördömelse. Hotet om att få brinna i den eviga elden blev för gossen något påtagligt och medförde en stark oro och ängslan.»

[44] M. Waller, *Människan som få kände*, cit., p. 25: «få en förnimmelse om de kval som måhända väntade honom själv en gång.»

[45] J. Bjarup, *Reason, Emotion and the Law. Studies in the Philosophy of Axel Hägerström*, Aarhus Universitet 1982, pp. 10 ff.

[46] Letter from end of March 1885. See M. Waller, *Människan som få kände*, cit., p. 39: «Du kanske förundrar dig över, att jag ej vill taga prästexamen nu först. Men, ser du, förhållandet är det, att jag ej kan riktigt bestämma, om jag känner mig kallad därtill av Gud.»

[47] M. Waller, *Människan som få kände*, cit., p. 62: «jag vill icke så komma i beroende av någon med avseende på mitt yttre liv och därför vill jag ej bli präst, allrahelst som jag ej äger någon representativ förmåga som därtill fodras.»

[48] Axel avoided the family house that summer. He gave private courses for his livelihood. In another letter from June, he makes an appeal to an argument that sounds very similar to his later thesis on right and justice: «The sense of justice and the sense of duty are eminently individual and delicate» (quoting from M. Waller, *Människan som få kände*, cit., p. 67).

[49] Besides the "magical" references in *Der römische Obligationsbegriff* and *Das magistratische Ius*, we should also mention his review of Birch-Reichenwald Aars' *Gut und Böse* from 1907; the

abandoned what he called his "anti-theological way of thinking." Yet, he developed a profound understanding of the role religion plays in the life of the single individual as well as in human civilisation. This is one of the major keys to understanding Hägerström's influence on Swedish theology in the second half of the twentieth century.[50] Margit Waller probably detects well the sentiment of her father when saying that «his position was characterised by great respect for other people's faith and he held religious sentiment to be so central that it induced him to consider it as the core from which his conception of religion as consisting essentially in an emotion sprung.»[51] There is no trace of the aggressive anticlericalism usually associated with viewpoints such as the sense of demystification and empowering of Man, typical for Enlightenment, the strict nineteenth century scientific positivism and materialism or the twentieth century post-metaphysicism, all positions that have been in some way linked to Hägerström. His «studies of the nature and sources of religious beliefs do not lead him to an iconoclastic renunciation of religion as juvenile or as an outmoded vestige of primitive culture (...). All the liabilities of religion can be removed once it is recognized that religious dogma is only mythology.»[52] His religious background seems to have guaranteed a more relaxed attitude towards spirituality, even though not towards creed. According to him, «the only way to save religion from decline is to cut it loose from the question of truth.»[53]

Robert Sandin who dedicated his PhD thesis from 1959 to Hägerström's philosophy of religion holds that it has «both a negative and a positive aspect. From the negative side, it involves an uncompromising renunciation of metaphysics in its religious form and the declaration that religious assertions are, descriptively regarded, meaningless. On the positive side, it involves both a psychological-sociological-anthropological account of the sources of religious beliefs in certain identifiable

---

essays from the 20s in *Religionsfilosofi* edited by Fries in 1949 and those translated by Sandin in *Philosophy and Religion* in 1964, along with *Vergleich zwischen den Kraftvorstellungen der primitiven und modernen Kulturvölker* from 1933; but also the book on *Jesus*, edited by M. Fries in 1968.

[50] He seems to have influenced the so-called "Theology of Lund" (*Lundateologin*) of Gustaf Aulén, Anders Nygren and Ragnar Bring, a movement in theology which insisted on the incompatibility between metaphysics and science, in a way not far from Karl Barth's. The influence was not direct nor Hägerström's personally, even though Aulén did take private lessons from Hägerström in philosophy. It was rather the influence of the Uppsala School as such which led to the thesis that religion is not theoretical in its nature. In general, the theology of Lund reflected on how religion needs to overcome nihilism. «Therefore they can be put in relation to other contemporaries (...), like Barth and Bultmann, Troeltsch and Weber, Scheler, Heidegger and Wittgenstein» (S. Nordin, *Från Hägerström till Hedenius*, cit., p. 134).

[51] M. Waller, *Människan som få kände*, cit., p. 141: «Hans uttalanden utmärkes också av stor respekt för andras övertygelse samtidigt som han själv tillmäter den religiösa känslan en sådan central betydelse.»

[52] R. Sandin, *Axel Hägerström's Philosophy of Religion, with Special Reference to his Philosophy of Knowledge and his Concept of Reality*, Ann Arbor University Microfilm, Michigan 1959, p. 221.

[53] A. Hägerström, *Religionsfilosofi*, Natur & Kultur, Stockholm 1949, p. 168: «Det ges endast ett sätt att rädda religionen från undergång, det är att slita den helt lös från sanningsfrågan.»

feelings and the contention that religion is entirely justifiable as a human enterprise.»[54] If Hägerström struggles with authors like Auguste Sabatier, Friedrich Schleiermacher and Rudolf Otto,[55] it is not just to end up in sheer scienticism. But under the reductionist thesis «since God is indeterminate, he is not accessible in abstract thought; he is apprehended only as the content of mystic feeling»[56], the stake is of a higher intellectual standard.

What Hägerström called the "metaphysics of reality and metaphysics of the Self" (*Realitetsmetafysiken och Jagmetafysiken*) are essentially similar experiences since they are based on the generic human tendency to "besoul" the outer world (i.e., to project on worldly phenomena the "false" experience of an Inner-self, called the "soul"). Simply put, the ecstasy of the mystic clarifies what Hägerström considers to be the underlying contradiction of Christian dogmatism (determination versus contingency): Hence the question is whether it is conceivable that some of God's acts are contingent, because in that case the dogma of self-necessity (*causa sui*) cannot be. This obviously has strong implications for the problem of ethics and free-will. Some scholars have sought a link between Hägerström's ideas and those of George Santayana and Nikolaus Cusanus.[57] Perhaps it is more rewarding to investigate the connection between this standpoint and contemporary views on how the universe can be at the same time determinate and contingent. In any case, it is well-known that this meta-epistemological problem puzzled more than one of the twentieth century's great minds. After all, how is it possible that God plays dice, as Einstein used to put it? We will come back to these issues further on.[58]

## 1.2 The Formative Years in Uppsala

In the autumn of 1886, at the age of 18, Hägerström arrived in the city that his name would be linked to: Uppsala, the most ancient and renowned university town in Scandinavia. Founded in 1477, the university counted, among its alumni and professors, some of the most distinguished names in the history of the Nordic peninsula. Here, classes were held by Anders Celsius, the inventor of the thermometer whose degrees are still named after him, and the medicine school directory lists the great systematizer of botanics, Carl von Linné. Christopher Polhem, the genius of mechanical engineering who invented the *laboratorium mechanicum* was among the ex-alumni, along with the cantor and poet Carl Michael Bellman. When the young

[54] R. Sandin, *Axel Hägerström's Philosophy of Religion*, cit., p. 2.

[55] Special mention should be made of Hägerström's seminars on Schleiermacher from the spring 1921 and on Otto's *Das Heilige* from autumn 1924.

[56] R. Sandin, *Axel Hägerström's Philosophy of Religion*, cit., p. 160.

[57] Both these links are investigated by Robert Sandin in his thesis *Axel Hägerström's Philosophy of Religion*. Silvana Castignone reiterates the connection between Hägerström and Cusanus in *Diritto, linguaggio, realtà. Saggi sul realismo giuridico*, Giappichelli, Torino 1995, p. 15.

[58] See the last chapter.

and inexperienced Hägerström arrived,[59] Uppsala was in full expansion. The new library *Carolina Rediviva* which still preserves the Hägerström manuscripts had just been built, like the new observatory and the *Chemicum*. Just 4 years later, women were admitted to this small but vivacious environment.[60] As customary since the sixteenth century, students were organised in *nations* according to their provenience. So Axel Hägerström enrolled in the association of his region, *Östergötland*, in which he remained faithfully engaged all his life, becoming its "inspector" from 1925 until retirement in 1933.

Even if Scandinavian historians usually stress the importance of the Uppsala world and its intellectually fervid milieu, it is remarkable that this aspect seldom aroused the interest of scholars illustrating Hägerström's development, notwithstanding that his name is indissolubly linked to it. Despite an enduring aura of provincialism, the 1880s were rather "radical" years in Uppsala: In 1882 Karl Staff founded the cultural association Verdandi as a meeting place for the advocates of religious and civil liberties, an organisation that Hägerström frequented.[61] The eccentric economist Knut Wicksell (1851–1926) who, in a neo-Malthusian spirit, recommended birth-control to deal with poverty in a lecture during the academic year 1886–1887 was also a member of Verdandi. Hägerström did not attend this specific (and highly debated) address on the 16th of May 1887, but he was well-informed about the diatribe.

This lively environment aroused his interest in philosophy. In 1886, he first studied theoretical philosophy under the supervision of Erik Olof Burman (1845–1929) who later became his teacher, mentor and close friend. Burman originated from a very small community close to the Northern Circle and in 1872 he started teaching theoretical philosophy, becoming professor in practical philosophy in 1896; a chair Hägerström was also competing for. According to the standards of the time Burman was a travelled man: He made study journeys to France, Switzerland, Italy and foremost Germany, the very heart of the *Kultursphäre* Uppsala gravitated around. A quick look at his bibliography shows an increasing interest in German idealism around the years when he was coaching Hägerström.[62]

This milieu had not yet broken loose from nineteenth century idealism. It is true however that the student world in Uppsala was full of life and the air was

---

[59]The rumour has it that the young Hägerström, together with his older brother and his friends in one of the classical inns of the town, became the object of the waitresses' laughter because he was unaware of the custom of tipping. Since then, he was known for his generous tips (M. Waller, *Människan som få kände*, cit., p. 75).

[60]In the autumn 1897, Axel managed to convince his parents to send his sister Berta to Uppsala. He coached her in mathematics until her admission at the faculty of Chemistry in Stockholm where she graduated in 1905.

[61]In the early 1980s Thomas Mautner edited and published a lecture that Hägerström held at Verdandi the 21st of April 1909 on *Philosophy as Science*, now in «Filosofisk tidskrift», 1980:2, pp. 1–13 and 1981:3, pp. 45–47.

[62]Among Burman's most important titles, see *Die Transcendentalphilosophie Fichtes und Schellings dargestellt und erläutert* (1892) and *Schleiermachers kritik av Kants och Fichtes sedeläror* [*Schleiermacher's Critique of Kant's and Fichte's Doctrine of Customs*] (1894), besides

buzzing with new ideas. Hägerström was surely influenced by this new atmosphere. For example, he read Ibsen, Brandes, Strindberg: All authors that were innovating literature at the time.[63] In March 1893 he first read and studied Nietzsche with enthusiasm. Probably the reading was *Ecce homo*. The Scandinavian culture of the 90s and the *fin de siècle* is profoundly influenced by the receptivity to Nietzsche[64] and it has been suggested that his «great impact in the Nordic countries can of course be explained by various factors, but it definitely has to do with the strict and severe tradition of State-Church.»[65] In a letter from February 5$^{th}$, 1897 Hägerström communicated to his fiancée Esther his intention to write a monograph on Nietzsche.[66] But he never did. He changed his mind and preferred the academically much more viable Aristotle. However, as we shall see, it is in this setting that Hägerström matures the conviction of his own philosophical "conversion" and of his task as a thinker to operate a "Copernican revolution."

For the time being, however, his revolutionary intention was put on hold. His first years in Uppsala were tough. Struggling with financial problems, he gave up to 12 hours of private lessons a day.[67] His first academic achievements were not exactly ground-breaking: He lectured at the "Filosofiska föreningen" (the philosophical association) on pretty common themes such as ethics of stoicism in April 1890, on the evolution of medieval philosophy in October 1891, on Leibniz' monadology in 1892 and on the philosophy of Plato in 1893. Finally, on his birthday, September 6$^{th}$ 1893, at the age of 25 he was proclaimed doctor with a thesis entitled *The Principles of Aristotle's Ethical Thought and Its Theoretical Premises.*

It is a neat little work, well-suited for his academic purposes. It is philologically fine-tuned and up-to-date with the secondary literature, as shown for example by the parsimonious references to *Magna moralia*: Hägerström is apparently aware of Spengels' questioning its authenticity. It is a diligent exercise, conversant with the work of the major contemporary specialists like Zeller, Hertling, Ollé-Laprune,

*Kants kunskapslära* [*The Theory of Knowledge in Kant*] from 1884, that made a great impression on the young Hägerström (see *Axel Hägerström*, in R. Schmidt (ed.), *Die Philosophie der Gegenwart in Selbstdarstellungen*, Meiner, Leipzig 1929, vol. VII, p. 111).

[63] In 1899 he said to appreciate Kant and Fichte, but also Kierkegaard and Shelley, Byron and the very inventor of the word "nihilism," Turgenev. Among the Scandinavian authors he mentions Björnstjerne Björnson, Selma Lagerlöf, Gustav Fröding, Zacharias Topelius, Holger Drachmann and Harald Høffding.

[64] H. Beyers, *Nietzsche og Norden*, vols. I–II, Universitetsförlaget, Bergen 1957–1959. Perhaps Hägerström came into contact with the thought of Nietzsche through Georg Brandes who published his Copenhagen-lectures (*Fremmende personligheder*) on the German philosopher in 1889.

[65] H. Ruin, *Hägerström, Nietzsche och den svenska nihilismen*, in «Tidskrift för politisk filosofi», 2000, n. 1, p. 11: «att Nietzsche fick ett så starkt genomslag just i Norden kan säkert förklaras med hänvisning till flera faktorer, men otvivelaktigt spelar en sträng statskyrklig tradition en roll.»

[66] M. Waller, *Människan som få kände*, cit., p. 173.

[67] Hägerström regularly worked as a "preceptor" from 1885 to 1891. M. Waller, *Människan som få kände*, cit., p. 101 claims that in May 1896 he taught from eight in the morning to eleven at night. August Hahr, one of his students, claimed he fixed lessons between two and three in the morning (*I Vasaslottets skugga*, Nyblom, Uppsala 1943).

Ravaisson and Bonitz. Temperately welcomed among scholars, the booklet can be found in various erudite libraries through out Europe. Philosophically the core issue consists in the difference between the laws of the city-state and the unwritten laws of customs. It is striking that some topics he would later develop are already present: For instance he discusses teleology, a notion he comes back to in his later studies on Marxism.[68] Moreover, the role of philosophy is described in a way not too far from Wittgenstein's: «The task of philosophy is to solve (...) the contradictions at hand.»[69]

From the personal correspondence he seems convinced that he is on the way to a great discovery. He is convinced that he has a lot to offer philosophy. In an interview he gave in April 1939 he recalls to have had a "philosophical epiphany" in his early 20s which opened his eyes to the fact that reality «cannot be a mere content of our conscience.»[70] All this points to a difference between what the letters bear out and what he expressed publicly. Even though some allusions might be made to his later thought, the Aristotle-thesis is essentially a conventional and mainstream *exercise de style*. So why all this caution and tiptoeing? The easy, but unconvincing explanation is sheer academic opportunism. Closer to the truth, in all likelihood, is that his intellectual maturity was yet to blossom and he must have felt an uncomfortable shadow hanging over him; that of Boström.

## 1.3 The Long Shadow of Boström

Christopher Jacob Boström (1797–1866) taught practical philosophy in Uppsala from 1827 and became professor there in 1840. He is perhaps best known for his significant impact on philosophy of law, or *Staatslehre* as it was then called. In general terms Boström accomplished «the most successful attempt to build a school of Swedish philosophy.»[71] He dominated the national intellectual scene for over fifty years to such an extent that Jean-François Battail, commenting on this period in *Le mouvement des idées en Suède à l'âge du bergsonisme*, concluded «we always come back to Boström.»[72] And indeed the movement influenced by

---

68 A. Hägerström, *Aristoteles etiska grundtankar*, Berling, Uppsala 1893, pp. 17 ff.

69 A. Hägerström, *Aristoteles*, cit., p. 4: «filosofins uppgift är att (...) lösa dessa förfintliga motsägelser.»

70 H. Apéria-Meurling, *Axel Hägerström. Samtal med en svensk tänkare*, in «Ord och Bild», 1939, anno 48, p. 421: «blott ett innehåll i vårt medvetande.»

71 S. Nordin, *Den Boströmska skolan och den svenska idealismens fall*, Doxa, Lund 1981, p. 196: «det mest framgångsrika exemplet på skolbildning inom svensk filosofi.» See also by the same author, *Romantikens filosofi. Svensk idealism från Höijer till hegelianerna*, Doxa, Lund 1987, pp. 104 ff. R. Sandin, *The Founding of the Uppsala School*, in «Journal of the History of Ideas», 1962, pp. 497–499; A. Wedberg, *Den logiska strukturen i Boströms filosofi*, Almqvist & Wiksell, Uppsala 1937; E. Ryding, *Den svenska filosofiens historia*, Natur & Kultur, Stockholm 1959, pp. 73 ff.; R Sandin, *Axel Hägerström's Philosophy of Religion*, cit., pp. 55–77.

72 J.-F. Battail, *Le mouvement des idées en Suède à l'âge du bergsonisme*, Lettres Modernes, Paris 1979, p. 41: «On revient toujours à Boström.»

Boström «was all through determined by the existence of a Master»[73] who incarnated idealism as such. Idealism, as a byproduct of nineteenth century romanticism was no Swedish peculiarity, yet Boström shaped it to his own image. Contrarily to other Nordic countries and Northern Europe in general, the influence of Hegel was mitigated. Some of the basic ideas surely originated in German post-Kantism and idealism, but «Boström and his followers actively contrasted Hegel's influence.»[74] Moreover, he also kept his distances from the Historical School of Savigny, developing what would become an extremely reactionary philosophy of law. Undeniably, «Boströmianism never questioned its roots in the old society.»[75]

He elaborated an exceptionally dogmatic version of what was called "subjectivism." What exactly is meant by this term within this specific tradition is often hard to say,[76] but in Boström it reflects a gnoseological theory based on the perfect identity between conscience and its own content. All in all, knowledge is guaranteed by the ontological structure of the world, the Absolute or God, which in turn reflects only on our Self-conscience (through relative perception). Whatever label one might prefer, this strong anti-empirical stance, usually identified as "rationalism" or "idealism" substantially corresponds to what Edmund Husserl termed "psychologism" in his *Logische Untersuchungen* from 1900; i.e., the philosophical viewpoint according to which natural science (or any so-called "special science") can be reduced to the realm of psychology, or rather (since empirical psychology had not been developed yet) to a solipsistic conception of "Self-conscience" that Boström himself referred to as "anthropology." The only "real" form of knowledge was hence non-empirical in nature, and derived rationally from ontology.

However refined idealism became on the continent, it remained quite rudimental in Uppsala. «Compared to the German version, Scandinavian idealism can be understood as more dogmatic, both because of the Platonic and Leibnizian elements and (...) because of the feeble sensibility towards the gnoseological problems evidenced by Kant.»[77] Reason was held to be a manifestation of God, who in turn

---

[73] S. Nordin, *Den Boströmska skolan och den svenska idealismens fall*, cit., p. 196. What came to be known as "Boströmianism" was determined by group solidarity, team spirit, institutionalization efforts and wars over nominations in the academic world; basically, everything that makes a "school." And the center of this web of influences was Uppsala.

[74] J. Carlsson, *Statsabsolutismens rättsfilosofi. En studie av Boströms och Hägerströms rättsfilosofi med avseende på deras bakgrund, innehåll och konsekvenser för juridiken*, HT 2001, available at: http://www.jur.lu.se/Internet/Biblioteket/Examensarbeten.nsf/0/F7C0DCF9A3EB3E98C1256AE60047A1A9/$File/xsmall.pdf?OpenElement

[75] S. Nordin, *Den Boströmska skolan och den svenska idealismens fall*, Doxa, Lund 1981, p. 19: «Boströmianismen tvekade aldrig om sina rötter i det gamla samhället.»

[76] See the emblematic account in E. Cassirer, *Was ist "Subjektivismus"?*, in «Theoria», 1939, V, pp. 111–140; now in *Gesammelte Werke. Aufsätze und kleine Schriften (1936–1940)*, Bd. 22, Meiner, Hamburg 2006, pp. 167–192.

[77] E. Pattaro, *Il realismo giuridico scandinavo*, cit., p. 31: «Rispetto a quello tedesco l'idealismo scandinavo può essere considerato più dogmatico, sia in ragione delle accennate componenti platoniche e leibniziane sia (...) per la scarsa sensibilità ai problemi gnoseologici messi in evidenza dal Kant.»

appeared as the *Principium Primum* guaranteeing Reason. Everything in the phenomenal world is supposedly organised hierarchically according to their grade of rationality and hence ontological rank; a world, in a nutshell, arranged according to "the great chain of being", to use Lovejoy's phrasing. It is not hard to see why Hägerström like many others found this idealistic equivalence between God and Absolute Reason, combined with Berkeley's principle *esse est percipi*, very irritating: In the presumably cold winter examinations, Boström's key question used to be «Tell me sir, is that stove over there inside or outside me?" assuming that the freezing student would respond "inside me."[78]

What made this obscure and outdated "idealism" worse is that, contrarily to Hegel, it did not obey the logic of dialectics. In fact, this indigenous philosophy designed a static worldview, totally deprived of a philosophy of history and based on an unquestionable coherence theory of truth, according to which the basic law of thought is consistency. These aspects influenced heavily on Boström's philosophy of law. From 1833 he was officially appointed as instructor of the Royal House, a position that gave him a certain influence over the future King, Oscar I. As a professor he did what Max Weber called "preaching from the chair." To understand the great authority of his *Staatslehre* it is enough to say that, during the last decades of the nineteenth century, Boström's books were the only requested literature for the preparatory year at law school.[79]

According to Boström law was the phenomenal expression of the "eternal being" or "organ of God"[80] – the State – personified by the Monarch whose will, thus, was rational. In an apparent Hegelian paraphrase Boström affirmed «justice is rational and the rational is just.»[81] He was a severe critic of contract theory, but yet he refuted traditional natural law as a mere "impossibility"[82] while custom (*sedelagen*) was not considered legally binding.[83] Moreover, his analysis of the constitution brought him to conclude that the only rational form of representation of the people was the Swedish Diet of the Four Estates. Unsurprisingly Boström violently opposed

[78]The famed anecdote is told in G. Oxenstierna, *Vad är Uppsalafilosofien?*, Bonniers, Stockholm 1938, p. 43. For the original texts, see C. J. Boström, *Grundlinier till philosophiska statslärans propaedeutik*, Adolph Johnsons förlag, Stockholm 1901, pp. 6 ff.; *Grundlinier till philosophiska statsläran*, Victor Roos, Uppsala 1882 and the recent reprint *Filosofiska sentenser*, Hilaritas, Johanneshov 1998; *Den förnuftiga viljans etik*, J. Siöcrona (ed.), Hilaritas Johanneshov 2002.

[79]For these aspects, see T. Frängsmyr, *Svensk idéhistoria: bildning och vetenskap under tusen år*, vol. 2, Natur & Kultur, Stockholm 2000, p. 162; J. Carlsson, *Statsabsolutismens rättsfilosofi*, cit., pp. 15 ff. His influence continued during the beginning of the twentieth century; see for instance F. Lagerroth, *Boström och Kelsen. En jämförelse*, in «Statsvetenskaplig Tidsskrift», 1925, anno 28, pp. 1–37.

[80]C.J. Boström, *Grundlinier till philosophiska statsläran*, cit., pp. 8–9.

[81]C.J. Boström, *Grundlinier till philosophiska statsläran*, cit., p. 19: «det rätta är det förnuftiga och det förnuftiga är det rätta.»

[82]C.J. Boström, *Grundlinier till philosophiska statsläran*, cit., p. 17.

[83]C.J. Boström, *Satser om lag och lagstiftning med tillägg och anmärkningar*, Schultz, Uppsala 1871, p. 59.

the abolition of the Estates and the introduction of parliamentary rule in 1866. It must be kept in mind that the harsh criticism Hägerström developed against voluntaristic conceptions of law is grounded in the historical and political background of Boström's doctrine.

In fact, the later struggle against metaphysics, especially in law, carried out by Hägerström and, generally, by Scandinavian realism and the Uppsala School, has come to be considered as a reaction against the prevailing "subjectivism" of Boström.[84] However, a more nuanced picture is offered by Ernst Logren in his monumental study on Hägerström from 1944: «We encounter thoughts that Hägerström has partly picked up and reshaped and partly rejected. This twofold relation to the Boströmian logic passes through all his work (...) even if it is rarely expressed.»[85] Boström's legacy was not of the kind you just throw off.[86] In general terms, it has been stressed that «the idealistic tendency of Hägerström's early philosophy was also different from Boström's speculative metaphysical philosophy. [It] (...) has a critical idealistic tendency.»[87]

This paralleled the fact that the cumbersome legacy became increasingly criticised in Uppsala. The year Hägerström arrived, the Swedish novelist August Strindberg wrote that «Uppsala shows signs of obsoleteness and dissolution of a period that might be called the Boström-era.»[88] This was due to the so-called neo- or critical-Boströmianism, an evolution of Boström's philosophy more than a radical break, represented by Carl Yngve Sahlin (1824–1917) and especially by Erik Olof Burman (1845–1929) among others. They both played significant roles in Hägerström's life.

Erik Olof Burman directed Hägerström's thesis and became his mentor and good friend. Burman fundamentally examined the Boströmian legacy in its theoretical aspects. It has even been suggested that Hägerström's characteristic way of

---

[84]This is the central thesis in G. Oxenstierna, *Vad är Uppsalafilosofien?*, cit.

[85]E. Logren, *Huvuddragen av Hägerströms filosofi*, Lundequistska bokhandeln, Uppsala 1944, p. 7: «vi möta här de tankar, som Hägerström dels upptagit och ombildat, dels även avvisat. Denna dubbla inställning till Boströmianismens logik genomgår hela hans författarskap (...) fast det mycket sällan uttryckligen säges.» Among those who insist on the influence of Boström on Hägerström, see for instance M. Fries, *Verklighetsbegreppet enligt Hägerström. En systematisk framställning av grundtankarna i Hägerströms kunskapsteori med särskild hänsyn till hans lära om verklighetsbegreppet*, in «Uppsala Universitets Årskrift», 1944, 3, pp. XXV–XXVI; and A. Wedberg in *Den logiska strukturen hos Boströms filosofi. En studie i klassisk metafysik*, Almqvist & Wiksell, Stockholm 1937, p. 17.

[86]One of the reasons why Boström's legacy has not been investigated properly by scholars depends on the extremely limited knowledge of what he represented in Swedish culture, and also on the dearth of sources. There is very little literature on the history of thought in Sweden and obviously it is written in Swedish. See n. 17 of the Introduction for bibliographical details.

[87]M. Lyles, *A Call for Scientific Purity. Axel Hägerström's Critique of Legal Science*, Rönnells, Stockholm 2006, p. 44.

[88]A. Strindberg, *Tjänstekvinnans son* (1886): «Uppsala visar tecken till utgång och upplösning av en period, som kunde kallas den Boströmska.»

viewing philosophy as conceptual analysis was influenced by Burman.[89] He was fundamentally concerned with the "epistemological problem" of how it is possible to guarantee the objectivity of knowledge. This issue brought him a step away from Boström and a step back towards Kant. Already in 1885 Burman published a monograph on *Kant's Doctrine of Knowledge*. He deepened the focus on German transcendental philosophy with his *Die Transscendentalphilosophie Fichtes und Schellings dargestellt und erläutert* from 1892 and the book on *Schleiermacher's Critique of Kant's and Fichte's Doctrine of Customs* from 1894. This made a great impression on Hägerström: «In 1887 I was introduced to Kant's *Kritik der reine Vernunft* by the Uppsala-philosopher Burman's *Die Erkenntsnislehre Kants* which opened a new world to me.»[90] In general terms, it was «Burman's merit to have put the problems of Kant's theory of knowledge in a relative perspective; he stressed how these problems are grounded on tenuous premises rooted in the history of epistemology and he indicated analysis as the necessary way out.»[91]

Both Burman and Sahlin influenced Hägerström intellectually. In an interview for his 70th birthday made by Knut Hagberg, Hägerström explained: «I was certainly a disciple of Sahlin and Burman. How erroneous is the common idea that you cannot learn, in a grateful way, from thinkers who move in different directions than you do! The history of thought is determined by the fact that one thinker emphasizes and unilaterally stresses one aspect of the philosophical problems.»[92] The weight of the (neo-) Boströmian environment therefore accounts for Hägerström's so-called youth idealism.[93] In particular, what Hägerström seems to have taken from this tradition of thought was the idea of determinateness and self-identity of reality, the general accent on coherence and on the basic principles of logic (identity, non-contradiction and excluded third), as well as a certain interest in German transcendentalism.[94]

In any case both Burman and Sahlin seemed to believe in the young Hägerström and they did a lot for his career. Sahlin, diligently and with personal involvement, requested that he should be made docent the day after the discussion of his

---

[89] A. Phalén, *Adolf Phalén. Die Philosophie der Gegenwart in Selbstdarstellungen*, Meiner, Leipzig 1924, p. 166.

[90] A. Hägerström, *Selbstdarstellung*, cit., p. 111; *Summary*, cit., p. 33.

[91] E. Pattaro, *Il realismo giuridico scandinavo*, cit., p. 69: «Merito di Burman sarebbe stato quello di relativizzare i problemi della gnoseologia kantiana, avvertendo che essi scaturiscono dall'assunzione di premesse non sostenibili, formatesi nel corso della storia della riflessione sui grandi temi della teoria della conoscenza, e indicando che per uscirne è necessario il ricorso all'analisi.»

[92] M. Waller, *Människan som få kände*, cit., p. 79: «Jag var ju lärjunge till Sahlin och Burman. Hur felaktig är förresten inte den vanliga föreställningen, att man inte kan tacksamt lära av filosofer, även om man rör sig i tankebanor motsatta deras. Hela den filosofiska utvecklingen betingas ju av att den ene tänkaren med eftertryck, ja ensidighet, framhåller en sida av en aspekt på de filosofiska problemen.»

[93] On his idealistic tendencies, E. Logren, *Huvuddragen*, cit., pp. 6–9.

[94] See S. Nordin, *Från Hägerström till Hedenius*, cit., p. 28. Max Lyles, *A Call...*, cit., p. 40, underlines that «Hägerström's characterization of metaphysics as an essentially subjectivistic trend (...) can for instance be found in Burman's doctoral thesis *Om kunskapens möjlighet* (1872).»

Aristotle-thesis in 1893. From the autumn of 1888 Burman let Hägerström organise the seminars in his own classes, partly because of his recurrent health problems. From 1903 to 1910 Hägerström held the courses in Burman's place for eleven semesters, permitting him to develop his teaching skills and his reputation at the University. Again in 1910 Sahlin was a member of the commission for nominating the professor to replace Burman on the chair of practical philosophy: He defended Hägerström.

Nevertheless, both Burman and Sahlin eventually developed the feeling that they had nourished a foe.[95] In order to understand this change of heart, we have to shed some light on *der junge Axel* and his evolution up to 1910. Before doing that, however, there is still one more disappointing experience that Burman and Sahlin had to accept from their insubordinate pupil.

## 1.4 "Philosophy is Full of Fraud": The Declaration of Incompetence

In a letter from 1897 to his fiancée Esther Axel Hägerström denounced that "philosophy is full of fraud."[96] It reflects his state of mind well. Two years earlier, in 1895, Carl Yngve Sahlin left his chair vacant and Hägerström, even though at the very beginning of his career, saw his chance to acquire the position. That very year he published two minor books: *An Inquiry into the Possibility of Empirical Ethics, with Special Reference to the Main Modern Forms* and a longer essay entitled *On Feeling and Thrust in Morals as a Rational Phenomenon in the Main Forms of Modern Rationalism*. It is possible that he drew on material he produced for a lecture on February 22nd entitled *On the Relation between Mind and Body in Empirical Psychology*. That same year, in November, he held another lecture which might have been the outcome of his research: *On the Bad Use of Ethical Ideas and Formal Concepts*.

The *Inquiry into Empirical Ethics* is a short essay which starts with a criticism of utilitarian ethics as being too focused on atomistic individualism, since it presupposes a «conception of mankind as a formal aggregate of individuals considered to be entities having constant external relations with one another.»[97] Hägerström, in agreement with Hegel, Boström and a horde of anti-individualistic authors from

[95] In a letter to Vitalis Norström from 1910 Burman declared: «In Hägerström I found my real adversary – his work on the Principle of Knowledge is all through an attempt to defeat me.» (see S. Nordin, *Från Hägerström till Hedenius*, cit., p. 30). And Sahlin's anger after attending Hägerström's inaugural lecture is described in T. Mautner, *Moralfilosofins grundläggning*, cit., p. 10.

[96] M. Waller, *Människan som få kände*, cit., pp. 170–171.

[97] A. Hägerström, *Undersökning av den empiriska etikens möjlighet*, cit., p. 38: «utilitarismen utgår från begreppet om mänskligheten såsom ett formellt helt af individer betraktade som i ett konstant yttre förhållande till varandra stående enheter.» For Jes Bjarup's account, see *Reason, Emotion and the Law*, cit., pp. 39–43.

the nineteenth century, holds that «philosophy of law (...) must ground itself on a conception of mankind as a whole where the individuals have constant inner relations with one another.»[98] It is plain to see that the in/out dichotomy is here a standard of the contemporary philosophy: It is far from original. It is however interesting insofar as he will later claim that the in/out opposition, which corresponds, on an epistemological level, to the opposition between *Bewusstsein* and *Sache*, is no real opposition. In the 1895 essay, he is still far from this conclusion and still engaged with the philosophy of the thinker who is generally acknowledged as a founder of experimental psychology, Wilhelm Wundt (1832–1920). The latter also developed an inquiry into the social basis of higher mental functioning, which probably interested Hägerström. But what disturbed him was Wundt's ecclectic theory of knowledge combining introspection with laboratory techniques. Hägerström, after examining the topic "Ethics" in Wundt, concluded his detailed exposition affirming that «the principle of morals in Wundt is thus (...) unacceptable because of his empiricism.»[99]

This clearly anti-empiricist viewpoint was not only well-accepted in Uppsala at the time, it is also constant in Hägerström and present as well in the other 1895 essay *On Feeling and Thrust in Morals*. So, it is not a feature that can be held to be particularly original but rather, it should be interpreted in the light of concrete events of those days: Both *Inquiry* and *On the Feeling and Thrust* were swiftly composed so as to participate in the competition for the chair in practical philosophy. He submitted them at the end of September just before the closing of the competition, even though he knew his chances were meager. In January 1896 he was advised to retire from the competition. In a letter dated the 17th of January he wrote to Esther: «The fact is that I have opened a new path with my two treaties and therefore my work is rejected, just like everything new.»[100] Finally, in May 1896, his professor and mentor Erik Olof Burman succeeded Sahlin on the chair of practical philosophy and Hägerström was formally declared "incompetent" for the position.

Understandably, he was disappointed. As a result, he attempted to defend himself in *On the Scrutiny of My Thesis by the Experts Concerning the Appointment as Professor in Practical Philosophy in Uppsala 1896.*[101] This polemic and aggressive pamphlet on the "poor" judgment of the commission was completed in May 1897, but published with a slightly different title, *Om "Den empiriska etiken" och "Den moraliska känslan." Svar på kritik*, in July 1897, once the competition

[98] A. Hägerström, *Undersökning av den empiriska etikens möjlighet*, cit., p. 39: «en rättsfilosofisk betraktelse (...) bör utgå från begreppet af mänskligheten såsom ett helt af till hvarandra i ett konstant inre förhållande stående individer.»

[99] A. Hägerström, *Undersökning av den empiriska etikens möjlighet*, cit., p. 84: «Således är Wundt's moral princip (...) orimlig på grund af hans empirism.»

[100] M. Waller, *Människan som få kände*, cit., p. 93: «Förhållandet är nämligen, att jag genom mina båda avhandlingar brutit en alldeles ny väg, och därför förkastas de såsom allt nytt.»

[101] Original title: *Om den af de sakkunnige vid tillsättandet af professuren i praktisk filosofi Uppsala 1896 företagna granskningen af mina avhandlingar.*

had been concluded, since he did not want «to complain on the declaration of incompetence.»[102]

This embarrassing misstep is interesting because it poses a series of interrogatives as far as his intellectual development is concerned. In this period, he started to feel unsatisfied with the critical Boströmian idealism, at least regarding epistemology.[103] However it remains unclear to what extent this dissatisfaction can be said to correspond to a personal and original philosophical position. Could it not have been a young man's excessively high expectations or personal overestimation rather than incomprehension for his revolutionary ideas? Was his thesis really so groundbreaking that he could possibly have felt, like he claims, akin to Luther at the Parliament in Worms?[104] Was the commission appointed to replace Sahlin truly so blinded by prejudice? If this was only a matter of intellectual bigotry why would the protagonists of this ludicrous *gaffe* have offered him a hand in the future?

The commission was composed by Sahlin, whose position was to be replaced; K.R. Geijer, professor in theoretical philosophy in Uppsala, a little stuck in his aged idealism, and P.H. Leander, the professor of practical philosophy in Lund. The latter soon became Hägerström's main scapegoat whom he accused of arbitrariness (p. 53), ambiguity (p. 22) and, evidently, ignorance (p. 10).[105] In reality, the decision of the commission was not as dramatic as it might seem. Of course, Sahlin lamented the lack of reference to Boström, "founder of Swedish rationalism;" Geijer considered – *et pour cause* – the candidate to be prey of a «*Sturm und Drang*-period.»[106] Leander was a little sharper in his opinion claiming the candidate had made too much use of his fantasy and too little of his reason.

The overall judgment was definitely not a statement of prejudice. Indeed, when the air cleared, Sahlin helped Hägerström to obtain a royal donation in 1906 and Burman, the newly installed professor, helped his ex-rival to acquire a grant (Filénska legatet) as early as 1897. If they had thought Hägerström was an unruly radical, would they have given him financial aid? His private letters offer a more likely image. At the end of 1898, he wrote to Esther «now I highly regret that I started a fight over the declaration of incompetence. But once I started I had to finish.»[107] In 1896, at the age of 28, Hägerström had great hopes, but poor results. The

---

[102] See the preface of *Om "den empiriska etiken" och "den moraliska känslan." Svar på kritik*, cit., *passim*.

[103] M. Waller, *Människan som få kände*, cit., p. 171. In *Das Prinzip der Wissenschaft* (p. 41), Hägerström criticised Boström's philosophy as «eine Mischform von Empirismus und Rationalismus.»

[104] M. Waller, *Människan som få kände*, cit., p. 93.

[105] A. Hägerström, *Om af de sakkunnige vid tillsättandet...*, cit.

[106] In 1912, Geijer recalls Hägerström's childish self-righteousness in *Svensk filosofi – historik* (M. Waller, *Människan som få kände*, cit., p. 96).

[107] M. Waller, *Människan som få kände*, cit., p. 127: «jag ångrar nu så mycket, att jag någonsin bråkade om min inkompetensförklaring. Ehuruväl, sedan jag en gång börjat, ville jag föra det till slut...»

inglorious days of the declaration of incompetence were however significant: They were the prelude of his own philosophical awakening.

## 1.5 The Young Axel (1897–1910)

After the embarrassing parenthesis of the "declaration of incompetence," on the verge of his 30s, Hägerström enters a period as intense and productive as it is dark and mysterious for the scholar who wants to reconstruct it. Except for one aspect: His private life.

On the intimate side of life, the sun shines: In June 1896 he asks to marry Esther Nyander. The young girl he met during the summer in 1892 was the daughter of his father's best friend, Nils Johan Nyander who once upon a time accompanied Axel's father to ask for his mother's hand. This was no stormy relationship. She was always by his side. In April 1899, after years of meager teaching salaries, he finally managed to rent a small apartment in Uppsala and on the 28th of June, he married Esther. With plans on extending the family, in 1901 they moved to larger accommodation in *Trädgårdsgatan*, a prim and proper little street just a few minutes walking distance from the University building where he held his seminars and the Carolina library where he borrowed his books. The Hägerström family, with their two daughters, Margit and Rut, stayed there for 22 years. From an intellectual viewpoint he needed to settle down: In the peace of the new home, his scholarly life really took off. However, this is one of the most obscure pages in Scandinavian history of ideas.

The philosophical awakening of Hägerström is something of a mystery, so much so that, while commenting on this period of Hägerström's intellectual life, Enrico Pattaro concluded, in 1974, that «it would be very interesting to reconstruct the[se] moments (...); but the material for such research (...) is still partly unpublished.»[108] Over three decades later, I might say it again. Scholarly work on Hägerström found it tremendously easy to adopt hermeneutical formats developed for very different authors, like Wittgenstein for instance. One of the most recurrent theses is that «two periods must be distinguished.»[109] There would be a "first (idealistic) Hägerström" and a "second (realist) Hägerström."[110] While «the

[108] E. Pattaro, *Il realismo giuridico scandinavo*, cit., p. 37: «sarebbe quindi innanzitutto interessante poter ricostruire [quest]i momenti (...); ma il materiale per una tale ricerca (...) è ancora parzialmente inedito.»

[109] R. Sandin, *Axel Hägerström's Philosophy of Religion, with Special Reference to his Theory of Knowledge and his Concept of Reality*, Ann Arbor University Microfilm, Michigan 1959, p. 12.

[110] For some extreme interpretations of this kind, see I. Hedenius, *Om rätt och moral*, Walhström & Widstrand, Stockholm 1963, p. 10; A. Wedberg, *Axel Hägerström. Några minnesbilder och intryck*, in L. Bergström (ed.), *Ditt och datt. Festskrift till Harald Ofstad*, Sthlm University, Stockholm 1970, p. 5. The idea of a "first" and a "second" Hägerström can be found already in the 1944-essay by Ernst Logren, *Huvuddragen*, cit., p. 6. The thesis has been stressed in particular by interpreters who knew Hägerström and who, mostly, became affiliated to logical positivism and analytical philosophy. The hegemony of this reading has only started to be questioned from the 1990s onwards: I would like to mention the work of Svante Nordin and a recent article by Carl-Göran Heidegren, *Den nya Uppsala-filosofin och brytningen med trascendentalismen* [*The New Uppsala Philosophy*

first philosophical *credo* of Hägerström was substantially a synthesis (or juxtaposition) between what he had learnt from the dominant academic culture inspired by Boström and what he had drawn from the study of Kant's theory of knowledge,»[111] the "second Hägerström" instead embraced what Einar Tegen once called "critical objectivism"[112] opposed both to the "subjectivism" of idealists and to the naïf "objectivism" of empiricists – a position from which the Uppsala-school had sprung.

From being an idealist – it is argued – Hägerström became convinced that «the proposition which is regarded as self-evident in the history of philosophy, and elsewhere, that "consciousness itself is the only immediately given" is false.»[113] The theory contends that even vocabulary had changed. The "first" Hägerström still uses a terminology borrowed from subjectivism, as he admits himself in *Selbstdarstellung* from 1929.[114] Even after his change of heart occurred, as late as in *Das Prinzip der Wissenschaft* from 1908, his language suffers from a «Hegelian touch.»[115] To some extent the idea of a "break" in Hägerström's intellectual evolution echoes (and exaggerates) what he describes in *Summary of My Philosophy*.[116]

This reading has entailed a series of problems for the scholar who wants to reconstruct Hägerström's intellectual path. Here I present four difficulties which should lead us to an alternative perspective on *Der junge Hägerström*.

First, the prevailing reading focuses almost exclusively on Hägerström's "definitive" thought, but it can be convincingly argued that his "established" thought cannot be correctly understood and hence assessed, if his earlier production is not taken into consideration. Using desire of systematization as an alibi, many scholars adopted this hegemonic reading that leaves the early (and not always pleasantly readable) work easily falling into oblivion.

A second problem is that this "first and second Hägerström"-reading fueled a violent diatribe on the "paternity" of the Uppsala School: Was the founder Axel Hägerström or Adolf Phalén (1884–1931)? They were both active and had a series of followers in Uppsala and they both criticised what they held to be the prevailing and incorrect epistemological paradigm, i.e. "subjectivism." Unquestionably,

---

*and the Break with Transcendentalism*] in «Lychnos. Årsbok för idé- och lärdomshistoria», 2001, LXV, pp. 71–102 with a summary in English.

[111] E. Pattaro, *Il realismo giuridico scandinavo*, cit., p. 32: «Il primo credo filosofico del Hägerström si risolveva sostanzialmente in una sintesi (o giustapposizione) tra quanto gli veniva dalla dominante cultura accademica ispirata a Boström e quanto gli veniva dallo studio della gnoseologia kantiana.»

[112] E. Tegen, *Kritisk objektivism*, in «Theoria», 1936, II, p. 27. A slightly different version is available in German: E. Tegen, *Der antimetaphysische Objektivismus in Uppsala*, in *Actes du congrès international de philosophie scientifique*, VIII, 1936, pp. 38–47.

[113] A. Hägerström, *Selbstdarstellung*, cit., p. 4; *Summary*, cit., p. 36; *Filosofi och vetenskap*, cit., p. 115 (my trans.).

[114] A. Hägerström, *Selbstdarstellung*, cit., p. 7; *Summary*, cit., p. 37.

[115] E. Cassirer, *Axel Hägerström. Eine Studie zur schwedischen Philosophie der Gegenwart*, in *Gesammelte Werke*, Bd. 21, Meiner, Hamburg 2005, p. 14: «eine Hegelsche Prägung.»

[116] A. Hägerström, *Selbstdarstellung*, cit., p. 7; *Summary*, cit., p. 37.

«Hägerström was the initiator, the most prestigious figure and the most important promoter in the field of practical philosophy; Phalén might perhaps have been the best advocate in the field of theoretical philosophy.»[117] Hägerström was much older of course, even though Phalén was affected by intellectual precocity.[118] The paternity quarrel was already a hot issue when Hägerström was active. Sometimes he was aggressively accused of being "a concealed subjectivist." At any rate, what is undisputable is that the first and second decades of the twentieth century witnessed the formation of a new "philosophical" school in Sweden: The so-called School of Uppsala, which should be kept separate from Scandinavian legal realism. It did not only have a significant influence on the intellectual life of Scandinavia in the twentieth century, but it also presented original features in the history of thought: Since some claim that «the modern analytical movement, in Europe at least, arose independently in three places: Cambridge, Uppsala and Vienna,»[119] the stake in the fatherhood debate, is largely a question of claiming merit to European history of ideas.

A third problem is the chronological sequence. According to when Hägerström's so-called "break with subjectivism" occurred, the paternity must be attributed to him or to Adolf Phalén. This debate poses the *vexata quaestio* of when exactly the "conversion" from the "first" to the "second" Hägerström took place. If we look at dates, a glance at the state-of-the-art could drive a scholar into despair. According to Lyles' recent survey «the final break with subjectivism and idealism occurred when Hägerström became professor of practical philosophy at the Uppsala University in 1911;»[120] which substantiates the suspicion that all previous work was infested with academic opportunism. According to Enrico Pattaro's careful specification – which follows Martin Fries' timeline in the *Foreword* to *Filosofi och vetenskap*[121] – «the period of Hägerström's decisive evolution towards realism can probably be narrowed down to the time between 1904 and 1908.»[122] Hägerström's daughter,

---

[117]E. Pattaro, *Il realismo giuridico scandinavo*, cit., p. 39: «il Hägerström ne fu sicuramente l'iniziatore, la figura di maggior prestigio e il più importante esponente nel campo della filosofia pratica; il Phalén ne è stato forse il rappresentante più valido nel campo della filosofia teoretica.»

[118]Among Adolf Phalén's books, some are worth mentioning here: *Kritik av subjektivismen i olika former med särskild hänsyn till transcendentalfilosofien* (1910); *Om det kvantitativa betraktelsesättet i logiken* (1911); *Das Erkenntnisproblem in Hegels Philosophie. Der Erkenntniskritik als Metaphysik* (1912); *Beitrag zur Klärung des Begriffs der inneren Erfahrung* (1913); *Zur Bestimmung des Begriffs des Psychischen* (1914). He died prematurely of cancer in 1931.

[119]J. Hartnack, *Scandinavian Philosophy*, I, in *The Encyclopedia of Philosophy*, 7, Macmillan, New York 1967, p. 295.

[120]M. Lyles, *A Call...*, cit., p. 170.

[121]M. Fries, *Förord*, in A. Hägerström, *Filosofi och vetenskap*, Ehlin, Stockholm 1957, p. 9.

[122]E. Pattaro, *Il realismo giuridico scandinavo*, cit., p. 38: «il periodo della evoluzione decisiva del Hägerström verso il realismo può probabilmente essere ristretto tra il 1904 e il 1908.» This opinion is upheld by E. Cassirer, *Axel Hägerström*, cit., p. 79. On the difficulty of fixing the date of the conversion, see E. Logren, *Huvuddragen av Hägerströms filosofi*, cit., p. 6; and K. Marc-Wogau, *Axel Hägerströms filosofi* (now in) *Studier till Axel Hägerströms filosofi*, Prisma, Uppsala 1968, p. 18.

however, insists that the episode of the "declaration of incompetence" in 1896 is already connected to the "conversion" from idealism to realism and that Hägerström at that time, «started to feel estranged to the idealistic positions in theory of knowledge.»[123] Already in 1897, in fact, he laments that «Swedish philosophy is full of fraud and deceit» and by then he also holds that his monograph on *Kant's Ethics*, that he had just started to write, would constitute a «definitive bombarding of Swedish philosophy.»[124] If we presume that "Swedish philosophy" is here a form of idealism in some Boströmian fashion, by the end of the century Hägerström seems convinced that his own thought was incompatible with such "fraud."

If we bear in mind what Hägerström declared personally, the date might be pushed back as far as the mid-80s. In an interview that Hägerström gave to Hélène Apéria-Meurling in 1939, he recalls that he was serving as a preceptor (during one of the summers between 1886–1888) when he was struck by the idea that the relation between conscience and reality cannot be articulated in such a way that reality might be absorbed by our minds.[125] Konrad Marc-Wogau held this statement to constitute an «unsolvable dilemma» for all Hägerström-research.[126]

Conversely, if we take into account what was commonly contended in the universities, Hägerström was labeled "Boströmian" as late as 1919![127] Another significant circumstance should be remembered: The commission – composed by two philo-Boströmians and two philo-empirists – was appointed in October 1905 to nominate the professor for the chair in practical philosophy in Lund and it expressed a high opinion of Hägerström and considered his philosophical production similar to that of another candidate; Efraim Liljeqvist (1906–1930) who came to be remembered as "the last Boströmian" in Sweden.[128] A historian who has studied the official documents of the commission, Svante Nordin, concluded that «notwithstanding strong disagreement in the commission on whom to appoint as number one, there is a striking unison when it comes to number two. All committee-members nominate Hägerström.»[129] If a "break" had already occurred, it would be remarkable if his most distinguished colleagues had not noticed that he considered their philosophy to be "full of fraud!"

A fourth problem associated to the timeframe is *when* to declare Hägerström fully mature: Should we include or exclude *Das Prinzip der Wissenschaft*? And what about *Botanisten och filosofen*? On one hand, the chronology usually makes the so-called "second" Hägerström-period start with the impressive *Das Prinzip der Wissenschaft* in 1908. There are some uncontroversial reasons for this assumption.

---

[123] M. Waller, *Människan som få kände*, cit., p. 171.

[124] Letter to Esther Nyander, April 5th, 1897, in M. Waller, *Människan som få kände*, cit., p. 171.

[125] H. Apéria-Meurling, *Samtal med en svensk tänkare*, cit., p. 420.

[126] K. Marc-Wogau, *Studier till Axel Hägerströms filosofi*, cit., p. 18.

[127] See the opinion of Anathon Aall in *Filosofien i Norden*, Videnskapsselskapetsskrifter, Kristiania 1919.

[128] E. Liljeqvist also wrote a *Selbstdarstellung*, Bd. VI, Meiner, Leipzig 1927.

[129] S. Nordin, *Den Boströmska skolan och den svenska idealismens fall*, cit., pp. 168–173.

In the *Summary* of his own thought from 1929 Hägerström explicitly refers to this book as his major work, even more important than the voluminous *Der römische Obligationsbegriff* from 1927.[130] On the other hand, in the same writing he admits that in *Das Prinzip* he was still using a terminology taken from the subjectivist tradition in philosophy that started with Augustine and followed through Descartes (for instance, he uses expressions like "the Absolute.")[131] Hägerström suggested that he had used a subjectivist vocabulary only to make himself understood in the prevailing milieu.[132] This argument sounds a little captious.[133] Hence some have suggested that, in 1908, Hägerström still had a traditionally "subjectivist" world-view, and that he modified it only later as a consequence of his discussions with Phalén.[134] Hägerström sent a private letter to Phalén's successor to the chair in theoretical philosophy, Anders Karitz, which seems to corroborate this hypothesis. In this letter – dated November 3rd, 1927 – he confessed «*On one hand,* when I wrote *Das Prinzip der Wissenschaft* my purpose was to demonstrate that Consciousness cannot be the logical *prius* when it comes to knowledge (. . .). But *on the other hand,* my aim was to determine the *logical* relation between concepts and not between sensitive phenomena in time and space as such. And I understand very well that you find traces of Spinozian and Fichteian rationalism. But this means, as far as my deepest intentions were concerned, that I failed.»[135] All in all, we must conclude that if, as late as 1929, Hägerström still considered *das Prinzip* to be his major contribution, an exposition of his theoretical philosophy must be anchored in this text: It cannot be simply written off as "metaphysical" or as "ontological nihilism."[136]

Bearing in mind all these different problems, which raise historical as well as philosophical issues, the next chapter attempts to offer a reconstruction of Hägerström's intellectual path starting from a different hermeneutical device and a clearly delimited timeframe.

The choice of the timeframe is due to two major factors. Between 1897 and 1910, Hägerström developed his theoretical philosophy: After the publication in 1910 of the divulgative version of the *Prinzip*, entitled *Botanisten och filosofen*, he

---

[130] A. Hägerström, *Summary*, cit., p. 37.

[131] A. Hägerström, *Das Prinzip der Wissenschaft. Eine logisch-erkenntnistheoretische Untersuchung*, SKHVSU Almqvist & Wiksell, Uppsala 1908, p. 68.

[132] A. Hägerström, *Summary*, cit., p. 37.

[133] The sophistic argument is analysed in K. Marc-Wogau, *Studier till Axel Hägerströms filosofi*, cit., p. 62. Jan Carlsson considers this to be only an "*ex-post* rationalization" (efterrationalisering); *Statsabsolutismens filosofi*, cit., p. 55.

[134] See for instance G. Oxenstierna, *Vad är Uppsalafilosofien?*, cit.

[135] A lengthy extract is published in S. Nordin, *Från Hägerström till Hedenius*, cit., pp. 41–42.

[136] See M. Lyles, *A Call. . .*, cit., pp. 92, 100 and 104. This reading is based on K. Marc-Wogau's account in *Studier till Axel Hägerströms filosofi*, cit., *passim* and especially his comparison between *Prinzip* and *Selbstdarstellung*. However, this hermeneutical device is grounded in the thesis of discontinuity in Hägerström's thought, which contradicts the explicit declarations of the author. Moreover, such readings contend Hägerström's thought developed in a systematic way, which is hardly the case.

progressively conveyed his curiosity into practical philosophy and his epistemological and gnoseological observations are fundamentally inserted within the theoretical framework he had already built up. This does not mean, however, that there were no significant developments afterwards (for instance in his terminology).

Furthermore, the circle of philosophical followers is well established in those years. His later admirers will have different academic proveniences, from law to economics. Therefore, as far as his participation in the founding of the Uppsala School is concerned, this is the fundamental period. The years following 1911 only accomplish the consolidation of what had already been acquired.

Regarding hermeneutics, my suggestion is that probably all these problems would find a more adequate solution if the basic hermeneutical device is varied. Indeed, instead of thinking of a *first and second* Hägerström (according to a popular Wittgenstein-interpretation) or a *pre- and post-Umwälzung* (according to the dominant Kant-reading), perhaps we should start thinking of *der junge Axel* who – like most intellectuals – needed several steps (and setbacks) before maturing what handbooks in history of philosophy would later classify as the definitive thought. So if his "mature philosophy" focuses on «an attempt to secure the *objectivity* of scientific knowledge in contrast to the inherent *subjectivity* of metaphysical so-called knowledge» – i.e., if Hägerström's philosophical «overriding goal [is] to save object sciences from formalistic solipsism»[137] – our purpose must be to describe the steps he took to get there, to illustrate how, as he puts it himself, «all later positions were barely developments out of the first original position.»[138]

[137] M. Lyles, *A Call...*, cit., pp. 7 and 39.

[138] H. Apéria-Meurling, *Samtal med en svensk tänkare*, cit., p. 421.

# Chapter 2
# A Real Conversion: Hägerström on Theoretical Philosophy

*A definitive bombarding of Swedish philosophy*[1]

## 2.1 The Task of Philosophy and the Foundation of *Criterium Veri*

Hägerström's early work seems to deal more with morals than with theoretical philosophy. However, to deduce content from glancing at the titles is to catch a red herring.[2] In fact, the two essays swiftly composed in 1895 – *Inquiry into the Possibility of Empirical Ethics* and *On Feeling and Thrust in Morals* – concern some interesting theoretical issues. More specifically, the second essay on the moral feeling builds on the traditional dichotomies between abstract and concrete, rational and sensible. Hägerström's aim was, as early as 1895, to defend the existence of a real *and* rational world. We might say that he was more interested in *Wirklichkeit* than *Realität*, more concerned with *Vernuft* than *Verstand*.[3] By casting light on the

---

[1]Hägerström in a letter to his fiancée Esther during spring 1897 (M. Waller, *Människan som få kände*, Natur & Kultur, Stockholm 1961, p. 173).

[2]This does not imply that Hägerström did not make considerations in connection with the practical realm of philosophy but that these considerations are less relevant for the understanding of his own intellectual evolution.

[3]Following the Hegelian use, reason (*Vernuft*) is distinguished from understanding (*Verstand*) which makes sharp distinctions and regard them as fixed and unchanging. Insofar as reason reveals contradictions in the products of understanding it is dialectical and insofar it resolves such contradictions it is speculative. Understanding is overcome by the latter. In contrast with Kant – for whom understanding is the faculty of concepts, responsible for turning sensible data into empirical knowledge – to Hegel reason is cognitively superior to understanding even in the theoretical context and it implies the use of concepts in self-understanding. The understanding (*Verstand*) in Hegelianism is the intellect *qua* fixing and isolating concepts (in Newton's sense). Hägerström is familiar with this use and seldom disregards it when employing the Swedish terms *förnuft* and *förstånd*.

P. Mindus, *A Real Mind*, Law and Philosophy Library 87,
DOI 10.1007/978-90-481-2895-2_2, © Springer Science+Business Media B.V. 2009

specific Germanized vocabulary,[4] it becomes easier to understand why he remembered, many years later, that, by the 1880s, he had already comprehended that the real world could not be «a mere content of our consciousness.»[5] The young Axel discovered that we cannot ground a rational world *(förnuftig verklighet/vernuftig Wirklichkeit*[6]) through the use of discursive thinking since it would be a purely abstract activity, neither can we rely on concrete emotions since they are merely sensitive. No passage via the intellect or the senses could possibly ensure the existence of the *vernuftig Wirklichkeit.* The sought-after "real world" seemed out of reach. He discovered that the existence of the real world is grounded in an assumption that cannot be proven: «An element confirming the fact that actualised rationalism is

[4]Hägerström's jargon was basically inspired by German philosophy (transcendentalism, Hegelianism and early modern psychology and phenomenology, such as in Brentano and Husserl). This engenders some serious difficulties for English translations. Here Hägerström's vocabulary will be reconstructed foremost against the background of Hegelianism for two major reasons: It was by studying Fichte and especially Hegel, that Hägerström abandoned Kantian epistemology (and consequent vocabulary) and it was while lecturing on Hegel that Hägerström matured his own philosophical position. In addition to these motives, Hegelianism must be considered one of the most significant philosophical legacies of the time and I shall therefore assume that Hegel's vocabulary might not be unfamiliar to the reader. As guides to Hegel's philosophical terminology in English translations, I have used the following sources: R. Solomon, *In the Spirit of Hegel*, Oxford University Press, Oxford 1983, pp. 273–287; M. Inwood, *A Hegel Dictionary*, Blackwell, Oxford 1992; H. Kainz, *Notes to the Glossary* in Hegel's *The Encyclopedia Logic* (ed. T. Geraets et al.), Hackett, Indianapolis 1991 and Kainz's discussion on vocabulary in the *Introduction* to Hegel's *Phenomenology of Spirit: Selections*, Penn State Press, State College, PA, 1994, pp. 347–352. I have also taken into account J.M.E. McTaggart, *A Commentary on Hegel's Logic*, Cambridge University Press, Cambridge 1931 and A.V. Miller's translation of Hegel's *Science of Logic*, Allen & Unwin, London 1969.

[5]H. Apéria-Meurling, *Samtal med en svensk tänkare*, in «Ord och Bild», 1939, 48, p. 421: «blott ett innehåll i vårt medvetande.»

[6]The German equivalent to *verklighet*, *Wirklichkeit*, is usually rendered, in the prevailing philosophical terminology, with "actuality" and it refers to the fully-developed, explicit, stage of something which incorporates a reference to (teleological) necessity. While *realitet*, or in German *Realität*, might include the contingent and the irrational, such things are only appearance in *Wirklichkeit*. «Actuality is always the unity of universal and particular (...). Where this unity is not present, a thing is not actual even though it may have acquired existence» (G.W.F. Hegel, *Philosophy of Right*, § 270 Add). A curious observation I have made concerns Hägerström's use of the terms *Realität* and *Wirklichkeit*: He does not follow Hegel's distinction in any systematic way. An explanation might be that Hägerström rejected Hegel's idea that there can be "indistinct Being" (cf. infra Section 2.5.4. in Chapter 2) and therefore it would not make sense to blame *Realität* for being conceptually indistinct while praising the concrete experience of *Wirklichkeit*. For example, Hägerström declares «reality (*die Realität*), existence (*die Existenz*) or whatever you want to call it, is nothing but a kind of concept that, without self-identity, would make it meaningless to say that something exists» (A. Hägerström, *Das Prinzip der Wissenschaft. Eine logisch-erkenntnistheoretische Untersuchung*, SKHVSU Almqvist & Wiksell, Uppsala 1908, p. 64). In any way, it is remarkable that in his later writings Hägerström habitually prefers the expression *verklighet* (*wirklichkeit*).

dogmatic is that even Kant, Fichte and Hegel, as far as they carry their rationalism through, ground their statements in a dogmatic assumption.»[7]

This way of approaching the issue led him in 1895 to his first standpoint in theory of knowledge, which amounted to an undeclared form of scepticism that he would later describe as "nihilism" in *Selbstdarstellung*.[8] So in order to avoid the reductive formula of a "first" idealistic phase and a "second" realist phase in Hägerström's thought, I suggest a different way of illustrating his move toward theoretical philosophy: Tempted by scepticism, he initially turned towards Kant and transcendentalism. Since his intellectual evolution follows his readings which in turn follow history of ideas, it was because of his post-Kantian readings that he became unsatisfied by the Kantian approach. Then Hägerström progressively developed his own philosophy, centered on the so-called reality thesis. If this reading is correct, it becomes easier to understand why Hägerström believed he was on the way to a new philosophy as early as 1895. Whereas the commissioners entrusted to judge his work, in the university commission that same year, contended he was simply under a "*Sturm und Drang*"-influence (see Chapter 1), the declaration of incompetence led him to experience at first hand that this sceptical key was no solution to the problem.

---

[7] A. Hägerström, *Om den moraliska känslan och driften såsom förnuftiga i den moderna rationalismens hufvudformer*, vol. I: *Den moderna rationalismens hufvudformer*, Berling, Uppsala 1895, p. 147.

[8] *Axel Hägerström, ad vocem*, in R. Schmidt (ed.), *Die Philosophie der Gegenwart in Selbstdarstellungen*, Meiner, Leipzig 1929, vol. VII, pp. 111–159; partially translated into English by R. Sandin with the title *A Summary of My Philosophy* in *Philosophy and Religion*, Allen & Unwin, London 1964, pp. 33–74. This is a summary of his philosophy that he wrote for the Felix Meiner library of living philosophers. It was first published in 1929, some years after Hägerström had taken up the chair in practical philosophy, letting the theoretical aspects of the "Uppsala school" be handled essentially by Adolf Phalén. Without any need to presuppose that «Hägerström's theoretical philosophy stiffened and did not evolve after 1910» (K. Marc-Wogau, *Studier till Axel Hägerströms filosofi*, Prisma, Falköping 1968, p. 55), it is undisputable that Hägerström considered his major conquests in the theory of knowledge to have occurred around the first decade of the century. The comparison between *Das Prinzip der Wissenschaft* and *Selbstdarstellung* has occupied many scholars: The stake of the dispute is whether Hägerström had always maintained his anti-subjectivism (as many of his own allies claimed, like for instance Martin Fries in *Verklighetsbegreppet enligt Hägerström. En systematisk framställning av grundtankarna i Hägerströms kunskapsteori med särskild hänsyn till hans lära om verklighetsbegreppet*, Lundquistska Bokhandeln, Uppsala 1944) or if he had abandoned a certain "youth idealism" expressed in *Das Prinzip* for his ideas in *Selbstdarstellung* as a result of Adolf Phalén's criticism, as many of Phalén's followers affirmed. On this issue, see A. Wedberg, *Den logiska strukturen i Boströms filosofi*, Almqvist & Wiksell, Uppsala 1937, p. 38; G. Oxenstierna, *Vad är Uppsalafilosofien?*, Bonniers, Stockholm 1938; E. Cassirer, *Axel Hägerström. Eine Studie zur schwedischen Philosophie der Gegenwart*, Göteborgs högskolas årskrift, Göteborg 1939; now in *Gesammelte Werke*, Bd. 21, Meiner, Hamburg 2005, pp. 39–40; I. Hedenius, *Om Hägerströms filosofi*, in «Tiden. Socialdemoktratisk idé- och debattidskrift», 1940, 32, pp. 35–44; A. Wedberg, *Metaphysica est delenda. Axel Hägerström och Uppsalaskolan*, in *Filosofins historia*, vol. III, Thales, Stockholm 1966, pp. 366–377; K. Marc-Wogau, *Studier till Axel Hägerströms filosofi*, cit., pp. 53–83; A. Lundahl, *Det filosofiska arvet från Uppsala*, Nya Doxa, Nora 1997, pp. 87–88. I will not discuss the *Selbstdarstellung* here because of its much later drafting.

Three years later, in 1898, while he was starting to plan his Kant thesis, he published an essay entitled *On the Importance of Philosophy for Man*. Again, regardless of the existentialist-tone of the title, this 50-page-long essay presents some remarkable theoretical features. While comparing the importance of religion and philosophy, he favors the latter.[9] Apart from his romanticised view of the *philosopher*,[10] his conception of *philosophy* is of interest here, for it is understood as the deepest foundation of reality. Hägerström highly prised Kant's first methodological question in *Logik* (1800): What can we know? A superficial glance at this essay could lead to the hastened conclusion that Hägerström conceived philosophy as a traditional form of *principia prima* (metaphysics) in 1898, i.e., an idea poles apart from his later conceptual analysis. Conversely, it would be more accurate to conclude that he believed philosophy should primarily focus on epistemological problems. What is of crucial "importance for Man" is that knowledge should be grounded in secure and stable foundations.

This reading makes his declarations in his personal correspondence less mismatched: In 1897, he presented a view of philosophy which seems very close to what he would claim later in life. The task of philosophy is to «tear away the shroud of prejudice in which mankind is cloaked, perhaps *en route* to civilisation, but in which the holes are now so large a hand can pass through.»[11] Thus, «cold and pure the spirit must be, if it shall perceive clearly and distinctively in life.»[12] This view of philosophy as analysis was later adopted by Ludwig Wittgenstein and the analytical tradition.[13]

Even though Hägerström realised the use of the critical scalpel in philosophy, he had not yet elaborated any positive view of his own. A letter from 1898 is telling: To the philosopher, «all the things that other people revere are only mist; mankind's endeavor, our so-called progress in culture, in morals, in religion has no secure basis.

---

[9] See J. Bjarup, *Reason, Emotion and the Law. Studies in the Philosophy of Axel Hägerström*, Press of the Faculty of Law, Aarhus 1982, p. 43.

[10] Hägerström had a vivid imagination when it came to his own profession. He had a somewhat romanticized view of what a philosopher does. This conception of his own profession certainly must have influenced his students. On Hägerström's high opinion of the philosopher, see S. Nordin, *Från Hägerström till Hedenius*, Doxa, Lund 1984, p. 34 and Victoria Höög, *The Philosophers on the Market Square. Philosophical Modernism from Vienna to Uppsala* in T. Rønnow-Rasmussen, B. Petersson, J. Josefsson, D. Egonsson, *Hommage à Wlodek. Philosophical Papers Dedicated to Wlodek Rabinowicz* at www.fil.lu.se/hommageawlodek, pp. 1–15.

[11] Letter to Esther Nyander from September 1897, in M. Waller, *Människan som få kände*, cit., p. 118: «vi kunna slita bort det fördomarnas täckelse, varmed vårt släkte höljt sig, måhända till dess förkovran, men där hålen nu äro så stora att vi kunna sticka handen igenom.»

[12] Letter to Esther Nyander from the summer 1897, in M. Waller, *Människan som få kände*, cit., p. 125: «Kall och ren (...) måste anden vara, om den vill skåda klart och skarpt i livet.» The Cartesian vocabulary is here clear and distinct.

[13] See for example the famous Chapters 2 and 3 in A.J. Ayer's *Language, Truth and Logic*, Victor Gollancz, London 1936.

Everything that critical reason comes into contact with, falls to pieces.»[14] In effect, the 1898 essay is not particularly eloquent on what the foundations of knowledge are or should be. But Hägerström gives us one clue: In order for a representation or idea[15] to constitute knowledge, and not just a mental state, it «must have a *determinate* character and a certain *necessity*.»[16] The idea of the "determinateness of reality" is one of Hägerström's main arguments. He would never change his opinion on this issue: Reality is said to be determinate (*bestämd/bestimmt*)[17] because it is identical with itself (*självidentitet/Selbstidentität*)[18] in the sense that it is consistent.[19] Significantly, in a letter to his parents, he claimed that this was the first

[14]Letter to Esther Nyander from September 1898, in M. Waller, *Människan som få kände*, cit., p. 122: «Vi finna allt, som andra akta stort, vara blott dunst; hela människolivets ävlan, människosläktets så kallade framsteg i kultur, i moral, i religion finna vi vara utan någon säker bas. Allt, som vi vidröra med det prövande förståndet, faller samman.»

[15]The Swedish term *föreställning*, from the verb *att föreställa*, corresponds to the German *Vorstellung/vorstellen*. This terminology will be rendered with *representation*, *idea* and *conception* depending on context. One standard translation is the neo-latin "representation" as in Schopenhauer's *Die Welt als Wille und Vorstellung* that has in one translation *Will and Representation*. Enrico Pattaro, for example, uses this term for *föreställning*. One problem with this word is that the verb "to represent" has come to signify specific activities, especially in the legal and political realms that might jeopardize the correct understanding. Another possible translation is "idea." This alternative was adopted by Thomas Mautner in his English translation of Hägerström's inaugural lecture. This alternative can also be considered a standard rendition that follows another translation of Schopenhauer's *Will and Idea*. Nevertheless, it should be stressed that "idea" here does not correspond to Hegel's use of the term *Idee*, which indicates the unity of object and concept in which reality is sublated (*Logik*, § 213). A third alternative that I endorse is "conception" since it allows us to keep the same root for verb and noun (*Jag föreställer mig*/I conceive), but it does not always accord well with standard philosophical usage, because it might be confused with the generic use of "conception" as the equivalent of *uppfattning*, *Auffassung*. Thomas Mautner has pointed out to me that "conception" and related words suggest (rational) thinking of some kind, whereas "idea" has a wider application, and takes in imagining as well. In some contexts, however, "conception" is quite suitable and here it generally reflects a mental content, proposition, or belief whose (ir)rational or (un)scientific character has not been established.

[16]A. Hägerström, *Om filosofiens betydelse för människan* (On the Importance of Philosophy for Man), in *I vår tids lifsfrågor. Skrifter utgivna af Sydney Alrutz*, Skoglund, Stockholm 1898, p. 34: «bestämd karaktär och viss nödvändighet.»

[17]*Bestämdhet*, the abstract noun of *bestämd*, corresponds to the German *Bestimmtheit/bestimmt*, which is usually translated with "determinacy/determinateness" and "determinate." To determinate something is to conceptualize, articulate, identify, specify it. Determination and determinacy presuppose negation since a thing is determinate in contrast to another. In the broadest possible sense, determinacy consists of the features of a thing.

[18]In keeping with the Hegelian terminology, Self-identity implies some degree of independence, of having an identity or sameness that is maintained in becoming more determinate; it is not posited. This is why essence is held to be self-identical. Abstract self-identity implies that the thing lacks structure or determinate characteristics since features would contrast with those of another thing and would hence imply connections to it. Self-identity is instead self-related.

[19]Hägerström uses a variety of expressions for designating consistency, but he usually refers to it by *giltighet*, which is rendered in German *Gültigkeit*. (Hägerström sometimes suffers a typographical slip in *Das Prinzip* and spells the German word with the Swedish *i* instead of *ü*). *Giltighet*, from the verb *att gälla*, is linguistically related to the latin term *validus*, which gives *kräftig*,

time he had exposed ideas of his own and that he did not care if they were badly received.[20]

What we also know from the letters in this period is that he had started to work on Kant who had "opened a new world to him."[21] Actually, he had made significant progress: On March 19th, 1897 he held a lecture at the *Philosophical Association* entitled *On the Foundations of Kant's Ethics.* Kant also reverberated in his 1898 essay: Hägerström's best assumptions in theoretical philosophy seem full-handedly taken from Kant's transcendental philosophy. All in all, he rejected both the belief in the "independent" object ("realism") and the belief in the individual mind as a source of knowledge ("subjectivism") since knowledge can only be based on some form of "general human consciousness" (*allmänt mänskligt medvetande/das allgemeine Bewußtsein*).[22] It is present in all individual minds but it transcends concrete individuality, just as it transcends time and space. Such a general consciousness is logically grounded *a priori* and with necessity, and hence it must be presupposed for experience to take place. Without it experience could not lead to any stable knowledge. This is no orthodox Kantism, but it is not far from the "transcendental I."

## 2.2 *Zurück zu Kant!*

In 1902, Hägerström published *Kants Ethik im Verhältnis zu seinen erkenntnistheoretischen Grundgedanken. Systematisch dargestellt.* It is needless to stress that Otto Liebmann's battle cry "Return to Kant!" was starting to echo in Uppsala as well.[23] As they would later recall in their *Selbstdarstellungen* edited by Felix Meiner, the

---

*wirksam*, etc. in Germanized languages; related terms are generally translated into English with "valid"/"validity." *Gültigkeit* is hence rendered validity or consistency in philosophical terminology (as in Kant, Hegel, Bolzano and many others). Hägerström indicates the authority, validity, or bindingness or binding force (*Gültigkeit, Verbindlichkeit*) of something, as for example norms, but he also means its consistency, steadfastness or reliability in terms of logical coherence. This latter aspect recalls the use of the expression soundness in English as it is used for instance in mathematical logic where a logical system has the soundness property when its inference rules prove only formulas that are valid with respect to its semantics, which in most cases, comes down to its rules having the property of preserving truth. This idea is reflected in the German use of *Gültigkeit* as synonym for "logische Wahrheit." I translate Hägerström's *giltig* with valid or consistent.

[20] M. Waller, *Människan som få kände*, cit., p. 122 and p. 173.

[21] A. Hägerström, *Selbstdarstellung*, cit., p. 111; *A Summary of My Philosophy*, in *Philosophy and Religion*, Allen & Unwin, London 1964, p. 33.

[22] A. Hägerström, *Om filosofiens betydelse för människan*, cit., pp. 33–34. Consciousness is the standard translation for "medvetande" and its German counterpart *Bewußtsein.* In the standard use of post-Kantian and especially Hegelian terminology, consciousness stands for cognitive awareness. "Med-vetande" is linguistically constituted like "cum-scientia" but it is distinct from "conscience" in moral or religious terms (*samvete*). Hägerström thus speaks of "consciousness" not conscience. Both of theses terms appear in post Lockean-Enlightenment English, but the notion of *conscience* was increasingly defined in distinction from its emergent cognate *consciousness* (see G. Andrew, *Conscience and Its Critics: Protestant Conscience, Enlightenment Reason and Modern Subjectivity,* Toronto University Press, Toronto 2001, p. 7).

[23] Otto Liebmann's *Kant und die Epigonen* was first published in 1865.

two fathers of the Uppsala School, Axel Hägerström and Adolf Phalén, equally broke loose from the prevailing idealism in Uppsala by taking, so to say, one step back; more precisely to Kant. It was the search of solutions to the problems inherent in Kant's theory of knowledge that stimulated Hägerström.

This reconstruction is confirmed by a series of lectures held by Hägerström on the topic *The State and the Law* during autumn 1901. In accordance with the academic routine, Hägerström kept diaries over his lectures. Carl-Göran Heidegren, who studied these diaries, reached the following conclusion: «The diary notes show that Hägerström's turning away from Boströmianism occurred in parallel with his moving closer to the position of transcendental philosophy.»[24] For example, after a lecture on September 14$^{th}$, 1901, Hägerström noted down some interesting remarks on Kant and Boström: «Self-consciousness objectified by Boström (...). Conclusion: Transcendental philosophy [is] the only possibility to ground epistemologically critical inquiries.»[25] The Kant exegesis definitely ascertains his turning away from Boströmianism.

Again, the title of his 1902 Kant monograph easily misleads: The central aspect of this work is theory of knowledge, even though it also treats issues related to ethics. This is clear from the book's structure: The over 800-page-long study is composed of a preface, a lengthy study on the epistemological premises of Kantian ethics, an "analytic-progressive" part on the concept of autonomy and a "synthetic-regressive" part specifically on Kant's ethical thought. And in the same year, Hägerström sent a synopsis of his book to the newly founded review *Kant-Studien*, insisting on the reasons why epistemological issues were so important.[26]

What motivated Hägerström to write this long exegesis? He believed that the unwillingness of contemporary philosophy to understand that Kant had not based his theory of knowledge on psychological grounds reflected the failure of the prevailing culture to go beyond mere psychology. The late nineteenth century positivism exasperated the young Axel, according to whom the psychological reading of Kant was a «violent construction.»[27] By taking this stance, he announced his interpretative thesis: The Kantian *a priori* does not indicate a form of universal configuration of the human mind in psychological terms. «A purely sensualistic approach cannot hereby explain an *objective* necessity, but only a *subjective* necessity to perceive things in a specific way.»[28] Hägerström's understanding of Kant's epistemological crux is at issue: «To know signifies to move beyond representation towards

[24] C.-G. Heidegren, *Den nya Uppsala-filosofin och brytningen med transcendentalismen*, in «Lychnos», 2001, LXV, p. 75: «att Hägerströms vändning bort ifrån boströmianismen försiggick parallellt med att han alltmer närmade sig en transcendentalfilosofisk position framgår av diarieanteckningarna.»

[25] Quote from C.-G. Heidegren, *Den nya Uppsala-filosofin*, cit., pp. 75–76.

[26] A. Hägerström, *Selbstanzeige*, in «Kant-Studien», 1902, vol. 7, pp. 467–469.

[27] A. Hägerström, *Kants Ethik*, cit., p. 27: «eine heftige Konstruktionen.»

[28] A. Hägerström, *Kants Ethik*, cit., p. 72: «Hieraus liesse sich ebenso wenig wie auf rein sensualistischem Wege eine *objektive* Notwendigkeit erklären, nur eine subjektive Notwendigkeit, auf bestimmte Weise wahrzunehmen.»

objective necessity and the problem consists of precisely how this crossing is possible.»[29]

This means that any form of psychologism is ultimately inconsistent. It moves in circles. If knowledge is considered to be a merely psychological activity, when we need to explain how it is possible to acquire knowledge *about* the human mind (that we pose as an object), we confuse *explanandum et explanans*, the principle *thanks to* which we explain and *what* we want to explain through that very principle. Basically, «the consciousness in which I apprehend myself cannot be identical with the "I" which I apprehend.»[30]

So as to leave the vicious circle, reference has to be made to the "self-consciousness" (*Selbstbewußtsein*) which «precedes every objectivation and which therefore cannot be set as an object distinct from Thought, but is immanent to it as pure self-consciousness.»[31] In other words, the principle of all knowledge must be sought in the circumstance that no object can be posited without referring to the necessity of the *cogito*. What Hägerström called "the *I-think* thought" is the synthetic unity of apperception in transcendental philosophy. And this self-consciousness, defined by unity, informs all representations: It is hence the principle of knowledge, in the sense that it is equivalent to the logical condition enabling reality to be conceived.

However, «this unity does not consist of an actual occurrence in the consciousness. If that were the case, it would only make a representation subjectively necessary. On the contrary, it constitutes Being itself and the principle of all reality, as far as it can be at hand for me.»[32] The clue understanding for Hägerström is that «we have to distinguish rigorously between what subjectively forces me to conceive things in a specific way and what is necessary in the conception.»[33] This central thesis on Kant would later be summarised by Hägerström in the following terms: «It was clear to me that in any case the problem had to be solved in the way that Kant had indicated. Every attempt (...) to solve the problem of the objectivity of knowledge through a psychological investigation of the nature of human consciousness, seemed to me to be based on an incredible confusion of thought. Indeed, such

---

[29] A. Hägerström, *Kants Ethik*, cit., p. 185: «Für die Erkenntnis ist nach ihm *ein Hinausgehen über die Vorstellung selbst zur objektiven Notwendigkeit* erforderlich, und *das Problem* besteht eben in der Möglichkeit dieses Hinausgehens.»

[30] A. Hägerström, *Summary*, cit., p. 35.

[31] A. Hägerström, *Kants Ethik*, cit., p. 185: «Sie ist vielmehr auf das Bewusstsein zurückzuführen, das jeder Objektivierung vorhergeht und daher nicht selbst als von dem bestimmenden Denken getrenntes Objekt gesetzt werden kann, sondern in demselben als ein reines Selbstbewusstsein immanent ist.»

[32] A. Hägerström, *Kants Ethik*, cit., p. 99: «Diese Einheit ist nicht eine thatsächlich vorhandene Einrichtung des Bewusstseins. Sie würde solchenfalls nur ein bestimmtes Vorstellen subjektiv notwendig machen. Sondern sie ist das *Wesen* selbst und Prinzip *aller* Realität, soweit diese *für mich* vorhanden sein kann.»

[33] A. Hägerström, *Kants Ethik*, cit., p. 72. «Mit einem Wort: man muss scharf unterscheiden zwischen dem subjektiven Zwang, auf eine bestimmte Weise sich die Dinge vorzustellen, und der inneren Notwendigkeit des Vorgestellten.»

an investigation presupposes the possibility of (...) knowledge, which has to be explained.»[34]

What is striking with Hägerström's book on Kant is that he considered himself to be virtually the only one who had understood that the psychologistic reading of the German philosopher is misleading. For instance, as far as other scholars' interpretations are concerned, Hägerström reached the following conclusion: «They have one thing in common: They think that Kant, with our knowledge capacity or the knowing consciousness means our *psychological* mind and that "knowledge" – the possibility of which is inquired – denotes a mental phenomenon. It follows from here that their method is essentially psychological.»[35] Hägerström extended this opinion to authors like Hermann Cohen and Aloys Riehl.[36] Such an extension, nevertheless, can be questioned.

Actually, the philosophical panorama of those days was progressively being dominated by anti-psychologistic readings. From this viewpoint, Hägerström seems quite close to the neo-Kantian interpretation of the Marburg School, in Hermann Cohen's and Paul Natorp's readings for example. In *Kants Theorie der Erfahrung* from 1871, Cohen had rejected any psychologistic reading of Kant. Since the major concern of Kant was to find a principle in order to guarantee the objectivity of science, Cohen individuated this principle in the unity of consciousness and in apperception. He later developed this standpoint in *Die Logik der reinen Erkenntnis*, which was published in the same year as Hägerström's Kant study, where Cohen avowed a form of logicism in which reason confers unity to experience and the principle of non-contradiction is not just a formal law, but an element determining reality.

Ernst Cassirer who studied for Hermann Cohen shed light on these aspects. He believed Hägerström had not correctly understood the thesis in *Kants Theorie der Erfahrung*.[37] In all likelihood, Cassirer had a point. Notwithstanding the different Kant-interpretations, there are other reasons for mentioning Cassirer's observations. Despite the fact that Hägerström's overriding goal was to demonstrate the implausibility of any "subjectivist" or psychology-centered reading of Kant, some of his statements in the 1902 essay are rather puzzling indeed. At one point, for instance, he stressed how «Kant's entire theory of knowledge ends up in a psychological

---

[34] A. Hägerström, *Summary*, cit., p. 35.

[35] A. Hägerström, *Kants Ethik*, cit., p. 1: «Eins aber haben sie thatsächlich noch alle gemein, nämlich die Auffassung, dass Kant mit dem Erkenntnisvermögen oder dem erkennenden Bewusstsein das *psychologisch* gegebene Bewusstsein, und mit der Erkenntnis, deren Möglichkeit untersucht wird, eine *psychische* Erscheinung meint, womit gegeben ist, dass die Methode mehr oder weniger wesentlich psychologisch ist.»

[36] A. Hägerström, *Kants Ethik*, cit., p. 8.

[37] E. Cassirer, *Axel Hägerström*, cit., p. 30.

explanation of the universal methods that engenders psychologically the mathematical science of Nature.»[38] These ambiguities have led some to contend that Hägerström somehow felt that Kant was incoherent. Ernst Cassirer pointed to an interesting paradox: «As an interpreter of Kant, Hägerström wants to demonstrate that Kant was the one who really triumphed over psychologism and subjectivism; as a systematic philosopher he considers Kant to be captivated by subjectivism.»[39]

This paradox can be adequately resolved if one keeps in mind that in different moments in time Hägerström acted as the Kant exegete and as the "systematic philosopher." The reason why Cassirer failed to see this is because he treated the Kant thesis from 1902 on the same hermeneutical level as *Das Prinzip* from 1908. In the latter book, indeed, Hägerström listed Kant among the fathers of subjectivism. And in *Selbstdarstellung*, he even described Kant's viewpoint as "solipsistic."[40] Whereas, in 1902, Hägerström believed in the theoretical framework of transcendentalism, six years later, in 1908, he had developed his original approach. Even if his fully developed theoretical standpoint had not yet taken shape, in 1902, however, some elements of his later position can be detected. In particular, his anti-empirical stance was already present: In *Kants Ethik* he systematically points the finger at empiricism and its companion piece, psychologism.[41]

Moreover, it has been argued that a specific event in 1902 functioned as a "catalyst" for Hägerström.[42] In February the well-known Kierkegaard disciple and Danish philosopher Harald Høffding visited Uppsala. This modern man, with his typical *esprit positif*, who had once introduced Mill and Spencer in Scandinavia, held a three-week long series of lectures on the topic *Problems and Directions in Contemporary Philosophy*,[43] where he advocated an empirically grounded theory of knowledge. Even though Hägerström was well-acquainted with Høffding and his presence in Uppsala was a major event, he never showed up at the lectures. Even

[38] A. Hägerström, *Kants Ethik*, cit., p. 2: «die ganze Erkenntnistheorie Kants auf eine psychologische Erklärung der allgemeinen Methoden hinausläuft, durch welche die mathematische Naturwissenschaft psychologisch entsteht»; see also p. 8.

[39] E. Cassirer, *Axel Hägerström*, cit., p. 30: «Als Kant Interpret will Hägerström nachweisen, daß wir in Kant den eigentlichen Überwinder des Psychologismus und Subjektivismus zu sehen haben; als philosophischer Systematiker urteilt er, daß Kant noch ganz im Subjektivismus befangen und tief in ihn verstrickt ist.»

[40] A. Hägerström, *Selbstdarstellung*, cit., p. 2; *Summary*, cit., p. 35. It is however true that in a passage of *Kants Ethik*, Hägerström ambiguously affirmed that Kant was not totally free from psychologism (*Kants Ethik*, cit., p. 100).

[41] Even though psychologism had yet not assumed its pejorative connotations, Hägerström was among the first to clearly promote a criticism of it. See M. Kusch, *Psychologism. A Case Study in the Sociology of Philosophical Knowledge*, Routledge, London-New York 1995, pp. 101 ff.

[42] C.-G. Heidegren, *Den nya Uppsala-filosofin*, cit., p. 74.

[43] Later published in *Filosofiske Problemer* and translated to English as *The Problems of Philosophy*, Macmillian, New York 1905.

so he sent Høffding a letter, excusing himself for his nonattendance by referring to their very different "views."[44]

Whether or not Høffding's lectures worked as a catalyst, it is beyond doubt that by 1902 Hägerström had embraced a largely transcendental approach to epistemology, driven by a strong anti-empiricist stance. *Kants Ethik* was not yet the work of an original philosopher, but it facilitated his formation. Furthermore, this book gave him some notoriety abroad: Leo Rauschenbach reviewed it – not in the most flattering terms, we must add –; and August Messer dedicated a whole chapter to Hägerström's interpretation in his homonymous book *Kants Ethik* from 1904.[45]

In 1902, he had not yet developed this overall view. He followed the path of the history of ideas and focused on the post-Kantian legacy.[46] By studying Fichte and especially Hegel, his doubts on the solidity of Kantian epistemology deepened. Probably, Pattaro's impression is correct: «Hägerström accepted the idealistic criticism of Kant's theory of the phenomenon, but he did not share the answer that Idealism gave.»[47] But before moving beyond Kant, Hägerström adventured into the legal realm.

## 2.3 Stat och rätt

In 1904, in view of his second chance to compete for a chair in philosophy – in Lund, this time – Hägerström took his first steps into the jurisprudential jungle; the setting which harbored much of his later intellectual achievements (see Chapters 4 and 5). He published *Stat och rätt*, a text destined to fall into oblivion, or to be dismissed as an error of youth.[48] Contrarily to some of his key works, Hägerström did not spend much time preparing this essay. To a large extent, it is based on results

[44]The letter can be found in Høffding's correspondence at the Royal Library in Copenhagen. It is quoted in length in C.-G. Heidegren, *Den nya Uppsala-filosofin*, cit., p. 75. Hägerström's good friend and follower Karl Hedvall (1873–1918) attended one of these meetings and attacked Høffding with arguments that might have been discussed with Hägerström. See C.-G. Heidegren, *Idealistisk systemfilosofi kontra den positiva andan i finsk och svensk universitetsfilosofi*, in S. Nygård, J. Strang, *Mellan idealism och analytisk filosofi: den moderna filosofin i Finland och Sverige 1880–1950*, Atlantis, Stockholm 2006, pp. 43–45.

[45]L. Rauschenbach, *Vierteljahrsschrift für wissenschaftliche Philosophie und Soziologie*, 1904, 28, p. 254; A. Messer, *Kants Ethik: Eine Einführung in ihre Hauptprobleme und Beiträge zu deren Lösung*, Veit & Comp, Leipzig 1904, Chapter 12; L. Nelson, *Die kritische Methode und das Verhältnis der Psychologie zur Philosophie: Ein Kapitel aus der Methodenlehre* in «Abhandlungen der Fries'schen Schule: Neue Folge», 1:1 [1904], Vanderhoeck & Ruprecht, Göttingen 1906, p. 84.

[46]See his acknowledgments in *A Summary*, cit., p. 34.

[47]E. Pattaro, *Il realismo giuridico scandinavo*, cit., p. 33: «Credo si possa dire che il Hägerström risentisse della critica idealistica della teoria kantiana del fenomeno, ma che non condividesse la soluzione che la filosofia idealistica gli prospettava.»

[48]Two comments on *Stat och rätt* can be found in E. Logren, *Huvuddragen av Hägerströms filosofi*, Lundequistska bokhandeln, Uppsala 1944, pp. 116–181; and M. Lyles, *A Call for Scientific Purity. Axel Hägerström's Critique of Legal Science*, Rönnells, Stockholm 2006, pp. 429–446.

from *Kants Ethik*. He developed the idea of obligation and duty which had been the final focus in the 1902 monograph. In the preface of *Stat och rätt*, he referred to his study on Kant; he delimited his object of research to «the lowest idea of right concerning the relationship between the State and the Law.»[49] Within this "lowest rank" this book only dealt with «the idea of external obligation.»[50] In fact, following the distinction between internal and external obligation in the section on philosophy of law in Kant's *Fundamental Principles of the Metaphysic of Morals* from 1797, Hägerström explored only on "the practical reality of the idea of duty" (external obligation) since jurisprudence does not concern the unconditional, internal duty or categorical imperative. As «law is pervaded by ideas of unconditional bonds»[51] his inquiry started with the *prima facie* idea of duty: «In every particular case I am aware of the fact that I ought to act in a specific way *because* that action is the right one in relation to what is unconditionally good.»[52]

Here, a word concerning translation is required. Hägerström's book is called *Stat och rätt*. In Swedish, "rätt" has the same ambiguity as its German counterpart *Recht*: It indicates law, but it has a broader connotation in philosophical usage as well. This is particularly evident in the English translations of Hegel's *Grundlinien der Philosophie des Rechts*, which is currently translated into *Philosophy of Right*, not *of law*.[53] The *Philosophy of Right* constitutes, along with Hegel's *Philosophy of History*, the penultimate section of his *Encyclopedia*, the section on Objective Spirit, which deals with the human world and its array of social rules and institutions, including the moral, legal, religious, economic, and political as well as marriage, family, social classes, and other forms of human organisation. Even though, the German word *Recht* is often translated as law, Hegel clearly intends the term to have a wider meaning that captures what we might call the fully-developed system of justice, teleologically "rightful" in its structure, composition, and practices. Now, Hägerström probably intended to deepen a philosophy of "right" in the sense in which Hegel uses the term. Law, in its technical jurisprudential meaning, is only one part of what is called "right." Indeed, only if we consider Hägerström's *Stat och rätt* to be involved with a philosophy of right can we understand why he claimed that he was interested only in the *lowest level* of the idea of right, external obligation, which he found first and foremost in law, more specifically in positive law.

In order to grasp this, it might be useful to compare Hägerström's analysis with that of Hegel. At the very beginning of the *Grundlinien*, Hegel states that the Idea of

---

[49] A. Hägerström, *Stat och rätt*, cit., p. IX: «den lägsta rättsidéen om förhållandet mellan Stat och rätt.»

[50] A. Hägerström, *Stat och rätt*, cit., p. IX: «yttre förpliktelse.» See pp. 137–250.

[51] A. Hägerström, *Stat och rätt*, cit., p. 28: «Rätten är genomträngd af idéer om ovillkorlig förbindelse.»

[52] A. Hägerström, *Stat och rätt*, cit., p. 50: «Jag är i hvarje särskilt fall medveten om att jag bör handla på ett visst sätt *därför* att handlandet är riktigt i förhållande till något obetingat gott.»

[53] See for example ed. A.W. Wood, trans. H.B. Nisbet, *Elements of the Philosophy of Right*, Cambridge University Press, Cambridge 1991.

right, the concept together with its actualisation, is the proper subject of the philosophical science of right. Hegel is emphatic that the study is scientific in that it deals in a systematic way with something essentially rational. He further remarks that the basis of scientific procedure in a philosophy of right is explicated in philosophical logic and presupposed by the former. Hägerström, in turn, focuses on the definition of *rätt* (*rättsdefinitionen*) and he dedicates the first part of the book to methodological issues (pp. 1–32) stressing the importance of the consistency of reasoning.

Furthermore, Hegel is at pains to distinguish the historical or legal approach to "positive law" (*Gesetz*) and the philosophical approach to the Idea of right (*Recht*), the former involving mere description and compilation of laws as legal facts while the latter probes into the inner meaning and necessary determinations of *Recht*. The bulk of the book is hence devoted to discussing the three spheres of "right" – each one larger than the preceding ones and encompassing them. The first sphere is abstract right, in which Hegel discusses the idea of non-interference as a way of respecting others. He deems this insufficient and moves onto the second sphere, morality. Under this, Hegel proposes that humans reflect their own subjectivity in others in order to respect them. The third sphere, ethical life (*Sittlichkeit*), is Hegel's integration of individual subjective feelings and universal notions of right. Under ethical life, Hegel then launches into a lengthy discussion about family, civil society, and the state. Now, Hägerström seems to start from this last "moment." Accordingly, he is interested in the state as the *ratio essendi* of "right" in the following terms: «That the title of the present book is *Stat och rätt* and not *On the Concept of Right* (...) finds its explanation (...) in the fact that the solution to the problem of the State's capacity to oblige its members through law (...) always becomes the main task in the kind of inquiry on the concept of right that is made here.»[54]

So Hägerström restricts his inquiry to encompass fundamentally the state, the positive law and thus "the lowest level of right." His chief problem is therefore the binding character of law from which obligation springs: «In any philosophical treatment of the problem (...) the inquiry concerns (...) the ability of (...) law to create an obligation.»[55] The reason why this binding capacity – at the core of the philosophical inquiry concerning external obligation – is related to the State (and not, as it is in Hegel's *Philosophy of Right*, to the family and to civil society as well) is that the State is «the highest setter and maintainer of law.»[56]

---

[54] A. Hägerström, *Stat och rätt*, cit., p. 32: «att titeln på föreläggande skrift är "Stat och rätt" och icke "om rättsbegreppet" (...) har sin anledning (...) däri att lösningen af problemet om statens förmåga att genom rätten förplikta sina medlemmar (...) alltid blir huvuduppgiften vid den slags undersökning som här rättsbegreppet underkastas.»

[55] A. Hägerström, *Stat och rätt*, cit., p. 1: «Vid den filosofiska behandlingen af problemet (...) undersöker man (...) rättens (...) förmåga att förplikta.»

[56] A. Hägerström, *Stat och rätt*, cit., p. 1: «den förnämsta rättssättande och rättsuppehållande faktorn.»

In other words, if we want to understand what external obligation is and how the practical reality of the idea of duty works, we need to understand how law functions. And not natural law, rational law or any other "subjective reflections over an ideal order (*en ideal rätt*)" but positive law. On one hand, «it is in the opinion of the author that any inquiry of philosophy of law, which does not satisfy itself with more or less subjective reflections on what is right, must, as its constant point of departure, use positive law. On the other hand, it is essential to the study of jurisprudence itself, provided that it wishes to clarify its own fundamental concepts, that a philosophical investigation is conducted, which must be performed without reference to the results of a philosophical research on these concepts. In the following it will be shown how palpable the lack of proper philosophical knowledge becomes in modern legal literature, if any attempt to clarify one's own foundations is made at all.»[57] It is worth noticing that the insistence on the "external obligation" will be important in Hägerström's later disquisitions on the legal realm (See Chapters 4 and 5).

What is interesting here is Hägerström's understanding of the connection between legal dogmatics and philosophy of law (it indicates relevant features of the role of philosophy as a meta-science). In *Stat och rätt*, Hägerström wondered in what manner philosophy, with its theoretical inquiries, can be valuable to legal science. Philosophy of law deals with «the preconditions of principle on which all judicial ideas rely.»[58] Unless these preconditions are cleared out, there can be no coherent system, no real legal *science*. The epistemological obstacle to sorting out these basic assumptions arises from a tendency in Jurisprudence to reificate judicial concepts entailing a hermetic closure.[59] Jurists seem to assume that «concepts, especially the

[57] A. Hägerström, *Stat och rätt*, cit., pp. VIII–IX: «det är förf:s mening, att en rättsfilosofisk undersökning, som ej nöjer sig med mer eller mindre subjektiva reflexioner öfver en ideal rätt, måste taga till beständig utgångspunkt den positiva rätten själf i dess faktiska bestånd. Å andra sidan är för juridiken själf, såvidt den vill komma till klarhet i sina egna grundläggande begrepp, en filosofisk undersökning nödvändig, som omöjligt utan hänsyn till resultaten af den på dessa begrepp riktade filosofiska forskningen kan bedrivas. Det skall då ock i det efterföljande visa sig, huru kännbart bristen på egentligt filosofiskt vetande gör sig gällande i modärn juridisk litteratur, då man öfverhuvud söker komma till klarhet öfver sina egna förutsättningar.»

[58] A. Hägerström, *Stat och rätt*, cit., p. 17: «principiella förutsättningar, hvarpå alla rättsidéer hvila.»

[59] I use the verb reificate and/or reification in a broader sense than its traditional use that gained currency especially in neo-Marxism and in sociology through Lukács in the 1920s. Here it does not designate turning something into a thing, or improperly regarding something like a thing. Rather, I refer to a process of *objektification* or *objektivising* (from the Swedish verb *att objektivisera*) in which notions, especially normative ones, appear as or are taken to be designata of predicates, and thus seem to be properties, which apply objectively, independently from the subject. Thomas Mautner has pointed out to me that introducing "reification" in this context would deviate from the terminology widely used among those philosophers who discuss for and against non-cognitivism. Yet it would allow us to avoid the confusion between "objectivation" and "(moral) objectivism." I therefore use it, with the mention however that it means to treat something *as if* it belonged objectively to certain actions or to certain states of affairs.

concept of what is right, possess an objective existence, connected to words, that science should discover. By discovering this [existence], knowledge is increased in the same way as a zoologist, through an investigation of a certain animal, gains further knowledge about the characteristic features of that animal. In other words, according to this view, the concept of what is right is firmly connected, through words, to an objective norm, according to which, what is right can be distinguished from what is not.»[60] Hägerström called this reification of concepts "mediaeval realism"[61] and, under this label, he brought together authors like Bierling, Savigny, Puchta, Jhering, Schäffle, Jellinek, Thon, and his compatriots Karl Bergbohm, Nils Stjernberg and Vilhelm Sjögren. On the whole, it seems that Hägerström detected this "concept-reificating realism" foremost in the scientific program of *Begriffsjurisprudenz*. He thus accused legal science of exoterism.[62]

What is important to stress is that some of Hägerström's statements in *Stat och rätt* are premonitory signs of his later thesis. For example, we find elements of axiological nihilism. Values already appear to be triggered by emotion. «Determinations of value cannot be related to the reality that Reason sets as independent from the existence of the [human] knowledge-ability, because, so as to have a specific meaning, they always presuppose a subjective element: Emotion.»[63] He used the same wording as in his more famous work: «In "you shall" there may be a "you

[60] A. Hägerström, *Stat och rätt*, cit., pp. 20–21: «begreppen, särskildt rättsbegreppet, äga en slags vid orden knuten objektiv existens, som vetenskapen har att uppsöka. Med finnandet af den samma vinnes en kunskapsutvidgning på liknande sätt, som zoologen genom undersökning af ett visst djur vinner ytterligare kunskaper i hvad som för detta djur är utmärkande. Rättsbegreppet står med ett ord efter en sådan föreställning fast såsom en vid orden knuten objektiv norm, efter hvilken det, som verkligen är rätt, kan skiljas från hvad som icke är det.»

[61] In late classical and mediaeval philosophy, realism was a development of the Platonic theory of forms, and held generally that universals like "horse" or "blue" have an independent, objective existence either in a realm of their own or in the realm of God. Mediaeval realism is usually contrasted with nominalism, and the classic criticisms of realism from this point of view were provided by Peter Abelard and William of Occam. In connection with this classic opposition, Hägerström accuses *Begriffsjurisprudenz* of confusing the universal concept and general representations. As Benedetto Croce claimed in *What is Alive and What is Dead in the Philosophy of Hegel* (1906), the philosophical concept is universal, not merely general, and it should not be confused with general representations, as for instance "house" or "blue" etc., which are usually termed concepts, owing to a custom which Hegel terms barbaric. This establishes the difference between philosophy and the empirical or natural sciences, which rely on types and class-conceptions. Such general representations are, in Hegel's view, mere determinations of understanding. It seems that Hägerström did not disagree. According to the tenets of Hegelianism, from the standpoint of understanding, which holds theses distinctions in rigid opposition, only individuals are real while the universal has no real existence. This defect of the understanding is overcome with reason which relies on the primacy of the universal. (See *infra* 2.6 in Chapter 2).

[62] A. Hägerström, *Stat och rätt*, cit., p. 22.

[63] A. Hägerström, *Stat och rätt*, cit., p. 4: «Värdebestämningar kunna icke hänföras på den verklighet, som af förståndet sättes såsom något oberoende af kunskapsförmågan förfintligt, därför att de alltid för att äga bestämd betydelse förutsätta ett subjektivt element, känsla.»

ought," not as a will, but as a belief (. . .), a judgment with an imagined knowledge-value.»[64] This is probably the earliest version of Hägerström's argument in ethics (see Chapter 3).

Therefore, as far as theory of law is concerned, we find several ideas in *Stat och rätt* that Hägerström would develop analytically in his later work. Whilst he criticised the ambiguity of subjective or individual rights,[65] of common good[66] and so on, he ended the book with a critical exposition of what he called the "theory of norms." It concerned the idea that the legal norm is a command of a specific will (a crucial element in his later criticism of the so-called will-theory).[67] This exposition led him to question the consistency of duty as an "external obligation" which «rules over the Consciousness of Law.»[68]

As far as theoretical philosophy is considered, however, Hägerström was still a convinced transcendentalist in 1904: «The very thought is – as we suppose according to the fundamental idea of transcendental philosophy – the ultimate foundation of knowledge; the truth itself.»[69] We would have to wait until 1905 for Hägerström to abandon this view, partially because of his post-Kantian readings.[70]

## 2.4 1905: The Year of Turning?

In 1905 Hägerström took his second chance to gain the chair in philosophy: It did not go well this time either. Even so, 1905 is a year to remember. At the age of 37, his position in theoretical philosophy underwent a radical change. He would later call this change of heart his "Copernican revolution." In this case, however, the Kantian paraphrase was not so much stimulated by Kant himself, as by another great thinker: George Wilhelm Friedrich Hegel. According to Carl-Göran Heidegren, who, as far as I can see, is the only scholar to have elaborated a plausible account of the 1905 turning, there is a clear path from Hägerström's Hegel lectures in 1905 to *Das Prinzip der Wissenschaft* from 1908. In the scholarly literature on Hägerström, most parallels have been explored but Hegel remains the unspoken name.[71] Yet it is not farfetched to compare Hägerström's point of view

[64] A. Hägerström, *Stat och rätt*, cit., p. 52: «I "du skall" kan ett "du bör" ligga inneslutet icke som vilja, utan som föreställning (. . .) ett omdöme med föreställt kunskapsvärde.»

[65] A. Hägerström, *Stat och rätt*, cit., p. 106. For comments on this issue see Chapter 6.

[66] A. Hägerström, *Stat och rätt*, cit., pp. 241 ff.

[67] A. Hägerström, *Stat och rätt*, cit., p. 240. See Chapter 4 for comments.

[68] A. Hägerström, *Stat och rätt*, cit., p. 241.

[69] A. Hägerström, *Stat och rätt*, cit., p. 66: «Tänkandet självt är ju, såsom vi här i enighet med transcendentalfilosofiens grundtanke antaga, den yttersta grunden till all kunskap – är sanningen själv.»

[70] In *Stat och rätt*, Hägerström initiated an enduring dialogue with Hegel and he referred extensively to *Grundlinien der Philosophie des Rechts* (in particular: §§ 5, 21, 71, 84 and 102).

[71] An exception can be found in S. Nordin, *Från Hägerström till Hedenius*, cit., pp. 39 and 221.

with Hegel's rationalism.[72] Nevertheless, as we shall see, to claim that Hägerström shared Hegel's "anti-subjectivism" does not mean that Hägerström shared Hegel's *pars construens*.

«All in all, it is possible to affirm that the outline of *Prinzip der Wissenschaft* can be observed already in Hägerström's diary notes from February-March 1905.»[73] A clearer arrangement of *Das Prinzip* can be seen in the 1906 lectures on *The Foundation of Knowledge*, edited by Thomas Mautner in 1987.[74] «Sometime during 1904, Hägerström got in contact with [Leonard] Nelson's *Die kritische Methode*. And under this influence, he amended his Kant-interpretation. The conclusion was now that even Kant is guilty of psychologism and subjectivism. However, Hägerström did not follow the Fries-and-Nelson inspired interpretation of Kant as a psychologist. Instead, he set on a new route and attempted to "cut out the corner stones for the new house" as he wrote to his parents in November 1904. In connection with his Hegel lectures during the spring term in 1905, specifically in February–March, he developed his theory of general reality as the *criterium veri* that all knowledge must presuppose.»[75] And this was the key to the Copernican revolution.

---

[72]In 1905, Hägerström's friend and follower Karl Hedvall, who in all likelihood was in the audience during the Hegel-lectures, wrote *open letters* addressed to two members of the committee appointing the new professor in Lund. These letters are of some importance since they enable us to understand how people around Hägerström then comprehended his philosophical position. Hedvall, who was protesting against the Lund-nomination of the idealist Efraim Liljeqvist instead of Hägerström, claimed: «Hegel is, according to me, in the history of philosophy the closest thinker to Hägerström, because of his pronounced anti-subjectivist (or anti-psychological) principle which is clearly stated in the beginning of the *Science of Logic*» (K. Hedvall, *Öppna bref till professorerna Hans Larsson och Harald Höffding*, Almqvist & Wiksell, Uppsala 1905, p. 22; «Hegel är i viss mening, nämligen just med afseende på sin prononcerat antisubjektivistiska princip (eller antipsykologistiska) princip, klart uttalad i inledningen till logiken, den i filosofiens historia, som står Hägerström enligt min åsikt närmast.») Cf. G.W.F. Hegel, *Wissenschaft der Logik* (1812–1816), Theorie Werkausgabe, Bd 5, Suhrkamp Verlag, Frankfurt a.M. 1969, p. 43. Another allusion to Hegel can be found in Martin Fries, *Verklighetsbegreppet enligt Hägerström*, cit., p. xxxii where Fries claimed that the Hegel-lectures from 1905 are "fundamental for understanding" *Das Prinzip der Wissenschaft*.

[73]C.-G. Heidegren, *Den nya Uppsala-filosofin*, cit., p. 83: «Sammantaget kan det sägas att konturerna av *Das Prinzip der Wissenschaft* börjar avteckna sig redan i Hägerströms diarieanteckningar från februari-mars 1905.»

[74]The reference goes to the manuscript *H 105:6* (spring term 1911) published under the title *Moralfilosofins grundläggning*, (ed.) Thomas Mautner, Almqvist & Wiksell International, Stockholm 1987.

[75]C.-G. Heidegren, *Den nya Uppsala-filosofin*, cit., pp. 87–88: «Någon gång under loppet av 1904 stiftar Hägerström bekantskap med Nelsons *Die kritische Methode* och reviderar under dennes inflytande sin Kant-tolkning. Slutsatsen lyder nu att även Kant gör sig skyldig till psykologism och subjektivism. Hägerström ansluter sig dock inte till en Fries-Nelson-inspirerad psykologisk Kanttolkning. I stället slår han in på nya vägar och söker, som det heter i ett brev till föräldrarna från november 1904, "hugga ut de stenar som skola utgöra grundvalen för det nya huset." I samband med sin Hegel-föreläsning under vårterminen 1905, närmare bestämt redan i februari-mars, vinner han så fram till det allmänna realitetsbegreppet såsom det kriterium veri som är förutsatt i varje särskilt vetande.»

## 2.5 The End of Idealism? The Principle of Science

Hägerström's intention in *Das Prinzip der Wissenschaft* from 1908 was to ground the *principium sapientiae*. In other words, his aim was to give a correct formulation of the great problem of knowledge, the eternal question of epistemology: How is it possible to gain objective knowledge? In the opening pages, he declared that he would carry out this task from a twofold perspective; from the viewpoint of our consciousness *(Bewußtsein)* and from the viewpoint of the whole (unity of knowledge). In *Das Prinzip*, he explored only the first viewpoint (*Die Realität*).

The significance of the lengthy research lies, in fact, in the so-called "reality thesis." The importance of this idea could hardly be underestimated since the reason most commonly adopted for calling Hägerström's position *realist* and also for naming the jurisprudential movement inspired by him "Scandinavian legal *realism*" is that this labeling is supposedly rooted in Hägerström's "reality thesis", first developed in *Das Prinzip*.[76]

It is important however to stress that Hägerström did not identify his own position in terms of realism. Instead he explicitly distanced himself from idealism and from what he called "realism." Quite frequently he used the term "subjectivism" so as to refute these two viewpoints, and what he described as "realism" is on other occasions called sensualism or empiricism. So, we should bear in mind that in Hägerström's own vocabulary, "realism" is the theory according to which objects "out there" are, so to speak, ontologically autonomous; a circumstance which in turn – according to Hägerström – engenders irremediable problems for the theory of knowledge, since it is based on the claim that we can "reach" the object through a mere collection of experimental data, for example. Notwithstanding the different labeling, what we need to do in order to grasp the core of the reality thesis is to go from etiquettes to understanding, "from sounds to things."[77]

### 2.5.1 The Method and the Copernican Revolution

«Whatever the theory is and whatever it is about, it has to account for the possibility of producing the very theory.»[78] This observation by Edgar Morin could have been stated by Hägerström who adopted a very specific methodology indeed: Any theory has to explain how it is possible to formulate the very theory at hand or – which is the same thing – it has to account for the possibility that a person is concerned

[76] S. Castignone, *Diritto, linguaggio, realtà. Saggi sul realismo giuridico*, Giappichelli, Torino 1995, p. 29; J. Bjarup, *Reason, Emotion and the Law*, cit., p. 432. Jim Harris claimed that the Scandinavians are better called "sceptics" than "realists" (in *Olivecrona on Law and Language – The Search for Legal Culture*, in «Tidskrift for Rettsvitenskap», 1981, 94, pp. 625–646).

[77] A. Hägerström, *Selbstdarstellung*, cit., p. 48; *Summary*, cit., p. 74.

[78] E. Morin, *Le sfide della complessità*, in *La sfida della complessità* (eds.) G. Bocchi, M. Ceruti, Feltrinelli, Milano 1985, p. 55.

with a problem to which the theory has to respond. Explaining phenomena ultimately means to insert them into a larger context (*Sammanhang/Zusammenhang*). This methodological premise would be sentenced to infinite regress, if there was not an ultimate, definite context above which no other can be identified. And this "ultimate context" can only be "reality" (there is no such thing as the "reality *of* the reality"). In other words, the reason why it is impossible, according to Hägerström, *not* to presuppose the real world (which equals the world in time and space) is because if we ask ourselves questions – which we obviously do – then we also *assume* our own existence and hence the existence of the spatially and timely determinate world. This methodological outlook is the key to understanding the so-called "Copernican revolution."

«Something is, objectively considered, directly impossible to think as non-existent: Reality, in its concept, is immediately identical with itself, i.e. absolute knowing. This constitutes the Copernican revolution in the theory of knowledge. That the world only exists in the thinking mind of Man is a thought which is just as impossible as the earth resting on the back of an elephant.»[79]

In short, Hägerström's "Copernican revolution" is a re-volution in the etymological sense. It is, so to say, a way of turning Kant inside out, a "reversal of philosophical causality" from the subject to the object. According to this revolutionary idea, the *principium sapientiae* cannot consist in the «*I think*-thought» (what transcendental philosophy also called self-consciousness), but it must rely on the "thought of reality as self-identical." «In all knowledge it is stated: it *is* so, it is *valid*, things are *really* that way. (...) The concept of reality constitutes hereby the logical condition of all particular knowledge.»[80] In all knowledge – judgments, sentences, propositions – that consciousness can be concerned with, the determinate reality is always assumed, presupposed, implied. Reality is, so to say, *embedded* in all (meaningful) judgments. «Even so, it is said consequently that reality is immanent to the concept, i.e. it is identical to the concept.»[81]

This Copernican revolution also presents an existential aspect. In *Das Prinzip*, one of the examples adopted to corroborate the new perspective is the going astray experienced by the subject who tries to cut loose from reality-as-self-identity: «All in all, the proposition is valid according to which just as I am directly conscious – without deduction or abstraction – of my own existence, through an act of reflection

[79] A. Hägerström, *Prinzip*, cit., p. 77: «Eines allein ist, objektiv gesehen, direkt unmöglich als nicht existierend zu denken, und das ist die Realität als ihrem Begriff nach unmittelbar mit sich selbst identisch – d. h. das absolute Wissen. Dies ist die kopernikanische Umwälzung in der Erkenntnistheorie. Dass die Welt nur bei dem denkenden Menschen existiert, ist ein Gedanke, der ebenso unmöglich ist wie der, dass die Erde auf dem Rücken eines Elefant ruht.»

[80] A. Hägerström, *Prinzip*, cit., p. 27: «In jedem Wissen wird ausgesagt: dieses *ist* so, es hat *Giltigkeit*, es verhält sich *wirklich* so. (...) Daher ist der Realitätsbegriff logische Bedingung für jedes besondere Wissen.»

[81] A. Hägerström, *Prinzip*, cit., p. 68: «Damit ist aber gesagt, dass die Realität im Begriff immanent, d. h. mit diesem identisch ist.»

towards within, I am also conscious of *every* reflection of the aforementioned concept [i.e. reality-as-self-identity] as given its own consistency, without any deduction or abstraction. Rather, the problematic representation in all reflection and abstraction is an outermost aid point. It is, so to say, the sheet-anchor that Man affixes to all acts of reflection in order not to be pulled away as a piece of wood on the sea of sentiments and reflection.»[82]

This revolution entails that consciousness and its content cannot be identical. In the "definitive" version, the thesis states: «The proposition (...) that consciousness itself is the only immediately given, is false.»[83] As Edmund Husserl was also discovering in the same period, consciousness must always be "consciousness *of something*." Indeed, for Hägerström it is not possible that a conscious being (*medvetet väsen, bewußtes Wesen*), such as Man, can conceive its own *Dasein* (*tillvaro*) as being a mere "idea" (*föreställning, Vorstellung*).[84]

Even though Hägerström had not (yet) quoted the school of act-psychology, some influence from this movement should not be excluded. Pattaro, for example, stressed «the family resemblances, whether accidental or derivate, between Hägerström's realism and the form of realism from the late nineteenth century and the beginning of the twentieth century, that started off with the teachings of Franz Brentano.»[85] Indisputably, the distinction between consciousness and its content was a current idea in authors such as Alexius Meinong.[86]

In any case, one of the major problems of reconstructing the sources that Hägerström used concerns those of his ideas on epistemology, especially in books such as *Das Prinzip der Wissenschaft*. Cassirer insisted on this aspect asserting that «while presenting his fundamental ideas in theory of knowledge [Hägerström] followed his own road without caring about what was going on around him. It

[82] A. Hägerström, *Prinzip*, cit., p. 79: «Im ganzen gilt da der Satz, dass ebenso unmittelbar wie ich bei nach innen gewandtem Reflektieren mir meiner eigen Existenz bewusst bin – ohne alles Schliessen oder Abstrahieren – ich auch bei *allem* Reflektieren mir des ebengenannten Begriffs als in sich selbst Bestand habend bewusst bin – ohne alles Schliessen oder Abstrahieren. Vielmehr ist die fragliche Vorstellung bei allem Schliessen und Abstrahieren als äusserster Stützpunkt gegenwärtig. Sie ist sozusagen ein Anker, den der Mensch bei allem seinem Reflektieren auswirft, um nicht wie ein Holzstückchen auf dem Meere seiner Gefühle und Reflexionen umhergetrieben zu werden.»

[83] A. Hägerström, *Selbstdarstellung*, cit., p. 4; *Summary*, cit., p. 36; *Filosofi och vetenskap*, Ehlin, Stockholm 1957, p. 115.

[84] M. Fries, *Verklighetsbegreppet enligt Axel Hägerström*, cit., pp. 526–528.

[85] E. Pattaro, *Il realismo giuridico scandinavo*, cit., p. 44: «ciò che (...) importa notare è (...) la parentela, sia esso casuale o derivata, tra il realismo del Hägerström e quel filone del realismo di fine Ottocento, inizio Novecento, derivante dall'insegnamento di Franz Brentano.»

[86] Hägerström criticised Meinong (but also Lipps and Brentano) in *Kritiska punkter i värdepsykologien* from 1910 and he commented extensively on Meinong in *Värdepsykologi*, his lectures from the years 1909–1910. See Bo Petersson, *Axel Hägerströms värdeteori*, Filosofiska föreningen vid Uppsala universitet, Uppsala 1973, pp. 30, 79–80. In any case, Meinong's theory of objects was precedent to Hägerström's *Prinzip*.

seems that in this field he did not feel the need to confront himself with others.»[87] Interestingly enough, Cassirer laid particular emphasis on the lack of reference to Edmund Husserl. Even if Hägerström did not mention his elder colleague from Halle, as far as I see, there seems to be some good evidence for claiming that Hägerström had read the *Logische Untersuchungen*: First, the *Untersuchungen* were generally read in Uppsala, which is clear for instance in Adolf Phalén's *Zur Bestimmung des Begriffs des Psychischen* from 1904, which was published four years earlier than Hägerström's *Prinzip*.[88] Moreover, the denigration of psychologism in *Das Prinzip* recalls Husserl's remarks in the *Logical Inquiries* both as far as arguments and style are concerned.[89] Last but not least, when Hägerström finished *Das Prinzip*, he sent an autographed copy to the father of modern phenomenology: It can now be found in the Husserl archive in Leuven in Belgium.

Regardless of whether Husserl was a source or not,[90] the Copernican revolution led Hägerström to uphold an interesting form of inter-subjectivity, or rather a form of cognitive interdependence. It is Reality as *Selbstidentität* or determinateness that guarantees the cognitive interdependence between Consciousness (the subject) and what is externally the focus of knowledge (traditionally, the object). The idea of reality-as-self-identical guarantees that an object can be an object of human knowledge. Using the vocabulary of phenomenology, we could say that «the determinateness (...) enables us to relate to the object.»[91] In other words, «Hägerström's

---

[87] E. Cassirer, *Axel Hägerström*, cit., p. 22: «Denn er selsbt ist in der Darstellung seiner erkenntnistheoretischen Grundgedanken seinen eigenen Weg gegangen, ohne nach rechts oder links zu blicken. Das Bedürfnis nach einer Auseinandersetzung mit anderen Forschern scheint er auf diesem Gebiet nicht empfunden zu haben.»

[88] Hägerström was not unaware of Phalén's work: He explicitly mentions it in *Selbstdarstellung*, cit., p. 6; *Summary*, cit., p. 38.

[89] I refer to the famous thesis according to which «every doctrine is *ipso facto* relativistic, a case of specific relativism, if, with the empiricists, it treats the pure laws of logic as empirical, psychological laws. It is likewise relativistic, if, with the apriorists, it deduces these laws, in more or less mythic fashion, from certain "original forms" or "modes of functioning" of the (human) understanding (...), from the *intellectus ipse* which, as an innate (generally human) disposition, precedes all actual thought and experience. All the objections we have made to specific relativism also affect such doctrines.» This implies that «specific relativism makes the assertion: Anything is true for a given species of judging beings that, by their constitution and laws of thought, must count as true. This doctrine is absurd. For it is part of its sense that the same proposition or content of judgment can be true for a subject of the species *homo*, but may be false for another subject of a differently constituted species. The same content of judgment cannot, however, be both true and false: This follows from mere sense of 'true' and 'false'. If the relativist gives these words their appropriate meaning, his thesis is in conflict with its own sense» (E. Husserl, *Logische Untersuchungen* [1900]; Eng. trans. by J.N. Findlay, *Logical Investigations*, Routledge, London, New York 2001, p. 82 and p. 79).

[90] For a comparison between Hägerström's and Husserl's standpoints, see J. Bengtsson, *Den fenomenologiska rörelsen i Sverige: mottagande och inflytande 1900–1968*, Daidalos, Göteborg 1991, p. 88.

[91] E. Pattaro, *Il realismo giuridico svedese*, cit., p. 43: «La determinatezza (...) consente che ci si possa rapportare all'oggetto.»

ontology holds that both the subject and the object exist in the same physical realm of reality, whereby correspondence between the two becomes possible.»[92] In order for the epistemological problem to be meaningful, the world and human consciousness, object and subject, must be in such a relation that they both persist in the knowledge process. The only way to maintain such a link between the parties is to presuppose that they are both located within the same context: Reality. If an epistemological link is upheld, then subsequently a correspondence theory of truth can be endorsed in science.

One might ask, however, whether this standpoint – reality as determinate and self-identical which ultimately is the foundation of knowledge (i.e. a link between the "I" and the "object" of knowledge) – is a metaphysical assumption. If this were true, Hägerström would fall into his own trap. While *prima facie* this might seem to be the case, a closer look shows that his "Copernican revolution" is intellectually a little sharper than that. He never attempted to offer any proof or evidence of the existence of the world. If he did so, he would obviously end up in metaphysics. "It is not how things are in the world that is mystical, but that it exists" as Wittgenstein would put it a few years later.[93]

Hägerström did not intend to demonstrate that the world of experience truly exists. He realised that every attempt to demonstrate anything implies the assumption of the world's reality and this, in turn, means that denying reality must be inconsistent. Hägerström's argumentation followed the logic of Aristotle's elenctic proof of the principle of non-contradiction, an argument which he had studied since his twenties. By showing the inconsistency of the opposite thesis, his assumption is left to be the only one standing (however, *that* the world *exists* remains a postulate: It cannot be proven in any positive terms). Only in this very narrow sense, is reality *presupposed* or *embedded* in all judgments and therefore in all knowledge. This is quite an elegant way of arguing which is based on the principle of non-contradiction which «more than expressing a law of thought, tells us what reality is.»[94]

### *2.5.2 Knowledge Between Scylla and Charybdis*

As commonly known, one of the best ways to comprehend what a thinker suggests is to understand what he rejects. So in order to clarify what Hägerström meant by reality, we shall first point to the two positions he attacked.

In *Das Prinzip*, the great problem of knowledge is beset on both sides by Scylla and Chaybdis. On one hand, the risk is to fall into solipsism (which ultimately ends up in sheer nihilism or scepticism, invalidating the very search for *principium sapientiae*); and on the other hand, the risk is to be too Kantian, that is «one can in

---

[92] M. Lyles, *A Call...*, cit., p. 55.

[93] L. Wittgenstein, *Tractatus logico-philosophicus*, Routledge & Kegan Paul, London 2001, 6.44.

[94] E. Pattaro, *Il realismo giuridico scandinavo*, cit., p. 47: «il quale, più che esprimere una legge di pensiero, dice che cosa è la realtà.»

the subject presume determinations which are valid beyond the subject, so-called determinations *a priori*.»[95] This latter argument sounds just like a criticism to his previous transcendental position. The problem with this viewpoint is that we have to assume that the principle guaranteeing the objectivity of knowledge resides both *in* the subject and *beyond* it. According to Hägerström, in his *post*-Copernican revolution stance, the inquiry is hence badly formulated and misleading; because whenever we search for the principle of knowledge, we are already assuming that something can be knowledge *for* us. This implies, consecutively, that we do assume the reality of the world and consciousness. Ultimately, this means that, in order to make the epistemological problem meaningful, we always assume the idea of "reality-as-self-identical." According to the Copernican swift of perspective, the determinateness or self-identity of reality must hence constitute the very point of Archimedes: «The problem of the theory of knowledge has now completely changed shape. It is no longer concerned with how I can gain certitude about this or that fact. It is concerned with establishing the consistency of an object, assuming the known object as consistent; in doing so the object [of knowledge] is set in relation with the absolutely valid concept.»[96]

Once Hägerström had completed his Copernican revolution, he was free to hit his targets. First of all, he attacked the *ingénue* empiricism or "realism" that considers the objects of the world to be "out there," removing any role whatsoever from the subject in the search for knowledge.[97] His sword was directed towards the naïf faith that Dr Johnson gave expression to in his refutation of Berkeley; a viewpoint that made a come-back in the late nineteenth century as a form of hymn to positivism. A powerful image of this kind of over-assurance is expressed by the botanist in Hägerström's 1910 popular essay *Botanisten och filosofen* (see *infra*). Against the empiricist's belief in the senses and experience, Hägerström used the traditional Kantian argument against Hume: Experience leads to knowledge only if it is based on causality which, in turn, cannot be grounded on experience, but only presupposed. The more empirical evidence the empiricist presents, the more Hägerström sees his own point proved: «With every degree of modification or with every step to extend the significance of experience, it becomes clearer to see that the general reality is a condition of experience in its extended significance.»[98]

---

[95] A. Hägerström, *Prinzip*, cit., p. 9: «Man kann bei dem Subjekt selbst Bestimmungen annehmen, die eine Giltigkeit [sic] besitzen, welche sich über dasselbe hinaus erstreckt, sog. apriorische Bestimmungen.»

[96] A. Hägerström, *Prinzip*, cit., p.13: «Das erkenntnistheoretische Problem hat nun ganz und gar seine Gestalt geändert. Es gilt nun nicht zu erörtern, wie ich dieser oder jener Sache gewiss sein kann. Sondern es gilt, von dem gedachten Objekt selbst aus seine Gültigkeit dadurch zu entscheiden, dass es mit dem absolut gültigen Begriff in Verbindung gesetzt wird.»

[97] A. Hägerström, *Prinzip*, cit., pp. 54 ff.

[98] A. Hägerström, *Prinzip*, cit., p. 36: «Bei jedem Grad seiner Modifizierung oder bei jedem Schritt zu einer Erweiterung der Bedeutung der Erfahrung tritt in immer schärferen Konturen die allgemeine Realität als Bedingung für die Erfahrung in ihrer erweiterten Bedeutung hervor.»

This attack on empiricism, considered as a doctrine which confuses the whole and its parts, can be found in Hägerström's diary notes from the Hegel lectures. He shared Hegel's sharp criticism of naïf empiricism and on February 22nd, 1905 he lectured on the topic «General reality as the primary [element] in relation to the particular [reality]. Empiricism criticised from this viewpoint.»[99] On March 4th, he continued his attack on empiricism and its attempt to «derive general reality from the particular reality as the immediately given.»[100] Hence, it seems that this part of Hägerström's *Prinzip* was already clear to him in 1905.

On the other hand, he criticised «the assumption of a determinate subjective certitude as *criterium veri.*»[101] In this latter case, the target of the criticism is the Berkeleian drift of idealism that was particularly palpable in the local admiration for Boström: This whole ideology was an exercise in which «l'objet est escamoté.»[102] In this case it is not the subject, but the object that is disregarded in the quest for knowledge. Hägerström contested that we can abstract from all but the *res cogitans*, consciousness. The error is that, insofar as «the abstraction consists in an act [i.e. mental state], it is placed in time and its reality is hence only time-dependent.»[103] Hägerström's aversion for such a thesis is evident in *Das Prinzip*. He virtually started off where he had ended his *Kants Ethik*.[104] As a matter of fact, «it is believed that the theory of knowledge is conducted when a psychological construction of experience can be made in accord with Hume and a psychologistic reading of Kant.»[105] Hägerström's argument is that transcendentalism used a term of the relation as if it were the very relation. Hägerström's argumentation is said to be very close to that of George Edward Moore,[106] who focused on the impossibility

---

[99] A. Hägerström, Diarier Uppsala Universitet: «den allmänna realiteten såsom den primära i förhållande till den särskilda. Kritik av empirismen i detta avseende»; quote from C.-G. Heidegren, *Den nya Uppsala-filosofin*, cit., p. 82.

[100] A. Hägerström, Diarier Uppsala Universitet: «härleda den allmänna realiteten ur den särskilda såsom den omedelbart givna»; quote from C.-G. Heidegren, *Den nya Uppsala-filosofin*, cit., p. 82.

[101] A. Hägerström, *Prinzip*, cit., p. 8: «die Annahme einer bestimmten subjektiven Gewissheit als Kriterium veri.»

[102] J.-F. Battail, *Le mouvement des idées en Suède à l'âge du bergsonisme*, Lettres Modernes, Paris 1979, p. 177.

[103] A. Hägerström, *Prinzip*, cit., p. 76: «Soweit die Abstraktion ein Akt ist, fällt sie in die Zeit und hat ihre Realität nur als zeitlich.»

[104] A. Hägerström, *Prinzip*, cit., pp. 9–12 and 76–77.

[105] A. Hägerström, *Prinzip*, cit., p. 10: «Man glaubt es sei Erkenntnistheorie, wenn man in Übereinstimmung mit Hume und einer pschologischen Auffassung von Kant eine psychologische Konstruktion der Erfahrung geben kann.»

[106] A. Hägerström, *Prinzip*, cit., pp. 76 ff. See also *Filosofi och vetenskap*, cit., pp. 120 ff.; *Summary*, cit., pp. 38 ff. This analogy has been stressed by A. Wedberg, *Den logiska strukturen i Boströms filosofi*, cit., p. 38; K. Marc-Wogau, *Studier till Axel Hägerströms filosofi*, cit., pp. 16–20; E. Pattaro, *Il realismo giuridico scandinavo*, cit., p. 41; Bo Petersson, *Axel Hägerströms värdeteori*, cit., p. 115. A commentator opposing this prevailing view is S. Nordin, *Från Hägerström till Hedenius*, cit., p. 51. This is one of the controversial points of the Uppsala School since it is often upheld that it was really discovered by Adolf Phalén (see Wedberg, *loc. cit.*). On the reasons why Hägerström could not have been aware of Moore, see K. Marc-Wogau in *Studier till Axel*

of defining "simple notions", such as "good" or "yellow" by pointing to good or yellow objects.[107]

### 2.5.3 The Reality Thesis Unfolded

If we look a little closer to what "reality" meant for Hägerström's theoretical philosophy, it is possible to say that there are three ways of being real.[108]

The first sense of reality is determinateness or self-identity, i.e. consistency.[109] Actually, *Selbstidentität* is the German term Hägerström used in *Das Prinzip* and it reflects his "subjectivistic" or "idealistic" vocabulary which he consecutively modified. Some years later, he preferred the expression "determinateness."[110] Already

---

*Hägerströms filosofi*, cit., p. 19 who claims the only copy of the review "Mind" in Uppsala was unavailable. Another opinion is expressed in Stig Strömholm, Hans-Heinrich Vogel, *Le "réalisme scandinave" dans la philosophie du droit*, LGDJ, Paris 1975, p. 39. On G.E. Moore's eventual influence on Hägerström, see also J. Bjarup, *Ought and Reality. Hägerström's Inaugural Lecture Re-considered* in P. Wahlgren (ed.), «Scandinavian Studies in Law», vol. 40, Almqvist & Wiksell, Stockholm 2000, pp. 11–72.

107 G.E. Moore, *Principia Ethica* (1903), Cambridge University Press, Cambridge 1954, pp. 7–10: «My position is that "good" is a simple notion, just as "yellow" is a simple notion; that, just as you cannot, by any matter of means, explain to anyone who does not already know it, what yellow is, so you cannot explain what good is (...). "Good" has no definition because it is simple and has no parts. It is one of those innumerable objects of thought which are themselves incapable of definition, because they are the ultimate terms by reference to which whatever *is* capable of definition must be defined (...). Consider yellow for example. We may try to define it, by describing its physical equivalent (...). But a moment's reflection is sufficient to show that those light-vibrations are not themselves what we mean by yellow (...). This view I propose to call the "naturalistic fallacy".»

108 Cf. K. Marc-Wogau's *Axel Hägerström's Ontology*, in R.E Olson, A.M. Parel (eds.), *Contemporary Philosophy in Scandinavia*, John Hopkins Press, Baltimore 1972, pp. 479–490. This does not mean that there are three degrees of reality: It would be misleading to think of any gradual structure of reality. As we shall see, the reason why existence cannot be gradual is because Hägerström did not admit the logical possibility of "nothingness." Any dividing of reality into degrees traditionally presumed a mix between Being and Nothingness. Hägerström rejected the possibility of such a mix. It is not possible to be "more or less" real: Something is real or it is not. «Die Wirklichkeit selbst hat keine Grade» (*Selbstdarstellung*, cit., p. 129). For a list of the ways in which Hägerström used the term *reality*, see J. Hemberg, *Religion och metafysik*, Diakonistyr, Stockholm 1966; and S. Castignone, *La macchina del diritto. Il realismo giuridico in Svezia*, Edizioni di Comunità, Milano 1974, pp. 37–38; L. Hierro, *El realismo jurídico escandinavo. Una teoría empirista del derecho*, Torres, Valencia 1981, p. 142.

109 See *supra* n. 19.

110 A. Hägerström, *Selbstdarstellung*, cit., p. 18; *Summary*, cit., p. 50; Hägerström claimed that, after *Das Prinzip*, he preferred using the expression "determinateness" instead of "self-identical." K. Marc-Wogau (*Studier till Axel Hägerströms filosofi*, cit., pp. 55–59) has particularly studied this change of vocabulary and the consequences that he believed the change entailed. An account in English can be found in M. Lyles, *A Call...*, cit., pp. 94–106. For Hägerström, determinateness and self-identity are synonyms and this is also clear, for example, in the French translation of Ernst Cassirer's book on Hägerström: Joël Gaubert translates "self-identity" with "non-contradiction"

in the 1905 Hegel lectures, Hägerström had been analysing the specific meaning of this "self-identity." On May 27th, he registered in his diary that his lecture concerned «Identity with self = identity between being and the concept.»[111] In more general terms, "self-identity" means the same thing as the expression – common both in post-Hegelian and phenomenological vocabulary – that something is "immediately given." Traditionally, modern philosophy held consciousness to be "immediately given," since the certitude of *cogito ergo sum* needed no mediation to be experienced. As we have seen, this is no longer true for Hägerström, who instead held "reality" to be immediately or primarily given (*det allena omedelbart givna/das allein unmittelbar Gegebene*); that is immanent or embedded in all judgments.[112]

This also clarifies Hägerström's otherwise rather mysterious use of the term "absolute." In the prevailing philosophical jargon, the "absolute" (*absolut, das Absolute*) indicated what is complete, self-contained and all-encompassing (a.k.a. God, or a hypostatic version of Thought) as in Hegel's definition «the Absolute is Mind» (*Philosophy of Mind*, § 384). Hägerström used the expression with a clear etymological reference; *ab-solutus* is said about something that has no ties, linkages, or bounds. So "absolute" is reality for Hägerström, the unavoidable premise and foundation of all our judgments; the principle from which all descends but that cannot be said to derive from something else.[113]

Hägerström claimed that reality as determinateness or self-identity is the simple element, the principle of all knowledge. «It is clear that we are dealing with an intuition that cannot be furthermore dissociated. Every additional attempt to analyse this concept inevitably ends up in a vicious circle. As far as (...) self-identity is concerned, we need to think about what we mean when we designate an object as determinate in this and that way.»[114] So in order for something to be real, in this first sense (1), it has to be logically consistent. The customary counterexample is, of course, the "circular square."[115] Once we have specified what "determinate" means,

---

following the tradition of Aristotle's *Metaphys.* A (E. Cassirer, *Éloge de la métaphysique. Axel Hägerström. Une étude de la philosophie suédoise contemporaine*, Cerf, Paris 1996). See also S. Nordin, *Från Hägerström till Hedenius*, cit., p. 40.

[111] A. Hägerström, Diarier Uppsala Universitet, «identitet med sig själv = identitet mellan varat och begreppet»; quote from C.G. Heidegren, *Den nya Uppsala-filosofin*, cit., p. 98.

[112] A. Hägerström, *Prinzip*, cit., especially pp. 54 ff.

[113] For a different interpretation of the concept of absolute in *Prinzip*, see Bo Petersson, *Axel Hägerströms värdeteori*, cit., pp. 28–29.

[114] A. Hägerström, *Prinzip*, cit., p. 87: «Es ist klar, dass er sich dabei um eine nicht weiter auflösbare Intuition handelt. Jeder Versuch, diesen Begriff weiter aufzulösen, gerät in einen unvermeidlichen Zirkel. Was (...) die Selbstidentität betrifft, so haben wir daran zu denken, was wir meinen, wenn wir einen Gegenstand als ein bestimmtes Dies bezeichnen.»

[115] We will not discuss here to what extent mathematical formulas can "square" the circle. It is worth noticing that Hägerström usually argued on purely linguistic grounds. This is also true in his analysis of the proposition or judgment "Man-does-not-breath-with-gills," where the semantic content is never assessed. These features however are more related to Hägerström's theory of language than, strictly speaking, to his reality thesis.

it is clear to see that "indeterminate" does not simply mean linguistically "vague" but rather logically fuzzy or so complex as to result ungraspable. In other words, in this first meaning, nothing says that Huckleberry Finn, Moby Dick and Hamlet are not, in some ways, real. From this viewpoint, indeed, Mme Bovary appears to be far more "real" than most women we meet in everyday life.[116]

Since we need to insert a phenomenon into a larger context (*zusammenhang*) in order to explain it, "real" also means (2) that something is determinate and belongs to a specific context that, however, only indirectly belongs to (or can be inserted into) the world in space and time. This is the second sense of reality. Hägerström usually referred to this second meaning by calling it "subjectively real." It depends on the fact that someone (a subject with consciousness) has an idea of it.

In a third or narrow sense (3), "real" means that a certain "conception" or "idea" belongs to the all-encompassing spatio-temporal natural world of experience. In *Das Prinzip*, Hägerström for instance held that a mental state, such as an abstraction, indirectly belongs to the all-encompassing spatio-temporal world of experience «in so far as (...) it is placed in time and its reality is hence only time-dependent.»[117] A simply mental phenomenon is hence indirectly real, since it belongs to a person's mind, set in time and space. That does not mean it has direct or objective reality. It has been stressed that "objective" means both object-related and logically coherent.[118] Ultimately, «the principle of non-contradiction is the principle of reality, because the object that does not appear to be intrinsically coherent does not subsist as an object: The representation (*föreställning/Vorstellung*) which involves a contradiction reveals the subjectivity of its content easily.»[119] Using Hägerström's vocabulary, we might say that when an idea or conception is inconsistent it cannot form a concept, but only an impression.

According to whether the content is coherent or not and whether the context into which it is inserted is coherent or not (whether it forms a system or not), the content (4) will amount to subjective or objective reality, direct or indirect reality.[120] In order to be more than just the content of a subjective mental state – which however is real in the second sense: It belongs to the world in space and time indirectly, since it occurs in a subject – the content of a conception or representation (4) has

[116]This means that Hägerström had a theory of error according to which the indeterminate and contradictory proposition is no real proposition and therefore all "real" propositions are to some extent also "true." See S. Nordin, *Från Hägerström till Hedenius*, cit., p. 44 and p. 56; K. Marc-Wogau, *Studier till Axel Hägerströms filosofi*, cit., p. 57.

[117]A. Hägerström, *Prinzip*, cit., p. 76: «Soweit (...) fällt [die Abstraktion] in die Zeit und hat ihre Realität nur als zeitlich.»

[118]M. Lyles, *A Call...*, cit., p. 74.

[119]E. Pattaro, *Il realismo giuridico scandinavo*, cit., p. 53: «il principio di non contraddizione è il principio della realtà, perché l'oggetto che non si presenti come intrinsecamente coerente non sussiste come oggetto: la *föreställning*, la *Vorstellung*, che rechi in sé la contraddizione rivela direttamente la soggettività del suo contenuto.»

[120]Bo Peterson (*Axel Hägerströms värdeteori*, cit.) also speaks of reality in a wide and a narrow sense: pp. 16–23, 37–39, 47–53, 121 and 177 ff.

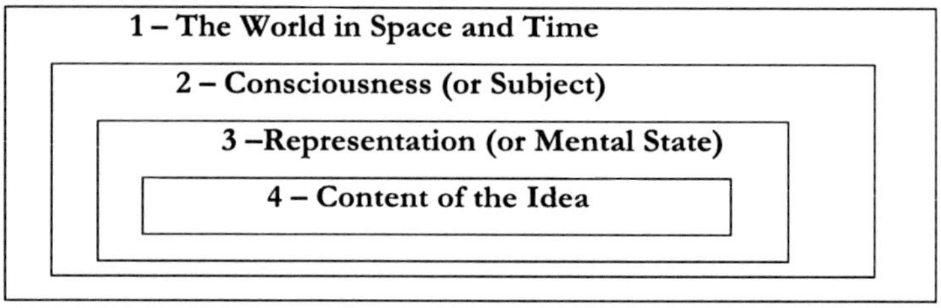


to be internally consistent (real in the first sense) and form a coherent system with the other pieces of information that together constitute our conception of reality in space and time (real in the third sense). Only if all three meanings of "real" match perfectly and coherently can the content of an idea be considered to have "full" reality. The three meanings of reality constitute, so to speak, a set of Chinese boxes, which can be illustrated as follows:[121]

The reality thesis has triggered rather different interpretations. One issue that has been debated is whether Hägerström considered that determinateness (and/or self-identity) implied existence. Now, it is true that Hägerström used the expression "real" so as to signify both existence and logical consistency. Konrad Marc-Wogau stressed that there are three meanings overlapping in Hägerström: *real, verklig, existerande* which we might translate with consistent, real and existing.[122] This, in turn, has implications as far as the ontological status of possibility is concerned. At any rate, Hägerström himself does not seem to have focused specifically on this issue. In *Prinzip*, he tellingly speaks of «reality, existence or *whatever you want to call it...*»[123] even though this issue has been the object of readings in the secondary literature that are poles apart.[124] And if we look at how Hägerström developed his

---

[121] Hägerström developed this thesis in his later work, especially in *Kritiska punkter i värdepsykologien*. More elaborate tables of synthesis of Hägerström's ontology can be found in Konrad Marc-Wogau's *Axel Hägerström's Ontology*, cit., p. 481; and with some differences in E. Pattaro, *Il realismo giuridico scandinavo*, cit., pp. 55 ff; L. Hierro, *El realismo jurídico escandinavo*, cit., p. 144. For comments, see Bo Petersson, *Axel Hägerströms värdeteori*, cit., pp. 18–27.

[122] K. Marc-Wogau, *Studier*, cit., p. 117. Liborio Hierro also insisted on this fact in *El realismo jurídico escandinavo. Una teoría empirista del derecho*, cit., p. 138.

[123] A. Hägerström, *Prinzip*, cit., p. 64: « ...die Realität, die Existenz, oder wie man es nun nennen will, nichts anderes ist als ein Begriff, ohne dessen Selbstidentität es überhaupt keine Bedeutung hätte, dass etwas existierte Daher muss auch die empirische Realität, die Realität in Zeit und Raum rein logisch hinsichtlich der Forderungen nach ihrer Selbstidentität bestimmt werden.» The reason of the logical interchangeability of reality and existence seems to depend on *Wirklichkeit* as bringing into existence what has *ratio essendi* (on the implications of this idea, see Chapter 6 on Hägerström's philosophy of history).

[124] According to Max Lyles, for example, «one must (...) note that Hägerström does not claim that all formally valid judgments (real judgments) predicate the existence of the object of the judgment in question. Far from it, formally valid judgments only predicate the necessary reality of the object, that is the object's self-identity, but not the object's actual existence.» (M. Lyles,

theory, this very controversy on determinateness and existence becomes easier to overcome.

### *2.5.4 Hägerström vs. Hegel:* Die Bedingung

Historical evidence, as mentioned, suggests that Hägerström developed his autonomous standpoint on the principle of knowledge while lecturing on Hegel; more specifically, while criticising the beginning of Hegel's *Science of Logic*.

Hegel opened his *Wissenschaft der Logik* with three "moments:" Being, Nothingness and Becoming (*Sein, das Nichts, das Werden*). At the very start, Hegel presented the indeterminate being, *das reine Sein*. Because of its lack of determinateness, pure being ends up as Nothingness, *das Nichts*. The whole intellectual route that the Spirit (*Geist*) accomplishes goes from *Sein* to *Ideen*, which mimics the determining of Being which becomes the determinate Being, *das Dasein*. On February 18th, 1905 Hägerström lectured on the «passage from being to nothingness and vice versa.» His diary annotation stated his opinion on Hegel's famous opening of the *Logic*: «Idle sophism. Confusion between nothingness subject to thought and nothing thought.»[125] This is an interesting gloss. While Hegel believed that the indeterminate Being is *das Nichts*, Hägerström contrarily affirmed that *das Sein* can never be *reine* since Being cannot be conceived without determinateness (i.e. self-identity).[126] Indeed, in *Das Prinzip*, reality is characterised by two "moments" – Being and self-identity. According to Hägerström, it is not possible to think of Being and of self-identity separately. Therefore, Hegel is wrong to believe that Pure Being equals Nothingness because, once Being is purified from determinateness, what is left is not Nothingness (*das Nichts*), but *nothing* (*nichts*). «Being without self-identity, or Being which is not thought as a determinate being, is nothing and so is the predicate "being" because of this indeterminacy. Consequently, [Being] is a logical impossibility when it is represented this way [indeterminate] – it goes against the principle of identity which is absolutely consistent and therefore [Being]

---

*A Call...*, cit., p. 68.) Existence and reality are thus not synonyms: «If a thing exists, then it is real, while conversely if a thing is real, then it may exist.» (p. 99). But the opposite idea has also been very popular: Anders Wedberg, for instance, maintained that Hägerström's reasoning in *On the Question of the Notion of Law* and Alf Ross' in *Kritik der sog. praktischen Erkenntnis* and *Virkelighed og gyldighed i retslaeren* rested on a confusion between existence and determinateness or rather on «the erroneous premise according to which every judgment as such is an existential-judgment.» (A. Wedberg, *Den logiska strukturen hos Boströms filosofi*, cit., pp. 198–200: «den oriktiga förutsättningen att varje omdöme såsom sådant är ett existentialomdöme»).

[125] A. Hägerström, Diarier Uppsala Universitet: «övergången från vara till intet och tvärtom. Idel sofistik. Det tänkta intet och ingenting tänkt förväxlas»; quote from C.-G. Heidegren, *Den nya Uppsala-filosofin*, cit., p. 82.

[126] One of the few interpreters who stressed this is Liborio Hierro, *El realismo jurídico escandinavo. Una teoría empirista del derecho*, cit., p. 140.

cannot constitute a moment of this principle.»[127] Anyone familiar with Hegel will recognize this particularly abstruse vocabulary. Using Hegel's lexis in *Logic*, we might say that what Hägerström asserted is that *Unbestimmtheit* cannot constitute *das Unbedingte*.

By refuting the possibility of *Das Nichts*, Hägerström does not fall back into traditional metaphysics, into the arms of Parmenides who claimed "what is, is and there is no Not-Being."[128] Rather, Hägerström listened carefully to Hegel's reproach of empiricism and his synthetic overcoming of traditional rationalism. In fact, the very distinction between empiricism and rationalism was a cornerstone of Hegel's *History of Philosophy*, and Hägerström used this distinction very often. By claiming there is no such thing as Nothingness (*Das Nichts*) – and therefore *die Wirklichkeit selbst hat keine Grade*[129] – Hägerström took a step further than Hegel just to serve him some of his own medicine: Hägerström accused Hegel of being too abstract! This is clear in Hägerström's appraisal of empiricism as, historically speaking, a fresh awakening from the dogmatic sleep of traditional rationalism. «Empiricism is historically justified because it drove rationalism away from the insecure and void image of Being, towards the concrete concept of being, as this latter is alive in the role of the highest logical condition [*Bedingung*] of everything called science.»[130] Heidegren is therefore correct when commenting «this formula encompasses a short-version of the history of nineteenth century philosophy: from Hegel to Hägerström.»[131]

### 2.5.5 Coherence vs. Correspondence Theory of Truth

Leaving aside these historical aspects, it is remarkable that Hägerström was looking for that very ultimate condition or premise – *die Bedingung* – that Hegel, in his *Logic*, affirmed was an error. According to the latter, *die unbedingte Bedingung*, i.e., the foundation that is not in turn founded on something else, is a groundless idea. Contrarily, Hägerström held that the determinate, practical, and concrete reality is ultimately the basis of all judgments and that this basis is not grounded in something else. Only if we understand this point does it become possible to resolve the

---

[127] A. Hägerström, *Prinzip*, cit., p. 88: «Das ohne Selbstidentität gedachte Sein oder das nicht als ein bestimmtes Dies gedachte Sein entbehrt infolge dieser seiner Bestimmungslosigkeit auch der Bestimmtheit des Seins, ist nichts. Damit ist es auch, wenn es so gedacht wird, eine logische Unmöglichkeit – wiederstreitet dem absolut giltigen Identitätsprinzip, kann dann auch nicht ein Moment dieses Prinzips sein.»

[128] For such a conjecture see J. Bjarup, *Reason, Emotion and the Law*, cit., pp. 277–286.

[129] A. Hägerström, *Selbstdarstellung*, cit., p. 129.

[130] A. Hägerström, *Prinzip*, cit., p. 18: «Der Empirismus hat seine historische Berechtigung darin, dass er den Rationalismus von dem leeren unsicheren Bilde des Seins hinweg zu dem konkreten Seinsbegriff hintreibt, wie dieser in allem, was Wissenschaft heisst, als höchste logische Bedingung lebt.»

[131] C.-G. Heidegren, *Den nya Uppsala-filosofin*, cit., p. 89: «i denna formulering ryms en kortversion av 1800-talets filosofihistoria: från Hegel till Hägerström.»

epistemological problem concerning whether Hägerström developed a coherence or correspondence theory of truth.

This topic has polarized scholars for generations.[132] The stake of the issue is basically whether Hägerström is a proto-logical positivist, a semi-god for all twentieth century scientists (who, of course, upheld a correspondence theory of truth), or if he is just a small-town metaphysician stuck in the mediaeval-scholastic *querelles des universaux* (with a strong belief in a coherence theory of truth).

This unfruitful diatribe is somehow missing the point. Apart from applying notions (correspondence vs. coherence) elaborated by twentieth century scholars in a rather different situation, it fails to see that the whole problem concerns what Hegel called *die Bedingung*. In order for there to be any correspondence theory of truth (upon which experimental sciences, concerned with *a posteriori* corroboration, obviously have to rely), there has to be pure coherence between reality and the concepts through which we recognize it, on the level of *principium sapientiae*, according to Hägerström. The reason why it is not possible to distinguish between reality and (the principle of) identity is because «reality, existence or whatever you want to call it, is nothing but a kind of concept that, without self-identity, would make it meaningless to say that something exists. Therefore empirical reality, the reality in space and time, also needs to be determinate on purely logical grounds according to the requirements of the principle of non-contradiction.»[133] This is why every demonstration or proof already presupposes «the logical necessity or absolute validity of the concept of reality as self-identical.»[134] In other words, there can be no correspondence without the logical guarantee of coherence. That does not mean formal validity is enough to make good science, but at least it means that the theory of knowledge, as a philosophical subject matter, has to be based on coherence.

By formulating the issue this way, it becomes much easier to appreciate Hägerström's position both on so-called "propedeutics" and on the role of conceptual analysis. Propedeutic philosophy – consisting in anthropology, phenomenology, logic and history of philosophy – was not only an important subject matter in philosophy in those days but, most of all, a way to grasp the principle of knowledge.[135] This view was held by Hägerström's neo-Boströmian teachers, Carl Yngve Sahlin and Erik Olof Burman. In the diary notes from 1904, it appears that Hägerström's

---

[132]Just to mention some who insist on Hägerström's attachment to the much more fashionable correspondence theory of truth: K. Marc-Wogau, *Studier till Axel Hägerströms filosofi*, cit., pp. 91 and 182–183; B. Petersson, *Axel Hägerströms värdeteori*, cit., pp. 50–51 and pp. 74–75. For the opposite thesis, see for instance J. Bjarup, *Emotion, Reason and the Law*, cit., pp. 270–277; Id., *Axel Hägerströms filosofi, värdenihilism och rättspositivism*, in «Juridisk Tidskrift», 2004–2005, anno 16, n. 1, pp. 25–41.

[133]A. Hägerström, *Prinzip*, cit., p. 64, see note 123 in Chapter 2 for extensive quote.

[134]A. Hägerström, *Prinzip*, cit., p. 56: «die logische Notwendigkeit oder die absolute Giltigkeit [sic] des Begriffs der Realität in ihrer Selbstidentität»; see also p. 65.

[135]See Hägerström's autumn course from 1908 entitled *Till den praktiska filosofiens propedevtik*.

teachings involved a criticism of this very idea, especially as developed by Sahlin.[136] Moreover, we know from Margit Waller that Hägerström had openly attacked Sahlin on several occasions (among which March 22nd, 1905). The same source also tells us that he held a number of discussions with Burman, supposedly offering the groundwork of his ideas in *Das Prinzip*.[137] Burman held propedeutics to link natural science and *Geisteswissenschaften*, while Hägerström denied the latter the status of science.

In *Das Prinzip*, Hägerström discussed the topic claiming that «in particular, a positive form of propedeutics, as a logical course to the principle, seems impossible. Otherwise it would be possible to acquire knowledge about the principle in a mediate way.»[138] According to Hägerström this propedeutical teaching, just like any experience, cannot lead to the principle of knowledge. It only provides personal certitude: «The subjective method only consists of a system of prudential rules for the individual thinking, determinated by the object itself and by the nature of the thinking subject.»[139] This is fundamentally what propedeutic philosophy amounts to. Hägerström distinguished between "what is thought *in the* analysis" and "what belongs to the concept of analysis as a concept", i.e. on one hand, the personal experience of whom – through propedeutics or some other practice – is enlightened and understands; and on the other, the principle as the ultimate starting-point of all consistent analysis.

Conceptual analysis is thus a precondition of experience; the principle of knowledge (determinate reality) is an unavoidable logical precondition (*Bedingung*) of all concrete experiences. It guarantees, on purely logical grounds, that experience does not evaporate – as Cassirer put it – in a "rhapsody of the senses." No experience can ever lead to the principle of knowledge. And without it, we would not know what to count as experience, what to ask Nature. So, according to Hägerström, before all forms of verification and/or falsification, we still need to ask the classical Greek question: *Tí estí? What is it?*

Hägerström's opinion on this issue ignited the debate with his own mentor, Burman. The difference of opinion sheds light on how Hägerström's theoretical standpoint was perceived by someone who knew him well and who shared his puzzling lexis. In October 1910, Burman wrote to Professor Vitalis Norström in

[136] C.-G. Heidegren, *Den nya Uppsala-filosofin*, cit., p. 100. See also *Stat och rätt. En rättsfilosofisk undersökning*, vol. I, Almqvist & Wiksell, Uppsala 1904, pp. 108 and 166, where he lists Sahlin as part of "Boström's school."

[137] This is documented both in M. Waller, *Människan som få kände*, cit., p. 182 and in a letter Burman sent to Vitalis Norström, which today can be found in the University library in Göteborg. For extensive quotes, see S. Nordin, *Den Boströmska skolan och den svenska idealismens fall*, Doxa, Lund 1981, p. 177.

[138] A. Hägerström, *Prinzip*, cit., p. 13: «Besonders scheint eine positive Propädeutik als ein logischer Fortgang zum Prinzip unmöglich zu sein, da für dieses damit direkt die Möglichkeit vorläge, vermittelt gewusst zu werden.»

[139] A. Hägerström, *Prinzip*, cit., p. 16: «Die subjektive Denken, bestimmt teils durch die Sache selbst, teils durch die Natur des denkenden Subjects.»

Göteborg about his pupil Axel that he now considered to be "his real opponent:" Hägerström's «writing on the principle of knowledge is throughout an attempt to refute me.»[140] In his brief portrayal of Hägerström's theoretical philosophy Burman finely summarised the accomplished Copernican revolution: «Hägerström's standpoint is *absolute* (against all transcendentalism), *intellectualist* (practical life is apparent) and *objectivist* (the thinking consciousness falls beyond and beneath reality which is pure identity).»[141]

While in *Das Prinzip* Hägerström had argued against both transcendentalism and the subjectivist equivalence between consciousness and its content, the third idea that Burman identified – the appearance of practical life or the minor importance of experience – was developed to a greater extent in the 1910 book *Botanisten och filosofen*.

## 2.6 The Botanist, the Philosopher and Conceptual Realism

In 1910, Hägerström returned to epistemological issues with *Botanisten och filosofen*. A first sketch of this popular version of *Das Prinzip*[142] was written as early as 1903 with the title *Philosophical Dialogue on the Elysian Fields in the Twentieth Century* (*Filosofisk dialog å de elyseiska fälten i tjugonde seklet*). The text had two later editions; an abridged version published in 1910 and a lengthier and more comprehensive draft entitled *Is Philosophical Epistemology Supererogatory?* (*Är filosofisk kunskapslära överflödig?*) from 1908, edited in 1957 by Martin Fries in *Filosofi och vetenskap*.[143]

This is a very peculiar text. It is a Platonic dialogue with an autobiographical touch. The discussion opposes the botanist – an empiricist and positivistic scientist with an August Comte-like self-assurance, modeled on the professor of physiology at the Uppsala University in those days, Hjalmar Öhrvall[144] – and the philosopher, embodiment of Hägerström himself. During a hike in the wilderness, these two acquaintances start a methodological inquiry on the principle of knowledge. The

[140] E.O. Burman, Letter to Norström, 1910: «hans skrift om vetenskapens princip är alltigenom ett försök att vederlägga mig» (quote from S. Nordin, *Den Boströmska skolan*, cit., p. 176).

[141] E.O. Burman, Letter to Norström, 1910: «Hägerströms ståndpunkt är *absolut* (mot all transcendentalism), *intellektualistisk* (det praktiska livet är fenomenalt), *objektiv* (allt filosoferande medvetande faller nedom och utom verkligheten, som är den rena identiteten)» (quote from S. Nordin, *Den Boströmska skolan*, cit., p. 177).

[142] Hägerström described it this way in *Selbstdarstellung*, cit., p. 5; *Summary*, cit., p. 37.

[143] Comments on the labourious genesis of this book can be found in T. Mautner (ed.), *Moralfilosofins grundläggning*, Almqvist & Wiksell International, Stockholm 1987, p. 18. Most of the work seems to have been done while preparing for the autumn lectures 1908.

[144] This information can be found in M. Fries, *Förord*, in A. Hägerström, *Filosofi och vetenskap*, cit., p. 9. Another source is the manuscript *H 5:3* which includes a pencil drawing with the title "the scientist and the philosopher" where Öhrvall wears glasses and holds a dying plant, whereas the philosopher wears a pince-nez, just like Hägerström, and holds a healthy plant.

philosopher leads the botanist into doubt by casting light on the necessity of presupposing causality in all experiences. By using an argument which Karl Popper made fashionable some decades later in *The Problem of Induction* (1953), but that can already be found in Giacopo Zabarella, Hägerström stressed that the botanist's investigation would be beyond doubt only if he had observed *all* the particular specimens of the vegetal species investigated, as well as «the infinite amount that has existed during the past centuries and that will exist in the future.»[145] Hägerström denounced the unfounded faith of his "brother empiricist"[146] on the basis of pretty common arguments in the history of epistemology, such as the idea that experience is meaningful only in reference to categories, like time, space, causality, which are preconditions of the observation and not its derivates. So the main argument is that we cannot ground science in sensualism, or rather use a purely empirical foundation, since any act of knowledge presupposes the use of concepts, which cannot be induced from experience.

This position does not only concern the law of causality, but also general representations overall. Indeed, according to Hägerström – like in many twentieth century epistemologists – the perceiving subject cannot distinguish physical objects from one another without using "abstraction," such as categories and concepts. The example is that the unprepared subject, a child for instance, cannot perceive the colors of the rainbow in any distinct way.[147] The empiricist is therefore able to make inductions from experience only because of the form (*Gestalt*), color, etc. of the object. Only through this conceptual determination does the object of experience become «distinguished in its nature from other things in a determinate way.»[148] If this were not the case, the empiricist would be left with only «conceptually void impressions.»[149] Discussing the example of a rose, the philosopher highlights that «you cannot reach existence on the basis of observation, on the contrary, in order for you to know that you are seeing [the rose] you already have to know it exists.»[150]

In the first part of *Botanisten och filosofen*, Hägerström lets the philosopher express standpoints very similar to his own ideas from the beginning of the century. By the end of Chapter 2, however, the botanist presents an argument which silences the philosopher: «The nature of the principle of truth is to be logically valid, but then I must retort: if *you* are not the principle of truth, in what do you ground this assumption if not in your own certitude? (...) The philosopher did not

[145] A. Hägerström, *Filosofi och vetenskap*, cit., p. 17: « den otaliga mängd som under århundradens lopp har funnits och som i framtiden skall finnas.»

[146] A. Hägerström, *Filosofi och vetenskap*, cit., p. 27: "broder empiriker."

[147] A. Hägerström, *Filosofi och vetenskap*, cit., p. 85.

[148] A. Hägerström, *Filosofi och vetenskap*, cit., p. 79: «blott därigenom blir den på ett bestämt sätt till sin egen natur skild från annat.»

[149] A. Hägerström, *Filosofi och vetenskap*, cit., p. 83: «begreppslösa intryck.»

[150] A. Hägerström, *Filosofi och vetenskap*, cit., p. 59: «Du kommer icke till existensen på grundvalen av ditt seende, utan för att kunna veta att du ser saken, måste du redan veta existensen.»

speak. He somehow recalled a chess player so eager to attack that he forgot to guard his king.»[151]

The philosopher, representing Hägerström in his early position on the theory of knowledge, is accused of subjectivism, as the bitter fruit of transcendental idealism. Chapter 3 opens with «a decade had passed» and, indeed, the philosopher encounters the botanist and they reengage in the same discussion, but this time the philosopher has assumed Hägerström's new "realist" position. After pondering for a decade on "the problem of problems"[152] he understood that consciousness is always consciousness *of something*, i.e. thought cannot equal its own content[153] – and the ultimate reality must form a consistent system: «All contents of consciousness (...) must belong to an identical time and therefore to an identical context.»[154]

What Hägerström refused is not empirical evidence as such – which clearly is fundamental for science in order to progress – but empiricism as an epistemological doctrine. His aim was to «secure the very preconditions of experience through a purely logical and epistemological inquiry» to use the wording from the 1908 manuscript *Är filosofisk kunskapslära överflödig?* In *Botanisten och filosofen*, he emphasized his purpose: «Much would be gained if empirical questions were dealt with empirically, and the preconditions of experience, and generally the concepts with no empirical significance that we continuously use, were subjected to conceptual analysis.»[155] Ernst Cassirer stressed this point when professing that Hägerström «does not object to empiricism that reality can be scientifically determinated only through experience, but he denies that experience in its scientific meaning, *sensu eminenti*, can be constituted on the basis of mere impressions.»[156] This is also the way we should understand the claim in *Das Prinzip*: «It is the very content of experience (...) through its capacity to determine reality in a non-contradictory way, that determines its own consistency.»[157]

This way of arguing is based on Hägerström's equivalence between reality and self-identity. According to Cassirer, this means that reality is independent from the

---

[151] A. Hägerström, *Filosofi och vetenskap*, cit., p. 42. Bjarup misses this point: See *Reason, Emotion and the Law*, cit., p. 433.

[152] A. Hägerström, *Filosofi och vetenskap*, cit., p. 43.

[153] A. Hägerström, *Filosofi och vetenskap*, cit., p. 46.

[154] A. Hägerström, *Filosofi och vetenskap*, cit., p. 52: «alla medvetenhetsinnehåll (...) höra till en identisk tid och därmed till ett identiskt sammanhang.»

[155] A. Hägerström, *Filosofi och vetenskap*, cit., p. 16: «mycket vore vunnet, om den åskådningen kunde tränga igenom, att empiriska frågor skola empiriskt behandlas men empiriens förutsättningar och öfver huvud de begrepp med icke-empirisk betydelse, hvaraf vi ständigt använda oss, skola genom ren begreppsundersökning prövas.»

[156] E. Cassirer, *Axel Hägerström*, cit., p. 41: «Er bestreitet dem Empirismus nicht, daß die Wirklichkeit wissenschaftlich nur durch Erfahrung bestimmt werden kann; aber er leugnet, daß die Erfahrung in ihrem spezifisch wissenschaftlichen Sinn, sensu eminenti, sich aus bloßen Empfindungen aufbauen kann.»

[157] A. Hägerström, *Prinzip*, cit., p. 62: «es ist der Erfahrungsinhalt selbst, der (...) durch sein Vermögen, auf eine widerspruchslose Weise die Realität zu bestimmen, seine eigene Giltigkeit [sic] bestimmt.»

thinking subject, nonetheless, it obeys the fundamental law of thought; *in primis*, the law of non-contradiction. Reality is necessary *in itself*, apodictically true, and it is not grounded in facts of any nature.[158] In other words, for Hägerström, the rational structure of the world offers the only guarantee for the conditions of the possibility of knowledge.

Hägerström therefore conferred great weight to "conceptual determination." Since experience cannot in itself guarantee access to "reality" we need to look for a "logical formation" in order to obtain access. Now, this logical formation is the concept (*begrepp*). «The concept is the "Open Sesame!" which unlocks the doors of reality. Both concept and reality are determinated by the same requirement, i.e. the principle of non-contradiction and self-identity (...). It is no longer possible to draw a line of demarcation between "concept" and "reality." They are not only correlated but they coincide in their fundamental meaning.»[159] In the name of the principle of non-contradiction, this means that reality-as-self-identity is immediately given as its own *ratio essendi*. This also explains why Hägerström attributed so much importance to conceptual analysis as the philosophical inquiry par excellence.

However, at this point of the dialogue, the botanist comes up with a different allegation: Nominalism. The empiricist claims that «concepts are (...) no realities, but only subjective means of reproduction, given in words»[160] but the philosopher – Hägerström – retorts: «If the content of the concept is *per se* determinated and certainly (...) *sensu eminenti* determinate, then it is *eo ipso* real.»[161] So, according to Hägerström, words do not amount to concepts. Hence *lógos* is distinct from *lektón*.[162] A thing that exists has «concepts built into it.»[163] Concepts are immanent in our world[164] and lie beyond time.[165] While the botanist affirms that he has never seen the concept of a birch tree,[166] it seems that Hägerström, by assuming there is something like the "universal birch tree" falls flatly into the sophism of Antisthenes; there is no such thing as the 'horsehood' of horses!

---

[158] E. Cassirer, *Axel Hägerström*, cit., p. 39.

[159] E. Cassirer, *Axel Hägerström*, cit., p. 42: «Der Begriff ist das "Sesam öffne Dich!", das uns die Pforten der Realität erschließt. Denn beide: Begriff und Realität, werden durch ein und dieselbe Forderung, durch die Forderung der inneren Widerspruchslosigkeit oder der Selbstidentität" bestimmt. (...) Ein Trennungsstrich zwischen„ Begriff" und„ Wirklichkeit" läßt sich jetzt nicht länger ziehen; beide sind nicht nur korrelativ aufeinander bezogen, sondern sie fallen ihrer Grundbedeutung nach zusammen.» As far as correlation is concerned, a critique can be found in K. Marc-Wogau, *Studier till Axel Hägerströms filosofi*, cit., pp. 58–61 and p. 118.

[160] A. Hägerström, *Filosofi och vetenskap*, cit., p. 80: «Begreppen är (...) inga realiteter, utan blott subjektiva reproduktionsmedel, givna i orden.»

[161] A. Hägerström, *Filosofi och vetenskap*, cit., p. 81: «om begreppets innehåll är något bestämt för sig och visserligen (...) *sensu eminenti* bestämt, så är det också *eo ipso* realt.»

[162] A. Hägerström, *Filosofi och vetenskap*, cit., p. 92.

[163] A. Hägerström, *Filosofi och vetenskap*, cit., p. 84: «insprängda begrepp.»

[164] A. Hägerström, *Filosofi och vetenskap*, cit., p. 90: «begreppen är visserligen verkligheter, men immanenta i vår värld.»

[165] A. Hägerström, *Filosofi och vetenskap*, cit., p. 91.

[166] A. Hägerström, *Filosofi och vetenskap*, cit., p. 82.

This has led some commentators to question the kind of theory of universals that Hägerström embraced. Many, like Jes Bjarup, believe this level of discussion to be plain "metaphysics."[167] The most polemic, but also clearest account on this issue can be found in Ernst Cassirer: «Hägerström is the only modern logician, if I see correctly, who dared to walk the line of the old *querelle des universaux* and adopt a very precise position. He unreservedly upholds the reality of universal concepts. I am not sure if he intends to endorse the thesis of *universalia ante rem*, but he defends without hesitation *universalia in re.*»[168] Hence, according to Cassirer, who, by then, had already published *The Problem of Knowledge in Modern Philosophy and Science* (1906) and *Substance and Function* (1910), Hägerström saw empirical science as true knowledge only due to the postulate that "something is real according to its concept" on the basis of the correspondence and overlapping of reality and the concepts through which it is shaped. This is why Cassirer makes a (metaphysical) insinuation that would certainly have irritated Hägerström a great deal: «Are we not here directly confronted again with something *cuius essentia involvit existentiam*?»[169] At the end, Cassirer realised he had exaggerated and admitted that Hägerström's realism «is certainly not of the metaphysical kind and therefore we cannot speak of a new-fangled respect of scholastic "ontologism".»[170]

Another recent interpretation of the same difficulty in Hägerström is offered by Max Lyles, who claims that Hägerström considered concepts, such as those involved in geometrical definitions, as deprived of "objective reality, but that they nevertheless possess subjective reality."[171] This would imply that the triangle is real in the same way as a fantasy is real: Belonging indirectly to the all-encompassing spatio-temporal world of experience (i.e. the ultimate context of reality) since it is part of a mental act, present in the subject. It would also entail that if humanity were to perish,

[167] J. Bjarup, *Reason, Emotion and the Law*, cit., p. 208; Id., *Epistemology and Law according to Axel Hägerström* in «Scandinavian Studies in Law», vol. 29, Almqvist & Wiksell, Stockholm 1985, pp. 26–32; Id., *Ought and Reality. Hägerström's Inaugural Lecture Re-considered* in P. Wahlgren (ed.), «Scandinavian Studies in Law», vol. 40, Almqvist & Wiksell, Stockholm 2000, pp. 11–72; Id., *Axel Hägerströms filosofi, värdenihilism och rättspositivism*, cit., p. 27; Id., *The Philosophy of Scandinavian Legal Realism*, in «Ratio Juris», 2005, vol. 18, n. 1, pp. 3–4.

[168] E. Cassirer, *Axel Hägerström*, cit., p. 43: «Hägerström ist, wenn ich recht sehe, der einzige moderne Logiker, der es gewagt hat, wieder in die Bahnendes alten "Universalienstreites" einzulenken und in diesem Streit eine ganz bestimmte Stellung einzunehmen. Er setzt sich unbedingt für die Realität der Allgemein begriffe ein. Ich bin nicht sicher, ob er die These "universalia ante rem" aufrechtzuerhalten gedenkt; aber für die These "universalia in re" entscheidet er sich ohne jedes Bedenken.»

[169] E. Cassirer, *Axel Hägerström*, cit., p. 43: «Haben wir hier nicht unmittelbar wieder ein Etwas vor uns, "cuius essentia involvit existentiam?"»

[170] E. Cassirer, *Axel Hägerström*, cit., p. 47: «Dieser Realismus ist sicherlich nicht metaphysischer Art, und von einer Neubelebung des scholarischen "Ontologismus" werden wir hier in keinem Fall sprechen dürfen.»

[171] M. Lyles, *A Call...*, cit., p. 192: «Hägerström's concepts have *subjective reality*, but not *objective reality*. They are real, but not objectively existent. To have subjective reality means that something (...) is the content of a psychic act (...). To have objective reality means that an object exists independently of any subjective consciousness.» See also p. 188.

mathematical concepts would no longer exist. The same author, while commenting on *Botanisten och filosofen* and, more specifically, on the theory of universals in Hägerström, stressed that there are traces of «what strictly speaking is rationalism in Hägerström's philosophy – namely, it reliance on a logical principle.»[172] Yet it seems hard to believe that a rationalist would think that concepts enjoy the same ontological status as Moby Dick.

At any rate, it seems to me that Hägerström's use of the term "concept" (*begrepp*) is quite close to the technical term *Begriff* in Hegel. As mentioned, Hägerström elaborated his fundamental ideas in epistemology after having lectured on Hegel's *Science of Logic* and it would not be surprising if he had picked up the Hegelian use of the term. *Begrepp* is the Swedish equivalent of *Begriff*. The verb *att begripa*, just like its German counterpart *begreifen* (to comprehend), incorporates *att gripa/greifen*, to seize or to grasp. In Hegelianism, a concept is not (as in Kantism) a representation of what several things have in common. Instead, things are what they are through the activity of the concept that reveals itself in them: Concept is the outcome of the sublation of essence and being.[173] For Hägerström, concepts cannot be induced from experience. Instead they are logical formations, characterised by non-contradiction, that lets consciousness access reality and hereby determining its consistency. Such a view is quite close to what Hegel claims in the Preface to the Second Edition of his *Science of Logic*: «That which is genuinely permanent and substantial in the complexity and contingency of appearance and fleeting manifestation, is the concept of the thing.»[174] For Hegel as for Hägerström, «the concept is thus the inward living principle of all reality.»[175] So Cassirer, who is well-acquainted with Hegel, is correct to stress that "concept" and "reality" tend to overlap.

This "Hegelian" use of "concept" in Hägerström, according to which real concepts are not merely thought, but they are also determinations of real objects, does not mean that the concepts are real in the sense that they belong to the all-encompassing spatio-temporal world of experience world, i.e. the context that Konrad Marc-Wogau called "reality 3."[176] There is no such thing as a Platonic *hyperurania*. From this perspective, Marc-Wogau is correct to stress that Hägerström's philosophy is directed both against irrationalism (in the sense that reality is indeterminate and contradictory) and dualism (in the sense that there can

---

[172] M. Lyles, *A Call...*, cit., p. 187.

[173] Walter Kaufmann (*Hegel: Texts and Commentary*, Doubleday, New York 1965, p. 9) comments that «the ordinary meaning of *Begriff* is definitely concept. Because this is one of Hegel's most characteristic terms, and he associates more than its ordinary meaning with it, some nineteenth-century English translators felt that a less ordinary term was called for and hit on notion.» In Miller's translation of Hegel's *Phenomenology*, for example, the term was rendered with "notion." I do not use this term since it is utterly misleading and seems to suggest vagueness.

[174] G.W.F. Hegel, *Science of Logic*, Allen & Unwin, London 1969, § 23.

[175] T.M. Knox, *Translator's Foreword* in G.W.F. Hegel, *Philosophy of Right*, Oxford University Press, New York 1942, p. viii.

[176] K. Marc-Wogau, *Studier till Axel Hägerströms filosofi*, cit., p. 120.

be a "spiritual reality" besides the material world, defined in space and time)[177] and Thomas Mautner effectively emphasized that Hägerström's rejection of metaphysics is really a reaction against supranaturalism grounded in his ontological monism.[178]

To conclude, we might affirm that Hägerström defined «reality through the idea of *determinateness*, laying emphasis on this determinate character; this permanent relation between the elements of experience should not be confused with what generally goes under the name of "existence".»[179] From this viewpoint – a perspective based on the contemporary scientific paradigm of which David Hilbert (1862–1943) can be cited as the main representative – pure mathematics of which we hardly could predicate "existence" *in natura rerum* is listed among "real things" since the judgments in mathematics form a *system* where «determinateness is present all over; instead of having simply particular positions, we have a system of positions which are entangled and respectively conditioning one another according to a rule.»[180] If this perspective is adopted, the line that should be drawn is between real and unreal concepts. Such a line, according to Hägerström, must be drawn by philosophical analysis, that might show that «many ordinary concepts such as "thing", "force", "free", "prima causa" are not real concepts since they are contradictory.»[181]

Hägerström's reality thesis is the foundation upon which he ultimately built his vision of science.[182] «We can thus say that the task of science is to insert the determinate objects as sections in the concrete happening and in the physical world.»[183]

---

[177] K. Marc-Wogau, *Studier till Axel Hägerströms filosofi*, cit., pp. 20–21. We will not discuss here whether Marc-Wogau's description of concepts as belonging to "Reality 2" is correct.

[178] T. Mautner, *Hägerström's Practical Philosophy*, unpublished manuscript the author kindly gave me.

[179] E. Cassirer, *Axel Hägerström*, cit., p. 41: «Denn er definiert die Realität durch den Gedanken der Bestimmtheit, und er betont, daß diese Bestimmtheit, dieser durchgängige Zusammenhang, den die Erfahrungselemente unter sich besitzen, nicht mit dem verwechselt werden dürfe, was man gemeinhin unter dem Namen der "Existenz" begreift.» See also Cassirer's comparison between Hägerström and Nicolai Hartmann in *Was ist Subjektivismus?* in E. Cassirer, *Gesammelte Werke*, Meiner, Hamburg 2006, pp. 182–183 where Cassirer affirms: «Die Möglichkeit, daß der Gegenstand der Erkenntnis "alogische" Momente in sich fassen könne, daß er etwas "Irrationales" oder Transintelligibles sein könne, wird von Hägerström sowenig erwogen, daß er das Prinzip der "Selbstidentität des Wirklichen" geradezu an die Spitze seiner gesamten Erkenntnislehre stellt, und es für das "Prinzip der Wissenschaft" schlechthin erklärt.»

[180] E. Cassirer, *Axel Hägerström*, cit., p. 41: «Bestimmtheit ist überall dort vorhanden, wo wir, statt bloße Einzelsetzungen, ein System von Setzungen vor uns haben, die ineinander eingreifen und sich wechselseitig nach einer Regel bedingen.» On this issue, see also A. Hägerström, *Hägerström, ad vocem*, in *Filosofiskt lexikon* (eds.) A. Alhberg, Natur & Kultur, Stockholm 1925, pp. 85 ff.

[181] A. Hägerström, *Filosofi och vetenskap*, cit., p. 94: «om den filosofiska kritiken uppvisade, att vissa vanliga begrepp sådana som ting-, kraft-, frihets-, prima causa-begreppen i själva verket saknar begreppsnatur genom sin motsägande beskaffenhet.»

[182] «Like the German *Wissenschaftlich*, *vetenskaplig* has a wider meaning than "scientific" and suggests that the view or method is theoretically respectable and meets criteria of rationality» (T. Mautner, *Hägerström's Practical Philosophy*, cit.).

[183] A. Hägerström, *Filosofi och vetenskap*, cit., p. 99: «vi kan därför säga att det är vetenskapens uppgift att insätta de särskilda objekten såsom led i det konkreta förloppet och det fysiska universum.»

This implies that the fundamental question of epistemology must thus be: «How can the sensitive objects be conceptualised in order for them to be determinated by the necessary self-identity of reality?»[184] Philosophy of science later reformulated the same issue in new terms. How do we construct tests that demonstrate a thesis? How can we falsify a scientific hypothesis? How do we get nature to speak our language?

## 2.7 Uppsala: *die kleine Wien*?

The reality thesis, and especially the anti-subjectivism based on the idea that consciousness is always consciousness *of* something, are among the ideas around which most members of the so-called Uppsala school pivoted. Here we shall put aside the unfruitful diatribe on the paternity of the school, concerned with Hägerström's alleged "hidden subjectivism" in *Das Prinzip*, that was supposedly abandoned only as a result of the discussions with the "real" founder of the Uppsala School, Adolf Phalén.[185] Later this issue fueled some bitter disputes in the 30s. Whether or not it is true that Vilhelm Lundstedt pushed Hägerström to underrate Phalén's influence over him in *Selbstdarstellung*,[186] it is clear that Lundstedt saw the whole debate as an «underground work against Hägerström's deeds and reputation.»[187] In effect, most of Phalén's numerous followers condemned the bizarre atmosphere of orthodoxy surrounding Hägerström, as well as his alleged attempts to promote incompetent students (see the Svante Bohman case for example).[188] Hägerström sentenced in a Salomon way: «The decision in this matter I leave to an impartial future inquiry.»[189] Many inquiries were made, but they were often rather biased: An extreme defense of Phalén can be found in Gunnar Oxenstierna and an equally unreserved *plaidoyer* for Hägerström can be found in Martin Fries.[190]

---

[184] A. Hägerström, *Filosofi och vetenskap*, cit., p. 110: «huru låter sig de sinnliga objekten begripa såsom bestämda av realitetens nödvändiga självidentitet?»

[185] See R.T. Sandin, *The Founding of the Uppsala School*, in «Journal of the History of Ideas», vol. 23, New York 1962, pp. 496–512; K. Marc-Wogau, *Studier till Axel Hägerströms filosofi*, cit., p. 80; S. Nordin, *Från Hägerström till Hedenius*, cit., pp. 40–42.

[186] This often repeated allegation myth originates from the autobiographical notes of one of Hägerström's disciples, Einar Tegen (*Levernebeskrivning*, manuscripts at the Uppsala University Library, p. 36). However, it should be said that in *Filosofiskt lexikon* from 1925, four years (!) before writing *Selbstdarstellung*, Hägerström had already claimed that he had «upheld, even if not demonstrated» the basic tenets of his epistemology (*Hägerström Axel*, *ad vocem*, in *Filosofiskt lexikon*, cit., pp. 89–92; *The Philosophy of Axel Hägerström*, *Appendix B*, in *Philosophy and Religion*, ed. R. Sandin, Allen & Unwin, London 1964, pp. 313–316).

[187] V. Lundstedt, *Det Hägerström-Lundstedtska misstaget: sju föreläsningar samt efterskrift*, Geber, Stockholm 1942, p. 139: «mullvadsarbete mot Hägerströms gärning och anseende.»

[188] S. Nordin, *Från Hägerström till Hedenius*, cit., pp. 64 ff.

[189] H. Apéria-Meurling, *Samtal med en svensk tänkare*, cit., p. 422: «Avgörandet av den frågan lämnar jag åt en opartisk framtida undersökning.»

[190] G. Oxenstierna, *Vad är Uppsalafilosofien?*, cit.; M. Fries, *Verklighetsbegreppet enligt Hägerström*, cit.

At any rate, there were unquestionable differences between Hägerström and his younger colleague Phalén. While the first was a charismatic radical with eccentric left-wing sympathies, the latter typically represented small-town bourgeois boredom.[191] Intellectually, Hägerström accused Adolf of tendencies towards scepticism, and Phalén retorted that Axel was nothing but a subjectivist. They both engaged in crypto-criticism, making the neutral scholar's task highly unpleasant. They were both the product of the ongoing debate in the first years of the century. It is probably impossible to establish once and for all what idea was first developed by whom since they belonged to the same group of intellectuals who were then exchanging ideas on a regular basis: The so-called "philosophical club" (*filosofiska klubben*) which used to meet at a restaurant in Uppsala to discuss theoretical issues.[192]

In fact, the first years of the new century saw the formation of the primary circle of what was to become the School of Uppsala. In this first circle around Hägerström we find Viktor Alexis Rinander (born 1872), who afterward had little business with the school; Karl Hedvall (1873–1918), Hägerström's good friend who taught theoretical philosophy in Uppsala before taking his life during World War I; Hilding Barkman (born 1877) who discussed his PhD thesis on transcendental philosophy in Uppsala in 1901 and later became a journalist in Göteborg; Harry Meurling (1878–1938) who taught practical philosophy in Uppsala in the same years as Hägerström, author of the essay *On Conceptual Analysis* from 1928 (*Om begreppsanalys*); and, last but not least, the young Aldolf Phalén (1884–1931).

«The most significant proof of the existence of this group of philosophers is the plan to start a philosophical review.»[193] Karl Hedvall seemed to have been the man behind the idea. The review was supposed to be published in German, which means that it was intended for a larger international audience. Hägerström was supposed to be the editor.[194] The Uppsala formation was a school in the sense that, like most other philosophical schools, it was characterised by the existence of a master, a common *afflatus* in methodology, and common targets as well as, of course, a unified front in all academic battles. The Uppsala School was enriched, later on, by names such as Einar Tegen (1884–1965), professor of practical philosophy in Lund and in Stockholm, author of *Moderne Willenstheorien* in two volumes (1924–1928) and *The Basic Problem in the Theory of Value* from 1944. With the passing of time, the school became a two-headed Janus, with the theoretical face of Phalén and the practical side of Hägerström. Phalén, as mentioned, had many followers, among whom Carl Hellström (1892–1932) who taught theoretical philosophy in Uppsala until his suicide in 1932; Gunnar Oxenstierna (1897–1939) who taught the same

[191] I. Hedenius, *Om stora män och små*, Rabén och Sjögren, Stockholm 1980, p. 194.

[192] M. Waller, *Människan som få kände*, cit., p. 172.

[193] C.-G. Heidegren, *Den nya Uppsala-filosofin*, cit., p. 78. These plans are illustrated in M. Waller, *Människan som få kände*, cit., p. 181.

[194] During spring 1905, in a letter to his wife, he came back to the editing-plan, set out for 1906, but some financial problems seemed to have cancelled the plan.

subject and was the author of the 1938-pamphlet *What is Uppsala Philosophy?*; as well as three eminent names in the Swedish postwar analytical tradition: Konrad Marc-Wogau (1902–1991), Ingmar Hedenius (1908–1982) and Anders Wedberg (1913–1978). Among Hägerström's followers, we can mention Erik Jonson (1889–1958) who circulated at a certain distance (he spent most of his time sailing) and the ever loyal and faithful Martin Fries (1898–1969) – the «stoic epicurean» as he was once described by the students in Uppsala[195] – who spent decades classifying and typewriting Hägerström's huge *Nachlaß*.

It should be clear from this brief account that the Uppsala School of philosophy, unified by the method of conceptual analysis (in Hägerström's sense, or as Phalén's "denunciation of dialectics"), is a separate group from that of Scandinavian legal realism, in which Vilhelm Lundstedt (1882–1955) and Karl Olivecrona (1897–1980) were the central figures.[196] The famed Danish jurist, Alf Ross (1899–1979) came into contact with Hägerström after the latter accepted that Ross discuss his PhD thesis in Uppsala since his Kelsen-influenced outlook had been banned by Fredrik Vinding Kruse (1880–1963) from Copenhagen. Ross' *Kritik der sogennanten praktischen Erkenntnis* is dedicated to Hägerström. But all this hardly makes Ross "Hägerströmian" to any significant extent.[197]

From a strictly philosophical point of view, indeed, it is more relevant to point to the relation between what went on in Uppsala and what was happening in the same period in England and in Austria. So was Uppsala the Vienna to come? This is a very common thesis and to a certain extent it is true.[198] What Hägerström and the Uppsala group shared with the Vienna Circle, that nevertheless published after Hägerström, were the struggle against metaphysics, a strong faith in science, and the refusal of *Geisteswissenschaften*. In general terms, both in Vienna and Uppsala there were traces of militant scienticism, along with a social pathos and belief in human progress; all elements common to a certain *esprit positif* which was then growing in Europe.[199]

Most historical accounts on the Uppsala group insist that the similarity between Uppsala and Vienna is a likeness in spirit, «an unquestioned family resemblance»[200]

[195] See the student review «Ergo», 1926, n. 5, p. 74.

[196] Folke Schmidt's *The Uppsala School of Legal Thinking* (Scandinavian Studies in Law, vol. 22, Almqvist & Wiksell International, Stockholm 1978), one of the few accounts in English from the Seventies made the two groups overlap, creating some confusing ideas in non-Scandinavian scholars.

[197] See for instance L. Hierro, *El realismo jurídico escandinavo*, cit., p. 162.

[198] On this issue, see R.T. Sandin, *The Founding of the Uppsala School*, cit., p. 496; E. Cassirer, *Axel Hägerström*, cit., pp. 12 ff. K. Marc-Wogau, *Studier till Axel Hägerströms filosofi*, cit., pp. 65 ff.; E. Pattaro, *Realismo giuridico scandinavo*, cit., pp. 58 ff.

[199] See J. Strang, *Axel Hägerström och Gunnar Myrdal. Om den svenska värdenihilistiska traditionen*, in «Historisk Tidskrift för Finland», 2003:1, pp. 43–61; C.-G. Heidegren, *Idealistisk systemfilosofi kontra den positiva andan i finsk och svensk universitetsfilosofi*, cit., pp. 21–49.

[200] R.T. Sandin, *The Founding of the Uppsala School*, cit., p. 496.

more than grounded on any direct influence.[201] Such descriptions usually stress that «isolation in Uppsala was strong»[202] even though the very members of the School never considered their positions to be either outdated, or provincial. Anders Wedberg, for example, acknowledged that the difference between consciousness and its contents was the basis of "modern epistemology" by referring not only to Brentano, Husserl and Meinong, but also to G.E. Moore as the "father of the Cambridge School" and to the "neorealistic school" in America as well.[203] Therefore the isolation should not be overestimated. There were contacts: Phalén had been in Vienna, where he met Eino Kaila, in the same years Alfred Ayer studied there for Moritz Schlick. Einar Tegen participated in the first international congress for scientific philosophy held in Paris in 1935, organised to a large extent by the Viennese positivists. Åke Petzäll, director of the review *Theoria*, did a lot to introduce the ideas of logical positivism in Uppsala,[204] even though Ingmar Hedenius should be credited for connecting the Uppsala philosophy with the Cambridge and Vienna schools.[205] From the Viennese viewpoint, *Die Richtung Uppsala* was well represented in the 1935 edition of *Erkenntnis* over positivist thinkers.[206] In the foreword of *Logical Positivism*, Alfred Ayer mentioned "the Uppsala school of empiricists" as a movement set in the same direction as the Vienna circle.[207]

However, the specific differences between the philosophers in Uppsala and the Viennese men of science are seldom stressed.[208] Apart from generic

---

[201] In order to establish direct sources, we should perhaps look in different directions; the German Marburg School and the newly born phenomenology probably played a greater role in the formation of both Hägerström and Phalén.

[202] E. Tegen, quoting from S. Nordin, *Från Hägerström till Hedenius*, cit., p. 77. See also p. 232.

[203] A. Wedberg, *Den logiska strukturen i Boströms filosofi*, Almqvist & Wiksell, Uppsala 1937, p. 38: «I modern kunskapsteori förkastas som bekant allmänt antagandet att medvetenhetsakten och dess innehåll skulle vara identiska. Det motsatta antagandet utgör en grundläggande förutsättning för den aktpsykologiska riktning, som kan följas tillbaka till Bolzano och vars mest bekanta representanter äro Brentano, Husserl och Meinong. Den aktpsykologiska ståndpunkten har på ett originellt och skarpsinnligt sätt hävdats av den engelske filosofen G.E. Moore, Cambridgeskolans fader, i hans berömda *The Refutation of Idealism*.» For Neo-realism in the U.S. the reference is to Edwin B. Holt (ed.), *The New Realism: Cooperative Studies in Philosophy*, Macmillan, New York 1912. Anders Wedberg, however, also claimed that «in Bertrand Russell, the metaphysical character of empiricism and positivism is very marked» (*Bertrand Russell's Empiricism*, in *Adolf Phalén. In memoriam*, ed. by I. Hedenius, Almqvist & Wiksell, Stockholm-Uppsala 1937, p. 387).

[204] During the 30s, some of Adolf Phalén's followers participated in a debate on the review "Theoria" against the Vienna Circle, represented by Phillip Frank (1884–1966). This debate was later summarized by Gunnar Oxenstierna in *Sannolikhetens filosofi* from 1937. It centered on the critique of empiricism as being a form of subjectivism, an argument taken to a large extent from Hägerström.

[205] I. Hedenius, *Begriffsanalyse und kritischer Idealismus* (I) in «Theoria», 1939, vol. 5, n. 3, p. 287.

[206] See «Erkenntnis», 1935, vol. 5, pp. 427–428.

[207] A.J. Ayer, *Logical Positivism*, Free Press, New York 1959, pp. 5–7.

[208] The exception that confirms this is Johan Strang's forthcoming *Theoria and Logical Empiricism* in Vienna Circle Institute Yearbook 15 (Springer, Dordrecht).

assumptions – such as Sandin's lapidary «the Uppsala positivism is in general less cavalier, more sensitive to philosophical traditions, and more constructive than its Viennese counterpart»[209] – on three major issues the philosophical trends diverge: Conceptual analysis, modern logic and the theory of meaning on which Hägerström grounded his ethical emotivism.[210]

When it comes to the methodological preference for the analytical scalpel in philosophy, an undisputable similarity between Uppsala and Vienna is at hand. The attention for the so-called linguistic turn and conceptual analysis is clear from the Uppsala motto: «Let us determine the concepts!»[211] The strong emphasis both Hägerström and Phalén laid on conceptual analysis as the method for philosophical inquiries, and their way of viewing the task of philosophy in terms of eliminating misconceptions seems to fit like hand in glove to what Wittgenstein was then claiming. But there were differences on this point. According to Oxenstierna, for example, conceptual analysis is first and foremost a way of emphasizing the internal contradictions of concepts following a *dialectical* scheme: «The image of conceptual analysis in our view is so diverse from what usually goes under this name, that one feels faint. In the analysis we discover that what we considered solid ground, hard concepts on which to rely, turn out to be a swamp of contradictions. And what is then the content of our overall views if its grounds are uncertain? This is really quite unclear. Conceptual analysis has, in fact, uncovered a part of the veil, but on the whole we still fumble in the dark. We only know that our precedent assurance in the fundamental concepts was an illusion.»[212]

Another dissimilarity between Uppsala and Vienna was the role attributed to modern logic. Central in Austria, it remained marginal in Sweden. It is not hard to confirm the harsh opinion of the Finnish professor Eino Kaila, who first introduced logical positivism in Scandinavia: «According to me, when it comes to these [Uppsala] views, we should note, first and foremost, that they are out-of-date from the perspective of the most recent research. The entire Uppsala philosophy has an obsolete touch to it. It is remarkable that the philosophers in Uppsala who claim to be logicians do not seem to be aware of the existence of the huge developments in logic in the last decades, roughly speaking, subsequent to Sigwart and Erdmann: I mean the exact research represented in the old generation by Frege and Russell and in the new generation perhaps by Wittgenstein and Carnap. For those who are

---

[209] R.T. Sandin, *The Founding of the Uppsala School*, cit., p. 512.

[210] See next chapter.

[211] See K. Marc-Wogau, *Studier*, cit., p. 7.

[212] G. Oxenstierna, *Vad är Uppsalafilosofien?*, cit., p. 14: «Den bild begreppsanalysen ger av vårt tänkande är så helt i skild från allt man vanligen menar, att man i förstone gripes av svindel. Vad vi tagit för fasta marken, hårda, solida begrepp, som man tryggt kan lita på, avslöjar analysen som ett enda gungfly av motsägelser. Och vad är då hela vårt tankesätts innebörd, om själva dess grundförutsättningar visa sig så osäkra? Det är faktiskt i hög grad oklart. Begeppsanalysen har visserligen lyft en flik av slöjan, men i det hela treva vi fortfarande i dunkel. Vi veta endast, att vår tidigare säkerhet om grundbegreppens natur var en illusion.»

familiar with the results of these new investigations, it is funny to watch the Uppsala philosophy struggle with problems which were resolved a long time ago by exact logic, or at least brought into new light.»[213]

As a matter of fact, modern logic never really got a grip in Uppsala and this explains both the persistent interest in classical metaphysics and the eclectic methodology that distinguished Hägerström and his followers.[214] Hedenius, for example, refused Carnap's idea that metaphysics is a form of emotional manifestation because, for the Uppsala School, the logical element in metaphysics (what Phalén called its dialectics) is crucial, since it enables the Uppsala philosopher to show, at a macroscopic level, the contradictions inherent in the concepts used by common sense (*vardagsmedvetandet*).[215] Contrarily to Carnap, Wedberg also considered it important to study metaphysics given that «from the errors of metaphysics we study important conceptual distinctions.»[216] A major difference between the Uppsala School and the tradition of logical positivism and analytical thought is therefore that, in Uppsala, the study of classics in philosophy never became obsolete.[217] The attention for the history of thought, religion, science, law and morals, for the complex evolutionary schemes of the ideas we use in everyday life, was indeed an interest that never abandoned Hägerström and that he infused in the Uppsala atmosphere.

A third difference concerned emotivism in ethics.[218] Indeed, non-cognitivism in general, and emotivism in particular, were never part of the logic-empiric program in Vienna. Neither can such positions be deduced from the 1929 *Wissenschaftliche*

---

[213] E. Kaila (1933), quoting from S. Nordin, *Från Hägerström till Hedenius*, cit., p. 97: «I främsta rummet måste man mot tankesättet i fråga enligt min mening anmärka, att det, sett ur den nyaste forskningens synvinkel, är avgjort föråldrat. Hela Uppsalafilosofin bär en viss prägling av efterblivenhet. Det är ett märkvärdigt sakförhållande, att Uppsala-filosoferna som i främsta rummet vilja gälla som logiker, icke synas äga någon kunskap om existensen om hela denna väldiga logiska forskning, som uppstått och utvecklats under de senaste decenierna, efter låt oss säga Sigwarts och Erdmanns tidevarv; jag menar denna exakta forskning, vars mest bekanta representanter i den äldre generationen äro Frege och Russell, och ur den yngre kanske Wittgenstein och Carnap. För den som känner till resultanten av denna nya forskning, är det ett sällsamt skådespel att se hur uppsalafilosofin brottas med problem, som av den exakta logiken redan för länge sedan fullständigt löst, delvis bragts i en alldeles ny belysning.»

[214] See C. Faralli, *Diritto e magia. Saggio su Axel Hägerström*, Giuffrè, Milano 1982, pp. 160 ff.

[215] I. Hedenius, *Sensationalism and Theology in Berkeley's Philosophy*, Uppsala University (Diss.), Uppsala 1936, Introduction.

[216] A. Wedberg, *Den logiska strukturen i Boströms filosofi*, cit., p. 2: «lära vi av metafysikens misstag betydelsefulla begreppsdistinktioner.»

[217] Wedberg, for example, attributed much importance to what he called a "*philosophical* history of philosophy": Id., *Den logiska strukturen i Boströms filosofi*, cit., p. 1; and *Filosofins historia III. Från Bolzano till Wittgenstein*, Bonniers, Stockholm 1966, *passim*.

[218] Another difference is, for example, the Viennese interest in "special sciences," in particular "protocol sentences" as in Moritz Schlick's *Positivism and Realism*. For a criticism of these aspects within the Uppsala School, see for instance Einar Tegen's *Kritisk objectivism* in «Theoria», 1936, II, p. 39. A final difference was the Uppsala school's refutation of Einstein's theory of relativity and of Heisenberg's quantum mechanics (see the last chapter).

*Weltauffassung der Wiener Kreis.* Otto Neurath, Moritz Schlick and Karl Menger, to mention but a few, do not tend towards any "axiological nihilism" of the kind Hägerström developed. Of course, Rudolf Carnap and Alfred Jules Ayer, who wrote his famous *Language, Truth and Logic* after studying in Vienna, are often mentioned as having developed emotivistic standpoints in meta-ethics by the mid-thirties. But, as emphasised by Sven Danielsson, they had adopted this standpoint for very different reasons, especially as far as the theory of meaning is concerned. «To ask for a word's meaning, for Carnap and Ayer and the other logical positivists, is not a question of what psychological events the words is associated with in the users. To ask for a sentence's meaning was to inquire on a factual relation which could make the sentence true.»[219]

So in this time of widespread "rebellion" against idealism and metaphysics, there was one specific field in which Uppsala was really avant-garde: If we look at the tradition of non-cognitivism and emotivism in ethics, long before twentieth century milestones such as Ogden and Richards' *The Meaning of Meaning* from 1923, Alfred J. Ayer's *Language, Truth and Logic* from 1936 or Charles L. Stevenson's *Facts and Values* from 1963, Hägerström had set a new record: *On the Truth of Moral Ideas* is from 1911.

[219] S. Danielsson, *Några värdenihilismer*, in Å.E. Andersson (ed.), *Huvudinnehåll*, Nya Doxa, Nora 1993, p. 40: «att fråga efter ett ords mening var för Carnap och Ayer och de andra logiska positivisterna inte att fråga om efter vilka psykiska skeenden hos användarna som orden är förbundna med. Att frågan efter en sats mening var snarare en fråga efter de sakförhållanden som skulle göra satsen sann.»

# Chapter 3
# The Value of a Chair: The Moral Teachings

*The Moor – the God of men – has delivered his services.*
*He may leave*[1]

## 3.1 The Shock of Axiological Nihilism

In 1910, Hägerström's friend and mentor, Erik Burman – «the Socrates of Swedish Philosophy»[2] – retired from the chair in practical philosophy because of his frequent health problems. Even though Burman had considered *Das Prinzip* "an attempt to refute him" he did not hesitate to nominate Hägerström as his successor. This time, Hägerström did not leave anything to chance, so he rapidly composed two lengthy essays in order to secure his succession to the prestigious chair in Uppsala: *Critical Aspects in Psychology of Value* and the often forgotten *Contribution to the Analysis of Empirical Self-Consciousness*. In November, the commission formed by Carl Yngve Sahlin, Karl Geijer, and Vitalis Norström from Göteborg, finally nominated him for the position that had once been of Christopher Jacob Boström.

On March 18th, 1911 Hägerström held what was to become his celebrated and yet ill-reputed inaugural speech: *On the Truth of Moral Propositions*.[3] The room was

[1] A. Hägerström, *Om social rättvisa* (1913), now in *Socialfilosofiska uppsatser*, Bonniers, Stockholm 1939, p. 140: «Moren – människoguden – har gjort sin tjänst. Moren kan gå.» The Shakespeare inspired similitude is between the Venetian moor and traditional values.

[2] Opinion of A. Hägerström in an interview by H. Apéria-Meurling, *Samtal med en svensk tänkare*, in «Ord och Bild», 1939, 48, p. 420: «den svenska filosofiens Sokrates.»

[3] There are various versions of this text, among which we find the actual speech entitled "Reality and Ought" and the published version. See T. Mautner (ed.), *Moralfilosofins grundläggning*, Almqvist & Wiksell, Stockholm 1987, p. 18; which contains the famous inaugural lecture from 1911 (with explanatory remarks by the editor) and the manuscript *H 105:6* (spring course 1911) with notes by the students. Hägerström's inaugural lecture was reedited in the first edition *Socialfilosofiska uppsatser*, cit., pp. 37–65. English translation by R. Sandin, *On the Truth of Moral Propositions*, in *Philosophy and Religion*, Allen & Unwin, London 1964; by T. Mautner, *On the Truth of Moral Ideas*, ANU, Canberra 1971; German trans. by D. Lang, *Über die Wahrheit moralischer Vorstellungen*, in «Perspektiven der Philosophie», 1979, pp. 219–242; an Italian translation

P. Mindus, *A Real Mind*, Law and Philosophy Library 87,
DOI 10.1007/978-90-481-2895-2_3, 

full of people, including theologians, jurists and the two men who had nominated Hägerström, Burman and Sahlin. *Rector Magnificus*, Henrik Schück, presented the new member of the faculty and underlined the academic tradition of the chair, the importance of the legacy of Boström, the guardian of the orthodox State-and-Church *habitus* of all decent members of the community. In the midst of this early twentieth century student crowd, Hägerström started with the ultra classic reference to Herodotus and to the anonymous author of the *Dissoi logoi*:[4] «Herodotus relates that the Persian King Darius put the following questions to some Greeks who were visiting his court: "For what price would you be willing to eat the dead bodies of your fathers?". "Not for anything in the world!", came the answer. Whereupon Darius called in some representatives of an Indian Tribe, among whom that which was abhorrent to the Greeks was the custom, and he asked them for what price they would be willing to burn the dead bodies of their fathers. They vigorously repudiated every thought of anything so horrible.»[5]

Now, this standard anecdote on the relativity of customs was only the starting point for Hägerström. Actually his purpose was to criticise a series of conceptions of value – from Kant to Spencer, from Wundt to the *Wertphilosophie*[6] – in order to focus on his main argument: «The final result of this investigation is that a moral conception (*föreställning, Vorstellung*) as such – i.e., the idea that a certain action represents a supreme value – cannot be said to be either true or false.»[7]

The motive behind this argument is that «even if it is absolute, a reality can never include within itself a supreme value. The existence of a divine will or an inner demand can never imply in and of itself, that we ought to follow it, that to

---

was made by Giuliano Pontara but never published. See also T. Mautner, *A Summary in English [of Hägerström's manuscript 105:6 from 1911]* in A. Hägerström, *Moralfilosofins grundläggning*, cit., pp. 201–233. On the inaugural lecture, see J. Bjarup, *Ought and Reality. Hägerström's Inaugural Lecture Re-considered* in P. Wahlgren (ed.), «Scandinavian Studies in Law», vol. 40, Almqvist & Wiksell, Stockholm 2000, pp. 11–72; Id., *Axel Hägerströms filosofi, värdenihilism och rättspositivism* in «Juridisk Tidskrift», 2004/2005, anno 16, n. 1, p. 27; as well as the critical remarks in T. Spaak, *(Review of) Legal Theory (Peter Wahlgren ed. 2000)* in «Archiv für Rechts- und Sozialphilosophie», 2002, vol. 88, n. 2, pp. 298–304.

[4]Hägerström did not give the reference, but the «Greek sentence» he mentioned on the first page of the inaugural lecture can be found in Diels-Krantz B, 2, 18.

[5]A. Hägerström, *Philosophy and Religion*, cit., p. 77.

[6]Further criticism of contemporary thinkers on the conception of value can be found in *Kritiska punkter i värdepsykologien*, in *Festskrift tillägnad E.O. Burman*, Appelgrens boktr., Uppsala 1910, pp. 17–75, where he attacked Hugo Münsterberg's *Philosophie der Werte* (1908), Heinrich Maier's *Psychologie des emotionalen Denkens* (1908), Max Reischle's *Werturteile und Glaubensurteile* (1900).

[7]A. Hägerström, *Socialfilosofiska uppsatser*, cit., p. 59. I am quoting the translation by R. Sandin, *On the Truth of Moral Propositions*, cit., p. 92, but I have taken some liberty by translating *föreställning* with "conception" and "idea" instead of "proposition" since the latter is often misleading. For the use of the terms *föreställning*, *Vorstellung* and the translations into representation, idea and conception depending on context, see note 15 in Chapter 2.

follow it is of supreme value. Existence and value signify something entirely different.»[8] Hence, Hägerström emerges as a true defender of «Hume's guillotine»[9] and adversary of all regressive confusion between *is* and *ought*. His purpose is to defend a «positivistic» and «scientific» as well as «value-free» method, as opposed to the idealistic dogmatism then prevailing in the academic world.[10] His intention was to abandon every scientific program that reduces social complexity and human emotion to the traditional frame of a metaphysical principle upholding a system of morals, aesthetics and so forth. This is the reason why Hägerström stood out as a strong advocate for the radical separation between *Sein* and *Sollen*, *is* and *ought*. But what might seem "modern" in contemporary eyes, was then rejected as "shocking."

He ended the inaugural lecture with a sentence that would become the nutshell-variant of his practical philosophy: «*There can never be any teaching* in *morality, only* on *morals.*»[11] This was the straw that broke the camel's back: Sahlin, who listened to the discourse, was furious! A student of his, Ragnar Josephson, tells us that «after the lecture, I met my philosophy teacher, Sahlin (...). Lightning shot from his clear blue eyes when he expressed his criticism of Hägerström, sentencing: "He only showed that some people honor the dead by mourning dressed in black while others do it dressed in red. It remains to be proven that anyone considers it morally approvable to dishonor their deceased parents."»[12] As Thomas Mautner correctly observed, «it was already well-known that [Hägerström] nourished radical opinions on politics and religion.»[13] Suffice it to say that just a few weeks before, on the 1st of March, Hägerström had denied the existence of free will in a talk held by the scientist Oséen.[14]

In a wider perspective, Hägerström had developed an interest in normative thought as early as 1904 in the monograph *Stat och rätt*, in the limelight in Chapter

[8] A. Hägerström, *Socialfilosofiska uppsatser*, cit., p. 51; *On the Truth of Moral Propositions*, cit., p. 87.

[9] D. Hume, *A Treatise on the Human Nature*, book III, part I, Section I.

[10] On the prevailing idealism in Scandinavia, see J.-F. Battail, *Le mouvement des idées en Suède à l'âge du bergsonisme*, Lettres Modernes, Paris 1979; and S. Nygård, J. Strang (eds.), *Mellan idealism och analytisk filosofi: den moderna filosofin i Finland och Sverige 1880–1950*, Atlantis, Stockholm 2006.

[11] A. Hägerström, *On the Truth of Moral Propositions*, cit., p. 96.

[12] Quote from T. Mautner (ed.), *Moralfilosofins grundläggning*, cit., p. 10: «efter föreläsningen mötte jag min (...) lärare i filosofi, Sahlin (...). Det sköt blixtar ur hans klarblå ögon när han för mig utlade sin kritik mot Hägerström och slutade: "han har bara visat att ett folk hedrar sina döda genom att sörja dem i svart frack och att ett annat folk gör det genom att sörja dem i rö: det återstår att visa att det finns något folk som betraktar det som ett moraliskt värde att vanhedra sina döda föräldrar."» Sahlin's criticism was a very common misunderstanding of Hägerström's axiological nihilism: Its confusion with moral relativism or practical nihilism.

[13] T. Mautner (ed.), *Moralfilosofins grundläggning*, cit., p. 7: «[det var] redan välkänt att han [Hägerström] hyste radikala åsikter om politik och religion.»

[14] See E. Tegen, *Anteckningar* (*Notes*) at Uppsala University Library (UUB Okat. 453 G:2, block-notes no. 3).

2. However, the 1911 discourse is, so to speak, the nucleus of Hägerström's practical philosophy,[15] which left the general impression of bewilderment. As late as 1940, a newspaper article in *Göteborgs Handels och sjöfartstidning* – significantly entitled *Hägerström and Hitler* – recalled that «many still remember clearly how [Hägerström] on this occasion shocked a trusting and unsuspicious audience by explaining that there is no scientifically observable moral.»[16]

From this very general viewpoint – according to which Hägerström is a forerunner of "scientific" approaches in ethics, a predecessor of Carnap, Ayer, Stevenson and contemporary meta-ethics – it seems that Hägerström gave expression to something that was really "in the air." In point of fact, the rejection of *Geisteswissenschaften* in Dilthey's sense and the plea for a more scientific philosophy were rather recurrent topics in those days.[17] For example, Henri Poincaré (1854–1912) claimed that «there can be no scientific morals and no immoral science.»[18] Émile Durkheim (1858–1917), at the international conference in philosophy in 1911, distinguished between judgments of value and judgments on reality.[19] In the same period, the Austrian legal scholar and sociologist Eugen Ehrlich (1862–1922), in his *Freie Rechtsfindung und freie Rechtswissenschaft* from 1903 and the four volumes of *Grundlegung der Soziologie des Rechts* from 1913, emphasized that the legal norm relies on the intensity of the underlying emotion. Another famous example is Max Weber (1864–1920) with his polytheism of values. Some even affirm that Hägerström's philosophy is a step in the process of *disenchantment* and *rationalisation* of the world.[20] In this wider sense, Hägerström certainly participated in the "breakthrough of modernism" along with many others in art, literature and science. This generic approach aside, what should be stressed is the development of his moral teachings and, above all, what arguments uphold his so-called "axiological nihilism" or theory of value. Consequently we will be able to show why Hägerström «was the one who, for the first time, entirely formulated a non-cognitive moral theory.»[21]

---

[15] B. Petersson, *Axel Hägerströms värdeteori*, Filosofiska föreningen vid Uppsala universitet, Uppsala 1973, p. 189.

[16] T. Mautner (ed.), *Moralfilosofins grundläggning*, cit., p. 7: «Många har ännu i friskt minne hur han [Hägerström] vid detta tillfälle chockerade en intet ont anande publik genom att förklara att någon vetenskapligt fastställbar moral inte finns.»

[17] A. Hägerström, *Selbstdarstellung*, Meiner, Leipzig 1929, p. 158; *Filosofi och vetenskap*, Ehlin, Stockholm 1957, p. 180.

[18] H. Poincaré, *Dernières pensées*, Flammarion, Paris 1913, p. 225: «Il ne peut y avoir de morale scientifique, ni de science immorale.»

[19] E. Durkheim, *Jugements de valeur et jugements de realité*, in *Atti del congresso internazionale di filosofia* (Bologna), Formiggini, Genova 1911, vol. I, pp. 99–114.

[20] S. Källström, *Filosofi och politik. Axel Hägerström och samhällsdebatten*, in G. Bexell, H. Stenius (eds.), *Värdetraditioner i nordiskt perspektiv*, Lund University Press, Lund 1997, p. 155; S. Eliaeson, *Axel Hägerström and Modern Social Thought*, in «Nordeuropaforum», 2000:1, pp. 19–30.

[21] T. Mautner (ed.), *Moralfilosofins grundläggning*, cit., p. 25: «Det var han som först formulerade en genomförd nonkognitivistisk moralteori.»

## 3.2 The Norm Theory and Its Evolution (1907–1917)

Bo Petersson in his 1973 PhD thesis on the development of Hägerström's theory of value – which is probably the most elaborate attempt to follow the chronological evolution of his thought – asserted that «Hägerström puts forward two versions of his theory of value. In the earliest version, 1907–1912, he declares that no valuation is true or false, while after 1912, he assumes certain valuations to be neither true nor false and others to be false. His later theories are combinations of axiological nihilism and error-theory.»[22] This suggestion of "steps" in Hägerström's theory of value was first developed by Martin Fries in the preface to the essay collection *Moral Psychology* from 1952.[23] In the early version (1907–1912), Hägerström insisted on the meaninglessness of moral assertions in scientific contexts, while, around 1912–1913, he developed a mixed theory where, on one hand, semantic propositions including normative terms are said to be neither true nor false and, on the other hand, he stressed that normative ideas on rights and duties are simply false.[24]

The easiest way to sum up Hägerström's meta-ethical ideas is to underline how we «dress emotions in the form of judgments.»[25] All of our misconceptions in the realm of ethics stem from this original sin and they generate very real and concrete conflicts among us. His theory of value usually goes under the name of "axiological nihilism."[26] However it should be added that this appellative is nothing Hägerström invented. The expression was first coined by the Swedish journalist John Landqvist, a legendary adversary of Hägerström – at that time responsible for the political and cultural section of the daily newspaper "Aftonbladet"[27] – who rejected Hägerström's position as «culturally abnormal.»[28] The name was only adopted after Ingmar Hedenius' attempt to rescue it by «taking away its tenebrous associations unsupported by facts, that sometimes made this expression a weapon

[22] B. Petersson, *Axel Hägerströms värdeteori*, cit., p. 187.

[23] A. Hägerström, *Moralpsykologi*, Natur & Kultur, Stockholm 1952, p. 11. Another attempt to distinguish phases in Hägerström's theory can be found in K. Marc-Wogau, *Studier till Axel Hägerströms filosofi*, Prisma, Falköping 1968, pp. 132 ff.

[24] Comments on Hägerström's alleged inconsistency can be found in A. Mac Leod, *Tre uppsatser om Hägerström, Zenon från Elea och relativitetsteorin*, Filosofiska föreningen vid Uppsala universitet, Uppsala 1973, pp. 19–20.

[25] S. Källström, *Filosofi och politik*, cit., p. 145: «vi klär en känsla i omdömets form.»

[26] Hägerström's «axiological nihilism» is not the same thing as what many theorists today call «moral nihilism» which is just another name for error-theory (John Mackie), while «axiological nihilism» is a more comprehensive paradigm which, however, includes some positions later labeled as "error-theory" (see B. Petersson, *Axel Hägerströms värdeteori*, cit., pp. 125–135).

[27] For a detailed reconstruction of the debate on Hägerström's axiological nihilism in the media, see S. Källström, *Den gode nihilisten. Axel Hägerström och striderna kring Uppsalafilosofin*, Rabén & Sjögren, Stockholm 1986.

[28] The expression was used by Landqvist for the first time in his review on May 23rd 1931 of one of the first monographs on Hägerström: *Hägerströmstudier* by A. Vannérus (Bonniers, Stockholm 1930). See K. Marc-Wogau, *Studier till Axel Hägerströms filosofi*, cit., p. 202.

against the Uppsala philosophy.»[29] This appellative, however, did not bring good auspices to Hägerström's ideas.

Just like he opposed both idealistic subjectivism and empiricist objectivism in his theoretical philosophy, in his practical philosophy he opposed both what he called subjectivism and objectivism: The value is neither in the object, nor in the subject. This is important since it enables us to understand how he thought of the relation between theoretical and practical philosophy: «As far as the relation of theoretical and practical philosophy is concerned, a twofold relation is possible: The ultimate foundation in theoretical philosophy can be combined with the ultimate objective of practical reasoning or they can be separated. Accordingly there are two different standpoints in the history of philosophy concerning the ultimate objective, absolute Good. We can qualify them in such a way that the first is objective, and the second is subjective.»[30] Since the "evaluation" or moral representation is no real judgment, it is neither "real for the subject" nor present in the object.

If we look for the genesis of Hägerström's axiological nihilism, the starting point might be his review of Danish social scientist and psychologist Birch-Reichenwald Aars' *Gut und Böse*, published in Christiania in 1907.[31] In autumn the same year, Hägerström lectured on the *History of Christian Ethics* (the first part of which was later edited under the title *Jesus* in 1968). In this lengthy review, published in two parts, he explicitly mentions his distinguished Finnish colleague, the sociologist and anthropologist Edward Westermark (1862–1939), who wrote *The Origin and Development of Moral Ideas*[32] in 1906, as a major source for ascertaining that «all

[29] I. Hedenius, *Om rätt och moral*, Wahlström & Widstrand, Stockholm 1941, 1963², p. 13: «få bort de kusliga, sakligt ogrundade associationer, vilka någon gång gjort ordet i fråga användbart som tillhygge mot Uppsalafilosofin.»

[30] A. Hägerström, *Moralfilosofins grundläggning*, cit., p. 74: «Med avseende på ställningen mellan teoretisk och praktisk filosofi är ett tvåfaldigt förhållande möjligt. Man kan nämligen ställa den yttersta grunden, som man förmenar sig finna i den teoretiska filosofien ihop med det yttersta målet, som man tror sig finna i den praktiska. Eller man kan avsöndra dem från varandra. Allt därefter ha vi i filosofiens historia två skilda ståndpunkter med avseende på det yttersta målet, det hösta goda. Vi kunna bestämma dem så, att den första är objektiv, den andra är subjektiv.» On the relation between *theoria* and *praxis* in Hägerström, see also E. Cassirer, *Axel Hägerström. Eine Studie zur schwedischen Philosophie der Gegenwart*, Göteborgs högskolas årskrift, Göteborg 1939; now in *Gesammelte Werke*, Bd. 21, Meiner, Hamburg 2005; and H. Ruin, *Hägerström, Nietzsche och den svenska nihilismen*, in «Tidskrift för politisk filosofi», 2000:1, pp. 5–30, especially p. 20 where no immediate relation between theory and practical reasoning in Hägerström is admitted. However, Hägerström clearly stated the opposite thesis in the manuscript H 106:5, p. 105.

[31] A. Hägerström, *I moralpsykologiska frågor*, in «Psyke. Tidskrift för psykologisk forskning», 1907, anno II, vol. 5, pp. 273–287 and second part in 1908, anno III, vols. 1–2, pp. 85–99. Around 1907 Hägerström abandoned the belief that the aim of ethics was to search for the highest good as expressed in earlier writings (A. Hägerström, *Om filosofiens betydelse för människan*, in *I vår tids lifsfrågor. Skrifter utgivna af Sydney Alrutz*, Skoglund, Stockholm 1898, pp. 5–47).

[32] Hägerström studied particularly the first volume of Westermarck's *opus* published by Macmillan, London 1906. On Westermarck's influence, see K. Marc-Wogau, *Studier till Axel Hägerströms filosofi*, cit., p. 23; B. Petersson, *Axel Hägerströms värdeteori*, cit., pp. 93–97. On a comparison between Hägerström and Westermarck, see J. Sundberg, *The Swedish Philosopher Axel*

of our moral judgments are only expressions of the internal capacity of an action to arouse pleasure or displeasure.»[33] Westermark's anthropological and historical account of the development of moral systems, ultimately grounded in two original feelings, love and hate, is criticised by Hägerström because of the oversimplified equation between considering emotion to be an insuppressible part in moral assessments and the idea that value equals pleasure or displeasure. Indeed, by keeping his distance from both "naturalistic ethics" such as utilitarian ethics, and more traditional "supernatural ethics,"[34] his point is that «we do not need to contest that emotion equals the ability of understanding a value, in the sense that it is an essential side in our way of conceiving it (*värdemedvetande*). But it can be disputed that value, for the person making the evaluation, (...) necessarily means pleasure or displeasure. (...) If the patient feels disgusted by the medicine the doctor ordered, he does not hereby feel that he does not have to take it.»[35] Hägerström came back to these features the same year in the aforementioned lectures on *Jesus*, where he defined "moral feeling" as «pleasure at the idea of being in accordance with the requirements of what is right in itself.»[36] Here he also delineated the difference between religious and moral feelings because of their heteronymous and autonomous character respectively.[37]

One remarkable aspect of the 1907 review is that he clearly stated why he was so interested in morals. Since religion was the issue that first aroused Hägerström's interest in philosophical analysis as a way to avoid psychological setbacks for the unbeliever, it is worth asking why his attention shifted to moral systems.[38] «The thing is that, for the modern mind, the reality of religious representations does not provoke the equal amount of affection as moral ideas.»[39] So, his investigations into the psychology of value can be viewed as the prosecution with other means of the very same battle against theology and religion.

Among his later writings on the theory of value we should, first of all, mention the two essays Hägerström composed before his admission to the chair, the

---

*Haegerstroem and his Relationship to Finland's Struggle to Preserve her Legal Order 1899–1917*, Rothman, Littleton (Col.) 1983, pp. 10–14.

[33] A. Hägerström, *I moralpsykologiska frågor*, cit., p. 274: «alla våra sedliga omdömen äro blott uttalanden af handlingars inre förmåga att väcka sedlig lust eller olust.»

[34] A. Hägerström, *I moralpsykologiska frågor*, cit., p. 274.

[35] A. Hägerström, *I moralpsykologiska frågor*, cit., p. 283: «man behöver icke bestrida att känslan är värdets uppfattningsförmåga i den meningen, att den är en väsentlig sida i medvetandet om värdet. Man kan dock bestrida, att det som den värdesättande förstår med värde (...) nödvändigtvis är hans lust eller olust. (...) Om den sjuke känner avsmak för den anbefallda medicinen, icke känner han sig därmed förpliktigad att icke intaga densamma.»

[36] A. Hägerström, *Jesus. En karaktärsanalys*, Natur & Kultur, Stockholm 1968, p. 67: «lust vid medvetandet att vara i överensstämmelse med det i och för sig rättas krav.»

[37] A. Hägerström, *I moralpsykologiska frågor*, cit., p. 78.

[38] See Chapter 1.

[39] A. Hägerström, *I moralpsykologiska frågor*, cit., p. 275: «Saken är den, att för det moderna medvetandet de religiösa föreställningarnas realitet icke äger så stort affektionsvärde som de moraliska.»

aforementioned *Critical Aspects* in the *liber amicorum* for Burman, which contains a criticism of Meinong's theory of objects, and *Contribution to the Analysis of Empirical Self-Consciousness*, drafted in 1910, but published only in 1945, and probably the fruit of an open seminar from the spring term in 1910.[40] These two essays focus essentially on the psychological aspects behind the theory. A part of *On the Question of the Notion of Law* from 1917 also deals with some significant psychological questions. These issues were in the spotlight of the spring lectures from the same period, that were published only in 1952: In *Moral Psychology* (pp. 15–110), Hägerström presented a phenomenology and categorisation of four different types of moral evaluations (*moraliska värderingssätt*), including a rather interesting assessment of virtue. This collection of unpublished manuscripts edited by Fries, also contains two other significant texts on the topic: The spring lectures from 1921 on the relation between ethics and conceptions of the world and the lectures from February 11th to May 10th 1930 on *Truly Autonomous Morals*.[41] Besides the above mentioned lectures, we should also cite the lecture series from the spring term in 1918 entitled *Doctrine and Psychology of Value* (*Värdelära och värdepsykologi*); the spring course from 1930 *Emotive Thinking (känslotänkande)* which was later translated into German and published in the *liber amicorum* for Arvi Grotenfelt[42] with the title *Vergleich zwischen den Kraftvorstellungen der primitiven und modernen Kulturvölker*. The original text in Swedish was unfortunately lost.[43] All in all, Hägerström wrote extensively on ethics and the greater part of the primary and secondary literature of a philosophical, and not strictly legal nature, deals with these topics.

The development that Hägerström's thought underwent from 1907 to 1939 can readily be reformulated as attempts to redefine and delimit one single philosophical intuition: I cannot cognitively conceive something as *the right thing to do* unless I hold it to be *my duty* and is therefore emotionally drawn toward the action. This basic conception is expressed in relation to the argument of the so-called "ideal observer." Such an argument can be found as early as in David Hume. However, the impartial spectator does not guarantee the "objectivity" of values, nor their

---

[40] Hägerström never published this text. It was conceived as an *ad hoc* production for the university commission entrusted to judge him. According to his daughter the text was never released because he thought it had been drafted too swiftly. See M. Waller, *Människan som få kände*, Natur & Kultur, Stockholm 1961, p. 187.

[41] Some interesting viewpoints are also expressed in the essay collection *Socialfilosofiska uppsatser*. Much more material on ethics and the theory of value can be found at the Uppsala University Library. Hägerström lectured on the topic for over 30 years.

[42] Grotenfelt was professor in philosophy at Helsinki University and represented a form of "value idealism." He followed in the path of Lotze, as a passage from old idealism and new positivism. See C.-G. Heidegren, *Idealistisk systemfilosofi kontra den positiva andan*, in *Mellan idealism och analytisk filosofi: den moderna filosofin i Finland och Sverige 1880–1950*, Atlantis, Stockholm 2006, p. 37.

[43] The original text *Primitiv och modern kraftföreställning* was never found. Hägerström usually wrote in Swedish and had the text translated to German. The Swedish version available in Fries' 1933 edition was translated from the abovementioned German transcript.

purely subjectivistic tenure. Rather, this fictional device is introduced so as to demonstrate the non-cognitivist thesis on the meaninglessness of value reification.[44] The most celebrated formulation of this idea can be found in the 1911 inaugural lecture:

> «If we stand as cold observers before ourselves, that is, in reality interested not in what is observed but only in the investigation of what is observed, what can we discover? We recognize, in the midst of a manifold of other phenomena, a feeling of duty in connection with a judgment of value and a direct interest in a certain action. But all this yields nothing more than a certain kind of psychological event. That the action ought to be done is not at all part of what we can discover (...). We can establish that the action arouses the strongest appetite or the strongest desire or that it leads to my well-being or that of another. We can discover – let us feign the possibility – that it is commanded by a god or our unobservable being. But every attempt to draw out of the situation the conclusion that it is actually in the highest degree of value to undertake the action is doomed to failure. (...). That something is better than something else is meaningless for an indifferent observer. For him nothing is better or worse. But turn the situation around. We are considering an action, and different motives appear. Now it becomes immediately clear to us that we ought to act in a certain way (...). Note that in so far as we consider something is actually the case, i.e., that truth is present, we also consider that it is so entirely without regard for our subjective posture towards the fact, our feelings or our interests *vis-à-vis* the fact. Thus the result must be that in moral ideas as such we do not at all consider that obligatoriness actually belongs to the action.»[45]

## 3.3 Four Theses on Non-cognitivism

Hägerström anticipated some central issues still discussed in ethics today. He did this by elaborating four theses in meta-ethics. They are connected to his epistemology and ontology (see Chapter 2), as well as interrelated, but not in explicit terms, since they seem to have been developed in different moments in time. Three are prevailingly negative since they aim to demolish a certain view and not to introduce any alternative notion. The fourth thesis, however, also presents some constructive or positive elements. Each thesis responds to a fundamental problem in ethics. They also correspond to specific antitheses, i.e., positions put forth by major moral philosophies. The four meta-ethical theses consist of (1) ontological, (2) epistemological, (3) linguistic or semantic and (4) psychological arguments. I suggest the following scheme in order to tackle the different questions at stake:

---

[44] In the autumn lectures in 1911, *Moralpsykologiska frågor*, Hägerström deepened this argument by claiming that, typically, an agent is emotionally involved whereas an observer is not. He held that if an alien from another planet – without our emotional apparatus – were to collect information on the emotional behavior of humans, this information would be meaningless in moral terms. See B. Petersson, *Axel Hägerströms värdeteori*, cit., p. 115.

[45] A. Hägerström, *Socialfilosofiska uppsatser*, cit., p. 54; *On the Truth of Moral Propositions*, cit., pp. 88–89.

| Thesis | (1) Ontological | (2) Epistemological | (3) Semantic | (4) Psychological |
|---|---|---|---|---|
| **Problem** | What is goodness? | How can we know if something is moral? | What is the meaning of an ethical utterance? | What is the nature of moral judgment? |
| **Argument** | «There are no axiological facts» | «There can be no science in morality» | «Moral propositions are neither true, nor false» | «Moral conceptions are no judgments» |
| **Antithesis** | Moral realism, i.e., the doctrine that holds moral proprieties to exist | Rationalism, i.e., the doctrine that considers ethics as a system of knowledge | Cognitivism, i.e., the doctrine that holds that ethical propositions express beliefs | Kantism: moral assessments are grounded in practical reason. Moral sensualism: moral judgments amount to feelings |
| **Predecessors and/or successors** | John Mackie (argument from queerness) | Poincaré, Ayer | Berkeley, Hume Ayer, Stevenson | von Ehrenfels Stevenson |

### *3.3.1 The Ontological Thesis*

A primary thesis that appears in the background of Hägerström's argumentation concerns ontology. According to this perspective, there are no *axiological facts*. «The mere factual character of something – may it even be a question of lust and desire – does not signify value or disvalue for me observing it, unless I take a stance *vis-à-vis* the fact, liking or disliking it. For me, there are no values whatsoever in the fact that I state, because I am entirely impartial in respect of what exists in fact. Only where I critically assume a position in respect of the fact, does it acquire axiological character.»[46]

This position derives from Hägerström's reality thesis: All things, in order to gain full reality, must be logically insertable within the *ultimate context* of space and time in a system of perfect coherence with all our other experiences and impressions.[47] Of course, the plurality of axiological positions makes such a coherent conductibility problematic, as shown for example by incompatible customs. This

[46] A. Hägerström, *Kritiska punkter i värdepsykologien*, cit., pp. 61–62: «den blotta fakticiteten av något, må det också vara fråga om lust och begär, alls icke för mig, som betraktar det, betecknar vare sig värde eller ovärde, annat än såvidt jag tager ställning till det samma, gillande eller ogillande. För mig såsom blott konstaterande faktum finns inga som helst värden, därför att jag så till vida är fullkomligt likgiltig, mot vad som faktiskt är. Endast om jag kritiskt tager ställning till faktum, får det för mig värdekaraktär.»

[47] A. Hägerström, *Selbstdarstellung*, cit., p. 126 where a body is said to be real only if «derselbe Körper gleichzeitig zu dem räumlichen Komplex gerechnet wird, zu dem die Vorstellung selbst gehört.»

is, furthermore, the reason why Hägerström criticised the account on *Bedeutung* and *Wahrheit* in Rickert: «So a distinction will be made, like in Heinrich Rickert, between reality and value in such a way, that value is only *valid*, but *is* not. The meaning of this is (...) that truth, in the realm of value, *is* the factual rightness of an evaluation according to a given rule.»[48] The distinction between *giltighet/Gültigkeit* and *riktighet/Richtigkeit* was common in neo-Kantian philosophy, yet Hägerström did not hold these notions to be parallel or alternative ideas of truth.[49]

More interestingly, Hägerström's argument seems to be that even those who defend a descriptivist or objectivist moral theory acknowledge that no normative or axiological facts may be discovered separately from the "natural fact." Hägerström's adversaries do not really claim that an "axiological fact" appears alongside the "natural fact." Their point is that the value is intrinsic or entangled[50] with the fact in such a way that the «mythical given»[51] fact could not be observable without the adoption of certain values. Now, Hägerström never argued clearly against this idea, rather he turned the argument the other way round and noted that not even his critics avow the existence of "axiological facts." Hägerström underlined the unreasonable confusion between the perceived fact and the "value" it is supposedly entangled with or, in his lexis, the object and the emotion. In *Om primitiva rudimenter* published in 1935, for instance, he stressed the example of the adventurer in the desert who is surprised by the sandstorm. «How does it appear to him? It seems in itself dreadful, terrorizing, even if it is not the storm but the perception of it that provokes the fear (...). This way of understanding contains a projection of the content of the feeling of terror on the object, the perceiving of which induces the horror.»[52]

---

[48] A. Hägerström, *Moralpsykologi*, cit., p. 67: «så kommer man som Rickert att skilja mellan verklighet och värde på så sätt, att värdet endast *gäller* men icke *är*. Meningen därmed är (...) att sanningen på värdeområdet *är* den sakliga riktigheten av ett värderingssätt som sker enligt en viss regel.» Hägerström lectured on H. Rickert's *Die Grenzen der naturwissenschaftlichen Begriffsbildung* in his seminars during the spring term 1908.

[49] On this distinction and its grounds in Swedish philosophy, see J. Hansson, *Idealistisk vändning i svensk filosofi*, in «Insikt och handling. Hans Larsson Samfundet», 2000, vol. 20, p. 22.

[50] *Entanglement* is generically a phenomenon of synchronic mutual connection in quantum mechanics. With triple entanglement, «it is possible, for example, to create triads of particles in which every member is 100% correlated to the other two: Whatever happens to one of the three particles causes a similar, instantaneous change in the other two. So the three entities are inexorably linked to one another wherever they are» (A.D. Aczel, *Entanglement: The Greatest Mystery in Physics*, Four Walls Eight Windows, New York 2001, p. 3). This concept has been applied analogously to social sciences, primarily by Hilary Putnam. Accordingly, some facts would be so "thick" that they result incomprehensible on the basis of the strict distinction between descriptive and prescriptive elements. On this phenomenon and its use in normative reasoning, J.J. Moreso, *Teoría del derecho y neutralidad valorativa*, paper presented at XIII Congresso Italo-spagnolo di teoria analitica del diritto "Teoría analítica y enfoques socio-jurídicos" (september 2007), available at http://www.iisj.net, P. Mindus, *Deliberare, negoziare e argomentare sulle incerte sorti della legge di Hume*, in «Teoria politica», 2008, XXIII, 1, pp. 145–155.

[51] I am borrowing the term from John McDowell.

[52] A. Hägerström, *Om primitiva rudimenter*, now in *Socialfilosofiska uppsatser*, cit., p. 151: «Huru ter sig denna för honom? Den är själv hemsk, förskräcklig, trots att det icke är den själv utan

This ontological thesis responds to the classical and innermost question of ethics: What is goodness or, in other words, do good and evil exist? Hägerström's answer is directed against moral realism[53] i.e., the doctrine that claims that moral values exist objectively as a quality of the objects themselves, a view which is shared by John McDowell, John Finnis, Richard Boyd and Nicholas Sturgeon to name but a few. While moral realists believe that evaluative statements are (true or false) factual claims, Hägerström's anti-realist stance seems to be close to the idea that was later developed by John Mackie,[54] with the so-called «argument from queerness.»[55] According to this argument, «if there were objective values, then they would be entities or qualities or relations of a very strange sort, utterly different from anything else in the universe.»[56] Since it cannot be proven that goodness in itself has any independent role in our actions and hence it lacks any observable referent, Occam's razor would apply suggesting that no axiological proprieties exist.

Finally, an interesting implication of Hägerström's ontological thesis, which – strangely enough – has not received much attention, is that he confuted the argument of entanglement as it has been elaborated by Hilary Putnam and others.[57] Since there

---

förnimmelsen av den, som vållar skräcken. (...) Detta uppfattningssätt innesluter en överföring av det i skräckkänslan givna innehållet på det föremål, vars förnimmelse väcker skräcken.»

[53]A curious twist of the tongue comes from the two different meanings of realism employed, in epistemology and in ethics: As we have seen in Chapter 2, Hägerström was a realist because he believed that all facts must refer to reality in space and time in order to gain full, i.e. objective "reality." The moral realist instead holds that there are objective moral values of which we might have intuitive awareness (cf. moral intuitionism, like for instance in G.E. Moore) or of which we might have knowledge grounded in empirical facts (cf. moral so-called naturalism, like for instance in Alasdair Macintyre). The moral realist thus holds moral judgments to be true or false independently of our subjectivity.

[54]It has also been suggested that Hägerström's ontological argument is in some ways similar to an argument elaborated by Gilbert Harman in the 70s. See Id., *Change in View*, MIT Press, Cambridge, MA 1988; and S. Danielsson, *Några värdenihilismer*, in Å. Andersson, N.-E. Sahlin, *Huvudinnehåll*, Nya Doxa, Nora 1993, pp. 33–45.

[55]Mackie derived his famous error-theory from this anti-realist stance, holding that moral judgments, while cognitive, are all false since there are no moral facts (*Ethics: Inventing Right and Wrong*, Viking Press, London 1977). Some of the scholarly disagreement on whether Hägerström is an error-theorist *ante litteram* or not may hence be resolved. Hägerström shares Mackie's ontological view of moral properties, affirming there are no axiological facts, but he does not fully share Mackie's understanding of the nature of moral assessments which according to Hägerström are no judgments at all. For an explanation and contextualization of Mackie's argument, see M. Timmons, *Morality without Foundations: A Defense of Ethical Contextualism*, Oxford University Press, Oxford 1999, pp. 12–50. For a famous criticism, see Ch. Korsgaard, *The Sources of Normativity*, Cambridge University Press, Cambridge, MA 1996, pp. 166 ff.

[56]J.L. Mackie, *Ethics: Inventing Right and Wrong*, cit., p. 38.

[57]On the entanglement and the *is/ought* problem, see J. Searle, *How to derive ought from is* in «Philosophical Review», 1964, 73, pp. 43–58; W.D. Hudson (ed.), *The Is-Ought Question. A Collection of Papers on the Central Problem in Moral Philosophy*, Macmillan, London 1969; G. Carcaterra, *Il problema della fallacia naturalistica. La derivazione del dover essere dall'essere*, Giuffrè, Milano 1969; G. Schurz, *The Is-Ought Problem: An Investigation in Philosophical Logic*, Kluwer, Dordrecht 1997; H. Putnam, *The Collapse of the Fact/Value Dichotomy*, Harvard University Press, Cambridge, MA, 2003. For a criticism of the entanglement argument,

are no axiological facts, no entanglement between facts and values can be discovered. Bjarup is therefore correct when he stressed that «it follows that moral realism that holds the ontological or metaphysical view that there are moral facts and which is related to the epistemological or cognitive view that these facts can be known by means of experience or reason is false, if not meaningless (...). Hägerström's moral nihilism holds that moral concepts are not embedded in persons, actions, and states of affairs.»[58]

### *3.3.2 The Epistemological Thesis*

Hägerström also elaborated an epistemological thesis for non-cognitivism. It is intrinsically linked to the other theses and it is grounded in the idea that there can be no *axiological knowledge*. Since only judgments can lead to knowledge, it is no wonder – from the psychological viewpoint – that "evaluations" (*värderingar*) in ethics, which are a form of simultaneous associations involving emotion, cannot bring about such a result. Furthermore, it is clear that if we cannot formulate meaningful ethical propositions, it is hopeless to erect any moral science. In the lecture series *Rättsidéers sanningsvärde* from 1908, for instance, Hägerström emphasized that moral ideas, like emotions, cannot lead to knowledge. So his overall conclusion is that the task of "moral philosophy" conceived as a science can only be to indicate what is true, but it cannot tell us what we ought to do: There can never be any teaching *in* morality. We can learn more about how our axiological evaluations work, even if it will never lead to knowledge about values as such.[59]

This thesis responds to a fundamental problem of ethics: How do we *know* if an action is good or bad? According to the epistemological thesis, we cannot scientifically establish the goodness of an action since there is no such thing as goodness, or any fact that entails goodness. Hägerström's epistemological thesis is thus directed against cognitivism, since it holds that we can gain knowledge in the realm of ethics. This viewpoint is very similar to the opinion later adopted by Alfred Jules Ayer in *Language, Truth and Logic*, according to which moral "knowledge" cannot be translated into non-normative, empirical and verifiable terms and, consequently according to Ayer, ethics apply pseudo-concepts: «If I generalise (...) and say "stealing money is wrong" I produce a sentence which has no factual meaning –

---

O. Blomberg, *Disentangling the Thick Concept Argument*, in «Sats. Nordic Journal of Philosophy», 2007, 8, n. 2, pp. 63–78. On Hägerström and the Is-Ought problem, see my *À l'origine du non-cognitivisme moderne: Axel Hägerström*, paper presented at IIIème Rencontre de Théorie du Droit "Dichotomie fait/valeur en question. Points de vue croisés" organized by J.-Y. Chérot in January 2008 (Aix-en-Provence), now in P. Comanducci, R. Guastini, *Analisi & Diritto 2008*, Marcial Pons, Madrid 2009.

[58] J. Bjarup, *Scepticism and Scandinavian Legal Realists*, in T. Endicott, J. Getzler, E. Peel (eds.), *Properties of Law. Essays in Honour of Jim Harris*, Oxford University Press, Oxford 2006, pp. 57–58.

[59] See for instance, A. Hägerström, *Moralfilosofins grundläggning*, cit., p. 45.

that is, it expresses no proposition which can be either true or false.»[60] Ayer's idea of ethics as a system of pseudo-concepts fits like hand in glove to Hägerström's general outlook: In point of fact, Hägerström accused normative ethics of elaborating concepts (*begrepp*) which lack worldly reference.

However, the unfeasibility of founding moral science in any prescriptive sense does not imply that it is impossible to obtain knowledge about normatively oriented behaviour in the social universe.[61] On the contrary, legal sciences, sociology, history and psychology work and elaborate propositions on such phenomena. In order to understand how this is possible, we should mention a distinction that was never explicitly elaborated by Hägerström but that can be found in Hedenius: The distinction between authentic (or genuine) and inauthentic deontic propositions.[62] Whereas «you shall not covet your neighbour's house» is an authentic axiological proposition – and hence neither true, nor false in Hägerström's view – the statement «in the Christian tradition the 10th commandment is considered fundamental in the life of the believer» has an inauthentic character and is hence liable to verification or falsification, even though the reference, *Bedeutung*, in both cases is the same human behaviour. Therefore, "moral science" – in the sense the term acquired, say, within the movement of Scottish Enlightenment – is an achievable goal only in a value-free perspective, since all other practices are detrimental to cognitive pursuit. Its objects are inauthentic normative statements with their historical, sociological, etc. background. It shares the methodology of other special

---

[60] A.J. Ayer, *Language, Truth and Logic* (1936), Dover Publication, New York 1952, p. 107.

[61] Hägerström distinguished between moral "science" as the analysis *sine ira ac studio* of our actual moral judgments, that can, in his opinion, be ordered into (at least) four categories; and, moral "doctrines" that attempt to establish normative frameworks for moral judgments. See A. Hägerström, *Moralpsykologi*, cit.; T. Mautner, *Hägerströms lära i moral. Hägerströms värdefrihetstes*, in «Insikt och handling. Hans Larsson samfundet», 2000, vol. 20, pp. 27–48.

[62] I. Hedenius, *Om rätt och moral*, cit., Chapter 2 («äkta och oäkta rättssatser»). In Hägerström's published work this distinction cannot be found. However, Bo Petersson points to a passage in a manuscript on *Consciousness of Value* (*Värdemedvetandet*) from 1910 where it seems to appear: «The judgment: "this is valuable" has two meanings; on one hand, the sense it has in macroeconomics "this is valued by Påhl or Per" and, on the other hand, "this has real value." It is this latter meaning that is of interest» (translated from B. Petersson, *Axel Hägerströms värdeteori*, cit., p. 75). What Hedenius called «inauthentic deontic propositions» seems to be similar, if not identical, to what Ayer called «propositions describing the phenomena of moral experience, and their causes» and that he ascribed to science in Chapter 6 of *Language, Truth and Logic*. The difference between authentic and inauthentic deontic propositions have sometimes been connected to the internal/external point of view (See for instance, M. Lyles, *A Call for Scientific Purity. Axel Hägerström's Critique of Legal Science*, Rönnells, Stockholm 2006, p. 244), but such an overlapping hardly helps the understanding of Hart's and Hägerström's different standpoints. It should also be stressed that the distinction between authentic and inauthentic deontic propositions might have been developed at an embryonic stage already by one of Hägerström's main sources; Alexius Meinong. The latter distinguished between *werhalten* and *für wert halten* which might be rendered in English with *to value* and *to evaluate, to esteem* and *to estimate* (see S. Satris, *Ethical Emotivism*, cit., p. 13).

sciences. It has no inductive basis: «Specifically, in certain systems of moral philosophy one believes that one can often establish an objective moral principle by starting from our actual moral valuations. Since in modern civilisation these valuations always present certain common elements, because of similar life situations, one thinks that by uncovering and systematizing them one can determine the correct principle for judging actions. It is in this way, for example, that Spencer and Wundt proceed (...). It is clear that knowledge of actual valuations is by no means knowledge of value.»[63] In essence, for Hägerström, the knowledge that we cannot obtain is that of a *science* – with its systematization and empirical corroboration techniques – of norms proper. This is why Hägerström and the Scandinavians realists are concerned with the law as a condition of culture, not merely as a normative system.[64]

All in all, Hägerström's view of moral science echoes Milton's laments in *Paradise Lost* (bk. II): «Of good and evil much they argued then (...). Vain wisdom all, and false philosophy!» Indeed, one of Hägerström's most significant and persisting legacies, in the context of moral philosophy in the twentieth century, is in fact the switch of focus from traditional moral philosophy to meta-ethics. Today, meta-ethics commonly appears as the non-normative branch of moral philosophy, that does not attempt to evaluate specific choices, although it might have strong implications as to the validity and scope of ethical claims. While normative ethics consists of ethical theory and applied ethics, the meta-ethical realm deals with three major issues: The meaning of ethical terms, the nature of moral judgments and the ways to support such evaluations.[65] Hägerström had his say on all these three topics. The epistemological thesis affects our way of supporting evaluation, while the semantic and psychological theses cope with the other two issues.[66]

---

[63] A. Hägerström, *Inquiries*, cit., p. 90.

[64] A. Hägerström, *Review of Kelsen*, in *Inquiries*, cit., p. 257; J. Harris, *Olivecrona on Law and Language – The Search for Legal Culture*, in «Tidskrift for Rettsvitenskap», 1981, 94, pp. 625–646.

[65] Here I am following the classic suggestion of Richard Garner and Bernard Rosen, *A Systematic Introduction to Normative Ethics and Meta-ethics*, Macmillan, New York 1967. For an overview of the central issues in meta-ethics, see P. Comanducci, *Assaggi di metaetica*, Giappichelli, Torino 1992.

[66] We should add that Hägerström's analysis of morals, especially his assessment of command and duty, is also important for the development of twentieth century meta-ethics insofar as the ontological thesis is considered. He focused on the issue in a specific way: Before asking "what is the nature of this or that norm?" or "what logical structure does it have?" his fundamental dilemma was "what does it mean when we say that there *is* a norm?" Von Wright, for example, insisted on such a change of perspective. See G.H. von Wright, *Intellectual Autobiography*, in P.A. Schlipp, *The Philosophy of Georg Henrik von Wright*, Open court, La Salle (Ill.) 1989, p. 33; Id., *Norm and Action. A Logical Enquiry*, Routledge, London 1963, p. 77.

### *3.3.3 The Semantic Thesis*

The third thesis in meta-ethics offers a semantic form of non-cognitivism. It has been argued that this semantic approach has been the prevailing one among interpreters.[67] It certainly is conceived as a response to another fundamental problem in ethics, i.e., what is the meaning of a moral proposition? According to the semantic thesis, *moral propositions are neither true, nor false*. This is a purely negative thesis: Sentences including axiological or normative terms, such as good, bad, etc. do not have any content entirely susceptible of verification or falsification. For Hägerström, such propositions have the same cognitive value as exclamations or interjections. Sometimes, he seems to have included the aesthetic exclamation – "how beautiful!" – in this same repertoire.[68] This is due to the fact that moral appreciations have historically been intertwined with aesthetical appreciation.

This juxtaposition between normative and aesthetical propositions, however, does not occur in all Hägerström's production.[69] Moreover this overlapping is not just an unintentional slip or, worse, an inability to understand aesthetical issues, but it is a legacy of one of his major sources: Hermann Lotze (1817–1881). Indeed, «in Lotze there was a tendency to assimilate values not to the moral but to the aesthetic.»[70] Lotze can be viewed as a key figure at the roots of emotivism. In fact, the German philosopher has generally, at least since Wilhelm Windelband's *History of Philosophy* (1901), been depicted as the father of modern *Wertphilosophie*. Hägerström drew on this legacy, for example, when he interpreted the *kalokagathia* in Aristotle: «Apparently this way of valuating was strongly related to aesthetical evaluation which also occurs immediately when perceiving the object. Therefore the virtuous man became, for the Greeks, the beautiful man as well.»[71] Regardless of whether beauty can be considered as the origin of virtue, Hägerström kept his distance from any equivalence of the aesthetical proposition and the judgment on a state of affairs: «I can certainly consider it good, that a work of art exists, but it is only a question of the work of art as a *means* for the aesthetical culture as the highest

---

[67] S. Danielsson, *Hägerströms huvudargument*, in «Filosofisk Tidskrift», 1990, anno 11, n. 2, pp. 16–22.

[68] This is at least the understanding of Gunnar Oxenstierna, *Vad är Uppsalafilosofien?*, Bonniers, Stockholm 1938.

[69] He seems to have restricted his thesis on this issue, as shown by B. Petersson, *Axel Hägerströms värdeteori*, cit., p. 72. Cf. *Kritiska punkter i värdepsykologien*, cit., pp. 19 and 30. The evaluation is initially linked to the existence of a fact, but this condition seems to fade away in later writings.

[70] S. Satris, *Ethical Emotivism*, cit., p. 8. "Value" is a notion that evolved over time: From the original economic meaning of "prize" (in Hobbes for example) to the current wide deontic sense.

[71] A. Hägerström, *Moralpsykologi*, cit., p. 21: «uppenbart var detta sätt att värdera starkt besläktat med estetisk värdering som också äger rum vid en omedelbar betraktelse av föremålet. Därför kom också för greken den duktige mannen att bli den sköne.»

good (...). That the work of art is beautiful, in the meaning that it is beautiful that it exists; now *that* is something meaningless.»[72]

Hägerström's analysis is rooted in the so-called linguistic turn in philosophy. He developed this semantic thesis in connection with his theory of meaning and in particular against the then prevailing ideas of the linguist Adolf Noréen.[73] So, when Hägerström addressed the problem of moral meaning with this non-cognitivist semantic thesis he, at least implicitly, avowed a certain pragmatic theory of meaning. Some scholars have insisted on this because if we take into account the underlying theory of meaning, Hägerström's theory of value is closer to that of Stevenson, than to the theory of Ayer, a form of «unorthodox spin-off of logical positivism.»[74]

Although the semantic thesis is prevailingly negative, it also entails a positive element: The idea that moral propositions include commands or imperatives meant to change the attitudes and actions of others. This idea has often been considered equivalent of claiming that "moral judgments contain commands." The imperative character of moral propositions is strictly related to one of Hägerström's main arguments – the so-called substitution argument.[75] According to this argument, axiological nihilism can be demonstrated by pointing to interchangeable sentences in certain situations where we are about to engage in action.[76]

Moreover, the imperative features of moral propositions are at the core of Hägerström's famous analysis of command and duty.[77] This idea was later the central contribution in Charles Leslie Stevenson's account of moral sentences in his

---

[72] A. Hägerström, *Moralpsykologi*, cit., p. 22: «jag kan visserligen anse det gott, att ett konstverk finns till, men då är det endast fråga om konstverket som *medel* för den estetiska kulturen som det högsta goda (...). Att konstverket skulle vara vackert i den meningen, att det är vackert att det finns till – *det* är något meningslöst.»

[73] See B. Petersson, *Axel Hägerströms värdeteori*, cit., p. 58. Some criticisms can be found in *Till frågan om den objektiva rättens begrepp*, cit., p. 52 and *Socialfilosofiska uppsatser*, cit., p. 71.

[74] S. Satris, *The Theory of Value and the Rise of Ethical Emotivism*, in «Journal of the History of Ideas», 1982, vol. 43, n. 1, p. 109.

[75] A. Hägerström, *Om pliktmedvetandet*, in *Socialfilosofiska uppsatser*, cit.

[76] B. Petersson, *The Substitution Argument*, in *ThD 60. Philosophical Essays dedicated to Thorild Dahlqvist on his Sixtieth Birthday*, Philosophical Society and the Department of philosophy/University Uppsala Press, Uppsala 1980, p. 122: «(1') If X ["A is a duty"] can be substituted for Y ["Do A!"] in a certain situation, then X and Y have the same truth-value in that situation. (2') In the situation S the sentence "A is a duty!" can be substituted for an imperative "Do A!". [Therefore] (3') In the situation S "A is a duty" and "Do A!" have the same truth-value. (4') "Do A!" is neither true nor false in S. [Therefore] "A is a duty" is neither true nor false in S.» Petersson correctly stressed how this argument confuses the effect or social function of a sentences with its meaning.

[77] See, *inter alia*, A. Hägerström, *Till frågan om den objektiva rättens begrepp*, cit., pp. 60–64; *Rätten och staten*, Natur & Kultur, Stockholm 1963, pp. 4–14; 33–35; 79–80; *Philosophy and Religion*, cit., pp. 97 ff. For comments, see E. Tegen, *Nya riktlinjer inom rättsfilosofi och straffrätt* (1921), now in *I filosofiska frågor*, Almqvist & Wiksell, Stockholm/Uppsala 1927, pp. 125–138; K. Marc-Wogau, *Studier till Axel Hägerströms filosofi*, cit., pp. 26–31; C.D. Broad, *Hägerström's Account of Sense of Duty and Certain Allied Experiences*, in «Philosophy», 1951, pp. 99–113; S. Castignone, *La macchina del diritto. Il realismo giuridico in Svezia*, Edizioni di Comunità, Milano 1974, pp. 45–51; E. Pattaro, *Il realismo giuridico scandinavo*, Clueb, Bologna 1974, pp.

1937 dissertation on *The Emotive Meaning of Ethical Terms* and his *Ethics and Language* from 1944. In accordance with Hägerström's view,[78] Stevenson claimed that both imperative and ethical sentences are used more for encouraging, altering or redirecting people's aims and conduct than simply describing them. The emotive meaning, «the immediate aura of feeling which hovers about a word»[79] is however a little different in both cases: «The ethical sentence centers the hearer's attention not on his interests but on the object of interest, and thereby facilitates suggestion.»[80] Moral propositions are not only expressions of feelings, as Ayer had already stressed, but they are also meant to change the attitude of the receiver and therefore they have an imperative component.[81]

This aspect of Hägerström's work is the source of some of the major misconceptions of the theory of value. Many have been blinded by Hägerström's quite complex theory into considering that, for the Swedish thinker, «value judgments about right and wrong are *purely* emotive»[82] – leading to some rather irrationalistic accounts.[83] For Hägerström, nonetheless, the evaluation (*värdering*) is not conceivable without reference to emotion, but it cannot be reduced to it. Rather, it is grounded in a complex relation between a state of affairs and an emotional state which mimics – but is not identical to – the complex relation between the judicial norm and the "conative impulse" that makes the experience of the duty-holder akin to that of the receiver of a command. Feeling is indeed a key component, but – as Pattaro emphasized in his interpretation of "duty" – «there are also the will, beliefs, and ideas (even hypostatised ideas); there is *ett medvetande om skyldighet*, "a consciousness of an obligation," as Hägerström says in discussing the state of mind of those who (in Hart's usage) *accept* a norm. These ideas (...) result from a combination of *föreställning* ("representation") and a *viljeimpuls* ("conative impulse") – a phenomenon occasioned in us through social conditioning. And again, the feelings of restriction or compulsion connected with this phenomenon are not in themselves norms, but rather a typical, and important, accompaniment to them.»[84]

---

74 ff. and Id., *A Treatise of Legal Philosophy and General Jurisprudence*, Springer, Dordrecht 2005, vol. I, *The Law and the Right*, Chapter 8.

[78]Ch. L. Stevenson, *Facts and Values*, Yale University Press, New Haven-London 1963, p. 204, footnote 11: «I regret that my discussion there [in *Ethics and Language*] neglected the ethical writings of A. Hägerström, now available in Broad's translation from the Swedish.»

[79]Ch. L. Stevenson, *Facts and Values*, cit., p. 21.

[80]Ch. L. Stevenson, *Facts and Values*, cit., p. 25. On the differences between Hägerström's and Stevensons' theory of meaning, see B. Petersson, *Axel Hägerströms värdeteori*, cit., p. 70.

[81]This element has been related to the "performative fallacy" of doing things with words, see E. Pattaro, *Non si fanno cose con le parole. Il negozio giuridico nella prospettiva di Axel Hägerström*, in «Sociologia del diritto», 1981: 3, pp. 25–42; S. Castignone, *Diritto, linguaggio, realtà. Saggi sul realismo giuridico*, Giappichelli, Torino 1995, pp. 293–318.

[82]J.W. Harris, *Legal Philosophies*, cit., p. 98 (italics added).

[83]J. Bjarup, *Axel Hägerströms filosofi, värdenihilism och rättspositivism*, cit., p. 25.

[84]E. Pattaro, *A Treatise*, cit., vol. I, *The Law and the Right*, p. 138.

This part of Hägerström's argument clearly reckons the so-called "emotive theory of value." Hägerström is not seldom credited to be the father of modern emotivism. Still today this aspect of the theory arouses interest in scholars. For example, Richard Mervyn Hare, in his *Hägerström lectures* at the University of Uppsala in the late nineties, claimed that «the proponents of emotivism, of whom Axel Hägerström was the first in modern times, made the important step of suggesting that there *is* another element in the meaning of moral statements besides their syntax and their truth conditions [i.e. emotion] (...) bringing out the distinction between two elements in the meaning of moral statements, the descriptive and the evaluative.»[85]

The standard historical account, however, is that «the earliest statement of the emotive theory of value terms in the modern British-American tradition (as opposed to statements in such continental writers as Hägerström which became known to English-speaking philosophers only comparatively late and had no early influence) was (...) that given by I.A. Richards.»[86] Even if we accept this account, it is undisputable that Hägerström developed his theses before Charles Kay Ogden and Ivor Armstrong Richards introduced "emotive meaning" in 1923 when they famously argued that «the emotive use of words is (...) to express or excite feelings and attitudes (...). Under the emotive function are included both the expression of emotions, attitudes, moods, intentions etc. in the speaker, and their communication, i.e. their evocation in the listener.»[87] Ogden and Richards precisely pointed out that «this peculiar ethical use of "good" is, we suggest, a purely emotive use.»[88] Hägerström would have agreed.

This convergence brings us back to the roots of his philosophy. If we take emotivism to be primarily a theory of emotive meaning, a theory explaining how signs devoid of (scientifically valuable) informative content can arouse the sentiments of others bringing them to engage in or to refrain from action, then an interesting question is «how is it that emotivism comes into existence in different places at the same time? The very fact that there is no early influence between Swedish and Anglo-American emotivism suggests that perhaps the coincidence can be explained by locating a common source for both. Such a common source can in fact be found in the *Wertphilosophie* of Lotze, Windelband and others in Germany and more immediately in the *Werttheorie* of Brentano, Meinong, Ehrenfels and others in Austria.»[89]

As far as "emotive meaning" is concerned, it appears that – let alone some brief and generic accounts in the history of thought[90] – it was designed as a

---

[85] R.M. Hare, *Sorting Out Ethics*, Clarendon, Oxford 1997, p. 103.

[86] J.O. Urmson, *The Emotive Theory of Ethics*, Hutchinson University Library, London 1968, p. 15.

[87] C. K. Ogden & I.A. Richards, *The Meaning of Meaning* (1923), Kegan, London 1927[2], p. 149.

[88] *Ibid.*, p. 125.

[89] S. Satris, *Ethical Emotivism*, cit., p. 5.

[90] George Berkeley in *A Treatise Concerning the Principles of Human Knowledge* (1710), paragraph 20, famously stated that «the communication of ideas marked by words is not the chief

technicality by a student of Brentano, Anton Marty, in his *Untersuchungen zur Grundlegung der allgemeinen Grammatik und Sprachphilosophie*.[91] Here he distinguished between expressions that suggest representations (*Vorstellungssuggestive*), statements (*Aussagen*) and "Emotive" or "interesseheischende Äusserungen." These latter linguistic phenomena usually appear as neither true nor false. Therefore, «there seems to be some good reasons for claiming that Marty developed the semantic version of axiological nihilism in his great work in 1908, even if it was concealed and less clearly stated than in Hägerström.»[92]

In order to fully grasp the problem of moral meaning in Hägerström's thought, we need to look at the fourth thesis from which the semantic thesis seems to derive.

### *3.3.4 The Psychological Thesis*

Hägerström's primary thesis, both logically and chronologically, is the psychological one. This viewpoint prevailed in his writings until around 1910. From then onwards, he progressively took into account the semantic aspect of the issue.[93] This psychological thesis addressed the fundamental question of ethics: "What is the nature of moral judgment?" Hägerström held that *axiological conceptions are neither true nor false*. Or rather, that moral conceptions (*föreställning/Vorstellung*) are not judgments on reality but mental acts of a different kind. In order to understand this, it is necessary to emphasize the fact that Hägerström relied heavily on the so-called *Aktpsychologie* going back to, and influencing, Franz Brentano, Alexius Meinong, Christian von Ehrenfels and Edmund Husserl among others. In particular, he borrowed the idea of "simultaneous associations" from Wilhelm Wundt, whom he criticised on other occasions.[94]

---

and only end of language, as is commonly supposed. There are other ends, as the raising of some passion, the exiting to, or deterring from an action.»

[91] A. Marty, *Untersuchungen zur Grundlegung der allgemeinen Grammatik und Sprachphilosophie*, Niemeyer, Halle 1908. See S. Satris, *Ethical Emotivism*, cit., p. 17, who describes the intellectual legacy of Marty in Richards, Perry and Stevenson.

[92] S. Danielsson, *Några värdenihilismer*, cit., p. 39: «det förefaller alltså finnas goda skäl till att säga att Marty framförde den semantiska värdenihilismen i sin stora bok 1908, fast den där kom lite i skymundan och inte formulerades så pregnant som hos Hägerström.» For instance, Marty believed that some "Emotive" were similar to what Brentano called "adequate emotions."

[93] B. Petersson, *Axel Hägerströms värdeteori*, cit., p. 58; I. Hedenius, *Om rätt och moral*, cit., pp. 12–21. Hägerström's vocabulary is centered on ideas or conceptions – and not as in Robert Sandin's translation on "propositions" – which indicates that Hägerström conceived his theory as a psychological theory in the first place, even though most readings hold Hägerström's thesis to be a semantic thesis or at least that the semantic thesis follows from the psychological thesis.

[94] According to Petersson's reconstruction, in the 1908 lecture series *Rättsidéers sanningsvärde*, Hägerström coined the expression "complex or simultaneous association," an idea he was inspired to by Wundt. He criticised Wundt and Brentano on different occasions, such as in the unpublished manuscript *Analys av fråge-, utrops- och önskesatser* and *Kritiska punkter i värdepsykologien*, cit., especially pp. 64 ff.

This was the heyday of German psychology of value and, according to this prevailing approach, three major psychological types of phenomenon (*akt*) can be distinguished: (1) conceptions or *Vorstellungen* (which is a form of "mental image"), (2) judgments (which imply the belief in the existence of the former) and finally (3) emotions (which do not entail such a belief).[95] In "moral conceptions" – or in any other mental act where I conceive an action as being good, bad, right, wrong etc.[96] – there is always an emotive element. In other words, I cannot conceive an action to be right or wrong, without experiencing, at the same time, a feeling, which Hägerström described as a «conative impulse toward the action.»[97] I cannot distinguish between moral conceptions and the belief in their reality.[98]

It is not necessary to reconstruct Hägerström's rather intricate and not always easily intelligible theory of the human mind, nor do we need to corroborate the results of his introspections. What we should stress instead is that, if labels were to be attached, Hägerström appears to be non-cognitivist in a general sense as well as in critical terms, while he is an emotivist in a more narrow sense and in his *pars construens*. In essence, Hägerström's main argument, in respect of the human mind, is that evaluations are no judgments on reality, since the act of *evaluating* something implies the existence of an *emotion*, which however is not necessary in the act of *making a judgment*.

This approach is often said to have been developed by Hume, who in the *Enquiry Concerning the Principles of Morals* (1751) claimed that «the approbation or blame which then ensues, cannot be the work of the judgment, but of the heart; and is not a speculative proposition or affirmation, but an active feeling or sentiment.»[99] Hägerström's idea was at odds with any such reconstruction. In *Moralfilosofins grundläggning* from spring 1911, he explicitly kept his distance from this view, which he called "moral sensualism" and ascribed to Hartley, Hume and Smith: «That the moral feeling is upheld [to be the highest norm for good and evil] depends on the influence of ordinary moral consciousness. But one does not want

---

[95] In his philosophy of mind, Hägerström contended that judgment has three elements. With a famous example of a running horse, in *Das Prinzip der Wissenschaft* (Almqvist & Wiksell, Uppsala 1908, pp. 22–27), a person sees the horse running if three mental conditions are present: (i) the *Vorstellung* or "mental image" of the running horse (the only condition of truth for such a mental image is "determinateness" in the sense of consistency); (ii) consciousness of the mental image (i) as real; and (iii) full objective reality of (i). The content of (ii) is called *Urteil*.

[96] For Hägerström axiological conceptions seem to be a form of simultaneous associations involving a complex system of acts; see B. Petersson, *Axel Hägerströms värdeteori*, cit., *passim*, who attempts an analytic description of Hägerström's mental and psychological theories.

[97] A. Hägerström, *Inquiries*, cit., p. 152.

[98] See, *inter alia*, I. Hedenius, *Über den alogische Charakter der sog. Werturteil. Bemerkungen zu Ernst Cassirer: Axel Hägerström*, in «Theoria» 1939, vol. 5, no. 3, pp. 314–329; E. Tegen, *The Basic Problem in the Theory of Value*, in «Theoria», 1944, pp. 28–52; L. Fröström, *Axel Hägerströms analys av värdeupplevelsen*, in *Logik, rätt och moral. Filosofiska studier tillägnade Manfred Moritz*, Studentlitt., Lund 1969, pp. 49–60.

[99] D. Hume, *Enquiry Concerning the Principles of Morals* (1751), Appendix I. Concerning Moral Sentiment.

to maintain the setting of absolute values by the moral consciousness and hence it all leads to arbitrariness. This, of course, does not imply that the opinion in question is not important as a description of how our moral assessments really emerged.»[100]

Hägerström's view of the nature of moral evaluations challenged not only Kantism, and more specifically Kant's account of practical reason, but it also contrasted with all subjectivistic tendencies prone to construe a form of equivalence between axiological phenomena and pure emotion, according to a penchant for crude irrationalism (moral sensualism).[101] Hägerström's account, on the contrary, places the conative, affective, and social nature of human beings in the foreground, without cutting it loose from rationality.

Indeed, he insisted on this "humanistic" viewpoint from which it follows that only human beings are capable and prone to evaluate actions morally by taking an ethical stance. One interesting implication of Hägerström's psychological thesis is that it shows why today we use machines, namely computers, for legal purposes (information retrieval but also in deciding routine cases such as imposing traffic related fines, declaring undisputed divorce, etc.) As these cases seem to highlight, there is no need for "taking an emotive stance" in order to "make a judgment." However, it is plain to see that jurisprudence – not to mention ethics – offers much "harder" cases and these fields are therefore far more complex than these, to some extent, marginal matters.

A much more plausible predecessor to Hägerström's view than Hume, is Christian von Ehrenfels who first developed the basis for non-cognitivism in his *System der Werttheorie* from 1897, where he claimed that the evaluation (*Wertung*) is neither true nor false,[102] that «value is a relation between an object and a subject, which expresses that the subject either actually desires the object or would desire it in case he were not convinced of its existence»[103] and, finally, that one of the factors explaining change in values is "suggestion," which echoes what Hägerström later called the "suggestive effect" of authorities in society on our moral conceptions (see Chapter 5).[104]

---

[100] A. Hägerström, *Moralfilosofins grundläggning*, cit., p. 174: «att man upptar den moraliska känslan [till högsta norm för gott och ont] beror på att man finner sig påverkad av det vanliga sedliga medvetandet. Dock vill man ej fasthålla vid det sedliga medvetandets sättande av absoluta värden och så utlöper det hela i godtycke. Naturligtvis utesluter icke det sagda, att åsikten i fråga kan ha sin betydelse såsom en skildring av huru våra moraliska omdömen faktiskt uppstå.»

[101] On the tendency to present emotivism as irrational, see S. Satris, *Ethical Emotivism*, cit., p. viii.

[102] Ch. von Ehrenfels, *System der Werttheorie*, Reisland, Leipzig 1897–98, vol. I, p. 102. I am quoting S. Satris, *Ethical Emotivism*, cit., p. 14.

[103] Ch. von Ehrenfels, *System der Werttheorie*, cit., p. 65. I am quoting S. Satris, *Ethical Emotivism*, cit., p. 14. Cf. A. Hägerström, *Socialfilosofiska uppsatser*, cit., p. 20.

[104] Here we shall not discuss the analogy between von Ehrenfels' *Suggestion*, Hägerström's *suggestive effect* and Ch. L. Stevenson's *magnetic influence thesis* (term taken from R. Brandt, *Ethical Theory*, Prentice-Hall, Englewood Cliffs 1959, p. 226). On the origin of "suggestion" in French sociology, in particular in Gabriel Tarde, see Bo Petersson, *Axel Hägerströms värdeteori*, cit., p. 30.

As the years went by, Hägerström elaborated a distinction that came to play a certain role for understanding his meta-ethical stance. He distinguished between *primary evaluations* (*primära värderingar*), which are assessments made by a person who is about to make a choice in practice, and *value judgments* (*värdeomdömen*) which are independent from the concrete situation where the choice is made. While value judgments are always false since they are shaped as a theoretical judgment about something that is not (the axiological fact), primary evaluations are theoretically meaningless, in the sense that they are neither true nor false.[105] This is why Hägerström's theory of value is considered a mix between error-theory and non-cognitivism, but it might well be rendered by affirming that this distinction restricts the scope of the argument of the ideal observer elaborated in his inaugural lecture.

On many occasions, Hägerström insisted on the complex nature of the axiological act. It appears to be a combination between conceptions (*föreställningar*) and emotions (*känslor*).[106] One of the most interesting accounts on the relation between cognitive and emotional components in moral ideas can be found in the written, and more extensive, version of Hägerström's inaugural discourse, published by Mautner in 1987. Here the Swedish philosopher claimed that, if axiological communication between individuals occurs, it is necessary to enter not only in the other party's «world of thought, but also to engage in his emotional life and volition.»[107] On one hand, without the principle of empathy (*sympathia*), it is not cognitively possible to understand moral arguments: «The attempt to persuade a [person like] Cesare Borgia that a more social approach is objectively right is as absurd as if the sheep attempted to convince the wolf that it is wrong to bite so carelessly.»[108] On the other hand, the more information we have about the world, the more will we be able to develop moral feelings, just like «in the aesthetical field, deeper knowledge opens the spirit for new aesthetical values.»[109] Moreover, this is why «the fundamental

---

[105]On this issue and for a comparison with Meinong, Perry, Dewey and other theorists of value, see E. Tegen, *The Basic Problem in the Theory of Value*, in «Theoria», 1944, pp. 28–52.

[106]There seems to be an evolution in Hägerström's way of conceiving the mental act of "emotion." See *Kritiska punkter i värdepsykologien*, cit., p. 22, and *Om primitiva rudimenter i modernt föreställningssätt*. He upheld that emotion is, on one hand, a conception and, on the other hand, something that comes in adjunction with a conception. In *Om primitiva rudimenter* he affirmed the emotion is somehow projected on the content of the conception. For the theory of emotion in Hägerström, see B. Petersson, *Axel Hägerströms värdeteori*, cit., pp. 32–45.

[107]A. Hägerström, *Moralfilosofins grundläggning*, cit., p. 44: «den ene kan försätta sig in i ej blott den andres föreställningsvärd, utan även hans känslo- och viljeliv.»

[108]A. Hägerström, *Moralfilosofins grundläggning*, cit., p. 45: «Försöket att övertyga en Cesare Borgia om det objektivt riktiga i en mer social läggning är lika abderistiskt som om fåret ville bevisa för vargen, att det är orätt att bitas så oförsiktigt.»

[109]A. Hägerström, *Moralfilosofins grundläggning*, cit., p. 45: «på det ästetiska området vidgade kunskaper öppna sinnet för nya skönhetsvärden.»

moral evaluation is itself influenced by the knowledge of how things are in reality. For example, greater insight of people's suffering usually gives a more humane touch to the principle of moral assessment.»[110]

This mutual interdependence and respective augmentation of the cognitive and emotional components of our axiological evaluations explain why in Hägerström's view it is reasonable to engage in moral communication. Indeed, his meta-ethical thesis and his overall non-cognitivism enable him to perform three operations: (i) to *demonstrate* why a given axiological view has, historically speaking, functioned within a certain society; (ii) to *show* how a specific set of axiological conceptions or norms maintains society and maintains itself, by being for instance functional to the survival of the group; and (iii) to *distinguish* the question of the authentic evaluation or value judgment from the question concerning the criterion of relevance corresponding to the "value" retained. While the first matter (evaluation) necessarily follows our emotional nature and it is hence prone to be an object of persuasion, the latter issue (criteria of relevance) can be the object of rational inquiry. We might reformulate this with the better known vocabulary of Stevenson: If our disagreement in interest is actually rooted in disagreement in belief, and we come to understand this, then there is a chance that empirical method and reasonable argumentation may relieve some harshness from the quarrel.[111]

Notwithstanding, or perhaps because of this distinction, we should hope for a deeper understanding and engagement in ethics: The more we reflect on a normatively laden issue, the more likely it is that we discover and dismiss some criteria of relevance as mere prejudice. In this sense, it has been argued that «Hägerström was really a profoundly moral philosopher.»[112]

## 3.4 Misunderstandings

### *3.4.1 Ernst Cassirer and Moral Relativism*

Hägerström's theory of value, because it is quite complicated and not always well-defended, led to a series of misunderstandings or deformations of his thought. A first, and very common misconception, considers that axiological nihilism advocates a form of moral relativism.[113] It is remarkable that this misconstrued view was adopted by the otherwise so perspicacious Ernst Cassirer. The neo-Kantian

---

[110] A. Hägerström, *Moralfilosofins grundläggning*, cit., p. 45: «den grundläggande moraliska värderingen själv påverkas av kunskaper i verklighetens egna beskaffenhet. Den större insikten i människors lidande skänker exempelvis vanligen en mera human färg åt den moraliska värderingsprincipen.»

[111] Ch. L. Stevenson, *Facts and Value*, cit., p. 29.

[112] S. Källström, *Filosofi och politik*, cit., p. 156: «Hägerström var i själva verket en djupt moralisk filosof.»

[113] For an analysis of relativism and its implications, V. Villa, *Relativismo: un'analisi concettuale*, in «Ragion Pratica», 2007, 1, pp. 55–76.

philosopher lectured in Uppsala in September and October 1934 and held a chair in philosophy in Göteborg from September 1935 to May 1941. During this intense and prolific period,[114] he dedicated considerable effort to studing Hägerström's thought. His book from 1939 on Hägerström is the only one he wrote on a contemporary thinker. Until quite recently, the great impact of Cassirer's interaction with the Uppsala school on his own philosophy of symbolic forms was unknown,[115] since the most important texts that Cassirer wrote in response to this encounter remained unpublished until 1995 when the nine volumes of the *Nachlaß* from his Swedish years were progressively published.[116] Anyhow, Cassirer, who is probably one of the most refined interpreters of the father of Scandinavian realism, had a hard time understanding axiological nihilism. He claimed, «the sun of moral philosophy must then shine for Hägerström, so to say, for the unjust as for the just.»[117]

At the beginning of his examination of Hägerström's practical philosophy, Cassirer glossed: «Here in effect the overall intellectual posture seems to have undergone a sudden change. As a theoretician, Hägerström is a strict rationalist and objectivist (...). But all this changes at once when we go from the field of theoretical judgments to that of the so-called "practical judgments" (...). Subjectivism, which Hägerström relentlessly combated in the realm of theoretical knowledge, hence triumphs within moral philosophy (...). Total *relativism* is hereby erected into the principle of foundation in the field of moral ideas (...). Between this [ethics of sophism] and that of Hägerström, I cannot discover any real, systematic difference in essence. In order not to be misunderstood I have to stress that, with this statement, I do not intend to *judge* if Hägerström's moral philosophy is true or false, meaningful or meaningless. It is only a matter of establishing a historical fact. Sophistic philosophy – at least as it appears in its consistent theoreticians – did not intend to be a justification or glorification of "egoism." Rather, it assumed the thesis of the *equivalence* between all moral conceptions. Man is explained to be the measure of all things: Ethics is dissolved in psychology and anthropology.»[118]

---

[114] In Sweden, he wrote *Determinismus und Indeterminismus in der modernen Physik* (1936), *Descartes: Lehre, Persönlichkeit, Wirkung* (1939), *Axel Hägerström* (1939), *Thorilds Stellung in der Geistesgeschichte des 18. Jahrhunderts* (1941), *Zur Logik der Kulturwissenschaften* (1942), and *Das Erkenntnisproblem IV*. On the stay of Cassirer in Sweden 1935–1941, see J. Hansson, S. Nordin, *Ernst Cassirer. The Swedish Years*, Peter Lang, Berlin 2006.

[115] See for instance M. Ferrari, *Ernst Cassirer – Stationen einer philosophischen Biographie: Von der Marburger Schule zur Kulturphilosophie*, Cassirer-Forschung, vol. 11, Meiner, Hamburg 2003.

[116] E. Cassirer, *Nachgelassene Manuskripte und Texte*, K. Ch. Köhnke, J. M. Krois, O. Schwemmer (eds.), 20 vols., Meiner, Hamburg 1995 ff.

[117] E. Cassirer, *Axel Hägerström*, cit., p. 53: «Die Sonne der Moralphilosophie muß demnach nach Hägerström sozusagen über Gerechte und Ungerechte scheinen.»

[118] E. Cassirer, *Axel Hägerström*, cit., pp. 53–54: «Denn hier scheint sich die intellektuelle Gesamthaltung plötzlich zu verändern. Als Theoretiker ist Hägerström strenger Rationalist und Objektivist. (...) Aber dies alles ändert sich mit einem Schlage, sobald wir vom Gebiet der theoretischen Urteile in das der sogenannten "praktischen Urteile" übergehen (...). Der Subjektivismus, den Hägerström in bezug auf das theoretische Wissen unablässig bekämpft hat, triumphiert also innerhalb der Moralphilosophie (...). Damit ist im Gebiet der moralischen

It is clear that Cassirer did not notice that Hägerström's axiological nihilism, to a large extent, is a semantic thesis grounded in the linguistic turn in philosophy and, moreover, presents meta-ethical claims from which no normative assertions can be immediately derived.

As we have seen, Hägerström's theory of value is a far cry from the moral relativism of classic sophistic teaching. Indeed, as Hedenius pointed out, the homomensura-thesis of Sophistic moral theory that Cassirer incorrectly associated Hägerström with, accepted that value judgements can be true or false, contrarily to axiological nihilism.[119] Hägerström's theory of value may be labeled "modern" because it does not aim at any classic *epoché* or suspension of judgment, traditionally grounded in the finitude of human reason. Rather, it is intended as a device for partitioning reality into what can plausibly be subject to description, i.e. what is likely to be the object of scientific knowledge and, on the contrary, what transcends this distinction as human emotion does in his view. This separation mechanism is based on Hume's principle and it is construed as a technical device for reducing the complexity of our social and normative environment.

### 3.4.2 Theodor Geiger and Social Relativism

A second type of misunderstanding is exemplified by Theodor Geiger and later on, by many "sociological" readings of Hägerström's theory of value. According to this view, the value is neither in the object before me, nor in my head. Values must instead be discovered in society's power distribution.

With the German invasion of Denmark, the left-wing sociologist Theodor Geiger crossed the strait of Öresund into Sweden where he came into contact with the Uppsala school and, after returning to Aarhus where he founded the research institute for social sciences, he developed a form of sociology of law largely inspired by Hägerström's theory of value. Geiger basically agreed with the Uppsala "axiological nihilism." In *Ideologie und Wahrheit*, he explicitly referred to Hägerström, claiming that «the value judgment is thus a meaningless sentence in theoretical terms (...).

Ideen ein völliger Relativismus zum Grundprinzip erhoben (...). Zwischen ihr [eine "sophistische" Moral] und Hägerström vermag ich einen eigentlichen, systematischen Wesenunterschied nicht zu entdecken. Ich muß, um nicht mißverstanden zu werden, freilich betonen, daß ich mit dieser Behauptung keinerlei Urteil über die Wahrheit oder Falschheit, über Wert oder Unwert von Hägerströms Moralphilosophie fällen will; es soll sich lediglich um die Feststellung eines historischen Tatbestandes handeln. Die Sophistik wollte – zum mindesten in der Gestalt, in der sie uns bei ihren konsequenten Theoretikern entgegentritt – keineswegs eine Rechtfertigung oder Verherrlichung des "Egoismus" sein; sie geht vielmehr von der These der Äquivalenz aller moralischer Vorstellungen aus. Der Mensch wird als Maß aller Dinge erklärt: Die Ethik wird in Psychologie und Anthropologie aufgelöst.» The comparison between axiological nihilism and moral relativism was criticised by Ingmar Hedenius in *Über den alogischen Charakter de sog. Werturteile*, cit., pp. 314–329 – i.e. the prestigious Scandinavian review directed by Åke Petzäll that edited numerous articles on this issue in those years.

[119] I. Hedenius, *Über den alogischen Charakter de sog. Werturteile*, cit., pp. 314–329.

The reification of evaluation in an idea of value is an illusion. (...) Its illegitimacy depends on the inconsistency between its structure and its content. This is the object of content of ideology. It lies in the (...) theorisation of non-theoretical content.»[120]

However, in the book *Debate with Uppsala,*[121] he echoed Hedenius' distinction between authentic and inauthentic value-propositions, his intention being to radicalise and "improve" Hägerström's blow against metaphysics.[122] A norm is not just an idea in the heads of people, but a real, sociologically observable, phenomenon. This viewpoint was later harshly criticised by both Karl Olivecrona and Alf Ross.[123] Geiger distinguished between verbal norms and subsistent norms that could not be perceived as typical behaviour but only classified as norms if reactions to deviant behaviour could be observed. This led him to emphasize the idea that only enforced norms are valid, a view, as we shall see, which does not really correspond to Hägerström's much more refined conception.

Geiger defined his own position as «judicial pessimism»[124] and insisted on the historically growing gap between law and morals, an aspect that Hägerström failed to stress. «The law is no moral but a political phenomenon: It is a social phenomenon of power.»[125] The error of Uppsala is that «Hägerström's and Lundstedt's battle against superstition in science is honorable, but they do not seem to notice that their own (...) faith in the social usefulness of suggestion might be a superstition.»[126] In Geiger's reading, the problem with Hägerström's teachings is not, as in Cassirer's reading, that it stimulates relativism, eventually dismantling social cohesion, but instead that it is too prudent concerning what power really means for the instauration of ideology, ultimately ascribing too much importance to human belief and social symbolism over factual empowerment: «Obedience to the legal system does not generally depend on moral convictions about duty. Plainly stated: Law has nothing

---

[120] Th. Geiger, *Ideologie und Wahrheit. Eine soziologische Kritik des Denkens*, Humblot, Stuttgart 1953, pp. 63–64: «Das Werturteil ist somit eine theoretisch sinnlose Aussage (...). Die Objektivierung von Bewertungen in einer Wertidee ist illusionär (...). Ihre Illigitimität beruht auf der Unvereinbarkeit ihrer Struktur mit ihrem Inhalt. Dies ist der Sachverhalt der Ideologie. Sie liegt in (...) der Theoretisierung des A-Theoretischen.»

[121] Th. Geiger, *Debat med Uppsala om moral och ret*, Carl Bloms tryckeri, Lund 1946; now in German edition 1978. See also T. Agersnap, *Theodor Geiger. Pioneer of Sociology in Denmark*, in «Acta Sociologica», 2000, vol. 43, n. 4, pp. 325–330.

[122] S. Eliaeson, *Geiger, the Uppsala-school of Value Nihilism – and Weber*, in U. Fazis, C. Nett Jachen (eds.), *Gesellschaftsteorie und Normentheorie. Theodor Geiger Symposium*, Social Strategies, Basel 1993 (Monographien zur Soziologie und Gesellschaftspolitik, vol. 25), pp. 225–34.

[123] For references, see A. Hägerström, *Rätten och viljan*, Gleerup, Lund 1961, p. 1.

[124] Th. Geiger, *Debat med Uppsala*, cit., p. 3.

[125] Th. Geiger, *Debat med Uppsala*, cit., p. 220.

[126] Th. Geiger, *Debat med Uppsala*, cit., p. 217: «Hägerström-Lundstedts kamp mod overtro i videnskaben er al haeder vaerd, men de synes aldrig at have taenkt på att deres (...) egen tro på overtroens samfundsgavnlighed kunde vaere – en overtro.»

to do with morals.»[127] Geiger offered what we might call the "realist" criticism of Hägerström's view (in the sense of "political realism"). This, however, remained the opinion of a minority. The most common (and distorted) view was rather that Hägerström's axiological nihilism brought about practical nihilism.

### *3.4.3 Practical Nihilism: How Hägerström Fell into Disrepute*

A claim which was as widespread as it was misleading concerning Hägerström's axiological nihilism is that it opens the door to the worst of all evils: Practical nihilism. Distorting Dostoyevsky, it is commonly claimed that if no alethic discourse on values is possible then "all is permitted." The rumour even has it that the bishop of Uppsala was once surprised to hear that «Hägerström treated his wife and children kindheartedly.»[128]

Some events participated in the creation of an aura of decadent nihilism and universal neglect around Hägerström's theory of value, which in time came to discredit his theses in the eyes of the greater public. These events were essentially the Svante Bohman case, the literary competition arranged by the publishing house *Natur och Kultur* and finally a series of newspaper articles from World War II.[129]

The Bohman affair exploded at the beginning of 1934. The case concerned Hägerström's protégé Svante Bohman and his Phd thesis that presented a reading of the Swedish poet Esaias Tegnér in a common sense perspective, where the bard was portrayed as a product of contemporary societal conditioning, challenging the standard account of the national genius: Tegnér was depicted as influenced by Thomas Reid and not by German idealism. Hägerström and Lundstedt defended Bohman, who was subjected to some devastating allegations in the press, made by Fredrik Böök, professor of history of literature, and John Landqvist, both convinced anti-hägerströmians and heavy-weights in Sweden's cultural life. The motive of contention was that Bohman had castigated the great poet for not believing in God, in the name of the "cold" scientific analysis at odds with the "warm" traditional interpretation.

A few years later, in 1937, the director of the prominent publishing house *Natur och Kultur*, Johan Hansson, who was convinced that all moral members of society ought to fight axiological nihilism if any ordered community were to survive, organised a literary contest on the subject «Can an objective moral system be erected today and on what foundations?» The Göteborg newspaper did not fail to emphasize

[127]Th. Geiger, *Debat med Uppsala*, cit., p. 218: «lydigheden overfor retsordenen ikke i al almindelighed bero på det moralske pligtmotiv. Renud sagt: Retten har intet med moral at gøre.»

[128]M. Waller, *Människan som få kände*, cit., p. 190: «Ändock lär Hägerström vara snäll mot fru och barn.»

[129]For a detailed reconstruction of these issues and Hägerström's impact on cultural life in Sweden, see S. Källström, *Värdenihilism och vetenskap. Uppsalafilosofin i forskning och samhällsdebatt under 1920- och 1930 talen*, Acta Universitatis Gothoburgenis, Göteborg 1984; Id., *Den gode nihilisten. Axel Hägerström och striderna kring Uppsalafilosofin*, Rabén & Sjögren, Stockholm 1986.

how «the formulation of the question made Hägerström the number one enemy of the competition.»[130] One remarkable contribution to this literary contest was written by the Dane Knud Grue-Sörensen and emblematically entitled *Contemporary Moral Scepticism.*[131] This contribution illustrates well the unsophisticated mix-up between Hägerström's value theory and sheer practical nihilism. The author lamented that moral nihilism establishes perfect equivalence of all our actions, notwithstanding that Hägerström had just written a lengthy essay, *Om pliktmedvetandet*, to demolish this prejudice.

In the late thirties, attacking Hägerström's value theory and depicting it as the source of many ills in society became a favorite pastime for the press. Anders Örne discussed the practical consequences of axiological nihilism on the social-democratic review *Tiden.* With a pun on the Swedish word «meningslös» (meaningless) – which indicates the technical aspect of being "deprived of (scientific) meaning" but, in ordinary language, it also means "useless" – Örne claimed that axiological nihilism made discussion on values and moral action «totally useless» (*alldeles meningslös*) and that it was thus perilous in that very moment in history.

The journalist Lönnqvist, in his review of Hägerström's *Socialfilosofiska uppsatser*, insisted on the connection between law and power, right and might, discrediting Hägerström's belief in the link between fanaticism and objective values: «On the contrary, Hägerströmism and other similar philosophies abroad seem to have paved the way for the kind of philosophy of power that now grins at us, cynically explaining "Now that it is proven that there is no objective justice and ethics, I take what I believe is my right for I have the power to do so and I call this power my right!"»[132]

Alf Ahlberg, in *Why the Swedish People React* (his contribution to the eloquently entitled essay collection *Philosophy of Power and Axiological Nihilism* from 1941), affirmed that fascism, nazism and communism all bear the mark of value nihilism, a psychological state that emerges from moral relativism and the absence of universally recognized objective values, which in turn can be considered an outcome of Hägerström's hazardous teachings: «The ancient sophists with their moral relativism which ended up in moral nihilism, destroyed the spiritual preconditions of ancient democracy. The modern sophists with their axiological nihilism, which

---

[130] *Göteborgs Handels- och sjöfartstidning*, 21/12/1937: «Genom tävlingsfrågans formulering har Hägerström kommit att representera den lede fienden vars åsikter skola vederläggas.»

[131] K. Grue-Sörensen, *Vor tids moral skepticisme. Om muligheden af en objektiv etik* (1937). On the Danes' representing classical views on normative reasoning, see L.L. Hierro, *El realismo jurídico escandinavo. Una teoría empirista del derecho*, Torres, Valencia 1981, p. 127.

[132] C. Lönnqvist, *Hägerström och Hitler*, in «Göteborgs Handels- och sjöfartstidning», 03/07/1940: «Tvärtom tycks hägerströmianismen och liknande filosofiska riktningar i utlandet ha banat väg just för den maktfilosofi som nu grinar emot oss, cyniskt förklarande: När det nu är bevisat, att det inte finns någon objektiv rätt eller moral, så tar jag själv vad jag anser vara min rätt, för jag har makt att göra det och denna makt kallar jag för rätt!»

finally became an explicit form of value nihilism, erode in the same way the spiritual foundations of free society.»[133]

This rendering of Hägerström's theory of value in terms of practical nihilism became quite a popular theme in twentieth century Scandinavia. An excellent literary example of the confusion between non-cognitivism and practical nihilism can be found in Vilhelm Moberg (1898–1973) and his novel, *The Old Reign* (*Det gamla Riket*). It offers an outstanding caricature of the Uppsala school which is also a raw political satire, where the young protagonist Per Urban Secretessius journeys to the country of *Idyllia* to learn from the famous law professor Adam Haggard about its legal system based on secrecy, censorship and deceit, where individuals enjoy rights only as cogs in the machinery.[134]

### *3.4.4 The Call for Tolerance*

While many interpreters considered Hägerström's axiological nihilism to ultimately legitimate all actions alike,[135] he himself did not believe that his viewpoint implied any "dissolving effect in morals" (*moralupplösande*). «Science has only to indicate what is true, while it is nonsense to regard the idea of an obligation as true; so no science can have it as its task to indicate how we ought to act (...). Just as a science of religion cannot be based upon a religious consciousness, so a moral science cannot have as its basis a moral consciousness. In both cases it is a question of a subjective process of thought, which itself may be an object for science, but cannot be the foundation for any science.»[136]

From Hägerström's perspective, induction from normative casuistic may refine our psychological reactions before ethically complex situations, leading to further comprehension. But such a practice cannot ground any scientific approach to normative reasoning. Moral science can only understand the social and historical background from which a given set of norms evolved. By comprehending the genesis and evolution of normative systems we get rid of their unjustified weight. By approaching norms this way we become less blinded by emotions and interests,

[133] A. Ahlberg, *Maktfilosofi och värdenihilism*, in Id. (ed.), *Varför svenska folket reagerar*, Natur & Kultur, Stockholm 1941, p. 15: «Den antika sofistiken med sin värderelativism, som slutligen blev en värdenihilism, undergrävde den antika demokratins andliga förutsättningar. Den moderna sofistiken med sin värderelativism, som slutligen blev en öppen värdenihilism, undergrävde på samma sätt den andliga grundvalen för en fri samlevnad.»

[134] See on this caricature, S. Nordin, *Vilhelm Moberg et l'école d'Uppsala dans* Det Gamla riket, in P. Bouquet, P. Voilley, *Droit et littérature dans le contexte suédois*, Flies France, Paris 2000, pp. 49–52.

[135] An alternative, but in my view implausible, reading can be found in Lyles who claims that Hägerström's «own moral theory and philosophy must be described as being that of a naïve idealist rather than that of a moral nihilist» (*A Call*, cit., p. 287).

[136] A. Hägerström, *On the Truth of Moral Propositions*, in *Philosophy and Religion*, cit., p. 95; *Socialfilosofiska uppsatser*, cit., p. 51.

more aware of the simultaneous associations that determine our way of thinking, and this, in turn, enables us to avoid falling into the trap of prejudice. Hägerström «attributes not only a philosophical importance to his conception, but also a pedagogical merit and he hopes that it will have a certain educational virtue.»[137] The call for scientific purity is therefore combined with a guiding principle for our practical behaviour: The call for tolerance.[138]

«The idea of one's own moral view as absolutely authoritative and thus as the only right one has led, and will always lead, to fanaticism (...). It is clear that if the consciousness of right in a society should disintegrate and each part should give to its own values an absolute sanctity, fanaticism would flourish (...). Once we have taken the final step and have left behind any patent or suppressed belief in the cosmic and thus objective significance of value, (...) morality will *not* die away. On the contrary, there is reason to suppose that, like a Phoenix-bird, it will be born anew out of the ashes of the old morality, with a more emancipated and farsighted vision. It will also bear the stamp of a milder judgment on all human aspiration, which follows from viewing things *sub specie aeternitatis*, from the insight that everything is only a moment in an endless natural context, in which nothing is in itself higher or lower.»[139]

*Écrasez l'infâme!* – Voltaire's formula for fanaticism – is exactly what must be rejected. The motive is essentially political, since the opposite behaviour brings on close-mindedness and dogmatism, i.e. a mental climate where the very prerequisites of any future inquiry would be doomed. In other words, the ban on dogmatic and fanatical attitudes is motivated on social and political grounds of opportunity: Innovation cannot be expected from closed societies, whereas meta-ethical non-cognitivism will tend to promote open-mindedness and critical thinking. More generally speaking, it is possible to claim that in the background of Hägerström's tendency toward tolerance and the search for consensus, the regulatory ideal or meta-value of autonomy can be distinguished.[140] Besides the great importance of

---

[137] E. Cassirer, *Axel Hägerström*, cit., p. 80: «Er spricht seiner Auffassung nicht nur einen philosophischen, sondern auch einen pädagogischen Wert zu, und er erwartet von ihr eine bestimmte erzieherische Wirkung.»

[138] Hägerström's call for tolerance is very different from Rudolf Carnap's "principle of tolerance" which refers to conventionalism or axiomatic reasoning (see R. Carnap, *Logische Syntax der Sprache*, Springer, Wien 1934, § 17).

[139] A. Hägerström, *On the Truth of Moral Propositions*, in *Philosophy and Religion*, cit., pp. 94–95; *Socialfilosofiska uppsatser*, cit., p. 62. See also *Om pliktmedvetandet*, in *Socialfilosofiska uppsatser*, cit., pp. 91–92.

[140] Mautner correctly highlighted the importance of autonomy, and the refusal of heteronomy, in Hägerström's moral philosophy. Hägerström's virulent attacks on "duty ethics" should also be viewed against this background. Heteronomy in moral valuations is, in Hägerström's phrase, nothing but "spiritual slavery" (*andlig träldom*: A. Hägerström, *Moralpsykologi*, cit., p. 204; *Moralfilosofins grundläggning*, cit., pp. 95 ff.) According to Mautner, Hägerström's claim from 1911 – «it is the religious element in morals that is false, not the moral element» (*det är det religiösa momentet i moralen som är det falska, ej alls det moraliska*) – should be understood «it is the authoritarian element in morals that should be rejected, not the moral element» (*det är*

the principle of tolerance in Hägerström's own life,[141] this very principle leaves the philosophical system as such unsealed.[142]

In this sense, Hägerström is clearly no "nihilist" at all.[143] Gunnar Fredriksson emphasized how «he had well-known opinions in morals, politics and even aesthetics (...). However values do not *exist*, they are not *facts* (...). In the end we must take responsibility for our evaluations and their consequences and then references to facts of a social nature and otherwise may be important for argumentation. The so-called axiological nihilism in Hägerström is rooted in personal responsibility. The world will not become a better place because we try to found morals on unquestionable authorities. Between World War I and II, he considered this rather as the ground for fanaticism, what we now call fundamentalism. In a time when fanatically conceived doctrines of absolute validity and obedience, race theories and other scientific doctrines of falsehood reigned in Europe, Hägerström maintained the idea that we cannot trust such notoriously conflicting authorities. The man who was called a value-nihilist was really a humanist in hard times.»[144]

---

*det auktoritära momentet i moralen som är det förkastliga, ej alls det moraliska*): T. Mautner, *Hägerströms lära i moral*, cit., p. 46.

[141] See for example M. Waller, *Människan som få kände*, cit., p. 133.

[142] T. Spaak, *(Review of) Legal Theory*, cit., p. 301: «Besides his main argument for non-cognitivism, Hägerström invoked other arguments, too. Thus he pointed to the fact that people in different cultures and in different social classes in the same culture often embrace conflicting values; and he suggested that acceptance of meta-ethical non-cognitivism would most likely lead to increased tolerance among people.»

[143] Since Bazarov in Turgenev's *Fathers and Sons*, passing by Friedrich Heinrich Jacobi and Nietzsche, down to Heidegger and Baudrillard, nihilism has assumed various meanings that share the etymology in *nihil*, according to the different realm considered (epistemological, metaphysical, existential, ethical and even legal nihilism should be distinguished). Here I use the generic term for profound indifference.

[144] G. Fredriksson, *20 filosofer*, Norstedt, Stockholm 1994, p. 207: «Han hade djupt kända, moraliska, politiska och även estetiska värderingar (...). Men värden "existerar" inte, är inte "fakta" (...). Vi måste till slut alltid själva ta ansvar för våra värderingar och deras konsekvenser och då kan förvisso hänvisningar till sociala och andra fakta spela en stor roll i argumenteringen. Den s.k. värdenihilismen i Hägerströms mening bottnar i krav på personligt ansvar. Världen blir inte bättre, menade Hägerström, om vi försöker basera moralen på odiskutabla auktoriteter. Det var tvärtom vad han under mellankrigstiden såg som en grund för fanatism, sådant som nu kallas fundamentalism. I en tid då fanatiskt omfattade läror med krav på absolut giltighet och lydnad, jämte rasteorier och annan falsk vetenskap härjade i Europa, stod Hägerström fast vid tanken att vi inte kan lita på sådana inbördes notoriskt stridande auktoriteter. Han som kallades värdenihilist var en humanist i en svår tid.»

# Chapter 4
# A Lawyer *Honoris Causa*: Criticising the Will-theory

*As if a will could make an utterance true*[1]

## 4.1 Five Arguments Against the Will-Theory

Axel Hägerström would certainly have been surprised on the cold morning of October 31st, 1917, if someone had told him that he would be remembered as the "spiritual father" of Scandinavian realism.[2] Yet, that very day was the first step along the way: The Uppsala University was about to confer upon him a *laurea honoris causa* in Jurisprudence. As we have seen, Hägerström had in fact already published *Stat och rätt* in 1904. While this early work was considered by some a mere opportunistic *exercise de style* in order to obtain the chair in practical philosophy,[3] others, like Erik Olof Burman, praised it as the great return of the Scandinavian tradition of legal thought.[4] Even if law was certainly not his only interest, maybe not even the main one, it was nevertheless not new to him.

Since his early youth, Hägerström had been looking towards the track of law.[5] Still a student, he followed with great interest the path of his brother Gustav, three

[1] A. Hägerström, *Inquiries into the Nature of Law and Morals,* K. Olivecrona (ed.), translated by C.D. Broad, Almqvist & Wiksell, Uppsala 1953, p. 252.

[2] D. Lloyd, *Introduction to Jurisprudence*, Stevens & Sons, London 1965, p. 292.

[3] An insinuation might be found in Ernst Cassirer, *Axel Hägerström. Eine Studie zur schwedischen Philosophie der Gegenwart*, Göteborgs högskolas årskrift, Göteborg 1939; now in *Gesammelte Werke*, Bd. 21, Meiner, Hamburg 2005, p. 55.

[4] Burman, who had long been Hägerström's professor and defendant, claimed in his statement that the importance of *Stat och rätt* depended on the fact that Hägerström had revived research in philosophy of law which in previous decades had been suffering a decline. See M. Waller, *Axel Hägerström. Människan som få kände*, Natur & Kultur, Stockholm 1961, p. 176. On the Scandinavian legal tradition, see S. Blandhol, *The Rhetorical Foundations of Nordic Jurisprudence*, in «Ideas in History. The Nordic Society for the History of Ideas», 2006, vol. 1, n. 1–2, pp. 33–56.

[5] See Chapter 1.

P. Mindus, *A Real Mind*, Law and Philosophy Library 87,

DOI 10.1007/978-90-481-2895-2_4, 

years his senior, through law school[6] while his uncle, Skarin, climbed to the top the jurisprudential ladder, becoming a high court judge (*justitieråd*) in Stockholm in 1886. As Hägerström spent most of his early years teaching in quite disparate subjects – stretching from history of ethics to epistemology, from psychology of value to logic in Hegel[7] – it must be added that his attention for law-related topics quite certainly deepened in the classroom.

For instance, in 1901 he held classes on "The State and the Law" which probably helped him focus on some of the issues later addressed in the 1904 study on philosophy of law. He then spent the autumn of 1908 lecturing on the truth-value of ideas on justice and law,[8] not to mention the many courses on the genesis of juridical ideas.[9] However, it was not until he finally became professor in practical philosophy in 1911 that he started to convey his attention more continuously into the subject. One reason seems to be that his teachings in moral philosophy and, more specifically his axiological nihilism found «their strongest application»[10] in the sphere of law.

Another reason possibly came from his personal acquaintances. Indeed, after his first summer spent in the deep forests of the Dalecarlia region in 1914, Hägerström was introduced by Arthur Engberg (a longtime friend and pupil) to a colleague 14 years his junior: Vilhelm Lundstedt, who had just become professor in civil law and roman law at the Uppsala University. It was the beginning of an enduring intellectual friendship which would contribute significantly to the rise of Scandinavian realism. Hägerström was not only known for his great oratory skills, but seems to have applied them well on the 32-year old jurist: Lundstedt was initially reticent to the meeting, fearing the philosopher would disrupt his worldview and ideas. As the discussion went along, he started to doubt whether his theses were well-founded and, as a matter of fact, it did not take long before the young scholar engaged in a radical renewal of legal science.[11]

---

[6] Gustav Hägerström studied law at the Uppsala University during the same period that his younger brother Axel dedicated himself to philosophy. Gustav graduated, by passing the *hovrättsexamen*, in 1888, and later became a lawyer in the southern Swedish town of Jönköping.

[7] This information may be found in the complete listing of Hägerström's courses and lectures in T. Mautner, *Vägledning till Hägerströmstudiet*, Almqvist & Wiksell, Stockholm 1994, pp. 69–84.

[8] A. Hägerström, *Rättsidéers sanningsvärde*, transcripted by Martin Fries in the Sixties and today listed under UUB signum 105:5B.

[9] Among the most significant series of lectures, we can mention *Rättidéers uppkomst* from 1917 and the lectures included in A. Hägerström, *Rätten och staten. Tre föreläsningar om rätts- och statsfilosofi*, ed. M. Fries, Natur & Kultur, Stockholm 1963.

[10] The clue is given by Staffan Källström in *Filosofi och politik: Axel Hägerström och samhällsdebatten*, in G. Bexell, H. Stenius (eds.), *Värdetraditioner i nordiskt perspektiv*, Lund University Press, Lund 1997, p. 46. On these features, see Chapter 3.

[11] Lundstedt himself described the meeting with Hägerström in *Det Hägerström-Lundstedtska misstaget*, Geber, Stockholm 1942, p. 185: «Hägerström was a great diplomat. He spoke very respectfully of what he knew of my writings. He asked if he could borrow my PhD dissertation (...). Next time I came he had read it. We now started to talk, that is he asked me to develop my views. He did this in a very discrete way, just as if he wanted to learn a little jurisprudence from me. But every question led to a trap (...). I quickly understood that nothing was consistent in my

In 1913 Hägerström had already published *Om sociala vidskepelser* (On Social Superstition) in the programmatic review of the social-democratic movement «Tiden.» Here, we find some of the thoughts that he will later develop: He summarily dismissed the idea of sovereignty and individual rights in a slightly rhetoric fashion against the background of an effectively brief and neat history of natural law. The article was based on a talk held at the radical student association *Verdandi* just a few weeks after his "appalling" inaugural lecture. It did not yet have the clear shape of his later position on legal science. A more developed standpoint on law and justice can be found in *Är gällande rätt uttryck att vilja?* (Is Positive Law an Expression of Will?) from 1916, i.e., Hägerström's contribution to the *liber amicorum* honoring Vitalis Norström,[12] as well as *Till frågan om den objektiva rättens begrepp* from 1917. In these two essays, Hägerström established his main thesis on the deliberate voluntary features in legal science, the so-called will-theory. The study, partly translated by Broad with the title *On the Question of the Notion of Law*, presents the German-style subtitle "The Will-Theory. Vol. I" (even though there never was a second volume).[13]

To complete the overview of Hägerström's main production on legal issues during these years, we still have to mention his first study published in a "real" legal review, the prestigious «Svensk Juristtidning»: *Naturrätt i straffrättsvetenskapen?* (Natural Law in Legal Science concerned with Criminal Law?) from 1920. Conceived as a contribution to the debate between Johan C.W. Tyrén, at that time professor of criminal law, and Hägerström's friend and colleague, Vilhelm

fundamental thoughts.» Lundstedt was Hägerström's close friend and follower; he was a member of the Social Democratic Party and a member of Parliament from 1929 to 1948, and held his view on politics and on legal science to form one single outlook. He is best known for his theory of "social welfare" and his criticism of International Law. His major contributions are *Föreläsningar över valda delar av obligationsrätten* (1920–1953); and the more reknown *Legal Thinking Revised* (1956). On Lundstedt, see S. Nordin, *Från Hägerström till Hedenius. Den moderna svenska filosofin*, Doxa, Lund 1984, pp. 118–123; J.-O. Sundell, *Vilhelm Lundstedt – A Biographical Sketch*, in *Perspectives on Jurisprudence. Essays in Honor of Jes Bjarup*, Jure, Stockholm 2005, pp. 465–478. Lundstedt is the least known of the Scandinavian realists, as Carla Faralli's overview of the available translations shows (*The Reception of Scandinavian Legal Realism*, paper presented at the IVR-meeting in Lund 2003, the abstract can be found in ed. C. Wong, *Law and Politics – In Search of Balance*, Media-Tryck, Lund 2003, pp. 61–62).

[12] Vitalis Norström was then professor at the Göteborg University. He was known not only for his studies on religion but also for his inclination towards philosophical idealism. He seems to have coined the expression "Hägerströmianism" as early as in 1910 in a letter to the great Swedish theologist Nathan Söderblom, then archbishop of Uppsala, where he dwelled on his «enemies, the Hägerströmian thinkers.» My source is *Moralfilosofins grundläggning*, Thomas Mautner (ed.), Almqvist & Wiksell International, Stockholm 1987, p. 8.

[13] A more suitable title might have been *On the Concept of Objective Law*. This is not the only time Hägerström started some grandiose work without ending it. In the 1904 study *Stat och rätt* he claimed that it is only the first volume (see p. IX) but there were never any follow-ups. To Jes Bjarup this seems to be reason enough to preclude overall scientific judgment (*Reason, Emotion and the Law. Studies in the Philosophy of Axel Hägerström*, Press of the Faculty of Law, Aarhus 1982, p. 52).

Lundstedt,[14] this study deals with the iusnaturalistic elements in the doctrine of some of the most eminent scholars of criminal law: Namely, Karl Binding, Johan Hagströmer and Tyrén himself. This essay is quite important since it illustrates not only Hägerström's opinion on the uselessness of the concept of "illegality" in criminal law but also his way of addressing the problem of founding the state's right to inflict punishment.

In order to address these issues, a fruitful way is to go back to the aforementioned essays. As Hägerström himself laid emphasis on,[15] the two studies from 1916 to 1917 form a single outlook so it appears to be a good starting point for illustrating his criticism of the will-theory.

One of the commonly known features of Scandinavian realism is its critical view of formalism as a dogmatic or "scholastic"[16] way of approaching the law. Scandinavian realism usually appears among the anti-formalistic currents of legal theory in the first decades of the twentieth century. One of the favorite targets in the theory of law hence became all sorts of voluntaristic features. This is also true for the groundbreaking criticism of the so-called "will-theory" put forth by Hägerström. It should be added that the "revolt against formalism"[17] typically goes along with sceptical theories of interpretation. Undeniably, this second characteristic can also be found in Hägerström.

On a more specific level, if we look for the reasons why Hägerström targeted the will-theory in the first place, he explained that this theory is «the prevailing theory as to the nature of positive law.»[18] Furthermore, it seems likely that «the reason for this allocation of effort is probably that the critique directed at the positivistic version of the will-theory affects voluntarism in natural law and legal positivism alike.»[19]

---

[14]Hägerström himself had harsh words for the debate: «Currently in Sweden there is a tough strife between Lundstedt and some other jurists who keep on defending, *pro ara et focis*, their hereditary methods of natural law» (in *Filosofi och vetenskap*, ed. by Martin Fries, Ehlin, Stockholm 1957, p. 177).

[15]A. Hägerström, *Till frågan om den objektiva rättens begrepp*, vol. I: *Viljeteorien*, SKHVSU Almqvist & Wiksell, Uppsala 1917. Partially translated by C.D. Broad with the title *On the Question of the Notion of Law*, in *Inquiries*, cit., pp. 56–256. The pages pp. 116–201 of the translation were reedited by R. Sandin in *Philosophy and Religion*, Allen & Unwin, London 1964, pp. 97–172 with the title *On the Idea of Duty*. Hägerström himself believed that the 1916 and 1917 essays were his major contributions; far more significant, strangely enough, than his *Obligationsbegriff*, which took him 20 years to compose. See A. Hägerström, *Appendix B. The Philosophy of Axel Hägerström*, in *Philosophy and Religion*, Allen & Unwin, London 1964, p. 315; org. ed. *Hägerström, ad vocem* in A. Ahlberg (ed.), *Filosofiskt lexikon*, Natur & Kultur, Stockholm 1925, p. 91. This is why I believe it necessary to start with a detailed comment of these two essays.

[16]The appellation is Lundstedt's. See his *Principinledning. Kritik av straffrättens grundåskådningar*, Norblad, Uppsala 1920, p. 5.

[17]The famous formula was once adopted by Morton Gabriel White, *Social Thought in America: The Revolt against Formalism*, Viking Press, New York 1949.

[18]A. Hägerström, *Inquiries*, cit., p. 56.

[19]M. Lyles, *A Call for Scientific Purity: Axel Hägerström's Critique of Legal Science*, Rönnells, Stockholm 2006, p. 326.

And this, in turn, provides the opportunity for Hägerström to show how the binding force of positive law actually comes from something other than itself.

Hägerström's criticism of the will-theory – held by Olivecrona to be one of the deepest of its kind[20] – grew out of earlier considerations on superstition in society. The 1916 essay *Är gällande rätt*[21] focused on the will of the state in a way that seemed to have sprung directly from what Hägerström stressed in the lecture at the *Verdandi* association on April 28th, 1911: *Sociala Vidskepelser* (Social superstitions).[22] Among the social superstitions he denounced, Hägerström explicitly listed the will of the State, i.e., the core issue of his later jurisprudential essays. When discussing the principle of sovereignty, he affirmed: «The Will of the Sovereign is considered (...) to be a rule of action, above all others, from a value standpoint. The will of the monarch, the highest law; that is the motto of the autocrat. Such a will is sacred and venerable. Hence, we are on the track of one of the deepest social superstitions there is.»[23]

Since he believed to be on "the track of one of the greatest social superstitions," it is no surprise that Hägerström choose to dig into the will-theory. So, when the time came to honour Vitalis Norström, Hägerström was ready to strike against the insidious and pervasive notion of "will." Malte Jacobson, with whom Hägerström maintained a regular correspondence, offered him the chance to participate in the aforementioned *liber amicorum*, provided he did not write more than two sixteenths.[24] The result was his 1916 essay on valid law.[25] Here, Hägerström used basically five different types of arguments against the will-theory, which in his

[20] K. Olivecrona, *Inledning*, in A. Hägerström, *Rätten och viljan. Två uppsatser av Axel Hägerström*, Gleerup, Lund 1961, p. 10.

[21] All important notions in Hägerström's legal thinking are already present somehow; for example, the concept of command, at the heart of *Till frågan om den objektiva rättens begrepp* from 1917, the idea of declaration of intention on which Hägerström will later focus in his 1935 essay *Begreppet viljeförklaring på privaträttens område*, the observations on criminal psychology central to the 1925 article *Kriminalpsykologiska reflexioner*, as well as his speculation on duty that he came back to in the 1934 paper *Om pliktmedvetandet*.

[22] The manuscript version of the lecture can be found under UUB signum 14:5. It served as the basis for the 1913 essay *Om sociala vidskepelser*, now in *Socialfilosofiska uppsatser*, Bonniers, Stockholm 1939, pp. 93–120.

[23] A. Hägerström, *Socialfilosofiska uppsatser*, cit., p. 100: «Suveränens vilja anses (...) vara en handlingsregel, som står över alla andra i värdesynpunkt. Monarkens vilja högsta lag, är självhärskarens devis. Den viljan är helig och vördnadsvärd. Men därmed har vi kommit på spåren en av de djupast inrotade sociala vidskepelser, som finnas.»

[24] See T. Mautner, *Vägledning till Hägerströmstudiet*, Almqvist & Wiksell, Stockholm 1994, pp. 85–98 for details on Hägerström's correspondance.

[25] For a discussion on possible translations of "gällande" see E. Pattaro, *Il realismo giuridico scandinavo*, vol. I: *Axel Hägerström*, Cooperativa libraria universitaria editrice, Bologna 1974, p. 78. The translation of the title of the 1916 essay suggested by Sundberg could fit well: «Is law in force a matter of will?» (see. J. Sundberg, *The Swedish Philosopher Axel Haegerstroem and his Relationship to Finland's Struggle to Preserve her Legal Order 1899–1917*, Rothman, Littleton, CO, 1983, p. 10). What should be stressed is that "valid law" is not simply "law in force."

view «exhaust the possible forms of the theory.»[26] The point is that law cannot be reduced to any idea of will.

### *4.1.1 A Circular Definition: The Will of the State Determined by Law*

According to the first line of argument, if the state is a *persona iuridica* it has no will. Hägerström targeted what was then highly popular among contemporary German-speaking jurists, like the young Hans Kelsen in *Hauptprobleme der Staatslehre*: «We can reject as circular the theory which regards will, whose content expressed in a certain way is to constitute law, as *itself determined by the law*.»[27] In a way, Hägerström reduced the problem to the classic dilemma *rex facit legem* or *lex facit regem*. What he pointed out is that one cannot have one's cake and eat it: If law is the will of the state, but the state is an entity only as a creation of law, the argument moves in circles. There is no way of arguing, at the same time, that law presupposes the state and vice versa without contradiction. In other words, «the concept in question, the will of the state, is demonstrated to have been defined by reference to *definiendum*, namely law itself, whereby the concept conveys no intelligible information (. . .). Hence, the real relationship between the will and the law remains unexplained and indeterminate.»[28]

Hägerström also examined another formalistic theory concerning the will of the state which he ascribed to Rudolf Stammler.[29] In this latter case, the argumentation is slightly different, but it substantially converges on the idea of the indeterminateness of any formalistic definition of will. So, «the fault with the formal definition of will is that the real will which is to serve as the substrate to law becomes indeterminate»[30] and, as we know from Hägerström's epistemological work, what lacks determinateness also falls short of reality. In other words, neo-Kantian attempts to formally define the will of the State end up in social superstition since they fail to prevent inconsistency.

[26] A. Hägerström, *Inquiries*, cit., p. 55; *Är gällande rätt uttryck att vilja?*, in *Festskrift tillägnad prof. Vitalis Norström på 60-årsdagen den 29 januari 1916*, Elanders Boktryckeri, Göteborg 1916, p. 210.

[27] A. Hägerström, *Inquiries*, cit., p. 18; *Är gällande rätt*, cit., p. 172.

[28] M. Lyles, *A Call. . .*, cit., p. 331.

[29] A. Hägerström, *Inquiries*, cit., pp. 35–37; *Är gällande rätt*, cit., pp. 190–192.

[30] M. Lyles, *A Call. . .*, cit., p. 341. Hägerström's argument against the Stammler version of a formal will of the state is that «it is impossible to leave unsettled the question of what is the subject to whom the unitary willing, which is alleged to be present in positive law, belongs. A subject which wills must be found, for willing cannot exist without one» (A. Hägerström, *Inquiries*, cit., p. 36; *Är gällande rätt*, cit., p. 191).

## 4.1.2 Is the Will of the State What We All Want?

The second strike against the will-theory concerns the idea of a collective will, a *Gesammtwille* or *Gemeinwille* in the German wording.[31] Law in force or valid law cannot be scientifically described as some form of common will. First of all, for Hägerström, it is obvious that law has nothing to do with the "will of all (members of society)":[32] Who would ever believe that a criminal really wants the law enforced on himself? In Hägerström's usual ironic tone, «do criminals as a rule feel such a burning desire that the judges shall apply the criminal law to them?»[33] Subsequently, he came up with a second proof of this inconsistency since he presupposed a connection between will and consciousness: Let us consider another victim who does not know his or her interests could be enforced by the law. How can you possibly want something you are unaware of? How can you desire what you do not know exists? There is no such thing as a general will that equals what everybody wants, because the «individual has no adequate knowledge of the rules of law which hold in his society, and therefore cannot demand that they shall be observed.»[34] The point does not concern the principle of *ignorantia legis non excusat*, being instead that «no particular rule of law can *be* a demand of the general will, on this view, since its special content is not demanded by that will but is a matter of indifference to it.»[35]

Hägerström's crusade against common or general will presupposes an interesting standpoint as to what "will" might be for the single person. There seems to be a "special absurdity" in the idea that «an individual can give orders to himself.»[36] Hägerström did not discuss the issue in the 1916 essay on valid law, although he would give us his opinion in other writings, by linking the concept of "will" to the phenomenological assessment of the idea of command and duty. Anyhow, it is worth noting that he seems to take for granted that there can be no room for the traditional

[31] Hägerström came back to this argument quite often. Any "common will," or worse, any form of *Volksgeist* keeping together people's desires is nothing but *Dichtung*, poetry. See A. Hägerström, *Der römische Obligationsbegriff im Lichte der allgemeinen römischen Rechtsanschauung*, vol. I, SKHVSU Almqvist & Wiksell, Uppsala-Leipzig 1927, p. 17 where he claimed: «Wenn man aus dieser des Rechtordnung eigentümlichen Kraft einen Gemeinschaftswillen, gerichtet auf die Aufrechthaltung des Rechts im Ganzen, macht, bewegt man sich auf dem Gebiete der Dichtung und nicht der Wirklichkeit.»

[32] A. Hägerström, *Inquiries*, cit., p. 20, or as the original version has it, "all active individuals belonging to the society in question" («den samfällda viljan hos alla de till ifrågakommande samhället hörande handlingsskickliga individerna»: *Är gällande rätt*, cit., p. 62).

[33] A. Hägerström, *Inquiries*, cit., p. 21; *Är gällande rätt*, cit., p. 175. Hägerström came back to this argument numerous times. See for instance *Stat och statsformer* from 1921 in *Rätten och staten*, cit., pp. 126 and 132.

[34] A. Hägerström, *Inquiries*, cit., p. 21; *Är gällande rätt*, cit., p. 175. This traditional argument about the impossibility to foresee all the detailed implications of a law is developed in *Rätten och staten*, cit., p. 132.

[35] A. Hägerström, *Inquiries*, cit., p. 21; *Är gällande rätt*, cit., p. 175.

[36] A. Hägerström, *Inquiries*, cit., p. 21; *Är gällande rätt*, cit., p. 175.

concept of autonomy and, *a fortiori*, no collective auto-determination. The "common will" cannot be conceived as the sum of fragmented singular wills. There is no possible composition of the various individual wills. Accordingly, in his discussion of Fischer,[37] Hägerström concluded that «the so-called "will of the majority" is therefore only a meaningless term. In reality the separate wills here are not thought of in the least as being unified through a common aim.»[38] Hägerström came back to this conclusion more than once, but he never developed it into a thorough argumentation.[39] For instance a few years later, in 1924, he stated in even clearer terms: «The will of the representative assembly (...) is merely legal fiction. Thus it cannot be defined as a real will directed towards the law.»[40] Besides, in the beginning of *Obligationsbegriff*, where Hägerström discussed some theoretical, and not yet historical issues, he came back to the fiction involved in the idea of a common will in Parliament.[41]

All in all, according to Hägerström, no single member in society would personally want the law enforced, although every single person might crave the enforcement on all other members.[42] Moreover, the only case where the single person would actually require the enforcement of law is that of «a possessor of a legal

---

[37] A. Hägerström, *Inquiries*, cit., pp. 23–24; *Är gällande rätt*, cit., p. 178.

[38] A. Hägerström, *Inquiries*, cit., p. 24; *Är gällande rätt*, cit., p. 178. It should be stressed that Hägerström already used the term "meaningless" (*meningslös*), not in the sense of "useless," quite common in Swedish, but technically as "without being" (*väsenlös*). For this use, see the manuscripts on Hegel's *Philosophy of Right* at the Uppsala University Library under *H 112:a*, p. 13.

[39] Sometimes he conceived will in a physiological fashion not far from cognitive science (see *Inquiries*, cit., p. 150). But he even went so far as to express doubts on the very existence of free will. See for instance the unpublished work on guilt and punishment, *Skuld och straff* (*H 19:4*) where his argumentation is based on the assumption that «it is obvious that [when we speak of Man's free will] powers are being presupposed in Man, powers that lie above and behind the real world» («Det är uppenbart [när man talar om att människan har kvar sin frihet i sin innersta natur] att man förutsätter krafter hos människan, som ligga över eller bakom den faktiska verkligheten», p. 1). In 1930, this position will be explicitly stated in *Om verkligt autonom moral*: «I decide my will without being myself under any causal law. The idea is obviously totally absurd (...). Nothing is more illogical than the idea of free will» («Jag bestämmer mitt viljande utan att själv därvid stå under någon som helst orsakslag. Positionen är naturligen fullkomligt absurd (...) Ingenting är mer ologiskt än idén om viljans frihet.») It should be said that the topic of Free Will was a hot debate in Uppsala back then: For instance, the Philosophical Association (*Filosofiska föreningen*) Hägerström usually participated in discussed the issue as early as in 1910. As far as I know, the only scholar insisting on this point is Jes Bjarup who claimed: «Hägerström's thesis of moral nihilism is based upon his denial of freedom of will» (*Reason, Emotion and the Law. Studies in the Philosophy of Axel Hägerström*, Press of the Faculty of Law, Aarhus 1982, p. 295).

[40] A. Hägerström, *Förhållandet mellan rätten och staten*, in *Rätten och staten*, cit., p. 265 (Lyles' translation, *A Call...*, cit., p. 334).

[41] A. Hägerström, *Der römische Obligationsbegriff im Lichte der allgemeinen römischen Rechtsanschauung*, volume II, *Über die Verbalobligation*, K. Olivecrona (ed.), SKHVSU Almqvist & Wiksell, Uppsala 1941, p. 13.

[42] A. Hägerström, *Inquiries*, cit., p. 21; *Är gällande rätt*, cit., p. 175. This seems to be a somewhat odd argument for someone who admired Socrates in the *Apologia* where the single citizen accepts his death sentence.

right [making claims] on another person in order to substantiate his right as being actual law.»[43] In no way does this mean that the law consists, or worse comes into being, through one's wishes to see one's right enforced. Such an argument ends up in a circular motion since it presupposes the existence of legal rights in the first place: Law is neither what we all want, nor what the majority desires.

### *4.1.3 The Will of the State as* Bonum Commune

As Rousseau used to put it, *la volonté général n'est point la volonté de tous*. Indeed, it might be argued that we are dealing with some form of supra-individual will, as the Historical School of jurisprudence or Hegel would have had it. When Hägerström drew his weapon for the third time he aimed at such a conception. He rejected any "general will" conceived as a *Magnus Homo* in the classical tradition of organicism:[44] Bluntschli, Spencer, Schäffle, and Fouillée are all wrong to think of «society (...) as a psycho-physical organism.»[45] Boström, although not explicitly mentioned, is also considered wrong in claiming that «the organism in question carries out its decisions in law-making through individuals as its organs.»[46] In accordance with his general theory of knowledge, Hägerström showed the absurdity of the organic perspective by using one of his favorite examples: The case of a monarch angrily sanctioning anarchism.[47] «If one is angry as a private individual, without any legal

---

[43] A. Hägerström, *Inquiries*, cit., p. 21; *Är gällande rätt*, cit., p. 175.

[44] Hägerström held organicism to be a somewhat puerile notion. In *Stat och statsformer* from 1921 he defined it as "fantasy" (in *Rätten och staten*, cit., p. 169). This position is echoed by his devout pupil Martin Fries in the introduction to *Socialfilosofiska uppsatser*, cit., p. 23: «The State is nothing but a plurality of persons that are bound to a certain territory and organised through law (...). The traditional conception of the State as *Will* is but a modern form of animism» («Staten är själv ingenting annat än en mängd människor, som äro bundna vid ett visst område och organiserade just genom rätten (...). Den traditionella föreställningen om staten som en *vilja* är blott och bart en modern form av animism»). Fries is actually paraphrasing what Hägerström claimed in *A Summary of My Philosophy* in *Philosophy and Religion*, cit., p. 73 where his definition of the state as being «a multitude of men who are connected with a certain locality and are organised simply through the law», seems very similar to Hans Kelsen's way of defining the State (See H. Kelsen, *General Theory of Law and State*, Harvard University Press, Cambridge, MA, 1945, Second Part, Chapter 1).

[45] A. Hägerström, *Inquiries*, cit., p. 25; *Är gällande rätt*, cit., p. 179. More than once, Hägerström comes back to the unsoundness of the holistic perspective. See *Till frågan om den objektiva rättens begrepp* on Ferdinand Tönnies and the "communal Will" of the Historical School of Jurisprudence (see *Inquiries*, cit., pp. 62–66), not to mention all the times he labels *Volksgeist*-theories as pure humbug.

[46] A. Hägerström, *Inquiries*, cit., p. 25; *Är gällande rätt*, cit., p. 180: «en överindividuell vilja, som har individerna till organ.» For a presentation of Boström and his relation to Hägerström, see Chapter 1. For a detailed criticism of Bostöm's theories, and their link to Hegel, see *Rätten och staten*, cit., pp. 156–158, 168, 177 ff., where Hägerström described Boström as «the philosophical flag-bearer of conservatives» («de konservativas filosofiske banérförare»).

[47] The example also emerges from Hägerström's correspondence. The anarchist and the monarch first appear in a letter to his fiancée Esther Nyander during spring 1899: The background is the

consequences, the feeling can be explained in the ordinary way»[48] but for the monarch, whose feelings seem to engender legal consequences, no explanation is at hand.

A similar absurdity arises from the second, rather more cited example Hägerström made. Let us consider a king reading a war dispatch. From an organic perspective, that would mean that «the organism of the state reads the dispatch through the monarch's eyes (...): but, from a natural standpoint, from an optical and physiological standpoint, how can one tell the reading made by the monarch as an organ [of the State] from the reading made as a tryout, a game or merely by a private person?»[49] The evergreen paradox that Hägerström emphasized so as to reject the organic viewpoint is the classic doctrine of the king's two bodies,[50] which he came back to more than once.

Even though no one seriously doubts that Alfred Fouillée actually confused the two bodies of the king, Hägerström used the argument to distinguish this gross standpoint from a more subtle version of the organic will. In fact, «there is (...) another way of conceiving the general will (...), as a purely spiritual reality, autonomous in relation to the psycho-physical context, which (...) determines [individuals] to perform certain actions.»[51] This is the case of theories like Gierke's and Jellinek's, which hold the State to be "a corporative unity" (*en korporativ enhet*) that governs through its organs on the grounds of a "unitary will," a form of purpose or final cause which is conceived as "an objectively valid goal" (*ett objektivt gällande ändamål*).[52] While confuting this theory which, to him, seemed extremely similar to a traditional form of iusnaturalistic *bonum commune*, Hägerström's terminology sounds more like Hegel's than a twentieth century analytical philosopher's. The point is made with a rather idealistic wording which proves that he has not yet given up the vocabulary of his youth: «It is maintained that the real unity in a corporation

1898 murder of the Empress Elisabeth, the wife of Franz Joseph by the Italian anarchist Luigi Lucheni. But the example gained new light with the Sarajevo murder in 1914.

[48] A. Hägerström, *Inquiries*, cit., p. 26; *Är gällande rätt*, cit., p. 180. Ordinary here means "in the natural way" (see the original version).

[49] S. Castignone, *Diritto, linguaggio, realtà. Saggi sul realismo giuridico*, Giappichelli, Torino 1995, p. 64.

[50] On this doctrine, see the account of Ernst Hartwig Kantorowicz, *The King's Two Bodies: A Study in Mediaeval Political Theology*, Princeton University Press, Princeton, NJ, 1957. See for instance, in the first volume of *Obligationsbegriff*: «Aber sagt man, hier ist nicht die Frage von den konkreten Personen, die Monarchen sind, sondern von dem Monarchen in abstracto, als einer ideeller Person, die kontinuierlich in den Personen der einzelnen Monarchen wiederkehrt. Die Fiktion ist offenbar. Es sind nicht die einzelnen Katzen, welche Mäuse fangen, sondern der Begriff der Katze, welcher sich bei allen Katzen findet!» (*Obligationsbegriff*, I, cit., p. 13). The argument of the King's two bodies through the cat and mouse image is from the 1921 lectures (*Rätten och staten*, cit., p. 172).

[51] A. Hägerström, *Inquiries*, cit., p. 26; *Är gällande rätt*, cit., p. 180.

[52] On this point, see the explanation in S. Castignone, *Diritto, linguaggio, realtà*, cit., p. 65. For a critique of *bonum commune* as being exceptionally ambiguous, see N. Bobbio, *La politica*, in V. Castronovo, L. Gallino (eds.), *La società contemporanea*, Utet, Torino 1987, I, pp. 567–587; now in M. Bovero (ed.), *Teoria generale della politica*, Einaudi, Torino 1999, pp. 161–183.

is the product of a synthesis, which is no doubt necessary but nonetheless *subjective*; and that there stands over against it the *objective* multiplicity of inter-related wills, whose unity is created only formally by the identity of their purpose.»[53] It is not the first time we find some "family resemblances" between the German philosopher and his Swedish counterpart (Chapter 2). After all, not long before writing the 1916 essay we are dealing with, Hägerström dedicated two semesters to the analysis of Hegel's *Philosophy of Right* and centered particularly on Hegel's determination of the "will."[54] In other words, Hegel's realism suggests yet another version of *die Shöne Seele* so that the argument goes: There is no such thing as a spiritual will governing our desires which makes us jointly accept laws and regulations. Such talk in fact belongs to the tradition of natural law.[55]

### *4.1.4 Is the Will of the State What the Mighty Want?*

If law is neither the "will of the State" nor some form of common will, is it perhaps what the mighty want? Another option, in effect, could be to claim that law can be identified with the will of the *de facto* power holders. This perspective does not seem to present any contradiction insofar as «law can be defined without circularity as a system of imperatives or declarations of intention issuing from certain independently authoritative persons or complexes of persons in a society, who are in a position to carry out the intentions thus expressed because the members of the society regularly obey them.»[56] By identifying the will of the state with that of "the *de facto* supreme personal authority"[57] in society, it is possible to avoid the first

---

[53] A. Hägerström, *Inquiries*, cit., p. 28; *Är gällande rätt*, cit., p. 182.

[54] The lectures can be found under UUB signum *112:9*. It should be noted that Hägerström explicitly calls for a review of Hegel's philosophy of law: «It is about time the distorted conception of Hegel disappeared. One only needs to read his Philosophy of Right» (p. 12: kunde vara på tiden att den förvridna Hegeluppfattningen försvinner. Behöver endast läsa hans rättsfilosofi). Hägerström also comments on the subjective and objective features of the Will (cf. pp. 17, 32). These lectures should be considered as a preparatory study for the will-theory criticism. Anyone familiar with Hegel knows how central will is. It is a bit surprising that no scholar has taken the Hegel lectures into consideration regarding this issue.

[55] A. Hägerström, *Inquiries*, cit., p. 27; *Är gällande rätt*, cit., p. 182: «Suppose that the law is regarded as the content of this will expressed in a certain way. Then, on this interpretation, it merely means that the individuals, in consequence of the common direction of their desires to this end, also jointly accept the regulations and declarations of intention which issue from certain persons who have been authorized to exercise power by this fundamental community of purpose. That is to say, we have come back to the notion of the general will, in the sense of the doctrine of natural law, as the subject of law.»

[56] A. Hägerström, *Inquiries*, cit., p. 29; *Är gällande rätt*, cit., p. 183.

[57] Hägerström's criticism of Bentham's and Austin's account of law being issued by the *de facto* power holders in society was later developed by Karl Olivecrona (See *Law as Fact*, 2 ed., Steven & sons, London 1971; Chapter 3). Hägerström never clarified what should be conceived as "supreme personal authority" (*den faktiska personliga makten i ett samhälle*). We clearly lack a theory or typology of power, such as the one we find in Max Weber for instance. Using

two traps: What the mighty want is not liable to circular argumentation and such a theory presents a notion of "will" compatible with scientific (neuropsychological) explanation. It is not some form of transcendent will, but the desire of people in flesh and blood.

This line of argument also derives from his 1913 essay on social superstition, where Hägerström had already elaborated this idea in connection with the concept of sovereignty. It stood clear to him that sovereignty cannot be «the highest *factual* power. Actually, both king and people appeal to sovereignty in order to keep their power.»[58]

Hägerström's polemical sword is not directly aimed at the traditional theory of the father of political realism, Thrasymachus of Chalcedon – "Justice is nothing other than the advantage of the stronger" (*Rep*. 339*a*) – even though it should be kept in mind.[59] More specifically, his target is John Austin's "analytical jurisprudence" or "naturalistic positivism."[60] Hägerström hints that the traditional argumentation that Plato ascribes to Thrasymachus is not incompatible with the "sociological approach"[61] to valid law. That is the reason why he insisted that Austin's model or any viewpoint holding validity of law to derive from the *de facto* power holders in society, is not grounded in constitutional states but on despotism (*herravälde, Herrschaft*).[62]

---

Weber's terminology, the "authority" in question might be political, ideological or even economic in its nature. Perhaps Hägerström did not hold explanation to be necessary because, in a monarchy like Sweden, it must have appeared obvious to whom the "supreme personal authority" belonged.

[58]A. Hägerström, *Om sociala vidskepelser*, in *Socialfilosofiska uppsatser*, cit., p. 99: «Klart är genast att det inte kan vara fråga blott om den *faktiska* högsta makten. I själva verket åberopa sig furste och folk på suveräniteten just för att kunna upprätthålla sin makt.»

[59]It is not a coincidence that while referring to Holland, Hägerström pointed out that the author of *The Elements of Jurisprudence* (1900) was strongly influenced by one of history's most Thrasymachian philosophers: Thomas Hobbes (See *Inquiries*, cit., p. 29, footnote).

[60]The naming is by Karl Olivecrona, *Rättsordningen*, LiberLäromedel, Lund 1976; I am quoting *Struttura dell'ordinamento giuridico*, Etas, Milano 1972, pp. 82 ff.; see also E. Pattaro, *Il realismo giuridico scandinavo*, cit., p. 88. Hägerström also discussed Salmond, Holland, Merkel, Berolzheimer and the Swedish legal scholar Reuterskiöld. In the 1921 lectures on *The State and Its Forms*, he developed this analysis of Austin (See *Rätten och staten*, cit., pp. 122 ff.) commenting also on E.C. Clark, *History of Roman Private Law*, Cambridge University Press, Cambridge 1914; and H. Rehm, *Allgemeine Staatslehre*, Mohr, Freiburg 1899.

[61]This tendency was labeled "sociological legal positivism" by Olivecrona because of its attempts to found law on sociological factors. See Karl Olivecrona's introduction in *Rätten och viljan*, cit., p. 15.

[62]A. Hägerström, *Inquiries*, cit., p. 35; *Är gällande rätt*, cit., p. 190: «It is pure despotism which serves as a model for the theory under discussion. In particular it has been occasioned by the idea (which is not adequately supported by facts) of the Roman emperor as "*princeps legibus solutus*." It has been assumed that all law must rest upon such a power not subject to any law.»

The motives Hägerström finds against this theory concern, first and foremost, the constitution. «The constitution, insofar as it regulates the activities of those in supreme power and delimits the sphere of their authority, is therefore devoid of all meaning.»[63] This happens because «if, in constitutional states, the supreme authority must base itself on the established constitution in all legislation, it follows that no constitutional rules as such can be described as a mere command or declaration of intention on the part of the possessors of power.»[64] The intellectual puzzle Hägerström presents can readily be reformulated: «Since the law and the sovereign's will have been equated with each other, the following problem arises: If the sovereign ceases to obey the constitution, then the constitution ceases to be valid, which in turn dissolves the existing identity between the will and the law.»[65] From such a perspective, it would be pointless to talk about unconstitutionality.[66]

Moreover, when Hägerström reflected on constitutional states, he did not only intend states that a contemporary political scholar would list under such a name.[67] Constitutional states, in Hägerström's sense, are all those forms of political organisation in which some form of *sécurité juridique*[68] prevails and that can hence be opposed to "pure despotism and mob-rule."[69] This explains why one of the examples cited by Hägerström in connection with constitutional rule is the *lex salica*.[70] In fact, what Hägerström suggests is an idea of the Constitution held separate from Constitutionalism. What he is looking for is not the content of the fundamental law, which may vary from place to place and time to time, but its function in relation to society.

---

[63] A. Hägerström, *Inquiries*, cit., p. 30; *Är gällande rätt*, cit., p. 184.

[64] A. Hägerström, *Inquiries*, cit., p. 34; *Är gällande rätt*, cit., p. 188.

[65] M. Lyles, *A Call...*, cit., p. 338.

[66] «Si dovrà ammettere (...) che, solo che i detentori del potere vogliano in un modo o in un altro non osservare le leggi costituzionali, queste nella misura stessa in cui siano non osservate (*id est* non volute), cessano di avere validità giuridica (...). Non si tratterebbe semplicemente di desuetudine – del fenomeno in ragione del quale una qualsiasi norma del diritto, se a lungo disattesa, cessa di avere rilevanza giuridica; si tratta, invece, di concepire come impossibile la incostituzionalità di qualsivoglia comportamento dei detentori del potere» (E. Pattaro, *Il realismo giuridico scandinavo*, cit., p. 89).

[67] Hägerström specified that his description of constitutional states did not take into account cases in which a constitutional court has been put in place. It is not surprising since he is writing in 1916. See *Inquiries*, cit., p. 34; *Är gällande rätt*, cit., p. 188.

[68] In *Inquiries* the formula is "with security for established rights" (p. 35). I prefer the French formula, used in parallel with *Rechtssicherheit*, since it expresses not only the "certainty of (the rule of) law" in the meaning of the established rights, but also "security" in the political meaning of an established state.

[69] A. Hägerström, *Inquiries*, cit., p. 35; *Är gällande rätt*, cit., p. 190.

[70] «Why should a rule of succession to the throne, which has been in force for generations, in an absolute monarchy, have any less legal significance, e.g., than an electoral law which determines the way in which the highest authority in a parliamentary state is to be constituted?»: A. Hägerström, *Inquiries*, cit., p. 35; *Är gällande rätt*, cit., p. 189.

### *4.1.5 The Will of the State, the Constitution and Some Puzzling Sources of Law*

What exactly is a constitution? By asking this question, Hägerström attempted to show why law is not what the mighty want. However, it remains unclear what precisely Hägerström had in mind when talking of "constitutional states."[71] It has even been suggested that constitution, in Hägerström's phrase, may not even be translated with the German tainted expression "fundamental law."[72] Although I find Sundberg's thesis hard to believe, he is correct in stating that «Haegerstroem's argument against the will-theory gains force first when given basis in a "constitutional state" which enjoys a *developed system of sources of law.*»[73] By linking the definition of constitutional states and the problem of *fontes iuris*, it becomes possible to grasp Hägerström's point.

Overall, the question of the priority – logical and chronological – of "political authority" on fundamental norms, such as constitutional law, is a somewhat false problem: «Must not constitutional law have first gained authority, no matter in what way this may have happened, in constitutionally governed states, in order that a certain person shall have any authority from the legal point of view?»[74] Taking this stance, it becomes clear why Hägerström concentrates on the quite controversial but yet illuminating examples of revolution and *consuetudo contra legem*. These two cases also happen to be text-book examples of *fons extra ordinem*. They certainly do not derive their validity from precedent laws and ordinances, but nevertheless they cannot be reduced to what this or that official wants. Indeed, as problematic

---

[71] Olivecrona in his introduction to *Rätten och viljan* (p. 16), while commenting this passage in the 1916 essay, interestingly enough used three different expressions for constitution: *konstitution*, *grundlagar* (i.e., in the more familiar German language: *Grundgesetz*) and *författning* (i.e. *Verfassung*). On the difference between *Verfassung* and *Konstitution* which developed in the nineteenth century with von Humboldt, Hegel and other German scholars of public law, see E. Böckenförde, *Die deutsche verfassungsgeschichtliche Forschung im 19. Jahrhundert. Zeitbundene Fragestellungen und Leitbilden*, Dunker & Humblot, Berlin 1961. Hägerström also used all three expressions as synonyms, which is reason enough to disagree with Sundberg's thesis (see below).

[72] J. Sundberg, *Haegerstroem and Finland's Struggle to Preserve her Legal Order*, cit., p. 18. While analysing the expression "despotism" that Hägerström contrasted to constitutional states, Sundberg discovered some resemblance with the very ancient "oriental despotism." It should be said that Hägerström used the expression *herravälde*, which is not synonymous with despotism. The Swedish translation of Machiavelli's *Principe*, for instance, used *herravälde* to translate "dominio." In German, the equivalent would be *Herrschaft*. Sunderg failed to investigate what Hägerström may have meant by "mob-rule" (*pöbelvälde*). My feeling is that it is hardly tantamount to democracy, as some form of "gouvernement de la populace." In all likelihood it could be understood as anarchy, or simply lawless mayhem.

[73] J. Sundberg, *Haegerstroem and Finland's Struggle*, cit., p. 25, (italics added).

[74] A. Hägerström, *Inquiries*, cit., p. 31; *Är gällande rätt*, cit., p. 185. On this "inversion" see S. Castignone, *Diritto, linguaggio, realtà*, cit., p. 67. Such argumentation about priority is somewhat of a trademark for Scandinavian realism: See for instance Olivecrona's argumentation about the chicken and the egg in *Rätten och viljan*, cit., p. 21.

sources of law they cannot be credibly explained on the basis of formal legitimacy imputation. However, they need to find an explanation.

The historical example of revolution Hägerström had in mind puzzled many great political and legal scholars in the twentieth century, i.e., the American Revolution.[75] «Now it is indubitable that what became the basis of the newly founded state (...), at the foundation of the American constitution, was not the *de facto* power of such and such persons. It was certain rules for exercising power within the region concerned, rules which derived their importance from being norms for the judges in carrying out the duties of their office. (...) Certainly English law had no longer force in this instance. Nor did the proceedings for founding the constitution rest upon it. But there were other rules for the exercise of power which here *governed men's minds and thereby had* de facto *effectiveness.*»[76] But what were these new rules? And why is it not possible to claim these rules were, in one way or another, what people like Jefferson and Madison wanted?

### *4.1.6 Rules with Factual Power over the Mind*

In Hägerström's reading of the American Revolution one of the key concepts is the *de facto effectiveness* which the constitutional charter enjoyed. More specifically, the new rules had factual power over the mind (*faktisk ideell kraft*):[77] «It was considered that the English crown had lost its rights over the colonies in question through wronging them, and that power had been transferred to its natural basis, the people. There were rules, regarded as belonging to the law of nature, according to which people themselves had certain fundamental rights.»[78] Hägerström is neither interested in testing the truth-value of these ideas, nor is he claiming to have discovered some natural law: He only affirms that the Founding Fathers were led

---

[75] It shall suffice to mention the accounts given by Charles McIllwain and Hannah Arendt on this very topic: Charles H. McIlwain, *Constitutionalism. Ancient and Modern*, Cornell University Press, Ithaca 1940; Hannah Arendt, *On Revolution*, Viking Press, New York 1963. Another historic example Hägerström had in mind without explicitly discussing it concerns what was then going on in Finland, where local civil servants opposed the Czarist incursion in the Finnish legal order, which led to the crisis of the Åbo and Viborg court of appeals when several Finnish judges were imprisoned and brought to Moscow. On this issue, see J. Sundberg, *Haegerstroem and Finland's Struggle*, cit. It must be said that the Finnish-Russian crisis was explicitly mentioned in the 1913 essay *On Social Superstition* and Hägerström systematically came back to this in his letters (see M. Waller, *Människan som få kände*, cit., p. 154).

[76] A. Hägerström, *Inquiries*, cit., p. 32, italics are mine; *Är gällande rätt*, cit., p. 187: «Men det fanns andra regler för maktutövning, som här behärskade sinnena och därigenom hade *faktisk giltighet.*»

[77] The English version states «rules that had actual power in the realm of ideas» but I prefer the original version, since the Aristotelian terms of the English translation easily mislead. Hägerström intended a form of power that Max Weber would have called "ideological." The grip of such an ideological power can be tested *de facto*, just as today we have sociological research on values.

[78] A. Hägerström, *Inquiries*, cit., p. 32; *Är gällande rätt*, cit., p. 187.

by such ideas about how power should be exercised in their design of the 1776 constitution, which, in turn, gave (legal) power to Jefferson, Madison and so forth. But this is quite far from having the Founding Fathers stating in the constitution whatever they fancied. Indeed, Hägerström seemed aware of this difference when he announced, in a tone that might have sounded prophetic in 1916: «The personal owners of power (. . .) may lose all importance after its [the constitution's] coming into force. Suppose, e.g., that a constitution, proclaimed by one of the heads of fortuitously collected armed forces, obtains their immediate support. Then it gains stability by causes which operate universally; e.g., its approximate agreement with the national ideas of justice, the people's need of peace, the lack of organisation among those classes with a rebellious tendency, etc.»[79] This is the fundamental problem with the "sociological" approach to validity: Its overestimation of brute force. «It is thus naïve of sociological jurisprudence to understand law as being merely a function of actual power. In reality it is the power itself that is determined by law.»[80]

But what is a constitution then? It cannot be the dead letter, but must somehow be rooted in life. Yet, «the practice cannot shun the previous norm (. . .) in the sense that there can be no practice without a norm which, by instigating the practice, makes it uniform, constant and ordered.»[81] Hägerström then made the argument for the other example of *fons extra ordinem*: The illegal custom. «If a constitutional custom comes into being, that of course merely means that certain rules for the exercise of power have gradually come to be applied without being embodied in laws. In that way they have certainly become (. . .) [valid] law. The law-creating power of the customs in question shows itself in the fact that regulations issued in accordance with them acquire actual application through the judges. If these rules conflict with the formal constitution, the latter has to that extent ceased to be in force, just as the old order ceased to be positive law in consequence of a revolution.»[82] In other words, an appeal to the formal constitution in absence of the "material constitution"[83] or – in a more English turn of phrase – an appeal to "law in the books" regardless of "law

---

[79] A. Hägerström, *Inquiries*, cit., p. 31; *Är gällande rätt*, cit., p. 185.

[80] M. Lyles, *A Call. . .*, cit., p. 339.

[81] «La prassi non può prescindere da una previa norma (. . .) nel senso che non vi possa essere prassi senza una norma che, ispirandola, la rende uniforme, costante, ordinata»: E. Pattaro, *Il realismo giuridico scandinavo*, cit., p. 97. This is, according to Pattaro, Hägerström's originality: (*Il realismo giuridico scandinavo*, cit., p. 90).

[82] A. Hägerström, *Inquiries*, cit., p. 33; *Är gällande rätt*, cit., p. 187. The translation into "regulations issued in accordance with customs" is not very clear. «According to the order emerging from customs» would perhaps fit better. The original version is more precise: «särskilt framträder ju den ifrågavarande sedens rättsbildande kraft däri, att bestämmelser, givna enligt denna ordning, komma till faktisk användning genom domarna» (*Är gällande rätt*, cit., p. 187). On the difference between customs and orders hereby created, see E. Pattaro, *Il realismo giuridico scandinavo*, cit., pp. 97–98.

[83] The concept comes from the Italian tradition of institutionalism and is defined by Costantino Mortati in *La Costituzione in senso materiale*, Giuffrè, Milano 1940. On this feature in Hägerström, see E. Pattaro, *Il realismo giuridico scandinavo*, cit., p. 98.

in the making"[84] i.e., formal doctrine divorced from constitutional *praxis*, is not an appeal to valid law, but, as Hegel would have put it, to abstract law.[85]

## 4.2 The Will of the State as a *Fictio Iuris*

If the «singularly mystical will»[86] of the state can be none of the aforementioned things, what is it then? To Hägerström, «the idea of a command or a declaration of intention appears as a mere juridical fiction.»[87] And to talk of the will of the state as the "will of the legal order" «is quite obviously a council of desperation.»[88] Even worse, the will of the state is the result of «that universal anthropomorphizing tendency which here, as so often, introduces fictious notions into science.»[89] In actual fact, the force that does operate in society and that jurists evasively call the "will of the state" is formed out of «a medley of all kinds of heterogeneous factors»[90] that cannot be reduced to sheer strength, such as «the habit of the people to obey decrees which present themselves with claims to authority, (...) popular feeling of justice, class-interest, the general inclination to adapt oneself to circumstances, fear of anarchy, lack of organisation among the discontent part of the people, and (...) the inherited custom of observing what is called the law of the land.»[91] By such sociological, historical and psychological factors «law is maintained without any will intervening.»[92] And in turn this means that «the power of the state is, in a word, a system of laws actually enforced.»[93]

---

[84]For this formula, see Carleton Kemp Allen, *Law in the Making*, Clarendon Press, Oxford 1930$^2$.

[85]See *Inquiries*, cit., p. 33; *Är gällande rätt*, cit., p. 188. As known, the first part of Hegel's *Philosophy of Right* is about the phenomenological figure of abstract law (See § 34–104). The terminology used by Hägerström distinguishes *rättssatser*, legal propositions or formal law, from *gällande rätt*, valid or substantive law. What Hegel called abstract law is usually rendered by Hägerström as "unrealised law" (See *Stat och rätt. En rättsfilosofisk undersökning*, vol. I, Almqvist & Wiksell, Uppsala 1904, p. 248) such as natural law for instance.

[86]A. Hägerström, *Inquiries*, cit., p. 38; *Är gällande rätt*, cit., p. 193.

[87]A. Hägerström, *Inquiries*, cit., p. 34; *Är gällande rätt*, cit., p. 189.

[88]A. Hägerström, *Inquiries*, cit., p. 101.

[89]A. Hägerström, *Inquiries*, cit., p. 41; *Är gällande rätt*, cit., p. 195. Later, he would find an even more scornful definition in *Summary of My Philosophy*, cit., p. 73; not to mention *Obligationsbegriff*, I, cit., pp. 14–17: «... dass der Staatswille als der das Recht tragende Wille eine reine Fiktion ist.»

[90]A. Hägerström, *Inquiries*, cit., p. 39; *Är gällande rätt*, cit., p. 193.

[91]A. Hägerström, *Inquiries*, cit., pp. 38–39; *Är gällande rätt*, cit., pp. 193–194.

[92]A. Hägerström, *Inquiries*, cit., p. 39; *Är gällande rätt*, cit., p. 194. It is worthwhile noticing that the factors Hägerström lists are all contributing to what scholars today would call "consensus." Yet it is not clear to what extent it is possible to claim that consensus does not have anything to do with human will. At least, it should be questioned what relation there is between tacit consensus and passive will, as the saying goes «silence implies consent.» Hägerström seems indirectly to conceive will only as an active capacity of Man. Hence, it would be a patent absurdity to claim that anyone could actually want a custom that only survives through absence of active desire to change things.

[93]A. Hägerström, *Inquiries*, cit., p. 54; *Är gällande rätt*, cit., p. 209.

However, if law is not the expression of some will, what is it then? Hägerström did not develop these ideas in the 1916 essay. Yet, it is quite clear that he echoed the *Zeitgeist* by appealing to the notion of interest. At a first glance, the reference goes to the so-called mature Jhering and his *Der Zweck im Recht*, or generally speaking to the *Interessenjurisprudenz* that developed in Germany in reaction to Conceptual Jurisprudence (*Begriffsjurisprudenz*) and focused on the application of law in order to criticise the dogma of completeness. It is not easy to establish what Hägerström really thought of this tendency. He quoted the theory favorably in *Stat och rätt*[94] and he came back to the point in his 1917 lectures on *The Genesis of Ideas of Justice.*[95] Nevertheless, he dismissed Jhering, and especially his idea of rights as legally protected interests, as blunder.[96] In the aforementioned lectures, *Rättsidéers uppkomst*, Hägerström claimed that if rights were to be considered as legally protected interests, the consequence would be that public and private law would be blurred, or actually that «all rights would be public.»[97]

Moreover, as Lyles mentions, «Hägerström's opinion was that the historical investigation of the legislator's intention, which the *Interessenjurisprudenz* advocates, is an aspect of interpretation that ought not to be overemphasized, as it fetters the interpretation and application of law to past interests rather than connecting it to the present.»[98]

Another influential source should be added. Even though we will come back to Hägerström's interest for Marx, it is worth noticing that when it comes to summing up the medley of factors grounding the law, he addressed the topic from a standpoint clearly influenced by Marx: «Law is, at any rate to a large extent, an expression of interests (...). Therefore the question of the intention and the significance of a law is a legitimate one (...). The real state of affairs (...) is that, in the conflict of interests within a society, certain interests come to express themselves in the form of laws.»[99]

---

[94] A. Hägerström, *Stat och rätt*, cit., pp. 30–32.

[95] A. Hägerström, *Rättsidéers uppkomst*, in *Rätten och staten*, cit., pp. 81–82 where he claims that the inadvertence of Jhering's theory may be adjusted. Nevertheless, in *Till frågan om den objektiva rättens begrepp* (Cf. for instance *Inquiries*, cit., p. 75), he continuously harasses the minor representative of the *Interessenjurisprudenz*, Philip Heck.

[96] See A. Hägerström, *The Conception of a Declaration of Intention in the Sphere of Private Law*, in *Inquiries*, cit., pp. 325–328; *Begreppet viljeförklaring på privaträttens område*, in *Rätten och viljan*, cit., pp. 131–135. He insisted on the criticism of Jhering's thesis in *Rättsidéers uppkomst* from 1917; and of rights as legally protected interests in the 1921 lectures *Stat och statsformer*: See *Rätten och staten*, cit., pp. 82–113.

[97] A. Hägerström, *Rätten och staten*, cit., p. 85: «alla rättigheter [blir] offentliga».

[98] M. Lyles, *A Call...*, cit., p. 636. See *On the Question of the Notion of Law*, in *Inquiries*, cit., pp. 74–105.

[99] A. Hägerström, *Inquiries*, cit., p. 41; *Är gällande rätt*, cit., p. 196.

## *4.2.1 Why Is the Will-Theory so Dangerous?*

Once we know the will-theory is only a form of *fictio iuris*, why all this fuss? After all, law abounds with such fictive notions. The will-theory «would still be relatively harmless, if it were not made the basis for deriving ostensibly scientific propositions with juridical content. What happens is that the supposed will of the state is used as a measuring-rod for judging the claims of other sources of law, e.g., custom, the spirit of the law, the nature of the situation, equity etc., to validity, in addition to the law in the strict sense.»[100] The commonplace account of *fons iuris* that legal positivism endorses, «cloaks in a shroud of science both the State-centered ideology and a heritage from natural law of which it is ignorant or unfamiliar.»[101] Hägerström's conclusion is that the will-theory must be rejected since it introduces unscientific elements into legal science and enhances arbitrary rule.[102]

The will-theory favours arbitrary rule through the unclear priority accorded to legislation among the sources of law. In order to show this, Hägerström used the example of a principled judicial ruling: «Suppose that a judge, in spite of everything, uses legal custom, the nature of the situation, and the spirit of the law *contra legem*. He may do this merely implicitly by putting a strained interpretation on the law, or openly in those cases where the application of the law would, because of special circumstances, lead to too great a shock to the sense of justice (...). If now the judgment acquires the force of law, what is the real will of the "organised power of society" (*samfundsmakten*) in this case?»[103] Not only will the rule of law suffer from such an unclear situation, but it will finally lead to an even more complicated state of affairs. Indeed, «the judicial decision, although it is not determined by statute, becomes part of the system of rules current in the society, as a concrete ruling, in spite of the fact that this system is essentially statutory.»[104]

---

[100] A. Hägerström, *Inquiries*, cit., p. 42; *Är gällande rätt*, cit., p. 196.

[101] E. Pattaro, *Il realismo giuridico scandinavo*, cit., p. 113: «nasconde sotto pretesi vesti scientifiche l'ideologia statualistica e un inconsapevole o non riconosciuto retaggio giusnaturalistico.»

[102] See for instance *Inquiries*, cit., p. 54; *Är gällande rätt*, cit., p. 208; *Till frågan om den objektiva rättens begrepp*, cit., pp. 122–126, 162–168; *Inquiries*, cit., pp. 201–205, 217–218; *Obligationsbegriff*, I, cit., pp. 6–7; *Das magistratische Ius in seinem Zusammenhang mit dem römischen Sakralrechte*, in *Minnesskrift utgiven av Juridiska fakulteten i Uppsala 1929 till hågkomst av dess första doktorspromotion 1629*, Lundequistska bokh., Uppsala 1929, pp. 1–5. This issue is also at the heart of the essay *Om svikligt förtigande*, in «Svensk Juristtidning», 1939, 24, pp. 311–335 which was never translated.

[103] A. Hägerström, *Inquiries*, cit., pp. 42–43; *Är gällande rätt*, cit., p. 197. A motive for Hägerström to use the latin formula *contra legem* instead of the Swedish expression *rättsstridighet* is that it refers explicitly only to *lex*, whereas its Scandinavian equivalent refers generally to *Recht*, the legal realm overall. Pattaro is correct in stating that "sources of law" for Hägerström basically means "types of law" or "legal norms" that "make themselves valid" or "keep themselves in force" (*göra sig gällande*). E. Pattaro, *Il realismo giuridico scandinavo*, cit., p. 113. C.D. Broad translated this evocative expression with «putting into force or into effect» (*Inquiries*, cit., p. 73).

[104] A. Hägerström, *Inquiries*, cit., p. 45; *Är gällande rätt*, cit., p. 200.

Moreover, the will-theory is grounded in unscientific legal reasoning. Statutory law (*lagrätten*) is not the will of the organised power in society. In a nutshell, whatever the parliament decides cannot be strictly equivalent to "law in force." The latter seems to be of a rather more complex nature. «If it is just statute law which through being in force, organises society, how can it be an utterance of the will of an organised society? It is as if one should say that a man can decide to create his own existence.»[105] This *ex nihilo* voluntarism is boldly at odds with any empirical explanation[106] of the legal phenomenon and this, in turn, means that «to make the "will" of an organised society into the measuring-rod for estimating the validity of these other sources of law is therefore quite meaningless.»[107] All in all, it brings us back to organicism and natural law.[108]

### *4.2.2 Statutory Law: A Cat Looking Like a King?*

Hägerström's polemic tone against what might seem to be a retrograde defense of traditional and non legislation-bound sources of law need to be explained on the grounds of two important elements: The historical context and the kind of legal system involved. First of all, when Hägerström was working on this essay, one of Sweden's most significant pages in contemporary history was being written. In these very years Swedish political life was largely dominated by strife between King and Parliament which would eventually lead to the establishment of a parliamentary political system.[109] It is telling that 1 year after the publication of *Är gällande rätt*, i.e., in 1917, a coalition of liberals and social democrats lead by Nils Edén and Hjalmar Branting won the election to the second chamber in Parliament. This was to be the end of the conservatory influences of the Crown in political affairs and

---

[105] A. Hägerström, *Inquiries*, cit., p. 44; *Är gällande rätt*, cit., p. 199. Broad's translation is a little different: «It is as if one should say that a man exists in virtue of his own voluntary decisions.» The original is less ambiguous: «det är som att säga att en man beslutar sin egen tillblivelse.»

[106] Hägerström is not interested in formal imputation, but in the causal nexus. This is obvious when he affirms about unapplied statutory law «how can anything which is ineffectual (*verkningslöst*: Without effect, *wirkungslos*) be an expression of the *power* of the State?» (*Inquiries*, cit., p. 48; *Är gällande rätt*, cit., p. 202).

[107] A. Hägerström, *Inquiries*, cit., p. 45; *Är gällande rätt*, cit., p. 200.

[108] See M. Lyles, *A Call...*, cit., p. 384 according to whom the will-theory damages the «time-honored systematic structure of law [... making] any agent of law other than the State redundant (...) for according to this theory the ultimately entitled party to a dispute is the state, not the creditor whose debtor has failed to perform.»

[109] Of course, the traditional Diet of Four Estates had already been abolished in December 1866 and replaced by a bicameral representative system. Although, the latter did not entirely hold back the Crown's interest in the political life of the country. Hägerström referred to this constitutional reform in *Förhållandet mellan staten och rätten* from 1924 (*Rätten och staten*, cit., pp. 233–235).

the ultimate triumph of parliamentary rule. In turn, the victory of the parliamentary system would in time come to entail greater weight attributed to parliamentary established statute law in the system of legal sources.[110]

Secondly, it should not be forgotten that Hägerström's assessment of the sources of law is grounded in the Swedish legal system, which cannot be inventoried among so-called codified countries, like the stricter formal systems of both German and French private law doctrines. His criticism of the priority conferred to statute law by legal science should therefore be viewed on the background of the similarities between the Scandinavian legal tradition and such legal systems as the United Kingdom's or the United States' common law.[111]

However, these contextual features only partly explain Hägerström's standpoint. At a closer look, he elaborated an hermeneutic argument about the sources of law: «Why should the decisions of statutory law concerning customary law be regarded as the only valid expression of the will of the state?»[112] The problem Hägerström pointed out cannot be easily resolved by including an article in the constitution or by adding another statute that determines the priority scale among the sources of law.[113] Indeed, the crux of the problem remains: «Why should just *that* utterance, in and through which the significance of various other utterances is determined, be decisive, if other expressions of the same will occur beside it, in which the forms demanded by the first utterance are not observed?»[114]

The doubts on the priority accorded to statutory law are developed in the first part of the 1917 essay *On the Question of the Notion of Law*. Hägerström recognized the predominance of statute centered legal systems in the Modern Age and admitted that «where statute law predominates, [there is enhanced...] regularity into the judge's performance (...) to the great advantage of legal security.»[115] Nevertheless, his inquiries into the history of law – from the Greek *nomothetes* to the Roman *praetor*, from the Frankish *court de justice* to the English Chancellor – helps him prove that «it is a perversely modernised interpretation of the facts to say that the state

[110] But when Hägerström worked on the essay such an evolution of the political and legal setting must have been hard to foresee and, scientifically speaking, far too risky to predict.

[111] In a vast literature, we can mention for instance B. Gomard, *Civil Law, Common Law and Scandinavian Law*, «Scandinavian Studies in Law», vol. 5, Almqvist & Wiksell, Stockholm 1961, pp. 27–38; S. Blandhol, *The Rhetorical Foundations of Nordic Jurisprudence*, cit., pp. 33–56.

[112] A. Hägerström, *Inquiries*, cit., p. 48; *Är gällande rätt*, cit., p. 202.

[113] For instance, such a priority scale may be found in the Italian legal system where art. 1 of the so-called "pre-leggi" determines the hierarchy of the different sources of law. Hägerström hinted at this issue when claiming that «we do not, of course, deny that the legislator can exert an influence on the application of law through promulgating special rules of interpretation, e.g. legal definitions» (*Inquiries*, cit., p. 96).

[114] A. Hägerström, *Inquiries*, cit., p. 47; *Är gällande rätt*, cit., p. 202. See also E. Pattaro, *Il realismo giuridico scandinavo*, cit., pp. 115–116.

[115] A. Hägerström, *Inquiries*, cit., p. 92.

gives binding force by an "express or tacit law" to "ancient customs".»[116] Indeed, to his eye, a custom «arises from the conditions of human social life through the direct influence which the modes of behaviour of others have on the individual.»[117] There is no *tacitus consensus populi* in this. To fully understand Hägerström's view on this issue it should be borne in mind that he did not consider will in its passive form, but just as an active willing, characterised by "a conative impulse."[118]

## 4.3 Is the Will of the State What Judges Apply? Towards a Sceptical Interpretation Theory

In the 1917 essay Hägerström developed the criticism of the will-theory in connection with the role of judges and of legal doctrine in the application of law (*rättstillämpningen*). Here, Hägerström criticised two of the major theories concerned with legal interpretation. Both the historical investigation into the presumed intentions of the legislator, and the exploration of the "reasonable meaning" or "objective interpretation" searching for the «thought behind the words»[119] are doomed. Not to talk about the flaws of the *ex analogia* principle.[120] The lack of systematization and completeness in the legal system creates embarrassing problems for anyone who wants to establish the original "will of state" by textual research.

[116] A. Hägerström, *Inquiries*, cit., p. 60. Hägerström was always sceptical about applying modern concepts to other epochs in history. See, for instance, *Obligationsbegriff*, I, cit., p. 605: «So wird die Rechtsgeschichte als eine Geschichte der Rechtsideen von Grund aus verfälscht.»

[117] A. Hägerström, *Inquiries*, cit., p. 63. It should be stressed that Hägerström's description of customs echoes what will later be the core of the French sociologist of law, Georges Gurvitch's classic account on "normative facts" (*Le temps présent et l'idée du droit social*, Vrin, Paris 1932, pp. 282 ff.). An interesting coincidence is that Gurvitch would come to develop interests close to those of Hägerström: It shall suffice to mention *La magie et le droit* (1938), Dalloz, Paris 2004.

[118] On these psychological features, C.D. Broad, *Hägerström's Account of Sense of Duty and Certain Allied Experiences*, in «Philosophy», 1960, 26, pp. 99–113; M. Fries, *Zur Interpretation einiger Gedanken in der Philosophie Hägerströms*, in «Theoria», 1951, pp. 39 ff.; L. Fröström, *Hägerströms analys av värdeupplevelsen*, in *Logik, rätt och moral. Filosofiska studier tillägnade Manfred Moritz*, Studentlitt., Lund 1969, pp. 49–60; D. Lang, *Wertung und Erkenntnis. Untersuchungen zu Axel Hägerströms Moraltheologie*, Rodopi, Amsterdam 1981; and especially the account in B. Petersson, *Axel Hägerströms värdeteori*, Filosofiska föreningen vid Uppsala universitet, Uppsala 1973. A brief summary of Petersson's thesis can be found in J. Carlsson, *Statsabsolutismens rättsfilosofi: en studie av Boströms och Hägerströms rättsfilosofi med avseende på deras bakgrund, innehåll och konsekvenser för juridiken*, Juridiska Fakulteten, Lund 2001, http://www.jur.lu.se/Internet/Biblioteket/Examensarbeten.nsf/0/F7C0DCF9A3EB3E98C1256AE60047A1A9/$File/xsmall.pdf?OpenElement, p. 57. It should also be said that Petersson's thesis is already present *in nuce* in the preface by Fries to *Moralpsykologi*, Natur & Kultur, Stockholm 1952, p. 11. See also the example in *Inquiries*, cit., p. 66.

[119] A. Hägerström, *Inquiries*, cit., p. 82.

[120] *Ibid.*, pp. 79–80.

Objective or rational interpretation is compelled to refer to what appears to be reasonable «*in the opinion of the interpreter.*»[121] As far as analogy is concerned, it is obvious that the judge does not apply «the legislator's *concrete intention*» and hence «the will-theory, according to which only the legislator's concrete intention at the time when he makes his decision has legal force, is set aside.»[122]

These theories of interpretation, however, are of great weight for what really goes on in the Courtrooms. It so happens that a judge uses problematic sources of law or even, say, the principle of analogy which is «never a purely logical argument»[123] when «the subsumption under the rule would lead to results which conflict too violently with certain moral, economic or general social values.»[124] But this, in turn, leads to assuming legal theory or doctrine among the sources of law. Indeed, «legal theory must play an important part, since it offers a fundamental systematization.»[125] Hence general rules of interpretation along with prevalent doctrine contributes to «the complex network of factors which operate in the application of law [that therefore is...] "not a science but an art".»[126] This means that prevalent doctrine, concerning «the *correct* principle for interpreting (...) are by no means judicial in the proper sense of the word. They belong to practical philosophy or sociology (...). If, e.g., an author recommends the historically philological method, he maintains at the same time that the legislator's real intentions *should* be made the basis for regulating social relationships (...). Only an investigation of the content of the rules which are *actually* applied in legal practice is genuine jurisprudence.»[127] In a nutshell, the doctrine's *iurisconsulti* seem to confuse *lex lata et lex ferenda*. This says a lot about how Hägerström thought about his own role and that of others.

## 4.4 Some Concluding Remarks About Philosophy of Law

Summing up this first chapter on Hägerström's legal theory, we need to insist on his purpose. Why would a full-blown philosopher, brought up on Plato, Aristotle, Kant and Hegel, ever enter something as distant as law? To answer this question we need to look a little closer at what philosophy meant for Hägerström. His general outlook on philosophy consisted of stressing its critical function. Philosophy can hence be applied to all special sciences. He shared this view with many early twentieth century philosophers (just think of Wittgenstein's classic formulation in

121 *Ibid.*, p. 77.

122 *Ibid.*, p. 80. On the role of the common law judges, cf. *Rätten och staten*, cit., p. 145.

123 *Ibid.*, p. 80.

124 *Ibid.*, p. 81. This hypothesis of a clash between the letter of the law and the expectations of justice echoes Gustav Radbruch's famous formula in *Einführung in die Rechtswissenschaft*. Cf. H. Adachi, *Die Radbruchsche Formel. Eine Untersuchung der Rechtsphilosophie*, Nomos, Baden-Baden 2006.

125 *Ibid.*, p. 84.

126 *Ibid.*, p. 85.

127 *Ibid.*, p. 104.

*Tractatus*).[128] The clearest account of Hägerström's opinion on the role of philosophy is offered by Cassirer: The "α and ω" of Hägerström's philosophy is nothing but «pure conceptual analysis which initially explains the sense of the terms we find in judgments that are usually called "philosophical" (...). Hence Kant's question on the possibility of the existence of metaphysics as science can not only receive a purely negative answer. (...) But he does not only want to fight metaphysics in its explicit form, the way it is adopted in particular philosophical "systems." What he wants to show is that the realm of metaphysics reaches further than is apparent from its historical manifestations (...). The unconscious metaphysics is more dangerous than the one of which we are aware (...). It hides beneath the propositions which, at a first glance, seem to have an innocent, purely empirical character. Hägerström wants to trail metaphysics into its very hidings and he finds it in places where one does not usually search for it. According to him, it is profoundly rooted in common consciousness and therefore develops like a veil of thought not only in philosophy but generally in everything that is called science.»[129]

What a philosopher must do is to go *from sounds to things*.[130] Hägerström applied this general view to different sciences, from law to physics. This has to do with Hägerström's view of the relation between philosophy and special sciences.[131]

---

128 See L. Wittgenstein, *Tractatus logico-philosophicus*, 6.53. See also the previously mentioned quote in n. 69, Chapter 1. While Wittgenstein, in the trenches of World War I was pondering upon this, Hägerström – unaware of the young Austrian – was finishing his jurisprudential essay: The year was 1917. Hägerström's view of philosophy is very similar to Wittgenstein's: As early as in 1897, he declared that the prime achievement of philosophy is to "tear away prejudices" (See M. Waller, *Människan som få kände*, cit., p. 118).

129 E. Cassirer, *Axel Hägerström*, cit., pp. 8–9: «die reinen Begriffsanalyse (...), die zunächst den Sinn der Termini klärt, die uns in den Urteilen begegnen, die wir als »philosophische« zu bezeichnen pflegen (...). Es zeigt sich, dass die Kantische Frage: die Frage, wie Metaphysik als Wissenschaft möglich sei, keine andere als eine rein negative Antwort zuläßt (...). Denn er will die Metaphysik nicht nur in ihrer expliziten Gestalt – in der Gestalt, die sie in den einzelnen philosophischen »Systemen« angenommen hat – bekämpfen. Was er zeigen will, ist, dass die Herrschaft der Metaphysik sich viel weiter erstreckt, als es ihre historischen Erscheinungsformen erkennen lassen (...). Die »unbewußte« Metaphysik ist bedenklicher als die bewusste (...). Sie verstreckt sich unter Aussagen, die auf den erste Blick einen völlig unverdächtigen, einen rein empirischen Charakter zu besitzen scheinen. Hägerström will die Metaphysik bis in ihre letzen Schlupfwinkel verfolgen, und er entdeckt sie an Stellen, wo man sie nicht zu suchen pflegt. Sie wurzelt nach ihm fest im gewöhnlichen Bewusstsein, und sie breitet sich deshalb wie ein Gedankenschleier nicht nur über die Philosophie, sondern überhaupt über alles, was Wissenschaft heißt.» The insistence on conceptual analysis as the essential feature in the methodology of Hägerström is common among scholars. See for instance the preface to S. Castignone, *Diritto, linguaggio, realtà*, cit.

130 The phrase, originally in English, is from *Axel Hägerström, ad vocem*, in R. Schmidt (ed.), *Die Philosophie der Gegenwart in Selbstdarstellungen*, Meiner, Leipzig 1929, vol. VII, p. 158; Eng. trans. in *A Summary of My Philosophy*, cit., p. 74; Swed. trans. in *Filosofi och vetenskap*, cit., p. 180.

131 As we have seen, Hägerström had already in 1910 cleared his mind about the relation of philosophy to science: «In reality, philosophy and the special sciences are dependant upon each other. Empirical research, without philosophy, lacks a comprehensive picture both over itself and over

Since jurisprudence, with the rise of positivism and the decline of natural law, has become a special science, there seems to be no room left for philosophy. One might well adopt a modified version of Alberico Gentili's adage *Silete philosophi in munere alieno...*

The issue found its mature formulation only in the 1935 essay, *The Conception of a Declaration of Intention in the Sphere of Private Law*: «Is Saul among the prophets? Roughly speaking, what has a philosopher to do with jurisprudence? Whilst it was still held that an objective rational law is of importance as the basis for interpreting actual laws, and even more so as something which stands over and above those laws, the line of separation between philosophy and jurisprudence was not hard and fast. But it has now entered into the common consciousness that only positive law can serve as a basis for legal decisions (...). So jurisprudence has become one of the special sciences (...). The representatives of the special sciences long ago issued to philosophers the command "Hands off!" But what induces a certain boldness in the philosophers, notwithstanding this command, is the fact that the notions which are used for describing what is actual may very well be delusive. (...) Ever since Socrates' times it has been held that one of the highest tasks of philosophy is to analyse notions which are in common use in order to attain a real world of scientific concepts, which must be internally coherent (...). Therefore no science which claims to describe reality can evade a conceptual analysis of this kind.»[132]

By evoking the Socratic *technai*-paradigm,[133] Hägerström called for a tough conceptual analysis applied to legal discourse. In his numerous jurisprudential essays, the object to which Hägerström applied his philosophical scalpel is not law, but rather legal science. Pattaro is correct in stating that Hägerström's «task [is] the analytic clarification of the concepts used by legal scholars (thus making philosophy of law [...] a meta-discourse).»[134] One crucial issue that comes back in most of Hägerström's production on law is the problem of whether legal science can

---

the soil on which it works. But philosophy, if thorn asunder from all that is empirical, withers away, because its principles apply precisely to the empirical world. Hence, all disputes concerning principles are in reality grotesque, and depend upon the fact that the adversaries in question are unclear about their own limitations» (*Botanisten och filosofen*, cit., p. 66, trans. di Lyles, *A Call...*, cit., p. 23).

[132] A. Hägerström, *Begreppet viljeförklaring på privat rättens område*, cit., pp. 99–100, I am quoting the Eng. trans. in Lyles, *A Call...*, cit., pp. 294–295. On the relation between special sciences and metaphysics, see the appendix A in *Philosophy and Religion*, pp. 309 ff. and Chapter 6 in *Filosofi och vetenskap*, cit., pp. 162 ff.

[133] For a reconstruction of these features in Socrates and Plato, see M. Kato, *Techne und Philosophie bei Platon*, P. Lang, Frankfurt-New York 1986; H.L. Roochnik, *Socrates' Use of the Techne-Analogy* in H.H. Benson (ed.), *Essays on the Philosophy of Socrates*, Oxford University Press, Oxford 1992; M. Vegetti, *Techne* in *Rep.* (trans. by Vegetti), Bibliopolis, Napoli 1998, pp. 193–208.

[134] E. Pattaro, *Il realismo giuridico scandinavo*, cit., p. 78: «il suo compito è la chiarificazione analitica dei concetti usati dagli scienziati del diritto (talché la filosofia del diritto è [...] un metadiscorso.)»

act as a source of law, implying that the task of philosophy basically consists of analysing «the formal validity of argument and argumentation, but not [in providing] positive law and jurisprudence with material principles of law (...). Finally, the main question regarding Hägerström's critique must therefore be whether or not legal positivism really followed its own scientific program»[135] and the answer is no. Positivism, for Hägerström, is not simply unscientific, but it is an unfinished research program.

The issue is of some importance for scholars. As mentioned, some view Hägerström and Scandinavian realism as a Third way, leading away from both legal positivism and any iusnaturalistic revival, which indeed corresponds to the traditional way of looking at it.[136]

Lately, however, another perspective has been emerging, according to which the difference between Hägerström's "realist" program and legal positivism should not be overrated. Accordingly, Hägerström no longer appears to be the groundbreaking revolutionary or radical avant-garde that most scholars in the twentieth century held him to be. Rather, he is reduced to a positivist, a strict legal scholar calling for scientific purity, basically a pedantic inspector. Marie Sandström, for instance, while commenting on *The Conception of a Declaration of Intention*, concluded that for Hägerström «every attempt to widen the field of legal science beyond the sources of positive law is doomed to failure. The picture of Hägerström as a revolutionary and nit-picker (*gnällspik*) fades away and is replaced with an unglamorous, but yet deeply sympathetic portrayal of a man, whose goal in life seems to have been protecting the good name of science.»[137]

Furthermore, Claes Peterson wondered «is it correct to say that it was Hägerström's intention to politicise legal science (...)? [No], on the contrary, the stake in Hägerström's critique of science is to draw a line of distinction between, on one hand, scientific argumentation and, on the other, discourses of different kind; in law, between legal dogmatics and politics of law (...). The normative side of

---

[135] M. Lyles, *A Call...*, cit., pp. 296–297.

[136] The idea of Scandinavian realism as a third way or as a groundbreaking movement opening positivistic approach to law to non-legal elements, including sociological factors is very common in literature. See, for instance, A. Verdross, *Abenländische Rechtsphilosophie; ihre Grundlagen und Hauptprobleme in geschichtlicher Schau*, Springer Verlag, Wien 1958, pp. 155–161. For a defense of this position, see E. Pattaro, *Il realismo giuridico come alternativa al positivismo giuridico*, in «Rivista Internazionale di Filosofia del Diritto», 1971:1, pp. 61–126.

[137] M. Sandström, *Axel Hägerström och realismen*, in «Juridisk tidskrift», 2001–2002, 4, p. 855: «Varje försök att utvidga rättsvetenskapens område utöver den positiva rättens källor är dömt att misslyckas. Bilden av revolutionären och gnällspiken Hägerström tonar bort och ersätts av en oglamorös, men samtidigt djupt sympatisk beskrivning av en man, vars livsmål synes ha varit att skydda vetenskapens goda namn.» Versions of this paper exist in German: *Axel Hägerström und der Realismus. Ein Beitrag zur Geschichte der Irrtümer*, in K. Modéer, H. Mohnhaupt (eds.), *Europäische Rechtsgeschichte und europäische Integration*, Rönnells, Stockholm 2002; and English, *Law – Fact, Fiction or In Between? Axel Hägerström's Quest for Legal Realism*, in *Perspectives on Jurisprudence*, «Scandinavian Studies in Law», *Essays in Honor of Jes Bjarup*, vol. 48, Jure, Stockholm 2005, pp. 329–340.

law is allocated outside the argumentation of legal science (...). When Hägerström restricted the boundaries of the argumentation in legal science (...), this cannot be considered anything but a quite undramatic expression of an old tradition of legal positivism.»[138]

By referring to the 1939 essay on fraudulent non-disclosure, *Om svikligt förtigande*, Max Lyles – aiming to show Hägerström's «dogmatic positivism»[139] – held that «if one looks at Hägerström's scientific ideal, one easily understands the Uppsala School's or Scandinavian legal realism's following development towards a "realistic" legal theory. Hägerström's incessant demand that legal science should and must use "real" methods (...) might be (mis)understood or (mis)construed as being demands for the inclusion of empirical research (sociological data) into jurisprudence. Hägerström never developed a realistic legal theory.»[140]

What is "revolutionary" in Hägerström is not really his criticism of positivism as such. Indeed, from that viewpoint, he really is a nit-picker. What he actually does is to attack what Francis Bacon called the *idola* of legal science. Just like the author of the *Novum Organum*, Hägerström's philosophy is made out of a *pars destruens* and a *part construens*. The latter corresponds to the pioneering element but it cannot be properly understood without the *tabula rasa* created by the former. More accurately, Hägerström strove to demolish the very four idols described by Bacon and applied to law. He struggled against *idola tribus*, i.e. the inaccuracies due to common errors in Man's mind; against *idola specus*, that causes us to err due to our psychological inclinations, personal habits and education; against *idola fori*, namely errors deriving from the (mis)use of language; and finally he fought against *idola theatri*, the mistakes we make because of the influence of traditional and well-established doctrines.

By destroying the idols, he moved towards his "groundbreaking" *pars construens*. He started to view the legal phenomenon in its relation to other aspects of human experience, aspects that today belong to such different fields as psychology, history, anthropology, sociology and cognitive sciences. This does not mean that legal science is free from epistemological boundaries, but it implies that there

---

[138]C. Peterson, *Uppsalaskolan och politiseringen av rättsvetenskapen*, in «Juridisk tidskrift», 2003–2004, n. 3, pp. 580–585. There is a German version of the paper: *Die Uppsala Schule und die Politisierung der Rechtswissenschaft* in K. Modéer, H. Mohnhaupt (eds.), *Europäische Rechtsgeschichte und europäische Integration*, cit.,: «Är påståendet riktigt att det var Hägerströms avsikt att politisera rättsvetenskapen (...)? [Nej]. Tvärtom går hela Hägerström's vetenskapskritiska gärning ut på att dra en skiljelinje mellan å en sidan vetenskaplig argumentation och å andra sidan andra diskurser, på rättens område mellan rättsdogmatik och rättspolitik (...). Rättens normativa sida hamnar utanför den rättsvetenskapliga argumentationen (...). När Hägerström begränsade den vetenskapliga argumentationens räckvidd (...) kan det inte betraktas som något annat än ett tämligen odramatiskt uttryck för en gammal rättspositivistisk tradition.»

[139]M. Lyles, *A Call...*, cit., p. 654.

[140]*Ibid.*, p. 656. It seems that for Hägerström legal dogmatics (positivism) and other discourses (such as sociology of law, but also psychology, politics, etc.) are grounded on different methodologies, but that does not say whether the different paths of knowledge run parallel or if another *methodos* can be found at the crossroads of science.

is more to life than law. This way of viewing the issue explains his otherwise puzzling legacy: From the "realist" tree sprouts have been growing over the last few decades in the most diverse directions, among which we find most critical legal studies-movements, centering – *et pour cause* – on the deconstruction of the legal realm.[141]

Finally, what should be appreciated is his method. He had learnt the classical lesson of philosophy well: The best way to win a dispute is to demolish it from the inside, by showing the contradictions of the opponent. No wonder he used legal science against itself, just as he used contemporary physics against Einstein. Perhaps, it is not farfetched to say that what Hägerström did was to operate a form of deconstruction. In doing so what must be remembered is that he was well-aware of Aristotle's elenctic proof of the principle of non-contradiction.

---

[141] This legacy is generally assumed to derive only from American legal realism, whereas Sweden would be largely untouched by any such developments. This is partly due to the fact that most of the so-called Critical Legal Studies were born in the U.S. See for instance G. Minda, *Postmodern Legal Movements: Law and Jurisprudence at Century's End*, New York University Press, New York 1995. I am well aware that Hägerström is more commonly associated with (such disparate things as) social engineering, state absolutism and the Swedish welfare model, but the continuous linking of Scandinavian to American realist traditions seems to have created a common ground for legacy appropriation. A quite telling example is offered by Anthony Carty in *Scandinavian Realism and Phenomenological Approaches to Statehood and General Custom in International Law*, «EJIL (European Journal of International Law)», 2003, vol. 14, n. 4, pp. 817–841. On the legacy issue, see C. Faralli, *The Legacy of American Legal Realism*, in P. Wahlgren (ed.), *Perspectives on Jurisprudence*, cit., pp. 75–82.

# Chapter 5
# A Realist Awakening: The Hidden Clockwork of Law

*The requirements of life are stronger than those of logic*[1]

One of the most renowned ideas of Scandinavian realism is law as a mechanism, a sort of clockwork. This thesis is usually said to parallel similar views in other anti-formalistic movements, particularly American realism.[2] Hägerström did speak of

[1] A. Hägerström, *Inquiries into the Nature of Law and Morals*, K. Olivecrona (ed.), translated by C.D. Broad, Almqvist & Wiksell, Uppsala 1953, p. 206. This quote sounds significantly similar to Oliver Wendell Holmes's famous remark «the life of the law has not been logic, it has been experience» that was later considered the "battle cry" of American Legal Realism. See M.J. Horwitz, *The Transformation of American Law. 1870–1960. The Crisis of Legal Orthodoxy*, Oxford University Press, Oxford 1992, p. 187.

[2] While handbooks in legal theory and philosophy of law have posited the two traditions of legal realism as parallel for decades, recent studies add doubt to the resemblance conjecture. It should be said that some doubts were expressed even earlier: W. Friedmann, *Legal Theory*, Columbia University Press, New York 1967, pp. 304–305; H. McCoubrey, N.D. White, *Textbook on Jurisprudence*, Blackstone Press, London 1999[3], p. 178; W. Twinning, *Talk about Realism*, in «New York University Law Review», 1985, vol. 60, p. 361; J.M. Kelly, *A Short History of Western Legal Theory*, Oxford University Press, Oxford 1992, p. 369. Among the recent emphasis on dissimilarity, Marie Sandström declared «in the aftermath, it is clear that it was not wise to bring together Hägerström's "realism" with, for example, Karl Llewellyn's. A closer study of the sources brings about the suspicion that the expression *realism* in Hägerström's writings and its use in the American legal realist-tradition represents a sort of *faux amis* in the History of Philosophy» (my translation); *Axel Hägerström och realismen*, in «Juridisk tidskrift», 2001–2002, 4, p. 849. For Gregory S. Alexander (*Comparing the Two Legal Realisms – American and Scandinavian*, in «The American Journal of Comparative Law», 2002, winter, vol. 50, n. 1, pp. 131–174), the reason why American scholars have failed to distinguish the American and the Scandinavian realist traditions largely depends on the fact that «they are unaware of the second of these» (p. 131), which is not unlikely. But the argument goes further: «Scandinavian legal realism was a version of legal positivism, seeking a strict separation between law and politics and law and morality. American Legal Realism, on the other hand, was an extension of Political Progressivism» (p. 132). See also M. Martin's account of the differences between Scandinavian and American legal realism, *Legal Realism. American and Scandinavian*, Peter Lang, New York 1997; I.M. Jarvad, *The Scandinavian Realism. A Critique. A Defense. A Restatement*, Institut for samfundsøkonomi, Roskilde 1984, pp. 21–26. More generally, B. Leiter, *Naturalizing Jurisprudence: Essays on American Legal Realism and Naturalism in Legal Philosophy*, Oxford University Press, Oxford 2007. An effort to reconcile the two traditions, through the elaboration of an "intersecting" model, is offered by Mauro

P. Mindus, *A Real Mind*, Law and Philosophy Library 87,
DOI 10.1007/978-90-481-2895-2_5, © Springer Science+Business Media B.V. 2009

such a mechanism, a metaphor that Lundstedt also used (*Rechtsmechanismus*). The mature formulation appears in an essay Hägerström published in the year he died, where he suggests that «the legal order is throughout nothing but a social machine in which the cogs are men.»[3] The idea, nonetheless, appears in much earlier work. As far as I know, the first time Hägerström used the image was in the essay *Jesus – Analysis of his Character*, which was written in 1906 but left unpublished until Martin Fries edited it in 1968. Here, the metaphor was fully developed and referred to Christianity and to the social order as such, not only to law: «The Christian religion (...) could be used by the mighty in society, like oil in the machinery of the social order (*samhällsmaskineriet*), so that the wheel would spin without too much of a shrill.»[4]

The most common interpretation has the metaphor standing for "Law as Fact" following Olivecrona's famous work.[5] In this context, it means that the legal order is basically a product of man. Hägerström insisted on this while describing man as a *zóon politikón* in the same essay from 1939. From this perspective, a significant difference between what Hägerström asserted and some basic features of positivism is not immediately obvious: In both cases the legal order is a result of human action. What should be stressed is the reference to the mechanical metaphor as such.[6] The basic elements of the clockwork of law that scholars usually mention are sense of duty and fear of sanction, aside from a generic social instinct.[7]

---

Zamboni in *Law and Politics in Legal Realisms* (Special workshop at the IVR-World Congress in Lund 2003), the abstract can be found in C. Wong (ed.) *Law and Politics – In Search of Balance*, Media-Tryck, Lund 2003, p. 65. For a more elaborate version of the theme, see M. Zamboni, *Legal Realisms and the Dilemma of the Relationship of Contemporary Law and Politics*, in P. Wahlgren (ed.), *Perspectives on Jurisprudence*, «Scandinavian Studies in Law», *Essays in Honor of Jes Bjarup*, n. 48, Jure, Stockholm 2005, pp. 583–606. The notion of "naturalism" has recently offered a way to claim that Scandinavian and American realism alike commit to it: «Even though the Scandinavians were primarily semantic and ontological naturalists, and the Americans were mainly methodological naturalists, two of the Scandinavian (Lundstedt and Ross) also embraced methodological naturalism and some of the Americans (Holmes, Cook and Cohen) also accepted semantic (and, it seems, ontological) naturalism.» (T. Spaak, *Naturalism in Scandinavian and American Realism: Similarities and Differences*, 25-year Anniversary Uppsala-Minnesota Conference 2008, available at SSRN: http://ssrn.com/abstract=1354154).

[3] A. Hägerström, *On Fundamental Problems in Law* (1939), in *Inquiries*, cit., p. 354. See also A. Hägerström, *Rätten och staten. Tre föreläsningar om rätts- och statsfilosofi*, Natur & Kultur, Stockholm 1963, p. 127.

[4] A. Hägerström, *Jesus. En karaktärsanalys*, Natur & Kultur, Stockholm 1968, p. 43: «den kristna religionen (...) kunde användas av de socialt mäktiga såsom olja på samhällsmaskineriet, så att hjulet gick utan att gnissla alltför starkt.»

[5] K. Olivecrona, *Law as Fact*, Steven & sons, London 1971.

[6] On the importance of the mechanical metaphor in the history of political thought, see the account by Otto Mayr, *Authority, Liberty and Automatic Machinery*, John Hopkins Press, Baltimore 1986. In the essay *Straffrättslig principundersökning* (now in *Socialfilosofiska uppsatser*, Bonniers, Stockholm 1939, p. 186) Hägerström fittingly gave the mechanical example of the driver whose will cannot explain how the engine of the car works.

[7] For a brief account, see S. Castignone, *Diritto, linguaggio, realtà. Saggi sul realismo giuridico*, Giappichelli, Torino 1995, p. 89. All these elements are cited in the 1939 essay *On Fundamental Problems in Law*.

Lyles interpreted this "machinery" as «fueled by human emotions, more precisely by fear»[8] while Castignone insisted on the centrality of "the organisation of force."[9] The emphasis on fear should not be overestimated: Hägerström is not Hobbes. He insisted on the plurality of factors contributing to the "social instinct"[10] which characterises Man as a society-building animal (*samhällsbyggande djur*), and specifically mentioned fear of sanction as one factor, but it is neither the first, nor the most important.[11] Historically, the most significant factor seems to be belief in God.[12] In his 1924 lectures on *The Relation between the State and the Law*, he affirmed that «law is not simply a regime of constraint, but it also decides over what is morally right and hence over our souls.»[13] In the aforementioned 1939 article, which appears to be something of an intellectual testament for Hägerström – *On Fundamental Problems in Law* – he stated "belief in divine power" as one of the four basic elements enabling the development of the legal order. I suggest looking a little closer at how this apparatus really works.

In the continuation of his 1917 essay *On the Question of the Notion of Law*, Hägerström developed his phenomenological assessment of command and duty.[14] This assessment is rather important for his moral teachings.[15] Cassirer correctly asserted that «the major task of Hägerström's practical philosophy is to free us from two idols; the theological and political idols. It lays off the absolutism of religion

---

[8] M. Lyles, *A Call for Scientific Purity: Axel Hägerström's Critique of Legal Science*, Rönnells, Stockholm 2006, p. 383.

[9] S. Castignone, *Diritto, linguaggio, realtà*, cit., p. 245. For Castignone, the "binding force of law" cannot be said to have a "factual reference" (in one of the three senses in which Hägerström used the word "reality"), and hence in a way it does not exist. Yet it cannot be understood as mere fiction ("fittizio" in Italian). The binding force of law actually operates in society, it is no fake force.

[10] A. Hägerström, *Socialfilosofiska uppsatser*, cit., p. 233. See also A. Hägerström, *Rätten och staten*, cit., pp. 250 ff. "Social instinct" engenders "legal morality" (*rättsmoral*) or "sense of lawfulness" which is one of the four factors enabling the existence of the legal order.

[11] A. Hägerström, *Socialfil. uppsatser*, cit., p. 236.

[12] A. Hägerström, *Socialfil. uppsatser*, cit., p. 237. This is due to the deification process first of the Monarch then of the State: See *Rätten och staten*, cit., pp. 228 ff.

[13] A. Hägerström, *Rätten och staten*, cit., p. 221: «Rätten är icke blott ett tvångsregemente, utan den bestämmer också över det moraliskt rätta och därmed över våra själar.»

[14] While Olivecrona believed «these pages are, perhaps, the most significant of all» (*Inquiries*, cit., *Introduction*, p. XXVI), Cassirer expressed doubts about the methodology as such. See E. Cassirer, *Axel Hägerström. Eine Studie zur schwedischen Philosophie der Gegenwart*, Göteborgs högskolas årskrift, Göteborg 1939; now in *Gesammelte Werke*, Bd. 21, Meiner, Hamburg 2005, p. 104. For an analysis of these pages in Hägerström, see S. Castignone, *Axel Hägerström e la nozione del dovere*, in «Annali della facoltà di giurisprudenza dell'università di Genova», Giuffrè, Milano 1966, now in Id., *Diritto, linguaggio, realtà*, cit., pp. 223–240; as well as E. Pattaro, *Il realismo giuridico scandinavo*, vol. I: *Axel Hägerström*, Cooperativa libraria universitaria editrice, Bologna 1974, Chapter III; L. Hierro, *El realismo jurídico escandinavo. Una teoría empirista del derecho*, Torres, Valencia 1981, pp. 148 ff. The idea of «conscience of duty» would be addressed later in the essay *Om pliktmedvetandet* published during spring 1934. It should be said that Hägerström came back very often to the idea of duty. For some English texts, see also *Philosophy and Religion*, Allen & Unwin, London 1964, note 47, 48. Comments in C.D. Broad, *Hägerström's Account of Sense of Duty and Certain Allied Experiences*, in «Philosophy», 1951, 26, pp. 99–113.

[15] See Chapter 3.

and of the state.»[16] However, what should be mentioned in order to fully comprehend his legal thought (and why it is commonly labeled realist) is that his perusal of command and duty brings into light the reification process which is at hand in our understanding of law.[17] Hägerström took on his *pars construens* by illustrating the "conglomerate of forces which co-operate in society" and hence added force to law.

His assessment of duty (*plikt*), as a form of state of consciousness akin to that in he who receives a command, has its outcome in the differentiation he established between what we might call (legal) obligation and (moral) duty, i.e. *plikt* in the strict sense of the word.[18] The belief in «duty in the sense in which the common-sense notion of justice understands that word»[19] is transformed into the conviction of «legal norms (...) as valid statements about obligation (...) being demanded by the legal will.» This passage is grounded in the «surrepititous notion of command.»[20] Simply put, the idea of a "sovereign or irresistible will commanding" is being objectified, reified and/or interiorised – through a series of factors contributing to the so-called "suggestive effect" of law (but also of morals, religion etc.) – that leads people to believe in "objectively existing rules" (legal, moral, etc.)[21] i.e.,

[16]E. Cassirer, *Axel Hägerström*, cit., p. 57: «Hägerströms praktische Philosophie sieht ihre Hauptaufgabe darin, uns von beiden Idolen: dem theologischen sowohl wie dem politischen, zu befreien. Sie lehnt den religiösen Absolutismus und den Staatsabsolutismus ab.»

[17]On the term "reification" see note 59 in Chapter 2.

[18]Hägerström certainly recognized «that "obligation" no doubt means [in the legal sphere] something rather different from what it means in the moral sphere.» Yet, as we shall see, «the idea of legal duty is co-ordinated with moral duty» (*Inquiries*, cit., p. 207). On the difference and resemblance between moral and legal duties, see *Stat och rätt. En rättsfilosofisk undersökning*, vol. I, Almqvist & Wiksell, Uppsala 1904, pp. 24 ff. Moral and legal duty is at the heart of the 1904 monograph on the "external obligation" which law gives rise to. The major difference depends on the kind of constraint, internal when moral and external when legal. His assessment is not very convincing, but it certainly facilitates the understanding of his idea of will since he believed external constraint is not directed towards our body, but towards our "will." Legal duty is therefore defined as "external constraint on the will" (*Stat och rätt*, cit., p. 125). On the connection between moral and legal duty, see *Rättsidéers uppkomst* from 1917 in *Rätten och viljan. Två uppsatser av Axel Hägerström*, Gleerup, Lund 1961, pp. 4–9; 12, 15–19.

[19]Here we have a categorical duty, grounded in religion and morals, without regard to positive norms, rather close to the traditional protestant idea of *Plicht*.

[20]A. Hägerström, *Inquiries*, cit., p. 201.

[21]This partly occurs because of improper use of language. In *Moralpsykologi*, Hägerström started to shed light not only on the mental states grounding law and morals, but also on linguistic propositions. He was initially interested in understanding which utterances provoke a specific kind of psychological state. In the unpublished manuscript *Analys av fråge, utrops- och önskesatser* from 1922 (for a comment, see B. Petersson, *Axel Hägerströms värdeteori*, Filosofiska föreningen vid Uppsala universitet, Uppsala 1973) he distinguished utterances in affirmative, imperative, interrogative, wishful forms etc. with the intention of differentiating the linguistic form from the psychological content that the utterance produces. For instance, "if he got well it would be good" is an affirmative proposition, apt to be a judgment, notwithstanding the grammatical form of the verb. It is therefore not tautological to claim that an imperative utterance expresses a command. It might be expressed differently, but we do have a tendency to communicate certain mental states

rules that ought to be obeyed not because they have been *ordered*, but because «the action is regularly thought of as being that which is *right* or *proper* under the actual circumstances.»[22] As we shall see, this viewpoint brings us, as close as possible, to what might be called the definition of "justice" in Hägerström.

In order to understand Hägerström's ill-formulated and at times frankly obscure *pars construens*, it is important to emphasize the idea that «the will-theory is of value scientifically only in so far as it brings to light an idea about law which exerts an actual influence in the life of a community subject to law, though it describes that idea unscientifically in fictional terms.»[23] So what exactly is brought to light with the unscientific will-theory? It shows a conception of the judicial and legal phenomenon that does have importance even though it cannot be said to be correct.[24] What needs to be stressed is that Hägerström's argumentation has an *as if* (*als ob*)-form. This kind of arguing might sound unfamiliar, but it illustrates his way of thinking well. He hardly ever gets into descriptions of what *he* thinks law is. What he usually does is, first, criticise what others think and then tell us what law is *not*.

So the reason why voluntarism-loving legal scholars keep on describing law in terms of will, no matter how implausible it might seem, is because people – legal scholars, jurists, ordinary citizens and politicians alike – *believe* that law works that way. They think of law *as if* it were an expression of will, they look at rights and duties *as if* they were "authoritative imperatives or prescriptions" and – mostly – those who live under a rule of law behave *as if* justice were some form of objective knowledge. What the legal order really is can be described as «a system of rules for the so-called organs of the state – themselves defined in the rules – a system of rules which is actually carried through.»[25] In order to deepen this argumentation, we need to look at one of Hägerström's key concepts: The suggestive effect of law.

---

through specific linguistic structures. That is why we grow up associating some formulations with specific mental states that corroborates the impression that the psychic reaction is "objectively" linked to the presence of the utterance. In the case of a judgment, however, «the very form of the utterance does not guarantee that reality is presupposed» (*Socialfilosofiska uppsatser*, cit., p. 70). Through his studies on Roman Law Hägerström drew the conclusion that what Austin would call performative utterances originally had a literal meaning. The interest for philosophy of language will later be developed by Olivecrona with reference to Austin: *Law as Fact*, cit., pp. 245 ff. Cf. also S. Castignone, *Le parole del fare*, in *Diritto, linguaggio, realtà*, cit., pp. 293–318.

[22] A. Hägerström, *Inquiries*, cit., p. 144. "Right" here means correct and flawless, in the sense of "corresponding to the rule"; "right and proper" as "regelrätt" in Swedish.

[23] A. Hägerström, *Inquiries*, cit., p. 253.

[24] A. Hägerström, *Inquiries*, cit., p. 254.

[25] A. Hägerström, *Appendix B. The Philosophy of Axel Hägerström*, in *Philosophy and Religion*, cit., p. 315; org. ed. *Hägerström, ad vocem*, in A. Ahlberg (ed.), *Filosofiskt lexikon*, Natur & Kultur, Stockholm 1925, p. 91. For an interpretation of this remarkable definition, see M. Lyles, *A Call...*, cit., pp. 347–357; on the definition of norm, see S. Castignone, *Diritto, linguaggio, realtà*, cit., pp. 247 ff.; E. Pattaro, *Il realismo giuridico scandinavo*, cit., pp. 100–101.

## 5.1 The Suggestive Effect: The Fuel of the Mechanism

Since the phenomenological assessment of command and duty leads to the conclusion that «the feeling of duty is akin to the state of feeling in the recipient of a command, in so far as in both cases a conative impulse independent of valuation»[26] is at hand, the following question arises: «What are the factors which in our experience, are capable of producing» such an impulse?[27] According to Hägerström, two experiences help to establish what these factors are. One is the already mentioned command and the other is, unsurprisingly for anyone familiar with Aristotle, "habit." What both have in common is that they parallel a «mental state, corresponding to (...) a feeling of conative impulse in connection with the action.»[28] It is not crucial to corroborate Hägerström's introspective results,[29] but rather to point out the unreflective element common to both experiences.[30]

On one hand, in order to elucidate the "suggestive effect of social power" (i.e., «the power possessed by the idea of an action, to evoke the feeling of conative impulse»[31]), Hägerström asked "what are the authorities with the power of command in a society?" He found a whole horde of them: Parents, teachers, lawmakers, priests and so on. «First we may mention the person who brings one up. The individual in his upbringing is subject to a whole mass of orders (...). Then there are the laws which hold in the society. The individual finds that the performing of some actions and the omission of others are bound up with reactions, in accordance with these laws, which are painful to him. It is no wonder that they come to represent for him an awe-inspiring power which commands and forbids. Then, again, the traditional belief in divine powers, who are held to issue commands and prohibitions,

---

[26] A. Hägerström, *Inquiries*, cit., p. 152; on these features see Chapter 3.

[27] A. Hägerström, *Inquiries*, cit., p. 153.

[28] A. Hägerström, *Inquiries*, cit., p. 154.

[29] While discussing the "conative power" of habit, it almost sounds as a comment on his own smoking habits: He never quit. See M. Waller, *Människan som få kände*, Natur & Kultur, Stockholm 1961, p. 111. On habit, see *Rätten och staten*, cit., p. 246; *Inquiries*, cit., p. 155.

[30] Hägerström also speaks of "reflexes which arise unconditionally" (*Inquiries*, cit., p. 138). In his essay translated with the title *On Fundamental Problems in Law* from 1939, he insisted particularly on this unreflective element: «I allmänhet oberoende av all reflexion» (*Socialfilosofiska uppsatser*, cit., p. 233).

[31] A. Hägerström, *Inquiries*, cit., p. 151. The concept of suggestive effect was first introduced in nineteenth century psychology. It has since been abandoned because of its all-inclusive character which makes it inadequate for scientific purposes. In Hägerström's time, however, it was a hot debate and quite some scholars in psychology believed the suggestive effect could explain some central problems of the human mind. Carla Faralli is right when affirming that Hägerström must be read against the background of the «positivistic studies in anthropology and sociology at the end of the nineteenth century and the beginning of the twentieth century» (*Diritto e magia. Saggio su Axel Hägerström*, Giuffrè, Milano 1982, p. 146). A brief overview of some authors Hägerström was interested in confirms this standpoint: It is enough to mention scholars such as Fustel de Coulanges, Henri Sumner Maine, Albert Post, Wilhelm Wundt, E.B. Tylor, James Frazer, Émile Durkheim, and Robert Henry Codrington.

plays its part.»[32] Considering the impressive amount of orders these authorities submerge us with, perhaps it would be appropriate to amend Hobbes' classic saying: *Auctoritas non potestas facit legem.*

On the other hand, as far as habit is concerned, the systematic repetition of all this "mass of orders" that society pours over the individual favours the "suggestive effect" even more. «Suppose, now, that the individual finds such a combination between the same actions and "must be done" or "may not be done." Then the belief naturally arises that a "must be done" (...) objectively belongs to certain actions (...). The idea of the "right" mode of action, which thus arises, carries unconditionally with it a feeling of conative impulse (...). Since the expression of command is regularly combined with the same ways of acting in all members of the group, it naturally follows that it is regarded as an objective property belonging to that way of acting.»[33] Methodical continuity and overlapping authority, as well as unreflective thinking, are obviously among the foremost efficient factors in the reification of customary rules. As Radbruch once claimed about the English common law, they suppose to apply *logos* where *ethos* really speaks.[34]

What the "suggestive effect" enhances could in fact be described as the makeover of *ethos* into *logos*. Moral conscience with its feeling of categorical duty «acquires for us a theoretical meaning, as pointing out the right action.»[35] The idea of duty stimulated by education – when not by some sheer form of civil religion (in Rousseau's sense) – participates in the reification of the "rightness of the action"[36] so that habit and social constraint *make* people *believe* that there is one *right thing to do,* in the sense of a correct, technically flawless, "objective" way of behaving in a specific situation. All the rest is *wrong*, deviating, improper, unjust.

The suggestive effect, which Hägerström came back to quite often in his work, is finally grounded in education. This is a feature that he laid particular emphasis on. During spring 1917, just after finishing his study *On the Question of the Notion of Law*, every Thursday and Friday he lectured on the topic of "moral psychology."[37]

---

[32] A. Hägerström, *Inquiries*, cit., p. 153.

[33] A. Hägerström, *Inquiries*, cit., pp. 154–155.

[34] G. Radbruch, *Der Geist des englischen Rechts und die anglo-amerikanische Jurisprudenz: Aufsätze* (1946), H. Scholler (ed.), Lit, Berlin 2006.

[35] A. Hägerström, *Inquiries*, cit., p. 157.

[36] See A. Hägerström, *Inquiries*, cit., pp. 167–9.

[37] This illustrates Hägerström's method well: He usually held courses and subsequently wrote the article or book. The motive behind such a method lies in Hägerström's endless and time-craving way of writing down his lectures. As a rule, he lectured in the morning, from 11 a.m. until noon. This timetable gave him the opportunity to write down his daily lecture after getting up at around five or six in the morning. Obviously, this method also explains the huge amount of handwritten lessons we now find in the Uppsala University Library, *Carolina Rediviva*. For a description of Hägerström's method of work, see Thomas Maunter's observations in A. Hägerström, *Moralfilosofins grundläggning*, Almqvist & Wiksell International, Stockholm 1987, p. 73. For his morning habits, see his daughter's account, M. Waller, *Människan som få kände*, cit., p. 14.

In these lectures, published by Martin Fries in 1952, we find a telling description of the role of the so-called "up-bringer" (*Uppfostraren*). While crypto-citing Rousseau, the grand master of modern political and pedagogical thinking, Hägerström affirmed that «the up-bringer (...) must not only try to imprint the way of thinking at hand as the only right (*riktigt*) one, but he must also try to guide the pupil to freely form himself the same conviction. The free conviction, based on one's own experiences, offers a quite particular force of continuity.»[38] *Persuader sans convaincre*, the motto of Rousseau's educator recurs in the mouth of a Swedish *Émile*. Indeed, education is about creating "unconditional reflexes" (*ovillkorliga reflexer*): «The up-bringer (...) leads the attention of the pupil towards specific persons who (...) immediately provoke determinate feelings in the pupil. These feelings recur automatically every time someone with similar characteristics appears.»[39]

## 5.2 The Feedback Effect: The Transmission Axis of the Machine

This reification process might be explained on historical, sociological and phenomenological grounds, which Hägerström also does in various studies. Here, it is interesting to stress the role that the suggestive effect plays in the world of law. I suggest the following scheme in order to shed light on Hägerström's view of the feedback effect that law has on individual identity and the autopoietic process this engenders or, in Hägerström's phrase, «the conglomerate of forces which co-operate within a certain group of men to maintain the legal system.»[40]

**Valid Law** **Suggestive Effect**

**What Legal Experts Do** **Consciousness of Law**

---

[38]The lecture is *Hägerström 112:4* (spring 1917), now in *Moralpsykologi*, Natur & Kultur, Stockholm 1952, p. 66: «Uppfostraren (...) måste (...) ej blott söka inprägla det ifrågakommande föreställningssättet såsom det enda riktiga utan även söka leda eleven mot att själv på egen bas fritt bilda sig samma övertygelse. Den fria övertygelsen, grundad i *egna* erfarenheter, erbjuder en alldeles särskild bibehållelsekraft.»

[39]A. Hägerström, *Moralpsykologi*, cit., p. 56: «Uppfostraren (...) leder elevens uppmärksamhet på enskilda personer, som (...) för eleven omedelbart framkalla vissa känslor. Dessa känslor infinna sig så av sig själva i varje fall, där en person med liknande egenskaper träder fram.» On the figure of the "educator" see also *Rättsidéers uppkomst* from the same year, now in *Rätten och staten*, cit., p. 11.

[40]A. Hägerström, *Inquiries*, cit., p. 250.

The aforementioned suggestive effect, together with the "auto-suggestion"[41] that occurs when people start thinking about such things as command, duty, rights, and obligations, exerts an effect on the so-called Consciousness of law. Consciousness of law (*rättsmedvetandet*) might be described as a form of "commonsense feeling of justice."[42] But there is more to this than meets the eye. "Consciousness of law" is also what Hägerström called "conviction of law" which is defined by its universality.[43] In other words, it is not only what is commonly held to correspond to "justice," i.e., what is just, fair, righteous, and blameless, but it is also «what one takes to be the positive law.»[44] Consciousness of law is both what I hold to be just and what I believe that the law actually states (valid law). That explains why Broad in the translation sometimes went over to calling it «consciousness of right.»[45] It is through this "consciousness"[46] that I grasp what is *right* (just, fair) to do, but also what I have *the* (legal) *right* to, and which ideas about positive law are *right* (correct).

Even though «it might be an exaggeration to suppose that the subjects in general "recognize" the law as the correct expression of what is just (...) in certain respects there is an inclination to do so.»[47] This explains the otherwise puzzling assertion that «if a tyrant's ordinances are astutely adapted to the current ideas of rightness, the people very readily come to regard them as authoritative confirmations of real duties.»[48]

Consciousness of law, along with the suggestive effect underpinning it, can hence be considered as the first two «forces which co-operate within a certain group of men to maintain the legal system.»[49] It should also be mentioned that the

---

[41] A. Hägerström, *Inquiries*, cit., p. 125.

[42] It is often defined this way: A. Hägerström, *Inquiries*, cit., p. 203. This is the meaning that Lundstedt borrows from his friend; Cf. *Superstition and Rationality in Action for Peace? Arguments against Founding a World Peace on the Common Sense of Justice. A Criticism of Jurisprudence*, Longmans, London 1925.

[43] A. Hägerström, *Inquiries*, cit., p. 65.

[44] A. Hägerström, *Inquiries*, cit., p. 65.

[45] See for instance, A. Hägerström, *Inquiries*, cit., p. 144.

[46] "Consciousness" is, on one hand, a conviction, persuasion or belief, and on the other, a *facultas* as more commonly understood. In this second meaning, Hägerström spoke of moral conscience (see *Inquiries*, cit., p. 157). *Rättsmedvetandet* should be compared to the German term *Rechtsbewusstsein*. It should be noted that *Bewusstsein* in Hegel can be understood as intuition (*anschauendes*), sensitive conscience (*sinnliches*) and, of course, reflexive understanding (*vorstellendes*). On these features in Hegel, see the classic account by E. Fleischmann, *La science universelle ou la logique de Hegel*, Plon, Paris 1968. Hägerström was acquainted with the use Hegel made of the word. *Rättsmedvetandet* might be rendered differently in English: The Hegelian term is ordinarily translated with "conscience" which also accounts for the etymology of the word (See, for instance, K. Deligiorgi, *Hegel. New Directions*, Acumen, Chesham 2006). See note 22 in Chapter 2.

[47] A. Hägerström, *Inquiries*, cit., p. 252.

[48] A. Hägerström, *Inquiries*, cit., p. 196.

[49] A. Hägerström, *Inquiries*, cit., p. 250.

Consciousness of law, sequentially, magnifies the suggestive effect. All in all, we now comprehend what Hägerström meant when, summing up his ideas a few years later, he asserted that «the explanation of legal propositions from the consciousness of law is false. For this consciousness is itself controlled by the interest in society.»[50]

In the 1921 lectures *The State and Its Forms* (*Stat och statsformer*), he defined the Consciousness of law as the "representation (*föreställning*) of a rational or natural order that regulates the rights and duties of individuals between themselves and with society." Unmistakably, he stated that «it is clear for everyone to see that the law made by the legislative bodies is by no means defined by the common good, but this law – especially private and criminal law – is determined by the Consciousness of law.»[51]

So «consciousness of law cannot be causative in relation to the rules of law, as the consciousness of law itself is enslaved by the law (...). Accordingly, in all likelihood, whatever the content of the popular consciousness of law is, it cannot constitute an idea of law that is autonomous in relation to the content of positive law.»[52] Hägerström explicitly came to this conclusion in the 1921 lectures: «Consciousness of law does not ground the legal order (...). Consciousness of law, in order to blossom, requires a safely upheld order. (...) Where does contract law come from? Apparently, it originates from the purpose to engender trust and hence bring about the general division of labour and distribution in society. Consciousness of law follows the path of social interests, it believes to be independent, but is only a tardy usher.»[53]

Additionally, consciousness of law weighs on what legal experts do since it influences their worldview. In particular, it helps them to see potential clashes between applying the letter of the law and the common sense of justice.[54] In turn, what legal experts do is obviously dependant on what they believe "valid law" is. «The individual investigator of law feels affected by the legal imperatives under consideration, and (...) they have for him, as for the people in general, an authoritative

[50] A. Hägerström, *Appendix B. The Philosophy of Axel Hägerström*, in *Philosophy and Religion*, cit., p. 316; org. ed. *Hägerström, ad vocem*, in A. Ahlberg (ed.), *Filosofiskt lexikon*, cit., p. 92.

[51] A. Hägerström, *Stat och statsformer* (1921), now in *Rätten och staten*, cit., pp. 187–188: «det ligger ju i öppen dag, att den rätt som blir bestämd av hänsynen till det allmänna bästa, utan denna rätt är, särskilt vad angår privaträtten och straffrätten, bestämd av rättsmedvetandet, dvs. föreställningen om en förnuftig eller naturlig ordning som reglerar individernas rättigheter och skyldigheter i förhållande till varandra och samhället.»

[52] M. Lyles, *A Call...*, cit., p. 367.

[53] A. Hägerström, *Rätten och staten*, cit., pp. 235–237: «Rättsmedvetandet är icke grund till rättsordningen (...). Rättsmedvetandet behöver för att kunna blomstra, en ordning som verkligen tryggt uppehålles. (...) Vari har kontraktsrätten sitt ursprung? Uppenbarligen just i syftet att väcka tillit och därmed möjliggöra den allmänna arbetsfördelningen och omsättningen i samhället. Rättsmedvetandet följer samhällsintresset i spåren, tror sig vara självständigt, men är blott en drabant.»

[54] See A. Hägerström, *Inquiries*, cit., pp. 42–43 and p. 81.

character as announcements of actual duties (. . .). Those who practice jurisprudence come therefore (. . .) to regard [legal imperatives] as valid assertions of what ought to happen.»[55] This is the reason why Hägerström stressed the bounds under which even the common law judge is held. Although he recognized that the common law judge is freer than his continental colleague, «it is certainly not so that the judge could be considered, because of the precedent, as creating law by his own will (. . .). The particular verdicts do not obtain their authority through the will of the judge, but only by being the correct expressions of an original, unwritten common law.»[56]

Valid law, as we have already stressed, brings about the suggestive effect by being, for instance, continuously applied. It also plays a significant role in underpinning the consciousness of law. However, because of the feedback effect, the opposite is also true: «Certain circumstances [such as a well-functioning suggestive effect and a compact consciousness of law] create a tendency to regard positive [here: valid] law in general as the true expression of existing rights and duties.»[57] Again, the way the legal phenomenon as such is represented by legal experts, lawmakers and the like fosters consciousness of law: «The legislative authorities consistently represent law *as if* it consisted in determining the public right of society and the rights of private individuals (. . .). That is to say, rules of law are represented as *correct* pronouncements about rights and duties, *in the sense in which they are understood in the popular notion of justice.*»[58] Lyles so accurately stressed that «the consciousness of law and positive law are codependent.»[59]

Hägerström seemed to think that this process, with its feedback effect, would not come to an end, even if internal contradictions occur. «It may be that the rules which the (. . .) [valid] law puts forward as objective determinations of rights do not satisfy the individual's demands for objectivity.»[60] This is the case, for example, of «an idealistic anarchist or a morally revolutionary innovator.»[61] Therefore, at a first glance, it seems that the entire mechanism would crack down. «But there is one respect in which the [rules of valid law] always fulfill their function, *viz.*, that the demand for their equitable application can be fulfilled by certain persons empowered thereto by the legal system, in particular by judges.»[62] Even in the hypothetical case of a conflict between what the individual regards as just and what legal experts,

---

[55] A. Hägerström, *Inquiries*, cit., p. 205. See also p. 250 where the «juridical way of thinking proves to be akin to rationalistic voluntarism.»

[56] A. Hägerström, *Rätten och staten*, cit., p. 145: «ingalunda är [det] så att domaren skulle betraktas såsom på prejudikatets väg själv genom sin vilja skapade rätt (. . .). De särskilda domsluten ha ej sin auktoritet genom domarens vilja utan blott och bart såsom de riktiga uttrycken för en ursprunglig, oskriven common law.»

[57] A. Hägerström, *Inquiries*, cit., p. 252.

[58] A. Hägerström, *Inquiries*, cit., p. 252, italics added.

[59] M. Lyles, *A Call. . .*, cit., p. 367.

[60] A. Hägerström, *Inquiries*, cit., p. 253.

[61] A. Hägerström, *Inquiries*, cit., p. 128.

[62] A. Hägerström, *Inquiries*, cit., p. 253.

through valid law, hold to be legally binding (and that hence the individual *should* have held to be objectively fair), there is no real clash. The apparent opposition does not account for the fact that both parties would still believe that the controversy could, at least theoretically, be decided on "objective grounds." They would both cry out for a "judge," a *tertès arbitrator*, the impartial Third, or Oddman, able to "recognize" the objective right.[63] To Hägerström there is no doubt that «confidence that the judge in legal controversies does really and truly express the objective norm for rights and duties (...) is still one of the corner stones of social peace.»[64] In the next chapter, we will have the opportunity to explore the communitarian features these assumptions bring about, but for now let's have a look at what triggers the validity of law.

## 5.3 Constitutional Procedures: The Trigger of the Gun?

In the lectures *On the State and Its Forms* from 1921, edited by Olivecrona in 1963, Hägerström dedicated the latter part of his course to the "concept of valid law." This often overlooked section is important in order to clarify some elements of his *pars construens* which were still foggy in the essays from 1916 to 1917.

Law is defined as a set of rules for action (*handlingsregler*) that are enforced (*genomförda*).[65] However, constitutional law is actually formed out of two different types of norms: Rules for normative production and rules for the attribution of competence. «Law is warded as follows: (1) Rules of action, really meant for the highest or higher so-called state authorities (*statsorganen*) (...). These are obviously rules for the lower authorities as well. But as the authorities respond on lower levels, the rules of action increasingly become rules for supervising and punishing transgressions (...); (2) the system provides rules for deciding who is to be considered overall as an authority in the state and for deciding the authorities' power to declare rules included in the system, like for example, rules for deciding who is the judge and rules for deciding his competence.»[66] Despite this specification, in Hägerström's description, constitutional law appears to be a sort of *causa sui*,

---

[63] Hence, in one way, the common sense of justice is always satisfied by the (existence of the) legal order. See S. Castignone, *Diritto, linguaggio, realtà*, cit., p. 240. For the oddman and impartial third, see P.P. Portinaro, *Il terzo. Una figura del politico*, FrancoAngeli, Milano 2006; W.I. Miller, *An Eye for an Eye*, Cambridge University Press, Cambridge 2006.

[64] A. Hägerström, *Inquiries*, cit., p. 89.

[65] A. Hägerström, *Rätten och staten*, cit., pp. 209 ff.

[66] A. Hägerström, *Rätten och staten*, cit., pp. 212–13: «rätten innehåller 1:a) Handlingsregler, egentligen för de högsta eller högre s.k. statsorganen (...). De äro visserligen även regler för lägre statsorgan. Men ju lägre dessa stå, desto mera få handlingsreglerna betydelsen av övervaknings-och straffregler, dvs. de överordnade organen övervaka att det handlas på visst sätt och straffa överträdelser (...). 2:a) systemet innehåller regler för bestämmandet av vem som i varje fall är statsorgan över huvud och för hans kompetens att bestämma till systemet hörande handlingsregler, t.ex. regler för bestämmandet av vem som är domare och regler för domarens kompetens.»

based on purely procedural measures, whereas other branches – or levels – in law, primarily administrative law, seem to be grounded in fear of sanction. The procedural features that Hägerström stressed, such as the majority vote in Parliament or the King's signature, enhance the impression that constitutional law is "grounded in itself"[67] or "functions automatically."[68]

In any case, fear of sanction is not the predominant motive for obeying the law, at least not at the higher levels of the judicial order, while «at the lower levels (...) the means of criminal law always acquire greater weight [than sense of duty].»[69] Whereas the ordinary judge holds himself to valid law because of his sense of duty, i.e., his unwillingness to pass unfair judgments and to be technically speaking a "bad" judge, fear of punishment still hangs like Damocles' sword over the common man: «Just like we need to presuppose that the ordinary judge does not want to pass unfair verdicts because (...) of his sense of duty, we could presuppose that the ordinary citizen would probably not follow the constraints if the sword of law did not hang over him.»[70]

In order to clarify what Hägerström had in mind when speaking of "valid law" and more specifically when claiming that the mechanism of law is grounded in "a conglomerate of forces which co-operate within a certain group of men," some light needs to be shed on the relation between (valid) law and its enforcement.

Enforcement cannot be the key concept for our understanding of law, for several reasons. First of all, the legal order could not survive in event of hypertrophy of litigation: «It is perfectly clear that if private persons in general (...) needed to take legal action and rely on executive bodies, the system as a whole would cease to work.»[71] Yet, enforcement of law is its *conditio sine qua non*: «The mere idea of rights and duties would not be powerful enough to maintain the necessary order (...). The menace of sanctions is therefore needed (...). Without it, even the ideas of rights and duties would lose their psychological grip.»[72] Nevertheless, enforcement is not the *conditio per quam* of the legal order, which should instead be identified in the consciousness of law which interiorises, and reverberates on, valid law. Consciousness of law, or rather its «ideas of rights and duties (...) does not belong

---

[67] A. Hägerström, *Rätten och staten*, cit., p. 210: «det är denna författningsrättens egen uppehållelse.»

[68] A. Hägerström, *Socialfil. uppsatser*, cit., p. 240.

[69] A. Hägerström, *Rätten och staten*, cit., p. 207: «hos de lägre instanserna (...) får dock alltid (...) straffrättsliga medel (...) en större betydelse [än pliktkänslan].»

[70] A. Hägerström, *Rätten och staten*, cit., p. 207: «Lika väl som man får förutsätta att genomssnittsdomaren av (...) pliktkänsla ej vill döma orättvist, lik väl får man icke förutsätta, att den privata genomsnittsmänniskan skulle hålla förbindelser om ej lagens svärd hängde över henne.»

[71] A. Hägerström, *Rätten och staten*, cit., p. 204: «det är alldeles uppenbart att om privata personer i allmänhet (...) måste anställa process och anlita exekutivmyndigheter, så skulle givetvis hela systemet icke kunna fungera.»

[72] A. Hägerström, *Rätten och staten*, cit., p. 205: «den blotta idén om rättigheter och skyldigheter skulle icke vara en tillräcklig kraft för uppehållande av den ordning som är nödvändig (...). Det behövs givetvis också alltid hotet med reaktioner (...). Därförutan skulle till och med idéerna om rättigheter och skyldigheter förlora sin egen psykiska kraft.»

to the rules of law in the way they are applied. But they are significant from a psychological viewpoint since they enable the application of the rules of law.»[73]

Consciousness of law is, on one hand, one of the foremost ingredients of the system and, on the other, it is "enslaved by law."[74] It cannot be truly causative in the spatial-temporal reality Hägerström had in mind. But this leaves the technical functioning of the mechanism unwarranted because if norms – whether those of valid law or those of consciousness of law – are only upshots of "fantasy," how can they cause so much fuss? Hägerström's solution is that «through the harmonisation between the rules of action that the specific authorities in the State enact before themselves, a system of rules of action given in fantasy is enforced on the whole.»[75]

What should be stressed here is the specific nature of norms. From Hägerström's viewpoint, the difference between norms and commands (*befallning*) is essential. He highlighted this point numerous times. Norms, contrarily to commands that necessitate a relation between the commander and the commanded, are what Olivecrona calls "independent imperatives."[76] The concept of "norm" in Hägerström finds an accurate explanation in Pattaro who wrote: «Let me stress here, against so many interpretations of Hägerström's thought, that what is crucial in his conceptual characterisation of norms is the consciousness of an obligation (. . .); also very important is the feeling of duty, because norms as motives of behaviour depend for their efficacy on the intensity of this feeling, but then Hägerström does not identify norms with any attendant feeling of duty or as ideas of norm.»[77] Indeed, a norm acquires a specific «apofantic sentence» which make people believe that there is a *real, objective* duty at hand. So «a norm's efficaciousness on a believing duty-holder will depend on the greater or lesser force of the duty-holder's sense of duty.»[78] As we have seen, the suggestive effect, sense of duty, education and other elements contribute to the upholding of a system of norms "given in fantasy" and it is because of this generalised reverence, «in virtue of such an attitude (. . .that) people are predisposed to obey. (. . .) They will obey on condition that they are told to do so in the proper form.»[79]

---

[73] A. Hägerström, *Rätten och staten*, cit., p. 204: «idéerna om rättigheter och skyldigheter (. . .) hör givetvis icke till rättsreglernas i den form vari de faktiskt genomföras. Det har dock betydelse ur psykologisk synpunkt såsom möjliggörande, att reglerna genomföras.»

[74] A. Hägerström, *Rätten och staten*, cit., p. 253: «Vi äro icke herrar över rätten utan dess slavar.»

[75] A. Hägerström, *Rätten och staten*, cit., p. 217: «Genom samstämmigheten mellan de handlingsregler som de särskilda statsorganen uppställa för sig blir i det hela ett i fantasien givet system av handlingsregler genomfört.» Hägerström insisted on the fact that norms are products of fantasy in his 1924 lectures *Förhållandet mellan rätten och staten*.

[76] K. Olivecrona, *Law as Fact*, cit., pp. 42 ff.

[77] E. Pattaro, *No Law Without Norms*, in *A Treatise of Legal Philosophy and General Jurisprudence*, vol. I, *The Law and the Right*, Springer, Dordrecht-NY 2005, p. 134.

[78] E. Pattaro, *No Law Without Norms*, cit., pp. 135–139.

[79] E. Pattaro, *No Law Without Norms*, cit., pp. 131–144.

The element that ultimately confers "validity" to the law seems to be, at its utmost, procedure. From this perspective, Hägerström appears to be something of a strict, formality-loving proceduralist. «It is so obvious that it needs no notice: A proposal for a new law gains validity through the votes of the majority according to parliamentary regulations, and not through the will of the members of Parliament.»[80] This is why Hägerström pointed out that the vote is valid even if members of Parliament regret their actions.[81] In the 1939 essay *On Fundamental Problems in Law*, he claimed that law is not such because it is promulgated, but because it "obeys the form" (*formenligt*).[82]

Accordingly, the norms of valid law function like a kind of domino game, or more precisely as a shot-gun: «The pulling of the trigger *may* naturally be caused by the will of the shooter (...). But this is totally irrelevant for the causal chain. (...) By pulling the trigger, the explosive is set off, and this in sequence ignites the gunpowder which sets the bullet in motion. This is exactly equivalent to the impact of a vote on the validity of a proposed bill.»[83] To vote in parliament is hence like pulling the trigger of law's powerful machinery, the ultimate explanation for the complicated web of factors enhancing validity of law. Independently of what the members of Parliament might wish in their hearts, the vote alone sets the "machine" in motion. «The consequence of the bill's passing is *that* they [who live in the state] are immediately and passively affected and feel committed to obedience; *that* those gaining benefices through the bill experience a particular sense of power (...); *that* the judges feel bound to judge in accordance with it; *that* the State officials feel obliged to enforce it.»[84]

To conclude this overview of Hägerström's reading, we might say that if law is a mechanism, it is no rusty tool, but rather *une pièce de haute horlogerie*. This technological refinement is the outcome of millennia of human coexistence, an instrument that can tackle the fine details of our social universe with its superficial accouterments, its unceasingly moving parts, and necessary arrangements. In order to recap, the following should be kept in mind: Law is a mechanism in which men are cogs.

---

[80] A. Hägerström, *Rätten och staten*, cit., p. 132: «Det är ju så uppenbart att det icke kunde behöva särskilt påpekas, nämligen att ett lagförslag som erhållit pluralitet i omröstningen enligt parlamentsreglerna gäller på grund av detta förhållande, på intet sätt på grund av parlamentsledamöternas vilja.»

[81] A. Hägerström, *Rätten och staten*, cit., p. 132.

[82] A. Hägerström, *Socialfil. uppsatser*, cit., p. 239.

[83] A. Hägerström, *Rätten och staten*, cit., p. 133: «Trycket på hanen åter *kan* naturligtvis ha sin orsak i den skjutandes vilja (...). Men detta förhållande är för orsaksserien fullkomligt likgiltigt. (...) Trycket på hanen bringar tändsatsen att explodera, denna explosion återigen föranleder krutets explosion, och denna sätter kulan igång. Alldeles motsvarande förhållande äger rum beträffande omröstningens betydelse för lagförslagets kraft.»

[84] A. Hägerström, *Rätten och staten*, cit., p. 134: «Följden blir den *att* de [som underordnas staten] genom det antagna lagförslaget omedelbart passivt träffade känna sig förpliktigade till efterlevnad; *att* omvänt alla som därigenom få fördelar erfara en särskild kraftkänsla (...); *att* domarna känner sig bundna att döma i enlighet med det antagna lagförslaget; *att* ämbetsmännen (...) känna sig bundna att efterleva den ...»

The trigger of the modern day device is constitutional norms. The four basic elements that enable the existence of the legal order and that explain its historical development are (1) the unreflective social instinct, that by becoming consolidated gives birth to a community; then, historically its (2) belief in divine power, which in turn paves the way for a (3) "legal morality" (*rättsmoral*) or "sense of lawfulness" that brings on the (4) fear of punishment and constraint as its outcome. None of these factors are by themselves sufficient motives for explaining why men obey the law. They need to be integrated with two stimuli that bestow, so to say, the engine capacity of the machine: (1) the pedagogic suggestion and (2) the feedback effect of law that guarantees the complex web of influences which continuously shape both consciousness of law and valid law, through the choices and actions of authorities in the State.[85]

## 5.4 The Theory of Justice

We still need to consider an essential, yet overlooked question in Hägerström's philosophy of law: His theory of justice. As we have seen,[86] Hägerström assumed a non-cognitivist standpoint in morals accordingly with his theory of knowledge (Chapter 3). This fact alone has led many scholars to conclude that there is no such thing as justice for Hägerström. Or rather, that Hägerström has no theory of justice and, properly speaking, cannot have one. However, since justice is one of Hägerström's main themes, it is crucial to investigate more closely whether the traditional assumption is plausible. What is puzzling about the traditional thesis is that, consequently, one must presume that Hägerström spent over three decades and thousands of pages pondering on something he did not think existed.

A good starting point for examining what I would like to call his "theory of justice" is the Greek vocabulary Hägerström was well acquainted with. Since his very first studies, he had become familiar with Greek thought and Aristotle in particular.[87] He often quoted the Greek originals as terms of art.[88]

The Greek semantic area for "justice" is constituted by three concepts, or meanings of "just" (*tò díkaion*), distinguishable according to their opposite: *adikía*,

---

[85] A complete listing and classification can be found in the article *On Fundamental Problems of Law*, in *Inquiries*, cit., pp. 233–236: This arrangement was one of the last things Hägerström did before dying.

[86] See Chapter 3.

[87] Hägerström's account of Aristotle's *Eth. Nic.* V should be mentioned. See A. Hägerström, *Aristoteles etiska grundtankar och deras teoretiska förutsättningar*, Berling, Uppsala 1893, pp. 191 ff.

[88] See for instance his comment on "kalokagathia" in A. Hägerström, *Moralpsykologi*, cit., pp. 21 ff.

*paranomía* and *pleonexía*.[89] Justice can thus be a predicate of three different kinds of behaviour:

(1) Behaving in a warranted way, that has no technical flaw, that is adequate for achieving a given purpose in the world. Here we have *díkaion* as roughly equivalent to *orthón*. In today's English, the idea is expressed in terms of right/wrong that can be replaced with true/false. In German, as well as in Swedish, there is a word for this adequateness: *Richtigkeit, riktighet*. Any question about *riktighet* can be answered with yes or no, i.e., true (*riktigt*) or false (*oriktigt*).
(2) Behaving in a lawful way, that does not break a rule in a given set of norms, that is approvable, generically worthy of being chosen for the sake of the game. Here, the opposite of *díkaion* is *paranomía*. It cannot be said to be true/false but only right/wrong in the sense of lawful/unlawful. In Swedish, this idea can be expressed with different terms: Following a moral set of rules, one acts *righteously* (*rättfärdigt*); following laws and regulations, one acts *lawfully* (*rättsenligt*).
(3) Behaving in a fair way, that is not excessive, partial, discriminatory. Here, *díkaion* is no longer a question of *orthón*: The opposite of *dikaiosýne* (justice) is clearly *pleonexía*, the iniquitous, undue, unfair chosen by a will which overflows, brims over, does not stand within its right proportions (*recta proportio*). English knows the autochthon and hardly translatable word "fair." In Swedish, the words for justice and injustice in general, *rättvisa/orättvisa* stand precisely for the conceptual couple *dikaiosýne/pleonexía* which means that justice here, to a certain extent, can be paralleled to the latin phrase *iustitia equatix*. The relational value of this latter "justice" can be determined in various ways but it is not in itself indeterminate. Most traditional definitions of justice are based on this meaning, as for instance in Ulpiano's formula *suum cuique tribuere*.

Hägerström, in his work on law and justice, as well as in his moral writings, used (and confused) the first two meanings of justice. I do not know any case where he clearly referred to the third meaning.[90] This implies that, on one hand, an action is the "right" one, because it is lawful, i.e., it follows from a set of rules (moral, legal...) that is in use, that people recognize as valid, that they hold to be true, or that in any other way "has factual power over men's minds" (*tò díkaion* as the opposite of *paranomía*). On the other hand, an action is the "right" one, because it is the adequate, correct, flawless way of behaving in order to achieve a certain goal; in a word, it is *riktigt* (*díkaion* as *orthón*). These two meanings should be kept analytically distinct even though they usually occur indistinctively in Hägerström's

---

[89] I am greatly indebted to Michelangelo Bovero who deepened, articulated and illustrated these three positions in reference to classic Greek literature and Aristotle's ethics during his spring lectures 2006 entitled *Che cos'è la giustizia?* We are waiting for an edited version of the thesis.

[90] The only clue in this direction might be the "law of justice itself" (*rättslagen*) that he mentions from time to time. But he never explained what he meant hereby. He just stated that this "law of justice" has a "divine" character. See for instance, *Socialfilosofiska uppsatser*, cit., p. 250.

jargon. It is important because it allows us to understand the reification process at hand in both law and morals.

This blurring of genres can be found throughout Hägerström's entire production. For instance, he assumed that *rätt* (right, just) means *riktig* (correct, adequate) ever since his first study in law. As early as the 1904 monograph *Stat och rätt*, he used *rätt* as an equivalent of "matching a technical rule" or "*orthón*" (*riktig*). Significantly, he declared that «philosophy of law seeks to render law righteous (*rättfärdiga rätten*) as a more or less adequate (*riktig*) mean for important purposes.»[91] In the same study, he defined duty in terms that echo the equivalence of *rätt* and *riktig*: «In any given case, I am conscious that I ought to act in a certain way, *because* that action is the right one (*riktig*) in relation to an unconditional good.»[92]

Furthermore, the idea that justice or right corresponds to a technicality or a question of "straight" reasoning is confirmed by the fact that Hägerström contrasted the feeling of justice to love. In his study on *Jesus* from 1906, Hägerström declared: «He was not characterised by any abstract feeling of justice, but rather by love. And love is incommensurable to the feeling of justice and has a completely different, personal color to it».[93] When analysing the "feeling of justice" (*rättskänslan*) in the same study, he claimed that «in this feeling it appears to be a duty to treat other persons in a certain way. This should be done regardless of my personal feelings, *only because it is right (riktigt) to do so following from an impartial rule above the persons.*»[94]

In another significant passage, in the section of *Moralpsykologi* entitled "truth and validity, reality and value" (*Sanning och giltighet, verklighet och värde*), Hägerström made clear what "normative reasoning" meant to him. By equaling subsumption in normative (moral or legal) reasoning to "right" in the first technical sense, he described the activity of judges as that of «the person who, in a certain case, passes a judgment technically well (*sakligt riktigt*) and consequently in a way that each and every person, confronted with such a case, *must* judge, if he wants to judge *well (riktigt)*.»[95] This passage should be confronted with the original text of the 1911 inaugural lecture *Om moraliska föreställningars sanning*, edited by Thomas Mautner in *Moralfilosofins grundläggning*, where Hägerström claimed that

---

[91] A. Hägerström, *Stat och rätt*, cit., p. 18, see also the explicit synonymical relation established on p. 102.

[92] A. Hägerström, *Stat och rätt*, cit., p. 50: «jag är i hvarje särskilt fall medveten om att jag bör handla på ett visst sätt, *därför* att handlandet är riktigt i förhållandet till något obetingat gott.»

[93] A. Hägerström, *Jesus. En karaktärsanalys*, cit., p. 46: «det var inte någon abstrakt rättskänsla som var utmärkande för honom, utan det var just kärleken. Och den är inkommensurabel med rättskänslan och har en helt annan, rent personlig färg.»

[94] A. Hägerström, *Jesus. En karaktärsanalys*, cit., p. 68: «i denna känsla framträder det som skyldighet att behandla andra personer på ett visst sätt. Detta skall ske utan hänsyn till mina personliga känslor, endast därför att det enligt en över personerna upphöjd, alltså opartisk regel är riktigt att så förfara.»

[95] A. Hägerström, *Moralpykologi*, cit., p. 66: «den som så dömer i ett visst fall, han dömer sakligt riktigt och därmed på så sätt som var och en i ett sådant fall *måste* döma, såvitt han skall döma riktigt.»

moral communication teaches us how to see the correct (*riktigt*) adjustment between means and end.

Yet another, particularly telling example of Hägerström's use of *rätt* in terms of *riktighet* can be found in the 1920 essay *Naturrätt i straffrättsvetenskapen,* where the standard formula of "unfair law" – echoing Equinas traditional *lex iniusta non est lex, est corruptio legis* – becomes "inadequate, inappropriate law" (*olämplig lag*).[96]

The quotations may be multiplied, but what is important here is to emphasize that, for a non-cognitivist like Hägerström, a law cannot be simply *iniusta* in the traditional meaning without specification. So it is not surprising that he needs to find another formulation. But, strictly speaking, what does one mean when one describes a law as "inadequate"? Inappropriate for *what*? As we shall see, law and jurisprudence, just like morals, can, in a certain sense, be judged (il)legitimate, (un)just on the basis of certain parameters, like for instance "social usefulness" and evolutionary aptitude or resilience of a social order (Chapter 6). This view unquestionably clashes with the traditional picture of the judgment-detached non-cognitivist scholar. It should therefore be viewed against the background of his philosophy of history and his political thought, issues that will be addressed in the next chapter.

For now, what should be underlined is that Hägerström had a specific theory of justice. To my knowledge, the most lucid analysis of "justice" in Hägerström is given by Pattaro who, for the purpose, proposed the quasi-neologism "justness" (*giustezza*) to describe Hägerström's position. Pattaro noted that *rätt* corresponds to *riktig,* i.e., the Swedish equivalent of *richtig* in German. This means that «right or just is intended more in the meaning of "rightness" (*rätthet*), in a way close to "correctness" (*riktighet*), than in the meaning of "justice" (*rättvisa, rättfärdighet*).»[97] According to the Italian scholar, this slippery connotation-gliding is due to the fact that «Hägerström, *because of that unconcerned disinterest in making himself clear*, fails to convey attention towards the difference between "justice" (*rättvisa* or *rättfärdighet*) and "justness" or "correctness" (*rätthet, riktighet*).»[98] What Pattaro

---

[96] A. Hägerström, *Naturrätt i straffrättsvetenskapen?*, in «Svensk Juristtidning», 1920:5, p. 333. In the 1921 lectures *Stat och statsformer*, he explicitly used the expression "regelenligt" (lawful, that follows a rule): See *Rätten och staten*, cit., p. 231.

[97] E. Pattaro, *Il realismo giuridico scandinavo*, cit., p. 160: «"giusto" si intenda, piuttosto nel significato di "giustezza" (*rätthet*), vicino appunto a quello di "correttezza" (*riktighet*) che non nel significato di "giustizia" (in svedese *rättvisa, rättfärdighet*).»

[98] E. Pattaro, *Il realismo giuridico scandinavo*, cit., p. 243: «anche se il Hägerström, per *quella sua certa trascuraggine di rendersi chiaro* al lettore, omette di richiamarvi l'attenzione – la differenza tra "giustizia" (*rättvisa* o *rättfärdighet*) e "giustezza" o "correttezza" (*rätthet, riktighet*)» (italics added). Since "just" can only be intended in terms of "justness" or "correctness," Pattaro concluded that, "just" does not mean "adequate for avoiding a sanction," "adequate for ensuring an interest," "an objective value," or "maximum pleasure." Furthermore, "just" would not mean "conform to a will" or "conform to autonomy" (See E. Pattaro, *Il realismo giuridico scandinavo*, cit., p. 160). He argues that any such equivalency must be grounded on an illegitimate reduction of justness to a mere question of a means to an end, whereas justness does not imply any «instrumental conception of justice (...) in view of an aim.» (*Ibidem*: «una concezione strumentale della giustezza (...) in vista dello scopo.») In effect, Hägerström did not have in mind any prudential calculus when discussing justice, but Pattaro failed to appreciate that justice is still a question of "adequateness

laid particular emphasis on is that «the idea of justness or correctness of a behaviour is connected with the idea that it is "fair" (*rättvis*) that the one who acts incorrectly (*orätt*) or who simply omits to act correctly (*rätt*) shall be obliged to correspond an equivalent service (*ekvivalent prestation*) to the correct behaviour omitted.»[99]

However these considerations lead us straight back to the puzzle of justice as a balance of equivalence between actions and subjects, i.e., the very essence of the *suum cuique tribuere*-principle. How can it be "just" that the person who has not upheld the "correct behaviour" be forced to perform an *equivalent service*? In this view, consequently, it is "correct" – in the sense of lawful, compatible with valid law – to claim that only the person who has not acted "correctly" (lawfully) can be liable to punishment in the realm of criminal law. This means that it is wrong to claim the opposite: No punishment can be "correctly" inflicted on those who act according to the law. Turning the problem the other way around: If justice does not exist, but only "justness" (*riktighet*), how can it be unfair to condemn an innocent party? Hägerström's own theory of justice brought him to this very dilemma.[100] It is relevant for understanding his conception of guilt and punishment, a central issue for any philosopher of law.

These paradoxical features in his theory of justice enable us to grasp why most of his mature studies on law focus on the issue of illegality, culpa, legitimation of liability and punishment. The very notion of illegality – the pivot of criminal and tort law, the core of "modern" prohibiting law[101] – is a central hub in Hägerström's legal thought. Commenting on the 1939 essay *En straffrättslig principundersökning*, Lyles highlighted the link between "justice" and the problem of justification of punishment: «Western penal theory defines punishment as being just, if and only if, the convicted person objectively deserves to be punished (. . .). But the delinquent is only perceived as being guilty if his actions have violated the absolutely binding *law of justice itself* (*rättslagen*).»[102] As we shall now see, the "doctrine of illegality" is the problematic outcome of Hägerström's reading of justice as such.

---

to an aim." Let alone the fact that adequateness does not necessarily imply prudential calculus; it might as well be intended as a generic form of *Zweckrationalität*, or even as a matter of *List der Vernunft*. Justice as adequateness in Hägerström should be understood on the basis of his evolutionary philosophy of history.

[99]E. Pattaro, *Il realismo giuridico scandinavo*, cit., pp. 243–244: «con l'idea di giustezza o correttezza di un comportamento è connessa l'idea che sia giusto (*rättvis*) che colui che tiene un comportamento scorretto (*orätt*) o che semplicemente ometta di tenere il comportamento corretto (*rätt*) sia costretto ad eseguire una prestazione equivalente (*ekvivalent prestation*) al comportamento corretto non tenuto.»

[100]Castignone saw the risk while commenting on Lundstedt: *Diritto, linguaggio, realtà*, cit., p. 340. Cf. also the comment on the Dreyfus affair in *Naturrätt i straffrättsvetenskapen?*, cit., p. 335.

[101]Hägerström developed this viewpoint as early as his PhD dissertation on Aristotle from 1893 where he claimed that «law in Aristotle does not correspond to a legal norm in the modern meaning. The former is essentially commanding (. . .), the latter essentially prohibiting»; *Aristoteles etiska grundtankar*, cit., pp. 191–192.

[102]M. Lyles, *A Call. . .*, cit., p. 501.

Finally, Hägerström's way of looking at justice in terms of *riktighet*, adequateness, also suggests how his name became, especially in Sweden, associated with "social engineering," teleological interpretation of statute law, and "state absolutism." This issue will be addressed in the next chapter where I propose a better understanding of Hägerström's philosophy of history to fully grasp the point.

## 5.5 The Critique of Legal Concepts

Once Hägerström realised the legal order actually functions like a well-oiled engine, a whole sea of corollaries appeared to him. Indeed, if Scandinavian realism is well-known for its critique of legal concepts, this must, to a great extent, be accredited to its founder. It can be argued that Hägerström, in his key essays from 1916 to 1917, at the age of forty-nine, established the basic features of his philosophy of law. Most of his later production on legal topics are specifications of this theory.[103]

Ever since his interest in the "external obligation of law" in *Stat och rätt* from 1904, he had got his eye on the problem of legality and illegality, lawfulness and unlawfulness, which he comes back to in the 1920 essay *Naturrätt i straffrättsvetenskapen?*, where the *Verplichtetsein* of legal science is labeled "magic through words" (*ordmagi*)[104] and therefore the duty to obey the state (*underordningsplikten*) must be founded anew.[105] He then focused on criminal and tort law since these areas pivot around the issue of (il)legality, holding a series of lectures during spring 1921, entitled *History and Critique of the Theories of Criminal Law* (*Straffrättsteoriernas historia och kritik*). A few years later, in 1925, he highlighted the problem of the "unlawful will" (*rättsstridig vilja*) in *Kriminalpsykologiska reflexioner*, where he analysed, from a psychological perspective, the case of the Raskolnikov look-alike convict, Winge, along with two other "criminal minds." From this investigation he concluded that consciousness of law is «the advocate of the most dreadful crimes.»[106]

This, in turn, led him to examine the vestiges of natural law-inspired concepts in positive law and contemporary legal science which he found abounds with "mystic elaborations." In 1933, he held a series of lectures on iusnaturalistic elements in

[103] I am not arguing about *Obligationsbegriff*. Indeed, his copious work on Roman Law, along with some other studies on the history of law should be viewed against the background of his genealogic methodology which leads him to search for the genesis and origin of fundamental legal concepts, like *obligatio* but also *dike*. On the concept of *dike*, see the lecture held at the Association for Classical Philology in Uppsala October 12th, 1928, under signum UUB *115:12*. We will return to his historical studies in Chapter 7. From his historical studies, I would mention the essay Das *magistratischen Ius* from 1929, his unpublished paper on *Forngrekisk rätt* from 1933, to a certain extent also *Nehrman-Ehrenstråles uppfattning* from 1934 and the article *Om handslagets ursprungliga innebörd* from 1938. A taste of what would come later can be found in his 1917 lectures *Rättsidéers uppkomst*.

[104] A. Hägerström, *Naturrätt i straffrättsvetenskapen*, cit., p. 323.

[105] A. Hägerström, *Rätten och staten*, cit., p. 176 on this duty.

[106] A. Hägerström, *Kriminalpsykologiska reflexioner*, now in *Socialfil. uppsatser*, cit., p. 194.

criminal law (*Naturrätt i straffrättsvetenskapen*) and in 1934 he devoted a lengthy article to the subject for the bicentenary of the Swedish Code (Sveriges Rikes Lag).[107] In the study *The Conception of a Declaration of Intention in the Sphere of Private Law* [108] from 1935, concerning what Germans refer to as *Willenserklärung*, he discovered that if the will-theory does not function in Public or Constitutional Law, it has no better ground in Private Law. In 1939, soon before dying, he finally issued two articles in the prestigious Swedish Law Journal on the doctrine of illegality: *En straffrättslig principundersökning*[109] and the almost forgotten *Om svikligt förtigande såsom straffbart efter 22:1 S.L.*[110]

## 5.6 The Doctrine of Illegality: A Judicial Theology?

In Leipzig, the town of publishing houses where Hägerström had some of his work published,[111] a German legal scholar who would come to be one of the great names of the twentieth century – Carl Schmitt – released the very first version of *Politische Theologie. Vier Kapitel zur Lehre der Souveränität* in March 1922. Even though his Swedish colleague tried to stay in touch with the German world, the natural gravitational pole for Swedes of his generation, Hägerström remained unaware of Schmitt's work.[112] Nevertheless, during the academic year 1921–1922, he had the opportunity to polish his German: He gave hospitality to a needy Austrian student,

[107] A. Hägerström, *Nehrman-Ehrenstråles uppfattning av grunden för ett löftes juridiskt bindande kraft, belyst genom å ena sidan romersk, å andra sidan naturrättslig åskådning* (Nehrman-Ehrenstråle's Conception of the Basis of the Binding Power of the Promise, Illustrated from, on one hand, Roman Law and, on the other, Natural Law), in *Minnesskrift ägnad 1734 års lag av jurister i Sverige och Finland*, Marcus, Stockholm 1934, vol. II, pp. 571–630; German trans. by K. Wührer, ed. K. Olivecrona, in *Recht, Plicht und bindende Kraft des Vertrages nach römischer und naturrechtlicher Anschauung*, SKHVSU Almqvist & Wiksell, Stockholm 1965. In this essay, Hägerström comments on the genesis of some ideas in the Swedish eighteenth century legal scholar David Nehrman-Ehrenstråle.

[108] For a comment, see J. Bjarup, *Scandinavischer Realismus*, Alber, München 1978; E. Pattaro, *Non si fanno cose con le parole. Gli atti negoziali secondo A. Hägerström*, in «Sociologia del diritto», 1981, VIII, 1, pp. 25–42; S. Castignone, *Diritto linguaggio, realtà*, cit., pp. 82 ff., p. 248.

[109] A. Hägerström, *En straffrättslig principundersökning*, in «Svensk Juristtidning», 1939, 24, pp. 209–225; it was published again in *Socialfilosofiska uppsatser*, Bonniers, Stockholm 1939, pp. 231–255 and again 1966[2], pp. 179–198; translated by C.D. Broad with the title *On Fundamental Problems of Law* in *Inquiries*, cit., pp. 348–366.

[110] A. Hägerström, *Om svikligt förtigande såsom straffbart efter 22:1 S.L.* in «Svensk Juristtidning», 1939, 24, pp. 311–335. It is the continuation of *Straffrättslig principundersökning*: It was never translated by Broad and never reedited in *Socialfilosofiska uppsatser*. Max Lyles has recently made a case study of this article in *A Call...*, cit., pp. 507–524.

[111] A. Hägerström, *Kants Ethik* from 1902. The original manuscripts were never found. When Thomas Mautner contacted the publishing house in the Seventies, he was told they were burnt in the Second World War bombings.

[112] Hägerström quoted *Gesetz und Urteil. Eine Untersuchung zum Problem der Rechtspraxis* in *Till frågan om den objektiva rättens begrepp* but does not seem aware of *Political Theology*.

in the small apartment in 23 Trädgårdsgatan where he lived with his wife and two daughters, Rut and Margit.

In that period, while gathering material for his *opus magnum – Der römische Obligationsbegriff* –, Hägerström became the target of some serious criticism. Just a few months after the publication of Schmitt's essay, in December 1922, Hägerström openly answers Lagercrantz's denigration in the Uppsala local newspaper.[113] This was the beginning of the raging debates that would develop in the thirties and that would give Hägerström his notorious nickname "axiological nihilist."

What is striking with the parallelism between Schmitt and Hägerström is that, regardless of one another, they seem to reach similar conclusions. The opening phrase of Schmitt's third chapter on sovereignty could almost have been written by Hägerström: «All significant concepts of the modern theory of the state are secularised theological concepts not only because of their historical development – in which they were transferred from theology to the theory of the state, whereby, for example, the omnipotent God became the omnipotent lawgiver – but also because of their systematic structure, the recognition of which is necessary for a sociological consideration of these concepts.»[114]

For Hägerström, not only are the main categories of the German *Staatslehre* a byproduct of theology, but this is basically true for any judicial notion. He used the genealogical perspective to dig up even older vestiges of theology and animism.[115] One of the significant differences between Schmitt's reading of the modern age and its legal and political theories and Hägerström's is terminological. Strangely enough, Hägerström seems largely unaffected by the concept of "secularisation."[116] He hardly ever used it.[117] Yet, what he described in several studies as the "deification process of Law and the State" fits Schmitt's thesis like hand in glove.[118]

What Hägerström usually did was to draw from far-ranging historic accounts in order to show that law and legal science, chiefly criminal law, are characterised by

---

[113]For details, see Thomas Mautner, *Vägledning till Hägerström studiet*, cit., p. 207.

[114]C. Schmitt, *Political Theology*, MIT Press, Cambridge, MA, 1985, p. 36 (from the second edition in 1934).

[115]An account of Hägerström's view of animism and his sources can be found in C. Faralli, *Diritto e magia. Saggio su Axel Hägerström*, Giuffrè, Milano 1982.

[116]One reason might be that Hägerström elaborated his ideas, between 1916 and 1920, before the start of the great debate on secularisation. Of course, Richard Fester's *Die Säkularisation der Historie* was published in 1908, and Ernst Troeltsch's *Die Bedeutung des Protestantismus für die Entstehung der modernen Welt* is from 1911, but to my knowledge Hägerström did not quote them. However other milestones in the secularisation debate had not yet been published: For example, Marc Bloch's *Les rois thaumaturges* is from 1924, the same year as Rudolf Bultmann's *Die liberale Theologie und die jüngste theologische Bewegung*; Friedrich Gogarten's *Kultur und Religion* was released in 1926 and Karl Barth's *Die Kirche und Kultur* is from 1928.

[117]An exception can be found in *Religionsfilosofi,* ed. M. Fries, Natur & Kultur, Stockholm 1949, Chapter 5.

[118]Another difference is that the reading of modernity did not lead Hägerström to any form of political realism. See next chapter on Hägerström and political philosophy.

a genealogically determined development rooted in a religious conception.[119] From animism and primitive religion sprung the original basis of criminal law: The law of vengeance (*hämndrätten*) which required that all infringements of the holy order must be vindicated so as to reestablish world-harmony. Higher and less primitive forms of theology led to the establishment of another conception: The *lex taglionis* or *vedergällningsrätten*[120] for which offences may be ranked and graded. Hence, the wrongdoer's intention starts to matter in the art of retribution and distribution of punishment.[121] History's path, along with the deification process of the modern State – a true «intellectual revolution»[122] – has led to a secular judicial order in which the State, on one hand, has the "monopoly of legitimate use of physical force" and, on the other hand, legal science has paved the way for unscientific notions, primarily lawfulness and legality. These pseudoconcepts are the poisoned fruit of this unconscious secularisation process that has brought God down from Heaven, into the State.

### *5.6.1 Cutting the Claws of the Tiger of Righteousness*

The core residue from previous superstitions and religious beliefs – that have been ultimately secularised in the modern state – is the battle cry of all vindictive notions: It is fair to punish the wrongdoer! But this is nothing more than «the objectivation of a primitive emotional way of thinking.»[123] In fact, in the review of Birch-Reichenwald Aars' *Gut und Böse*, Hägerström insisted on the primitive character of vengeance that can be adequately explained on the grounds of the most basic of all elements, attraction and repulsion, love and hate: «Hate contains both repulsion for the author of a suffering, and attraction towards the idea of punishing or destroying him (...). Love and hate [... are] the two most primitive forms of moral valuation.»[124] For Hägerström, «all vengeance (*hämndlust*), all hatred is senseless in its nature»[125] and «it is specific to all actions originating from vengeance and hatred that they tend to cloak themselves in a shroud of righteousness.»[126] This is

[119] See for instance the exemplary lectures from 1921 on *History and Critique of the Theories of Criminal Law* (*H 114:8*); *Rätten och staten*, cit., pp. 227 ff.; *Socialfil. uppsatser*, cit., pp. 241 ff.

[120] See the manuscript *H 119:4* from autumn 1923 (*Om skuld och straff*).

[121] An eloquent version of the thesis can be found in *Naturrätt i straffrättsvetenskapen* from 1920 where Hägerström claimed that criminal law works like a catechism, cit., p. 336.

[122] A. Hägerström, *Rätten och staten*, cit., p. 228.

[123] A. Hägerström, *Socialfilosofiska uppsatser*, cit., p. 159.

[124] A. Hägerström, *I moralpsykologiska frågor*, in «Psyke. Tidskrift för psykologisk forskning», 1907, II, vol. 5, p. 78: «Hatet innefattar dels olust vid upphovsmannen till ett lidande, dels lust vid idéen om bestraffande eller förintande af denne (...). Hatet och kärleken [... är] de två mest primitiva formerna för moralisk värdering.»

[125] A. Hägerström, *Kriminalpsykologiska reflexioner* (1925); now in *Socialfil. uppsatser*, cit., p. 214: «all hämndlust, all hatiskhet är till sin natur vettlös.»

[126] A. Hägerström, *Kriminalpsykologiska reflexioner* (1925); now in *Socialfil. uppsatser*, cit., p. 215: «det är egendomligt för ur hämndlust och hatiskhet framspringande gärningar, att de så lätt klädas i *rättfärdighetens* mantel.»

not only true for the «beastly instincts» which rule over international relations,[127] but generally for all "system of dogmas." «The tendency of the human kind towards moral systems of dogmas is a sword, that can serve society, but might as well be directed against it.»[128]

From this viewpoint, «the history of criminal law is to a large extent a struggle between the interest of society and private revenge in order to vanquish the consciousness of law.»[129] What is important is that society seems to have won the game. Hägerström continuously directs his polemic tone against «the perpetual circle of blood's vengeance» (*blodshämndens eviga circkelgång*) which was first interrupted by the institution of the "justice-courts of blood" (*blodsdomstolarna*) at the Aeropagos in Athens,[130] leading to the "significant revolution" which conferred upon the State the exclusive right to punish.[131] Perhaps, Hägerström's most eloquent description of this process can be found in the often neglected *Truly Autonomous Morals* from 1930: «The State cuts the claws and rips out the teeth of the tiger of righteousness and then makes it pull the carriage of the State (...). Under the course of civilisation, the barbarian thirst for revenge has been tamed and kept within precincts determined by the outer forms of the offense, as well as the intention of the offender. This is because of the requirements of society (...). The unlimited raging of vengeance is even more dangerous for general peace in society. Spilt blood cries out for more, as Aeschylos says.»[132]

### 5.6.2 Illegality, a Spurious Concept

The ultimate result of his inquiries on the secularisation process brings him to the thesis – outrageously bold for the jurists of the time – that the concept of legality

---

[127]The reference goes to the *Diktat* inflicted on Germany after WW1 held by the victor to be "nothing but fair" (*Socialfil. uppsatser*, cit., p. 217). It should be said that in 1917 Hägerström claimed that *ius gentium* was a form of adaptation of our moral system to evolution (*Rätten och staten*, cit., p. 12).

[128]A. Hägerström, *Socialfil. uppsatser*, cit., p. 207.

[129]A. Hägerström, *Socialfil. uppsatser*, cit., p. 215: «Straffrättens historia framställer till väsentliga delar en strid mellan samhällsintresset och den privata hämndlusten i deras strävan att var för sig överväldiga rättsmedvetandet.»

[130]Hägerström did not give any clue to his reference. It might be the Council which met on the Areios pagos, an organ which ever since the reforms of Efialtes in 462 B.C. had the competence to judge homicide cases of Athenian citizens. The law on homicide derived from Dracontes' statutes in the Archaic age and one of its objectives was to avoid vengeance being sought by the family members of the deceased (for a description of these features, M.H. Hansen, *The Democracy in the Age of Demosthenes. Structures, Principles and Ideology*, Blackwell, London 1991).

[131]A. Hägerström, manuscript *H 119:6*, pp. 6–7.

[132]A. Hägerström, *Verkligt autonom moral*, in *Moralpsykologi*, cit., pp. 190–191: «staten klipper klorna och drar ut tänderna på rättfärdighetens tiger, men sedan detta skett spänner den densamma framför sitt ekipage (...). Att nu den barbariska hämndlusten under civilisationens fortgång tuktats och hålles inom gränser, bestämda av såväl brottets objektiva yttringar som av uppsåtet hos brottslingen – det beror av samhälliga behov (...). Hämndlustens obegränsade härjningar i samhället äro farligare ändå för den allmänna samhälleliga freden. Det utgjutna blodet ropar efter mer blod, säger Aeschylos.»

and its opposite are useless for jurisprudence.[133] His conclusion is that «it should be doubted whether justice itself dears to live under the motto: *Fiat justitia, pereat mundi.*»[134] His thesis appears clearly in the 1920 essay on iusnaturalistic elements in Criminal Law, *Naturrätt i straffrättsvetenskapen?*, which was his contribution to the "debate" between Tyrén and Lundstedt.[135]

The latter had attacked the notion of causality in criminal law and law of torts, since both these legal disciplines unwarrantedly assume that legal causality works like natural causality. This, in turn, constituted the launch pad for an attack on the very notion of illegality. So what Hägerström does is essentially analyse «the different varieties of the doctrine of illegality that were about at the beginning of the twentieth century, theories whose only justification seems to have been to serve as a last line of scholastic defense for the doctrine of illegality.»[136] For instance, the doctrine of "faultless wrong" or *Schuldlose Unrecht*[137] according to which even natural elements can incur in guilt, or the doctrine of *objective illegality*, which leads to contradictory statements both in property law and law of torts.[138]

In particular, Hägerström lingered on the attack of the duty of indemnification in property and tort law since it is based on so-called "norm-adversity." Particularly telling is the example of "objective illegality," which according to Hägerström is "an absurd idea." «The absurd consequences of the theory that the infringement of a legal demand is a presupposition of executive coercion in the law of property and of the similar assumption in the case of adverse legal decisions and liability for damages have led to the following view.»[139] For example, «if a person in good faith possesses the rightful owner's property and the possessor is ruled against at a trial and is forced to part with the disputed object then the possessor is considered to have committed a wrong,»[140] more specifically an "objective wrong" independent

[133]The problem of illegality raised Hägerström's interest as early as in *Stat och rätt* where he was particularly interested in the "external obligation" of the state, i.e., the so-called "political obligation" (*underordnadsplikten*). However in this early study he set the problem in rather traditional terms, asking whether is it logically viable to subsume political obligation under a concept (obligation) which is taken from private law and only analogically applied to public law. This is a traditional argument against the social contract and can be found in several thinkers from the 18th and 19th centuries.

[134]A. Hägerström, *Naturrätt i straffrättsvetenskapen?*, cit., p. 336: «det är att betvivla att "justitia" själv vågar ställa den devisen: *fiat justitia, pereat mundi.*»

[135]Hägerström referred to this quite "hot" debate as the "the combat essays" (*stridskrifterna*) in the manuscript *H 119:4*, p. 12.

[136]M. Lyles, *A Call...*, cit., p. 473.

[137]He often criticised the doctrine of *Schuldlose Unrecht* according to which people deprived of full mental capacity or even objects may incur in guilt. See for instance *Inquiries*, cit., pp. 225–231; *Socialfil. uppsatser*, cit., p. 235; *Naturrätt i straffrättsvetenskapen?*, cit., p. 338.

[138]It should be stressed that both Hägerström and Lundstedt assume that "illegality" brings about similar problems in the private and public spheres of law. This is why the critique of criminal law runs parallel to that of propriety and tort law.

[139]A. Hägerström, *Inquiries*, cit., p. 229.

[140]Example by M. Lyles, *A Call...*, cit., p. 474.

of the *mens rea*. As early as in the 1917 essay *On the Question of the Notion of Law*, Hägerström insisted on the fact that, if one looks at certain examples taken from private law, guilt is not really a *conditio sine qua non* for punishment inflicted by the State.[141] Yet, jurisprudence holds the use of force to be legitimate only if the subject of a sanction has wronged.

In the 1939 essay *On Fundamental Problems in Law*, Hägerström concluded that illegality is «nothing else than the behavior, whether it be omission or positive action, which calls forth a certain coercive action in accordance with the rules for coercion which are in general applied (. . .). Legal duty (legality) (. . .) is nothing else than behavior with the opposite character.»[142] The bottom line of his argumentation is that illegality has an aloof character and lacks scientific tenure. For jurisprudence, it is a key concept: It is held to be a precondition to liability in criminal law (in the form of guilt) as well as in law of torts (in the form of indemnity liability). It is conceived as a precondition to the penalisation of behavior in criminal law.

Illegality does not imply anything other than the fact that liability follows from it. Above all, it does not imply that it necessarily flows from the action itself and it is therefore a meaningless concept when deciding whether or not a behavior is punishable.[143] Illegality merely claims that specific consequences (i.e., liability) follow from a particular norm. It is by no means a precondition for the existence of a norm. It is merely a precondition for declaring that certain consequences follow from an already valid norm. Something is liable to punishment because there is a norm that states that a specific action or omission is liable to punishment, not because it is *per se* "illegal." So "illegality" «is thus nothing more than a constructed fact (. . .). Hägerström's position was that positive law does not require that a *right*, or that a *law* must be *violated* (. . .) for the legal machinery to enter into action (. . .). Illegality is not a concept of substance, rather it is a function of law – illegality follows from law, but law does not follow from illegality (. . .). Despite the term's outward appearance of positivistic respectability (. . .), "illegality" is a haven for all kinds of non-legalistic arguments (. . .), thereby making it possible to use illegality as an argument to contend that certain types of behavior are criminal and punishable on account of the intrinsic illegality of the behavior in question.»[144] In other words, since criminal law is based on the principle *nulla poena sine lege*, liability follows from the norm, not from "illegality," which therefore becomes useless.

---

[141] He uses examples such as the debt of an infant or of a mentally incompetent person (*Inquiries*, cit., pp. 223–235).

[142] A. Hägerström, *Inquiries*, cit., p. 348.

[143] Lyles sees the patent absurdity of the claim: According to the prevailing doctrine of illegality «an action can be criminal, albeit not penalized, or penal, albeit not *illegal*; so an action may be *illegal* and yet not *illegal* (. . .) The customary use of the term illegality is in fact tautological» (*A Call. . .*, cit., pp. 496–7).

[144] M. Lyles, *A Call. . .*, cit., p. 474.

This construal of illegality is of importance since it leads directly to the problem of legitimating the state's right to punish and hence to the question of political obligation. Hägerström understands that every justification of the state's powers over its subjects, and the corresponding political obligation of those subjects, is ultimately based on the idea that certain conditions have intrinsic characteristics making them necessary. In fact, the debate on illegality brought on the question of the basis of punishment and Hägerström polemicized with both Johan Tyrén and Karl Binding since these authors held the state's right to punish as «a principle that is axiomatically given, simple and indubitable.»[145] This is due to the metaphysical elements that have been secularised into the state, a process of which legal scholars remain largely unaware. So Hägerström noted that jurisprudence uses the state's right to punish in the same way classical metaphysics uses the *causa sui.*[146] In line with his reasoning, since criminal law is necessary there is no need to search for pseudo-concepts – such as illegality – to ground the legitimacy of punishment. It is not the presence, but the absence of criminal law that requires justification. Probably, Lyles is correct to observe that «one weakness in Hägerström's argument is that he begs the question and justifies the penal system, by arguing that it needs no justification.»[147] Ultimately, the state's right to punish depends on the capacity of criminal law to underpin consciousness of law.

### *5.6.3 The Understanding of Punishment*

One of the consequences of Hägerström's interpretation of illegality is the view on punishment which, to a great extent, was shared by Scandinavian realism as such: «The Scandinavian realists were all oriented towards the preventive theory [of punishment] and of social welfare, and they attack the retributive theory.»[148] In effect, Hägerström's conception of punishment is different from some of the prevailing views.[149]

The retributive or absolute theory, according to which a sanction is inflicted as a consequence of the infringement of law by which the delinquent deserves his

[145] M. Lyles, *A Call...*, cit., p. 490.

[146] See A. Hägerström, *Naturrätt i straffrättsvetenskapen?*, cit., p. 336.

[147] M. Lyles, *A Call...*, cit., p. 492.

[148] S. Castignone, *Diritto, linguaggio, realtà*, cit., p. 334: «I realisti scandinavi sono tutti indirizzati verso la teoria preventiva e dell'utilità sociale, e attaccano la teoria retributiva.» See also V. Lundstedt, *Superstition or Rationality in Action for Peace? Arguments against Founding a World Peace on the Common Sense of Justice. A Criticism of Jurisprudence*, Longmans, London 1925, especially pp. 48 ff.; A. Ross, *Skyld, ansvar og straf* (1970), Eng. trans. *On Guilt, Responsibility and Punishment*, Berkeley University Press, Los Angeles 1975.

[149] Cf. L.H. Jakob, *Philosophische Rechtslehre oder Naturrecht* (1802); J.F. Abegg, *Die verschiedenen Strafrechtstheorien in ihrem Verhältnisse* (1835); K. Binding, *Grundriss des deutschen Strafrechts* (1879).

punishment – *quia peccatum est* – seems to be tautological and ultimately contradictory:[150] «According to the law of the taglion, it is fair to punish a person not because it is useful for society or for the person to suffer penalty, rather because the action itself is the ground for the righteousness of the sanction. Yet, how can it be righteous that the person shall suffer because of the action without any purpose other than the very suffering?»[151]

The theory of repentance – as in the traditional *poena medicinalis* – according to which the punishment's goal is to reconvert the criminal in view of moral redemption, seems to be most perverse. In the review of Bjerre's *Contribution to the Psychology of Murder* (*Bidrag till mordets psykologi*), Hägerström rejected both the theory of repentance – «punishment shall upright the crooked» – and the generic theory of prevention – «punishment shall assure public security.»[152]

To his mind, other problems emerge with the preventive theory – *ne peccetur*[153] – according to which punishment is inflicted not in reason of the past since it cannot be undone, but in view of the future so it will prevent further crimes, committed by the same tortfeasor (special prevention theory), or by others (general prevention theory). His argument against the special prevention theory is that we need to «understand how meaningless it is to regard punishment of such criminals [who are convinced to do no harm] as a form of vengeance and to try to *straighten* criminals through punishment (. . .). All punishment that is not required for the sake of other people who are really dissuadable and for the sake of public safety, only become a useless torture, due to ignorance and raw instincts of vengeance, just as barbarian as the punishment inflicted by the Inquisition so as to bring people to deny the faith on which their lives rested.»[154]

---

[150] The distinction between "*absolute und relative Theorien*" elaborated by German jurisprudence, and recurrent in most continental literature, corresponds to the Anglosaxon distinction between retributive and utilitaristic theories of punishment. Hägerström only considered the second type as viable, in line with his non-cognitivism. On the German distinction, cf. A.F. Berner's *Lehrbuch des deutschen Strafrechts* from 1857, as well as Jhering's disciple Franz von Liszt's *Lehrbuch des deutschen Strafrechts* from 1899.

[151] A. Hägerström, manuscript *H 119:4*, p. 17: «att personen straffas är efter vedergällningsidéen rättvist ej därför, att det är nyttigt för samhället eller för att personen själv att han straffas, utan gärningen själv är rättfärdighetsgrunden för straffet. Men huru kan det vara rättfärdigt, att personen får lida på grund av sin gärning utan något nyttigt ändamål med lidandet?» See also, *Socialfil. uppsatser*, cit., p. 253.

[152] A. Hägerström, *Socialfilosofiska uppsatser*, cit., p. 228. See also *Naturrätt i straffrättsvetenskapen?*, cit., p. 333.

[153] Hägerström, strangely enough, claimed that Anselm Feuerbach first introduced the *quia peccatum/ne peccetur*-dicotomy: See the manuscript *H 119:4*. The reference is to P.J.A. Feuerbach, *Anti-Hobbes oder über die Grenzen der höchsten Gewalt und das Zwangsrecht der Bürger gegen den Oberherrn*, Erfurt, Henning 1798 and *Revision der Grundsätze und Grundbegriffe des positiven peinlichen Rechts*, I, (1799), Scientia Verlag, Aalen 1966. Actually, the famous distinction between looking towards the past (*quia peccatum*) and the future (*ne peccetur*) when punishing is Seneca's: *De Ira*, bk I, Chapter XIX.

[154] A. Hägerström, *Kriminalpsykologiska reflexioner*, cit., pp. 217–218: «förstå huru meningslöst det är att se bestraffningen av sådana brottslingar som vedergällning liksom också genom straff

As far as prevention is concerned, Hägerström departed from the theory of Tyrén. According to the latter, the execution of the crime deters citizens while, for Hägerström, the deterrent factor is not punishment in itself. Rather, it is the fact that it is *regularly* inflicted and consequently this "knowledge" underpins the consciousness of law, as well as the activity of lawyers and judges. «Just like criminal laws are necessary for public safety, these cannot reach their aim if they are applied arbitrarily.»[155] It seems that Hägerström inclined towards what might be called a positive theory of general prevention, centering more on the threat of punishment than on the actual execution, and more on the fidelity and trust ordinary citizens would develop towards the judicial system than the deterent effect on deviant behaviour. Basically, the deterrent effect of punishment depends on the law-abiding habit prevailing in society and thus on "valid law."[156] Not only is it impossible to dissuade the single criminal through his particular punishment from pursuing his or her illicit doings, but it is equally impossible to dissuades others via an individual punishment.[157]

An interesting consequence is a shift of perspective from the effect (the crime in criminal law and the offense in law of torts[158]) to the cause: The law itself. Castignone, in her essay on Lundstedt's conception of punishment, commented: «If objective duty (...) does not exist, it is meaningless to talk about guilt, *mens rea*, and justice of punishment. Reverting what was standing on its head, we understand how punishment finds its premise only in social usefulness, i.e., without criminal laws society could not exist (...). The crucial element is not punishment, but rather the existence of criminal law. We should speak of the social function of criminal law, not of punishment.»[159]

---

söka *rätta* brottslingar (...). Varje annan bestraffning än den som tarvas för andra verkligt påverkbaras skull och till skydd för den allmänna säkerheten, blir i angivet fall endast en onödig, av okunnighet och råa vedergällningsinstinkter föranledd tortyr, lika barbarisk som den inkvisitorer övat för att bringa människor att avsvärja den tro, vari de förankrat sitt livshopp.»

[155] A. Hägerström, *Socialfil. uppsatser*, cit., p. 254: «likaväl som strafflagarna äro nödvändiga för den allmänna säkerheten, likaväl förfelas detta ändamål, om sådana godtyckligt tillämpas.»

[156] A. Hägerström, *Naturrätt i straffrättsvetenskapen?*, cit., p. 330.

[157] A. Hägerström, *Naturrätt i straffrättsvetenskapen?*, cit., pp. 332–333.

[158] For Hägerström, this happens not only in criminal law but also in law of torts and indemnity liability is therefore nothing more than «a residue of the private *lex taglionis*.» (See manuscript *H 119:4*, p. 20: «skadeersättningen [är] en kvarleva av den privata vedergällningsrätten.»)

[159] S. Castignone, *Diritto, linguaggio, realtà*, cit., p. 338: «se i doveri oggettivi (...) non esistono, allora non ha senso parlare di *guilt*, di *mens rea*, e di *giustizia* della punizione. Rimettendo sui piedi ciò che era stato posto sulla testa si vede come la pena trovi il suo presupposto esclusivamente nell'utilità sociale, cioè nel fatto che senza la legislazione criminale la società non potrebbe esistere. (...) L'elemento essenziale non [è] la pena, la punizione, bensì l'esistenza delle leggi penali. È della *social function of criminal law* e non della *social function of punishment* che bisogna parlare.»

A frequent objection to Hägerström's construal of punishment concerns the risk of convicting the innocent. This is not really the only preoccupation the question rises. A less emphasized point concerns social homogeneity as a precondition for his thesis. According to Hägerström – who basically registered what was actually going on in his day – crimes are rare and people's moral reaction towards them is substantially compact and direct. The idea is clearly expressed by Lundstedt who declared «criminals are only drops in the ocean formed of masses of people.»[160] The theory of punishment in Hägerström seems to rest, ultimately, on the communitarian conviction of a shared *Sittlichkeit* making crimes uncommon.[161]

However, Hägerström ultimately seems to support an alternative form of criminal law, no longer focused on the unscientific doctrine of illegality and with less dreadful castigation. Indeed, he appears to be a somewhat Northern counterpart of Cesare Beccaria: «Is it really a loss, from a social viewpoint, if the general desire for revenge would be silenced? Would it not be, on the contrary, an achievement if society could determine the punishment according to rational deliberation on what society requires, instead of following such feelings which, as experience shows, confuse the mind? (. . .) Cannot we understand that the [social desire for vengeance] awakes the beast in Man? It is always hard to chase away devils with the help of their principal, to curtail the beastly instincts with the most irresistible form of these.»[162] From this perspective, Hägerström seems to stand closer to the ideal of the Enlightenment to abandon vengeance and irrationality in criminal law, a request shared by Hobbes, Locke, Beccaria, Filangieri and Bentham, than the deterministic approach prevailing in positivistic sociology, as expressed for example in Gabriel Tarde's *La philosophie pénal* from 1890.

Perhaps, the most eloquent description of his proposal for future criminal law designs can be found in a manuscript dating from 1923: «If no backlash of superstition comes along, the criminal law of the future will motivate punishment

---

[160] V. Lundstedt, *Legal Thinking Revised*, Almqvist & Wiksell, Stockholm 1956, p. 223.

[161] Hägerström's conception of punishment should therefore be confronted with that of Émile Durkheim for instance. Cf. E. Durkheim, *De la division du travail social* (1893) where punishment is said to serve social cohesion.

[162] A. Hägerström, *Socialfil. uppsatser*, cit., p. 227: «Är det verkligen ur social synvinkel en förlust, om det allmänna vedergällningskravet skulle dämpas (. . .)? Måste det icke tvärtom vara en fördel, om samhället blir i stånd att bestämma straffet efter förnuftig överläggning om vad dess intressen kräva, och icke efter sådana känslor, som, såsom erfarenheten visar, förvirra förståndet? (. . .) Månne man icke förstår att de [sociala vedergällningskänslor] vädra vilddjuret i människan? Men det lär alltid vara svårt att utdriva djävlar med djävlarnas överste – att kuva vilddjursinstinkterna med den mest oemotståndliga formen för dessa.»

exclusively on social grounds, consequently in reference to its necessity for the preservation of the social order and thus for the satisfaction of those interest that are of primal importance for Man.»[163]

All in all, the legal order is far from being a purely scientific realm of knowledge. Rather, it is the poisoned fruit of an unconscious secularisation process that has brought primitive elements into the modern State. The *autodafé* Hägerström would like the modern legal scholars and state-theoreticians to perform is chiefly to recognize that they participate in the reification process at hand in law and morals and consequently in the deification process of the Modern State which leads to the confusion that we might call, by paraphrasing Kelsen's famous title: *Staat ist Gott.*[164]

This does not mean that Hägerström would desire the abolition of criminal law: He is no *schöne Seele*. On the contrary, these laws are necessary, just as fear of sanction is a *conditio sine qua non* for the functioning of the legal order. What he would like to see is jurisprudence free from the emotional constraint on scientific description due to the lasting, primitive, and superstitious elements that still make lawyers and laymen believe that punishment is "fair."

According to the tenets of Hägerström's conception, does this mean that we would be left with poorer principled judicial reasoning and, eventually, be deprived of the capacity of arguing against the punishment of the innocent? As we have already mentioned in relation to the theory of justice, at the first glance, Hägerström's conception of justice seems to leave the question of convicting the innocent, inexplicable and unsolved. Under closer examination, his argument is different: In the 1931 essay on *Social Justice*, when Hägerström asked «would it not be possible to become immediately upset facing human suffering, without believing in its injustice?»[165] – he also answered himself: «The feeling of revolt in such cases [in which an innocent is convicted or someone punished arbitrarily] will therefore always survive, even if the feeling, originated in superstition, had no longer power over our minds.»[166]

---

[163] A. Hägerström, manuscript *H 119:4*, p. 22: «den framtida straffrätten skall, såvitt ej ett bakslag till vidskeplighet kommer att ske, uteslutande motivera straffet ur sociala synpunkter, sålunda med dess nödvändighet för beståndet av en samhällelig ordning och därmed för tillgodoseendet av de intressen, som för människorna överhuvud äga betydelse.»

[164] On this issue, see *Rätten och staten*, cit., pp. 257 ff. where he analysed this "particular swap of absoluteness" that has made the state into an absolute power, apparently standing free from space and time.

[165] A. Hägerström, *Om social rättvisa* (1931); I am quoting from *Socialfilosofiska uppsatser*, cit., p. 139: «skulle man icke omedelbart kunna bli upprörd över mänskligt lidande utan att tro på dess orättvisa?»

[166] A. Hägerström, *Socialfilosofiska uppsatser*, cit., p. 255: «känslan av upprördhet i sådana fall skall därför också alltid leva kvar även om av övertro ursprungligt verkade känslor skulle förlora sin makt över sinnena.»

Man's natural empathy will ultimately endure without the superstructure of superstition, favoring both scientific perspicacity and greater tolerance for human behavior. The Swedish philosopher Ingmar Hedenius, who knew Hägerström well, even though they did not share the same views, was quite right when he concluded «ultimately, behind the criticism, lay the conviction of the Enlightenment: It served humanity."[167]

[167] I. Hedenius, *Om Hägerströms filosofi*, in «Tiden», 1940, 32, p. 44: «Bakom kritiken låg till sist upplysningsmannens övertygelse, att den tjänade mänskligheten.»

# Chapter 6
# The Father of Scandinavian State Absolutism? Hägerström on Politics

*The tradition of all dead ancestors encumbers like a nightmare on the mind of the living*[1]

## 6.1 Political Radicalism in Historical Perspective

Hägerström had a passion for politics, international relations, political history and the history of political ideas throughout his life. He also lived in a world of great changes: Born in a rural and static society, in one of Europe's oldest kingdoms, he died in a mass society where the industrial revolution had made possible such extremes as the *belle époque* and the world war. Besides, in his life time, parliamentary rule and constitutional democracy were solidly put in place in Sweden, the country that the twentieth century was to remember as the cradle of its welfare model.

The political panorama in Sweden in the early twentieth century had two significant issues on the agenda: Social reforms favouring the have-nots and the democratic turn in government. Both were central for Hägerström. After the Union with Norway came to an end in 1905,[2] the political debate in Sweden focused on the questions of parliamentary rule and universal suffrage. Hägerström followed the evolving situation quite closely, since he, as well as other family members, was generally interested in world politics and foreign affairs.[3] The loss of Norway

[1] A. Hägerström, *Marx och filosofin*, in «Tiden», 1933:25, p. 148: «Traditionen från alla döda släkten trycker som en mara på de levandes hjärna.»

[2] Sweden acquired Norway with the peace treaty signed in Kiel 1814.

[3] During the *fin de siècle*, for instance, he discussed the discovery of the North Pole as well as the *affaire Dreyfus* with his grandmother, the quite amazing Charlotte Skarin (1814–1903). For more details, see Chapter 1.


DOI 10.1007/978-90-481-2895-2_6, 

particularly interested him.[4] His opinion in favour of Norwegian independence has been considered a display of political radicalism.[5]

That same year, 1905, the political situation took a new turn. As the union crisis passed, attention was directed towards internal affairs. In the 1905 general elections, the social-democratic party, founded in 1889, and the liberal party, established only 5 years before, obtained the majority in the second chamber in parliament. The new government was led by Karl Staaff, who launched the radical student association "Verdandi"[6] at the Uppsala University in 1882, an association which Hägerström was involved in only 4 years after its founding. The main aspiration of the newly elected was the instauration of universal suffrage and consequently the abolition of census. Since such an innovation meant a change to the 1809 constitution requiring a majority in both chambers, Staaff was soon forced to resign, as the first chamber insisted on a conservative standpoint. The time being ripe, though, Arvid Lindman, who succeeded Staaff by royal appointment, presented a proposal for male universal suffrage: It was adopted in 1909, the same year Sweden faced up to its first massive confrontation between workers and employers: The great strike.

When the "great strike" broke out, Hägerström was lecturing on socialism, one of his main interests in those years.[7] In a letter to his mother, Augusta Maria Skarin, he wrote: «You ask for my opinion on the big strike. About its outcome there can hardly be more than one opinion: It will fail. So, it was a foolish deed in the first place that the leaders probably endorsed in sheer desperation since their position had become unsustainable through the lockout organised by the industrial companies, a lockout that the workers had no means of resisting. But on the other hand, I cannot share the general indignation from the right-wing side: It has the nature of class-egoism, to a large extent dressed in the coat of hypocrisy. That the workers are guilty of

---

[4] Already in April 1899, Hägerström was worried about the Swedish policies in relation to Norway, fearing it may evolve into a civil war and that Sweden might lose it. He was especially alarmed for the autonomy of Finland.

[5] G. Fredrikson, *20 filosofer*, Norstedt, Stockholm 1994, p. 202.

[6] Verdandi was a political association of students intentioned to promote political thought based on free speach as a common ground both to liberalism and the labour movement. The key issues of the association were awareness of the public opinion, internationalism, rule of law and public education. Verdandi, in the Old norse mythology, is one of the Norns, together with Urd and Skuld; the three powerful maiden giantesses that draw water from the well of fate. These female figures correspond to the Greek *Moirae* and Roman *Parcae* or *Fata*. The verb *verða* meant "to become" and *Verdandi* derives from the present tense of *verða*, "that which is happening." The political association was thus meant to stimulate critical thinking on the present time.

[7] Hägerström first started to lecture on socialism in 1904, when he held a quite popular course for the chair in practical philosophy instead of Burman. His interest in socialism grew during this first decade of the twentieth century. In 1907 he lectured on *The Driving Forces of Social Movement* and in 1908 and again in 1909 he dedicated a semester to the *History of Socialism*. The same year he published his first book on the subject: *Social teleologi i marxismen* (*Social Teleology in Marxism*, which was published in *Uppsala universitets årsskrift*, by Almqvist & Wiksell). Some lectures were later collected and published by Martin Fries in 1946 with the title: *De socialistiska idéernas historia*, Natur & Kultur, Stockholm 1946 that includes the now typed manuscripts *H 108:1* and *H 110:2*, which correspond to the preparatory notes for the classes during spring 1909.

contract breaking is beyond doubt (...). How impressive (...) the calm behaviour of a starving mass of 285 000 men with wives and children?»[8]

Bjarup is correct when stating that «Hägerström's philosophy addresses the burning political issue of his day, between the socialist class and the capitalist class, since "one fights better if one believes that one has right on one's side." Thus, if the capitalist belief that an action is right can be shown to be illusory it follows that the opposite socialist belief that the action is wrong is also illusionary. (...) If this is so, then political conflict can be neutralised, since people will realise that there is no reason to evoke any moral rights and to engage in any violent attack on the existing social and cultural institutions. As he puts it, "only barbarians make an assault on them by casting stone" (...). To be sure, one's values may be informed by scientific truths to promote a detached or tolerant view of people and their behaviour (...). For Hägerström, the supreme value is peace, and this can be achieved by means of the law of the land to regulate human behaviour in order to fulfil human needs and desires.»[9]

The other important political issue of the time was parliamentary rule. In 1911, the year Hägerström held his notorious inaugural lecture, the elections were won by the liberals and the social-democrats again. Since Sweden was engaged in the lengthy process of modernising of its military system – a debate that regularly monopolised the political scene – the army became the pretext for further strife between king and parliament: The reelected Staaff government disagreed with the project, upheld by the Crown, to invest in the navy. Finally, some 30 000 peasants marched into Stockholm in February 1914 to sustain the national defence plan, leading to Staaff's second resignation.[10] In Uppsala, meanwhile, during the so-called "political spring term" of the same year, students were polarized between royalists and radicals. Staaff was finally succeeded by Hjalmar Hammarskjöld, appointed by Gustav V, and new elections were indicted in March 1917.

This was not only a crucial year for Europe, it was a significant date for Sweden too. It also happened to be a cold and hungry year. The harvest was poor, because of the war the commerce routes were interrupted, so that small and extremely unpopular rations were introduced. All this fuelled strong malcontent towards the

---

[8] M. Waller, *Människan som få kände*, natur & kultur, Stockholm 1961, cit., p. 184: «Mamma frågar efter min mening om storstrejken. Om dess utgång kan det väl knappast råda mer än en mening, nämligen att den skall misslyckas. Därmed är också sagt, att den var ett oförståndigt företag från början, som väl igångsattes av ledarna i förtvivlans mod, emedan ställningen hade blivit olidlig genom arbetsgivareföreningens lockout, som arbetarna saknade medel att uthärda. Å andra sidan kan jag emellertid ej dela den allmänna indignationen från de "borgerligas" sida, som till stor del synes få karaktären av en klassegoism, som bra mycket bär skenlighetens kappa. Att arbetarna i sitt förtvivlade läge kommit att begå avtalsbrott, är ju otvivelaktigt (...). Imponerande (...) den lugna hållning som en hungrande massa på 285 000 man med hustru och barn (...) iakttagit.»

[9] J. Bjarup, *Scepticism and Scandinavian Legal Realists*, in T. Endicott, J. Getzler, E. Peel (eds.), *Properties of Law. Essays in Honour of Jim Harris*, Oxford University Press, Oxford 2006, pp. 58–59. The quote is from A. Hägerström, *On the Truth of Moral Propositions*, in *Philosophy and Religion*, Allen & Unwin, London 1964, p. 94.

[10] The issue regarded whether the king could legitimately give political declarations without the government being informed.

government led by Hammarskjöld, known by the infamous starvation-like nickname: Hunger shield (*Hungerskjöld*). When the election day arrived, a coalition of liberals and social-democrats, led by Nils Edén and Hjalmar Branting, won the majority in the second chamber of Parliament.[11] This event marked the end of the conservative influences of the crown in political affairs and the accomplishment of parliamentary rule. But it was also what made the social-democratic party, coming into power in October 1917, opt for the reformist agenda and drop the revolutionary alternative. Hägerström's hopes for neutralisation of social conflict hereby found a new strategy: To channel the revolutionary doldrums towards the struggle for political reform and democratisation. «It was against this political background that the Scandinavian Legal Realists [and Hägerström before them] developed their critiques of the then dominating schools of jurisprudence, the Historical School and the Idealist School (...), ideologies that legitimated an undemocratic status quo.»[12]

In the 1921 lectures *The State and Its Forms* (*Stat och statsformer*),[13] which are to a great extent a critique of John Austin and Georg Jellinek, Hägerström's own views on the democratic turn in government came to light. While discussing the various theories on popular sovereignty and representative democracy, Hägerström explicitly stated which position he preferred: «The English-French doctrine of representation as a delegation of the people, bound by mandate, is in itself scientifically implausible. But it should be preferred since this doctrine, with its fundamental ideas on the individual's liberty and equality, was the basis from which the representation of the people by means of mass voting – *one man, one vote* – historically developed.»[14] Some have insisted that Hägerström's philosophy of law – in particular, his criticism of both the historical school of jurisprudence and theories of natural rights – were inspired by the hope to «create more room for the expression of popular sovereignty through legislative law.»[15]

There are some reasons to doubt that Hägerström embraced the democratic ideology uncritically. More than once, he insisted on the questionable views that were held by many democrats. He stressed that there is no actual "common will in par-

[11] As mentioned in § 2.2 in Chapter 4.

[12] G.S. Alexander, *Comparing the Two Legal Realisms – American and Scandinavian*, in «The American Journal of Comparative Law», 2002, winter, vol. 50, n. 1, p. 168.

[13] Ed. by Martin Fries in *Rätten och staten*, Natur & Kultur, Stockholm 1963, pp. 119 ff.

[14] A. Hägerström, *Rätten och staten*, cit., p. 169: «den engelsk-franska doktrinen om representationen såsom folkets fullmäktige, bundna av uppdrag, [är] själv vetenskapligt sett orimlig. Den är emellertid att föredraga ur den synpunkten, att det är denna doktrin med dess grundläggande idéer om individernas frihet och jämlikhet, som historiskt legat bakom utbildningen av sättet för folkrepresentationens tillkomst genom väljarmassor, där var och en har sin röst.» For the arguments on this issue, see Chapter 5 for details.

[15] G.S. Alexander, *Comparing the Two Legal Realisms*, cit., p. 167.

liament"[16] but only the wills of the single members of parliament: «The will of the representative assembly (...) is merely legal fiction. Thus it cannot be defined as a real will directed towards the law.»[17] In general terms, Hägerström was suspicious of the overemphasis on popular sovereignty.[18]

Some interpreters have even gone so far as to accuse Hägerström of favouring an "aristocratically motivated socialism." Hans Ruin emphasized the influence of Nietzsche and his esthetical aristocratism: «This combination of Nietzsche and social-democracy can appear totally unreasonable. But (...) do not we already have the answer to this equation? Is it not Aristotle? In Aristotle there is a basis for the anti-Platonic (and therefore anti-Christian) aristocratically motivated communitarism that Hägerström (...) stimulates.»[19]

Such readings can be questioned.[20] In particular, Hägerström was far from being "communitarist" in any contemporary meaning of the term, and he did not uphold holism or organicism that he considered to be only "fantasy"[21] and "poetry"[22] and he rejected collectivism[23] and the metaphysical belief in "commonly shared values." To Hägerström, «for the modern man it is clear that we are not here for the sake of unity of society but, on the contrary, society exists for the individual.»[24]

However, it should be remembered that many intellectuals who followed in his footsteps did fall back on a community of shared values when legitimating democracy: «The fact that value nihilistic theory was closely associated with a progressive political movement was definitely one of the reasons for the intense debates (...) in

---

[16] A. Hägerström, *Der römische Obligationsbegriff im Lichte der allgemeinen römischen Rechtsanschauung*, volume II, *Über die Verbalobligation*, K. Olivecrona (ed.), SKHVSU Almqvist & Wiksell, Uppsala 1941, p. 13. See Chapter 6, § 2.

[17] A. Hägerström, *Förhållandet mellan rätten och staten*, in *Rätten och staten*, cit., p. 265.

[18] A. Hägerström, *Stat och rätt. En rättsfilosofisk undersökning*, vol. I, Almqvist & Wiksell, Uppsala 1904, pp. 12–13; see also Chapter 4, § 2.

[19] H. Ruin, *Hägerström, Nietzsche och den svenska nihilismen*, in «Tidskrift för politisk filosofi», 2000:1, pp. 5–30: «den kombination av Nietzsche och socialdemokrati kan till en början te sig alldeles orimlig. Men (...) har vi inte i själva verket redan svaret på denna ekvation? Och lyder den inte: Aristoteles. Hos Aristoteles finns grunden för det slags antiplatoniska (och därmed antikristna) aristokratiskt motiverade kommunitarism som Hägerström (...) framkallar.»

[20] See for example S. Danielsson, *Hägerström, Nietzsche och Hans Ruin*, in «Tidskrift för politisk filosofi», 2000, n. 2, pp. 45–52 and Ruin's rejoinder, pp. 53–56.

[21] Hägerström held organicism to be a puerile notion. In *Stat och statsformer* he defined it as "fantasy" (in *Rätten och staten*, cit., p. 169). A virulent attack on the organicism of the historical school of jurisprudence can be found in the manuscript *H 111:1a*, pp. 97–99, from autumn 1929.

[22] Any "common will" or *Volksgeist* is nothing but *Dichtung*, poetry: A. Hägerström, *Der römische Obligationsbegriff*, cit., p. 17.

[23] Jes Bjarup erroneously claimed that Hägerström upheld collectivism in *Reason, Emotion and the Law. Studies in the Philosophy of Axel Hägerström*, Press of the Faculty of Law, Aarhus 1982, p. 403. Hägerström's criticism of collectivism can be found in *Rätten och staten*, cit., pp. 82–113; see also Rätten och viljan. Trå uppsatser av Axel Hägerström, Gleerup, Lund 1961, pp. 131–135.

[24] A. Hägerström, *De socialistiska idéernas historia*, cit., p. 30: «för den moderna människan står det klart att vi icke äro till för samhällsenhetens skull utan tvärtom samhället är till för de enskildas skull.»

the 1930s and 1940s. Among leading intellectuals within the Swedish labour movement value nihilistic theory was used as an argument against the "metaphysics" of competing political ideologies. For example, it was argued that conservatism relied on a metaphysical idea of "right to ownership," that liberal economic theory was superstitious in its belief in a "natural harmony" in economics; and that Marxism failed because of its teleological historicism.»[25]

So Hägerström was deeply involved in the two major issues that concerned Swedish politics in the early twentieth century. Furthermore, let us look a little closer at some other important political questions that raised his attention and that were significant for Europe as a whole.

## 6.2 A Passion for Politics

As a matter of fact, politics certainly represented a great passion throughout Hägerström's entire life. He frequented some of the front-line politicians of his time, like the social-democratic party member Vilhelm Lundstedt, but also Arthur Engberg, who became minister in the 1930s. He also inspired many politicians of

[25] J. Strang, *Why Nordic Democracy?*, paper presented at the research seminar at the department of philosophy, Helsinki, October 2006, p. 5 (http://www.helsinki.fi/filosofia/tutkijaseminaari/whynordicdemocracy.pdf). The social-democratic movement counted on some very influential names, all allegedly inspired by Hägerström, like Ingmar Hedenius, Herbert Tingsten, Alf Ross and Alva and Gunnar Myrdal, who launched the concept of "Nordic democracy" in the mid-thirties as a rhetorical figure «aiming at distinguishing a Nordic democratic region (...) from the totalitarian chaos surrounding it.» (J. Strang, *Why Nordic Democracy*, cit., p. 3). These latter national strategists of the Labour party used Hägerström in the struggle for "Nordic democracy" on the basis of a presupposed community of shared values. In the name of *axiological nihilism*, Hedenius claimed that a common set of values is a prerequisite for a meaningful discussion on ethics and that this evaluative background of democracy is part of a greater system of attitudes that form a «cornerstone of our culture.» (I. Hedenius, *Om rätt och moral*, Wahlström & Widstrand, Stockholm 1941, p. 412; Id., *Filosofiska skäl för demokratin*, in *Nordisk demokrati*, edited by H. Koch, A. Ross, Halvorsen & Larsen, Copenhagen 1949, p. 213). Tingsten criticised the classical arguments for democracy in Rousseau, Mill and Bentham for being based on the metaphysics of natural law (a criticism taken full-handedly from Hägerström) and stressed the community of shared values at the basis of democracy as an "over-ideology" (H. Tingsten, *Idékritik*, Bonniers, Stockholm 1941). Alf Ross, a prominent name in the Danish debate on democracy, insisted on the principle of shared values, notwithstanding his formal view of democracy: In *Why Democracy?* from 1946, he discussed the problem of clashes within society due to religious and national minorities and advocated broadly for the social-democratic program of change so as to end the conflict between socialism and capitalism in such a way that the conservative elements had the time to adapt to the "common set of values" (A. Ross, *Hvorfor Demokrati?*, Munksgaard, København 1946, pp. 282–293; short version in *Hvad er demokrati?*, in H. Koch, A. Ross (eds.), *Nordisk demokrati*, cit.; Eng. trans. in J.A. Lauwerys (ed.), *Scandinavian Democracy*, Danish Institute/Norwegian Office of Cultural Relations/The Swedish Institute, Copenhagen 1958). Gunnar Myrdal, in the article *With Dictators as Neighbours* in «Survey Graphic. Magazine for Social Interpretation» from 1939, claimed that Sweden had maintained its democracy through its legalistic mind set and its tradition of freedom, so that «the frontier of democracy lies within our boundaries, and not at our borderlines» (quote from J. Strang, *Why Nordic Democracy?*, cit.).

the next generation, while he intensively lectured on and studied issues like popular representation, fundamental rights, constitutionalism, liberty and equality. Among the authors he systematically read and commented on we find the great names of modern political theory: Hobbes, Locke, Rousseau, Kant, but also Bentham and Mill.[26]

Even in his youth, his personal correspondence is filled with contemporary references. In April 1899, he expressed his sincere worries for the autonomy of Finland. A year earlier, in a letter to his fiancée Esther Nyander, he had analysed the 1898 murder of the Empress Elisabeth, the wife of Franz Joseph, by the Italian anarchist Luigi Lucheni.[27] In innovative terms, he criticised the moral condemnation of anarchism which does not account for its impact, favouring a sociological explanation of the appeal of anarchism on specific social groups.[28] Moreover, he favoured female emancipation. In the autumn of 1897, he managed to convince his parents to send his sister Berta to university. As mentioned, he personally coached her in mathematics until her admission to the faculty of chemistry in Stockholm, from where she graduated in 1905.

As a rule, Hägerström was always more open and explicit when he lectured than when he wrote for scientific purposes. He relaxed in the classroom. In *Social teleologi*, Hägerström labelled Hegel "conservative" and accused Spencer of being "an old liberal."[29] On another occasion, he depicted Boström as the "flagbearer of the conservatives."[30] A more elaborate example can be found in the lecture series *On the Relation between the State and the Law* from 1924, where he compared Tsarist Russia to an absolutistic state.[31] Actually, Hägerström's account of Russian

---

[26] No attempt has been made to study Hägerström's reading of these authors in any systematic way. Except on a few occasions where he concentrated on one specific author, like the monograph on Kant or the homonymous manuscript on Rousseau, the references to and crypto-quotations of these six thinkers can be found throughout his whole production. We might say that they represent his ideal interlocutors.

[27] As mentioned in n. 47 in Chapter 4.

[28] See letter in M. Waller, *Människan som få kände*, cit., p. 133.

[29] A. Hägerström, *Social teleologi*, cit., p. 70.

[30] A. Hägerström, *Rätten och staten*, cit., p. 168. One clearly anti-communitarian element we find in Hägerström is certainly his vehement criticism of Boström's traditional organicism that was revived in the thirties. In fact, the German edition of Boström's work was edited in the heydays of the Weimar republic (1923). In addition to this, the ideas of the political scientist Rudolf Kjellén, who declared his debt to Boström and who (in *Staten som lifsform,* Hugo Gerbers förlag, Stockholm 1916) upheld a geopolitical theory based on organicism, had a certain impact, especially in Germany, during the first world war (the impact of this thesis on the *Lebensraum*-idea later favored by Nazism has been investigated in N. Elvander, *Rudolf Kjellén och nationalsocialismen*, in «Statsvetenskaplig tidskrift», XX, 1956, p. 23). Hägerström also rejected the organicism of Efraim Liljeqvist (1865–1941, known as the last Boströmian, who withheld Boström as sole literature for his university course as late as 1930, and then became president of the pro-Nazi association *Riksföreningen Sverige-Tyskland*). See S. Nordin, *Den Boströmska skolan och den svenska idealismens fall*, Doxa, Lund 1981, p. 187.

[31] A. Hägerström, *Rätten och staten*, cit., p. 257.

political conditions had a prophetic tone. In 1916, a year before the October revolution, he stated: «Under modern conditions no [unitary will] normally exists. Whole strata of the population desire a revolutionary alteration in the foundation of the law (...). Russian law certainly does not depend *merely* (...) on the fact that a certain section of Russians desires that what the Tsar wills shall be carried into effect. It depends to a large extent also on such things as religious convictions about the person of the ruler, the indolence of the masses, army discipline and so on.»[32]

Notwithstanding that these politically loaded comments can be found all over Hägerström's production, it is embarrassingly difficult to extract any coherent political theory from this mass of information. The most telling fact is that Hägerström never wrote any such formally accomplished political theory. This explains why, apart from Ola Sigurdson,[33] no scholar ever attempted to examine his political doctrine. He analysed power and violence throughout his entire production, but he never developed a theory of power, such as Max Weber did in those very years. He recurrently addressed the problem of political obligation (*underordningsplikt*),[34] just like many scholars in Cambridge in the same period, and dedicated over a decade to the *Obligationsbegriff* in Roman law, but he never found the time to formalise his political philosophy with consistency. He might have believed that there are legal obligations that need to be explored on the basis of political obligation. By unmasking the inconsistency of obligation in law, and especially its very origin – Roman law – it would have become possible to ground political obligation anew without falling back into the violence of war and the destruction of revolution, the two phenomena that he always shunned.

In order to comprehend the meaning and consequences of this seemingly paradoxical behaviour towards politics – a personal attraction and yet no elaborate formalisation – we have to ask why Hägerström, who never developed a thorough political theory, became known as the father of state absolutism.[35]

---

[32] A. Hägerström, *Inquiries into the Nature of Law and Morals*, Almqvist & Wiksell, Uppsala 1953, p. 41; *Är gällande rätt uttryck att vilja?*, in *Festskrift tillägnad prof. Vitalis Norström på 60-årsdagen den 29 januari 1916*, Elanders Boktryckeri, Göteborg 1916, p. 195.

[33] O. Sigurdson dedicated a section to "Hägerström's political philosophy" in *Den lyckliga filosofin: etik och politik hos Hägerström, Tingsten, makarna Myrdal och Hedenius*, Östlings bokförl. Symposion, Eslöv 2000.

[34] See for instance, *Rätten och staten*, cit., p. 176.

[35] State absolutism is a quite generic term, with a clearly negative ring. In relation to Hägerström, the expression has lately appeared in Jan Carlsson who used the term as equivalent to a conception of society in which "justice" corresponds to the "rationally defined interest of the State" (*Statsabsolutismens rättsfilosofi: en studie av Boströms och Hägerströms rättsfilosofi*, Juridiska Fakulteten, Lund 2001, http://www.jur.lu.se/Internet/Biblioteket/Examensarbeten.nsf/0/F7C0DCF9A3EB3E98C1256AE60047A1A9/$File/xsmall.pdf?OpenElement, p. 36). It has been associated broadly with Lutheranism and the State church; with the Scandinavian welfare model; with forms of social engineering; with the lack of rule of law in the meaning of scarce principled judicial reasoning and teleological interpretation of statute law. We might

## 6.3 Father of State Absolutism?

In time, Hägerström's axiological nihilism as well as his account of the metaphysical character of rights and duties became associated with the infamous slogan that goes back to Thrasymachus of Chalcedon: "Might is Right."[36]

During the era commonly known as "the crisis of democracy" in the 1930s and 1940s, it was often suggested that axiological nihilism, such as that of Hägerström, was to blame for the collapse of European culture in general and for the rise of totalitarian regimes and antidemocratic movements in particular. It was suggested that axiological nihilism had left people in a spiritual void, which was easily exploited by anti-democratic, populist and power-focused political movements. It is noteworthy that this criticism often came from the left: For instance, the historian of philosophy Alf Alhberg claimed that «the deepest reason for the crisis of democracy lies in this value nihilism»[37] and the social-democratic member of parliament, Anders Örne, held Hägerström responsible for sweeping the way for «the modern totalitarian states.»[38]

The prejudice that was put in place in the thirties has never really been altered. A typical account of the connection of might and right in Hägerström is given by

say that it indicates (i) a form of society where the individual has a very limited residual liberty concerning foremost private life (generic use of the term); (ii) a discretionary political organisation where positive law is considered the only form of law and where the state is the principal setter of law (this use is not uncommon in Catholicism: In Razinger's *Freedom and Truth* («Communio: International Catholic Review», 1996, Spring issue; now at http://www.ewtn.com/library/THEOLOGY/TRUEFREE.HTM) for example, the expression is equivalent to arbitrary will of positive law or "the caprice of positive legislation"); (iii) a conformist and servile attitude among civil servants, and especially of judges (this is the more specific meaning the expression has in contexts related to Scandinavian legal realism; see for example Jacob Sundberg and Jes Bjarup). This form of "idiosyncratic legal positivism" has been described by Alexander Peczenik as the conviction which brings about "the obligation for Swedish Courts of Law to conform to the political values underpinning the law and to abstain from engaging in moral judgments" (A. Peczenik, *Lagstiftningen, domstolarna, rättsmedvetandet och rättsvetenskapen*, in *Löser juridiken demokratins problem? SOU. Rapport till Demokratiutredningen*, Fakta Info Direkt, Stockholm 1999, p. 12, my trans.). More recently, it has been claimed that the supposedly proverbial submissiveness of civil servants enhanced by massive bureaucracy – a feature that is, in turn, accused of bringing about illiberal practices and immoral behaviour – cannot be derived from any conception of legal positivism, whether embraced or not, by Scandinavian legal realism: Nicklas Berggren, *Rättspositivism och äganderätt*, in N. Berggren, N. Karlson (eds.), *Äganderättens konsekvenser och grunder*, Ratio, Stockholm 2005, pp. 180–215. Here I will not develop an in-depth analysis of the notion. I will instead look at the reasons why Hägerström has been associated with the ill-sounding appellative and try to illustrate why this is not any appropriate attribute: As we shall see, Hägerström's refusal of natural rights or rights transcending time and space is not reason enough for holding him to endorse any of the above-mentioned meanings of "state absolutism."

[36] M. Lyles, *A Call for Scientific Purity. Axel Hägerström's Critique of Legal Science*, Rönnells, Stockholm 2006, p. 340, nota 147.

[37] A. Alberg, *Maktfilosofi och värdenihilism*, in Id. (ed.), *Varför svenska folket reagerar*, Natur & Kultur, Stockholm 1940, p. 21 (quoting from J. Strang, *Why Nordic Democracy*, cit., p. 7.)

[38] A. Örne, *Uppsalafilosofin – reflexioner av en lekman*, in «Tiden», 1940, 3, p. 167.

Jes Bjarup, who (along with Jacob Sundberg) criticised Hägerström most severely on this issue: «Hägerström's moral philosophy implies that a discourse about social ends cannot be a cognitive question of argumentation and truth, but a non-cognitive question concerning suggestion and power.»[39] Hence, the theory of value (apart from being unscientific) would bring about practical nihilism, as it refers ultimately to (political) power, if not brute force: Hägerström is reduced to «a philosophical imperialist in analytical disguise!»[40] Sundberg recently voiced these recurrent allegations with his usual overstatement: «The Kingdom of Sweden was (...) hit early by the Uppsala school which provided, under the guidance of Professor Axel Hägerström, a more comprehensive philosophy of science which fitted excellently the dominating political power of the day – the Social Democrats (...) and the study of law was relegated to a kind of unscientific Siberia [... under] the "secret marriage" between the ruling social democrats and the Hägerströmian Uppsala school.»[41] This allegedly resulted in the circumstance that «in the past, Swedish Law had been characterised by a Hägerströmian encapsulation.»[42] This reading leads straight to the claim that Hägerström's philosophy is, in the end, responsible for scientific decay, illiberal practices and generic immoralism in Scandinavia, or at least in Sweden. From a very different standpoint, it has even been suggested that Hägerström and «Scandinavian legal realism dismissed the possibility of normative arguments about values» leading to the overall abandonment of normative political theory in the Nordic countries.[43] To some other scholars, axiological nihilism even appeared as a "Swedish ideology"[44] or a "national disease"[45] which brought about «an emotionally cold individualism, a massive bureaucracy and functional but gloomy grey concrete.»[46]

---

[39] J. Bjarup, *Axel Hägerströms filosofi, värdenihilism och rättspositivism*, in «Juridisk tidskrift», 2004/2005, anno 16, n. 1, p. 32: «Hägerströms moralfilosofi implicerar att en diskurs om sociala mål inte kan vara en kognitiv diskurs som är en fråga om argumentation och sanning utan en non-kognitiv diskurs som är en fråga om suggestion och makt.»

[40] J. Bjarup, *Reason, Emotion and the Law*, cit., p. 169.

[41] J. Sundberg, *A Chair in Jurisprudence*, in *Perspectives on Jurisprudence*, «Scandinavian Studies in Law», *Essays in Honor of Jes Bjarup*, vol. 48, Jure, Stockholm 2005, p. 434.

[42] J. Sundberg, *A Chair in Jurisprudence*, cit., p. 444. Variations on this theme can be found in J. Sundberg, *The Swedish Philosopher Axel Haegerstroem and his Relationship to Finland's Struggle to Preserve her Legal Order 1899–1917*, Rothman, Littleton, Co, 1983; Id., *Uppsalaskolan och den nationella inkapslingen*, in «Tidskrift utgiven av Juridiska Föreningen i Finland», 1999, pp. 170–180. For a criticism coming from a non-Scandinavian scholar, see S. Castignone, *Diritto, linguaggio, realtà. Saggi sul realismo giuridico*, Giappichelli, Torino 1995, pp. 341–344.

[43] A. Føllesdal, *Er normativ politisk teori død i Norden? Diagnose og prognose*, in «Distinktion»,7, 2003, pp. 129–138, quote from abstract.

[44] P. Colla, *La Värdenihilism comme « idéologie suédoise »? Une lecture de la pédagogie des valeurs dans la réforme suédoise*, in Ph. Bouquet, P. Voilley, *Droit et littérature dans le contexte suédois*, Flies France, Paris 2000, pp. 53–81.

[45] M. Berendt, *Tilfaeldet Sverige*, Chr. Erichsen, København 1983, p. 94.

[46] J. Strang, *Axel Hägerström och Gunnar Myrdal. Om den svenska värdenihilistiska traditionen*, in «Historisk Tidskrift för Finland», 2003:1, p. 43. Variations on this theme can be

But what about historical evidence appointed to sustain the idea of the "monstrous appearance of raw power" lurking behind the meta-ethical theses (in the negative reading)[47] or Hägerström's influence on the political figures behind the so-called Swedish model (in the positive reading)[48]? Many interpretations stress the influence Hägerström would have had on political scientists like Herbert Tingsten (1896–1973) and economists like the Nobel laureate Gunnar Myrdal[49] (1898–1987) and, last but not least, the first UN secretary general Dag Hammarskjöld[50] (1905–1961).

However, some scholars have started to point out that the influence of Hägerström's meta-ethical theses over the minds of the political protagonists has been significantly exaggerated.[51] «Axel Hägerström and value nihilism are usually mentioned as inspirational source for social engineering and the Swedish model (. . .). The importance of axiological nihilism was never really so comprehensive (. . .). It is easy to enumerate many influential names (. . .) that were inspired by Hägerström (. . .). It is interesting to notice that Hägerström's influence over them was rather generic.»[52]

As a matter of fact, what we should look at here is not strictly speaking Hägerström's political legacy (from such a viewpoint the case of Vilhelm Lundstedt would be more interesting). Rather, the question that needs to be asked is: What were the ideas of Hägerström that might be associated with illiberal political practices

---

found in J. Nergelius, *Konstitutionellt rättighetsskydd: svensk rätt i ett komparativt perspektiv*, Fritzes, Stockholm 1996, p. 94, pp. 611–13; A. Peczenik, *Den skandinaviska rättsrealismen*, in J. Nergelius (ed.), *Rättsfilosofi: samhälle och moral genom tiderna*, Studentlitteratur, Lund 2001, pp. 122–124.

[47] Another historical event singled out *ad hoc* to prove this, is the alleged negative influence of Scandinavian legal realism on the appointment of the members of the European Court of Human Rights and specifically on Alf Ross' role. See J. Sundberg, *A Chair in Jurisprudence*, cit., pp. 457–63.

[48] See S. Strömholm, H.-H. Vogel, *Le "réalisme scandinave" dans la philosophie du droit*, LGDJ, Paris 1975, p. 4 who claim Hägerström and Scandinavian realism are worthy of attention not just as a school but as *the* philosophy behind contemporary Swedish society.

[49] For a detailed reconstruction of Hägerström's influence, see O. Sigurdson, *Den lyckliga filosofin*, cit. On the relation between Hägerström and Myrdal, see J. Strang, *Axel Hägerström och Gunnar Myrdal*, cit., pp. 43–61.

[50] This latter influence is testified in a letter from 1958 that Hammarskjöld sent to Hägerström's daughter Margit Waller (*Människan som få kände*, cit., p. 207.)

[51] S. Danielsson, *Värdenihilismen i praktiken*, in *Forskningsprofiler. Uppsala Universitets Installationsföreläsningar, 1989/1990*, Uppsala University Press, Uppsala 1990, p. 19: «betydligt överdrivet.»

[52] O. Sigurdsson, *Den lyckliga filosofin*, cit., p. 247: «Axel Hägerström och värdenihilismen brukar nämnas som en av dem som inspirerat till social ingenjörskonst och den svenska modellen (. . .). Värdenihilismens betydelse har i själva verket aldrig varit så omfattande (. . .). Det går utmärkt att räkna upp många inflytelserika personligheter (. . .) som lärt av Hägerström (. . .). Det är intressant att notera att Hägerströms inflytande hos dessa gör sig bemärkt i tämligen allmänna ordalag.»

and social engineering[53] and made him earn, however erroneously, the nickname of being the father of Scandinavian state absolutism?[54]

## 6.4 The Motives Behind the Bad Reputation

Two major aspects should be stressed as motives behind the bad reputation. On one hand, Hägerström had a profound interest in Marx and, in an age of extremes such as the twentieth century, this fact alone seems to have induced some scholars to situate Hägerström on the opposite side to political liberalism and legal constitutionalism. However, his attention towards Marx was essentially linked to his view of history and the individual's role in it. On the other hand, Hägerström elaborated a specific theory of rights (and duties) as forms of "social superstition" which led him to dismiss (elements that can be considered fundamental in modern constitutionalism and political liberalism such as) the rule of law, the concept of sovereignty (including popular sovereignty), and both the ideas of private property and human rights as mere "phantoms of the imagination."[55] While a better understanding of this latter theory will provide a less unilateral portrait of this part of his political thought, first let us look at why Marx made such a lasting impression on Hägerström.

### *6.4.1 Hägerström Reads Marx*

Marx's intellectual breakthrough in Sweden lagged behind in comparison to the rest of Europe. Hägerström was one of the first scholars to discover the great unmasker of the nineteenth century. He first started to lecture on socialism in 1904, when he held a very popular course for the chair in practical philosophy instead of Burman because of the latter's poor health. The field of study was breaking news: In April 1906 the Russian Social Democratic Party held its congress in Stockholm, where Lenin, among others, participated. The year after, Hägerström lectured on *The Driving Forces of Socialism*. These lectures were then published in the book entitled *Social Teleology in Marxism* (*Social teleologi i marxismen*) in 1909, which launches an attack on historical materialism. During spring 1909 he continued to lecture on the *History of Socialist Ideas*, and theses lectures were eventually collected and edited by Martin Fries in 1946.

---

[53]The expression social engineering, as a form of "technical" expertise dealing with persons and aiming mainly at the solution of problems in the workplace, appeared in an essay from 1894 by the Dutch industrialist J.C. Van Marken and it seems to have received its last great impetus from the American social reformer W.H. Tolman in 1909. See D. Östlund, *A Knower and Friend of Human Beings, Not Machines*, in «Ideas in History», 2007, vol. 2, n. 2, available at http://www.ideasinhistory.org/cms/index.php?page=a-knower-and-friend-of-human-beings# main

[54]For the notion of "state absolutism", see *supra* note 35 in this chapter.

[55]This cryptocitation of Bentham's *Anarchical Fallacies* in not the only one. See *supra* note 26 in this chapter.

Hägerström's interest in Marx (particularly historical materialism and the notion of superstructure) did not decline with age. In 1922 he reviewed (in rather critical terms) Sven Helander's work on *Marx and Hegel: A Critical Study on the Worldview of Social Democracy* for the journal of political science (*Statsvetenskaplig tidskrift*). One of the enduring political topics that Hägerström dealt with was that of social justice, at the heart of the homonymous essay from 1932. He also contributed to this particular direction of research with additional work published in the review *Tiden*, an important social-democratic think-tank. For example, here he presented the essay *On Social Superstition* (*Om sociala vidskepelser)* in 1913 as well as his contribution to the fiftieth commemoration of Marx's death, *Marx and Philosophy* published in 1933. Significantly, Hägerström is said to be «definitely the greatest specialist on Marx in Sweden» as early as 1910.[56] Besides the *Manifesto*, the theses on Feuerbach and the *Misery of Philosophy*, Hägerström continuously referred to the *Kritik der Hegelschen Rechtsphilosophie* and *Zur Kritik der politischen Oekonomie*.[57] Moreover, Arthur Engberg, the aforementioned social-democratic minister and good friend of Hägerström, explicitly stated that Hägerström's «revolutionary new thoughts are intimately related to the fundamental thoughts of Marxism.»[58] Several elements do seem to point in this direction. In *Social teleologi* for instance, Hägerström repeatedly used his own vocabulary in "re-translating" Marx's ideas, leaving the reader under the impression that he shared his basic opinions. While describing the *Klasselöse Gesellschaft*, he claimed that «truly humane ethics will appear only when the opposition between the classes ceases, through the instauration of the socialist society.»[59]

Furthermore, Hägerström read Marx in parallel with Hegel. To him, Marx represented Western metaphysics: «The idea that the purpose of existence is to reach *true* reality is the basic idea of metaphysics in philosophy in general and it runs, so to speak, in Marx's veins. The idea that duty or purpose consists in *reason* (...) is part of transcendental philosophy and Hegelianism; an idea that Marx picks up.»[60] What Marx and Hegel share is «the view that the development of

---

[56]E. Hedén, Review of *Axel Hägerström, Botanisten och filosofen*, in «Tiden» 1910, p. 224: «Hägerström är säkerligen Sveriges störste Marx-kännare.»

[57]On Hägerström's sources in Marxian secondary literature, see his review of *Sven Helander: Marx och Hegel*, Fahlbeckska stiftelsen, Lund 1920, in «Statsvetenskaplig tidskrift», 1922:25, p. 258.

[58]Quote from S. Nordin, *Från Hägerström till Hedenius*, Doxa, Lund 1984, p. 243: «revolutionerande nya tankar är intimt besläktade med marxismens grundtankar.»

[59]A. Hägerström, *Social teleologi*, cit., p. 59: «Endast om klassmotsatsen en gång genom upprättande af det socialistiska samhället faller bort, skall en verklig mänsklighetsmoral träda fram.»

[60]A. Hägerström, *Sven Helander, Marx och Hegel*, cit., p. 255: «föreställningen att den *sanna* verkligheten är tillvarons mål är den allmänna filosofins genomgående metafysiska grundtanke och har så att säga gått Marx in i blodet. Och föreställningen att börat eller målet finnes blott för förnuftet (...) är ett led i transcendentalfilosofin och hegelianismen som Marx därifrån upptagit.»

society depends on a purpose that is achieved unconsciously.»[61] It is this conception of history as largely independent from individual choices that Hägerström rejected. Both Hegel and Marx are thus constrained by a teleological view of history that ultimately places the purpose (Absolute Spirit, Socialism) above mankind's endeavour for its own happiness. «I call [this] a social teleology, since the interest of *society* predominates (...). With this terminology I intend a process that is independent of human will in the sense that the need of society to produce for its own persistence is consistent, unconditionally and independently of individual consciousness.»[62]

Hägerström was thus far from being any orthodox Marxist. To him, there is no such thing as "objective evaluations" at the root of historical or dialectical materialism. For example, in *Social teleologi*,[63] Hägerström developed the idea that Marxism suffered from a teleological conception of history, essentially blinded by one single factor in explaining history, namely economic production: «The orientation of the necessarily coordinated people towards the production of what is necessary for life and its reproduction is the ultimate driving force in history.»[64] This is why Marxism, in the end, is just an expression of class interest, making the very ideology a means in the struggle: «The religious trust in the realisation of the moral goal that we find in Marxism was specifically appropriate to become the proletarian's gospel (...). It proves in scientific terms that the kingdom is near.»[65] Therefore, on Hägerström's reading, the father of modern communism indulged in wishful thinking.[66] Marx's error was an oversimplified philosophy of history that

---

[61] A. Hägerström, *Sven Helander, Marx och Hegel*, cit., p. 256: «betraktelsen av samhällsutvecklingen såsom bestämd av ett bakomliggande omedvetet verkande mål.»

[62] A. Hägerström, *Sven Helander, Marx och Hegel*, cit., p. 253: «jag betecknar [detta] som en social teleologi, emedan *samhällets* intresse dominerar (...). Med beteckningen avses en process, som är oberoende av mänsklig vilja så tillvida att samhällets behov att producera för sitt eget liv gör sig ovillkorligt gällande utan varje medvetande.»

[63] Hägerström elaborated his thesis on teleology in Marxism under the influence of Stammler's *Wirtschaft und Recht* (see A. Hägerström, *Social teleologi*, cit., p. 17). The title also recalls Max Adler's *Kausalität und Teleologie in Streite um der Wissenschaft* that Hägerström had read when it was first published in 1904. Hägerström seems to have been well-acquainted with Austro-Marxism (p. 23). Adler attempted to combine Marxism and neo-Kantism (Marburg School). Just like Hägerström, Adler refused the Rickert-inspired distinction between *Natur-* and *Geisteswissenschaften*, where the latter seemed incompatible with the method of comprehension (*Verstehen*), and the natural sciences appeared to be the only true science and hence causality is the only valid principle of explanation (*Aufklärung*). Adler however included man's practical will in the concept of "reality."

[64] A. Hägerström, *Social teleologi*, cit., p. 65: «de nödvändigt samverkande människornas samfällda riktning på produktion af det för det omedelbara lifvets uppehållande och förnyande är den yttersta drifkraften i historien.»

[65] A. Hägerström, *Social teleologi*, cit., p. 69: «det religiösa förtröstan på det moraliska målets förverkligande, som finnes i marxismen, specifikt lämpade sig till ett proletariatets evangelium. (...) På vetenskaplig väg visas det ju att riket är nära.»

[66] A. Hägerström, *Social teleologi*, cit., p. 69: «Marx exemplifierar (...) endast den alldagliga psykologiska erfarenheten, att man har benägenhet att konstruera verkligheten efter sina önskningar.»

stimulated the rise of a moral and even religious conception, which might suit the interests of the working class, but that are still nothing but "ideology" and "false consciousness."[67]

For the commemoration of the death of Marx in 1933, Hägerström had the opportunity to explain what kept his interest alive. In particular, historical materialism and the notion of superstructure were considered as steps towards conceiving history as a pattern of complex interactions between economy, politics, law, and technology. So, even though Hägerström challenged the deterministic features in Marx's philosophy of history, he still considered it to be a worthy and innovative attempt to understand the past. In particular, Hägerström was interested in «the theory according to which the order of production and redistribution is dependent on the development of technology and that the legal, moral and religious ideology in turn mirrors this order. It may be true that this conception needs to be subjected to substantial revision as far as empirical explanation of history is concerned (...). [But] Marx's account of legal ideology has been particularly stimulating for my research in the philosophy of law. The conception of rights *in se* is nothing real, but it is reality-based insofar as it is a superstructure of economic conditions.»[68]

Hägerström's relation to Marx was certainly complicated, but he could definitely not be univocally ascribed to the political camp of the latter. In particular, Hägerström disagreed with the use of revolutionary means and he consequently tended towards the reformist agenda.[69] From this viewpoint, it is interesting to stress what Gunnar Myrdal claimed about his old teacher: «Through his deep sceptical attitude to metaphysics of all kinds and his unrelenting insistence on clarity in the concepts used for social analysis, he contributed to saving the post-war generation of intellectuals in Sweden from becoming Marxists.»[70] It is no wonder then that a Marxist like Arnold Ljungdal did not like Hägerström at all.[71]

---

[67] A. Hägerström, *Social teleologi*, cit., pp. 57, 61, and p. 63.

[68] A. Hägerström, *Marx och filosofin*, cit., p. 147: «teorin, att den ekonomiska produktions– och fördelningsordningen är beroende av teknikens utveckling och att den rättsliga, moraliska och religiösa ideologin i sin tur avspeglar den nämnda ordningen. Det må vara sant att denna åskådning vid en empirisk betraktelse av det historiska förloppet måste bli underkastad djupgående modifikationer (...). Särskilt har för mig vid min rättsfilosofiska forskning Marx' framställning av rättsideologin varit tankeväckande. I sig själv är rättsidén realitetslös. Men den har som en överbyggnad på de ekonomiska förhållandena ett realitetsunderlag.»

[69] J. Bjarup stressed this aspect: «Hägerström rejects the Marxist call for a violent revolution in favour of a peaceful revolution to end the strife [between capital and labour] by bringing human beings to their senses that they are not only social but also intelligent animals with the capacity to use scientific knowledge to introduce and maintain the appropriate social structure by means of positive law» (*The Philosophy of Scandinavian Legal Realism*, in «Ratio Juris», 2005, vol. 18, n. 1, p. 5). Hägerström often had terrible words for wars and revolutions, see for example, the manuscript *Hägerström 119:5*, p. 8.

[70] G. Myrdal, *Vetenskap och politik i nationalekonomin*, Rabén & Sjögren, Stockholm 1971, p. 278.

[71] See G. Fredriksson, *20 filosofer*, cit., p. 209.

### *6.4.2 The Theory of Rights as Social Superstition*

The second motive behind Hägerström's reputation as the father of Scandinavian "state absolutism" brings us back to his rather unconventional conception of rights and corresponding obligations.[72] The text-book version of this thesis is that rights and duties were «mysterious, supernatural powers and bonds.»[73] Eloquently, in *The State and Its Forms* from 1921, Hägerström explained that «the boundary between reliance (...) of the type "God is my strength" and reliance on natural rights is definitely feeble.»[74] Ideas of rights ultimately derive from «the archaic magical conception of rights as exterior forces that can be transferred to others through magical means.»[75]

While Hägerström elaborated a non-cognitivist theory on the basis of the impartial observer in his meta-ethics (see Chapter 3), he also developed a *theory of rights* (and corresponding duties), which was *not* part of his non-cognitivist theory, and that is at odds with a long-standing tradition of considering rights. Sven Danielsson dismissed Hägerström's theory of rights as a mere "eccentricity."[76]

In fact, what is so eccentric with Hägerström's theory of rights is that it seems to clash with his axiological nihilism. Indeed, he asserted that normative evaluations are neither true, nor false, but there are some "norms" (like conceptions of rights, duties and the like) that are simply false. Torben Spaak recently emphasized that although non-cognitivism «is meant to apply to value sentences in general, an exception is to be made for right sentences, that is, sentences formulated in terms of rights. On Hägerström's analysis, right sentences are *false*, as they involve the ascription of magical powers to the right-holder, and such powers do not exist. Accordingly, we must describe Hägerström's theory of rights as an error-theory»[77] in the sense that it is a theory according to which all statements within a certain field of discourse are false.

---

[72]On the notion of "subjective rights" in Hägerström, E. Pattaro, *Il realismo giuridico scandinavo*, vol. I: *Axel Hägerström*, Cooperativa libraria universitaria editrice, Bologna 1974, pp. 201–226; L. Hierro, *El realismo jurídico escandinavo. Una teoría empirista del derecho*, Torres, Valencia 1981, p. 151; S. Castignone, *Diritto, linguaggio, realtà. Saggi sul realismo giuridico*, cit., pp. 86–87, 96, 247–255; G. Mac Cormack, *Hägerström on Rights and Duties*, in «The Juridical Review», 1971, pp. 59–78; M. Lyles, *A Call for Scientific Purity*, cit., pp. 445–456.

[73]G. Mac Cormack, *Scandinavian Realism*, in «The Juridical Review», 1970, p. 34.

[74]A. Hägerström, *Rätten och staten*, cit., p. 165: «gränsen mellan den förtröstan som ligger i detta (...) "Vår Gud är oss en väldig borg!" och förtröstan på naturliga rättigheter är synnerligen svag.»

[75]Quote from manuscript *H 119:3*, p. 3: «den urgamla magiska åskådningen om rättigheterna som yttre krafter, som genom vissa trollmedel kan överföras på andra.»

[76]S. Danielsson, *Värdenihilismen i praktiken*, in *Forskningsprofiler*, cit., p. 18.

[77]T. Spaak, *(Review of) Legal Theory (Peter Wahlgren ed. 2000)*, in «Archiv für Rechts- und Sozialphilosophie», 2002, vol. 88, n. 2, p. 301

It was this conception of rights and duties that influenced Scandinavian legal realism. For instance, Lundstedt famously argued there were no such thing as ownership and that talk of law violating rights was like a parrot's blather.[78] Olivecrona elaborated his famous comparison with the monetary unit[79] and stated that "right" was a "hollow word."[80] Alf Ross first treated "right" as an expression for an invisible and mystical power,[81] and then accused lawyers and laymen of conceiving "rights" as having a semantic reference which they actually lack.[82] In point of fact, to ask the question "what is a right?" is logically and conceptually quite different from asking "what is a table?"

This "error-theory of rights" has led to Scandinavian legal realism being described as a form of «substantive Naturalism» that reduced legal concepts to behavioural and psychological categories, an aspect which ultimately made it «more a museum piece than a live contender in the jurisprudential debate.»[83] This latter point of view is not entirely accurate, since it misses the fact that Hägerström's view of rights and duties cannot be simply reduced to the behavioural feature, which remains an important element but cannot in itself explain the "binding force of law" (see Chapter 5 for details). If any reductionism is possible, it is a genetic reductionism which historically demonstrates the determining origin of a specific set of norms: Rights and duties can, in fact, be traced back to their origin in Roman Law where the "original sin" – according to the tenets of Hägerström's argumentation – was that legal concepts stemmed from religious and magical ideas (see Chapter 7).

---

[78] Quote from S. Källström, *En filosof i politiken – Vilhelm Lundstedt och äganderätten*, in «Idéhistoriska uppsatser», Avdelningen för idéhistoria – Stockholms Universitet, 1991:23, p. 15: «Ty det finns ingen äganderätt och har i alla tider aldrig funnits någon äganderätt. Hela begreppet är blott en fantasiprodukt, logiskt otänkbar i verkligheten. Det finns överhuvud inga rättigheter (...). Talet om att en ny lag skulle kunna kränka äganderätten är lika meningslös som en papegojas pladder.»

[79] K. Olivecrona, *Legal Language and Reality. Essays in Jurisprudence in Honour of Roscoe Pound*, R.A. Newman (ed.), Bobbs-Merrill, Indianapolis-New York 1962, p. 173: «The case of the monetary unit is highly illuminating. We find here a noun ostensibly used as denoting an object. But there is no object; the word has ceased to denote anything at all. It nevertheless plays an important role when employed in certain ways according to law and social custom. By means of its use the whole exchange of goods and services is mediated.» See also C.J. Arnholm, *Olivecrona on Legal Rights. Reflections on the Concept of Rights*, «Scandinavian Studies in Law», Almqvist & Wiksell, Stockholm 1962, pp. 9–31; B. Bix, *Ross and Olivecrona on Rights*, in «Minnesota Legal Studies Research Paper no 06–14» available at SSRN: http://ssrn.com/abtract=892788

[80] K. Olivecrona, *The Legal Theories of Axel Hägerström and Vilhelm Lundstedt*, in «Scandinavian Studies in Law», vol. 3, Almqvist & Wiksell, Stockholm 1959, p. 143.

[81] See A. Ross, *Towards a Realistic Jurisprudence. A Criticism of the Dualism in Law*, Einar Munkgaard, Copenhagen 1946, pp. 189–200. See also E. Millard (ed.), *Special Issue of* «Droit & Société», *Is an Empiricist Theory of Law Possible?*, 2002, 50.

[82] See A. Ross, *Directives and Norms*, Routledge, London 1968, p. 134.

[83] B. Leiter, *Naturalism in Legal Philosophy*, in *Stanford Encyclopedia of Philosophy* (Fall 2002 Edition) available at: http://plato.stanford.edu/entries/lawphil-naturalism/

The point that should be stressed in this context is that, as far as rights and duties are concerned, we have to focus on the complex web of beliefs that surrounds theses notions because what Hägerström offered was essentially an «account of the beliefs which make the behaviour intelligible.»[84]

Nevertheless, Hägerström's theory of rights is rather intricate and here I shall try to outline it briefly. First, we look at what he meant by "rights" and "ideas or conceptions of right." Then I will try to give a clearer statement of the precise relationship between Hägerström's non-cognitivist theory and his theory of rights, since it has been stressed that this would be «of interest to anyone trying to understand Hägerström's philosophy.»[85]

### *6.4.3 What Rights and What for?*

Hägerström claimed that ideas about rights are social superstitions. This is the thesis of the homonymous essay from 1913. A first distinction that has to be made is that the "idea of right" (*rättsidén, idéen om rättigheter*) is not the same thing as moral ideas concerning values (*moraliska värdeidéer*): In his autumn course from 1917, *The Genesis of Ideas of Justice*, Hägerström clearly explained that «the idea of right is not therefore a moral idea of value.»[86] As we have seen, moral ideas are neither true nor false because they involve a conative impulse based on emotions: «A feeling is never true or false.»[87] The idea of right, however, is far more complex.

The "rights" we are concerned with are rights in the modern, subjective sense of the term,[88] as conceived in practical reasoning and in legal discourse alike.[89] Moreover, it should be noted that, for an ontological monist like Hägerström, it is meaningless to distinguish legal rights from moral rights following the Anglo-American tradition: Both conceptions ultimately refer to a "spiritual reality" or sphere of *Sollen* that makes all conceptions of *rights* «representations totally devoid of reality engendered by the influence of emotions on our way of conceiving

[84] G. Mac Cormack, *Scandinavian Realism*, cit., p. 36.

[85] T. Spaak, *(Review of) Legal Theory*, cit., p. 305.

[86] A. Hägerström, *Rätten och staten*, cit., p. 17: «alltså är icke rättsidéen en moralisk värdeidé.» See also pp. 15, 19, and 33.

[87] A. Hägerström, *Socialfilosofiska uppsatser*, Bonniers, Stockholm 1939, p. 154.

[88] In French and in German the same word (*droit, Recht*) serves as the noun which refers both to rules of law and the rights which are created by them, and therefore disambiguation is required through the description of rights as being 'subjective' (*droits subjectifs*; *subjektives Rechten*). Hägerström refers to this category, usually using the Swedish term *rättighet*, the abstract reflection of which is called "idea of right" (*rättsidén*).

[89] The question, central to analytical jurisprudence, of what we mean by rights has been combined, ever since the seventies, with the question, central to normative and practical reasoning, of what rights a certain right-holder can be said to enjoy.

reality and connected to a primitive way of imagining.»[90] Hart's classic definition of rights in terms of the «*normative* property belonging to the right-holder»[91] would certainly have irritated Hägerström. However, in the case of moral or natural rights, which lack impact on law, their unreal character is simply blatant. «The subjective right insofar as it is a moral right is, as I have said, a *power* or *force* to claim something from others independently of physical conditions (...). *Force* is always something inner or spiritual (...). The *force* as something inner or spiritual is given in an emotional experience.»[92] This is why one important and very polemic definition of rights is «a pure power of the Spirit.»[93]

If we look at how Hägerström intended rights, it is striking that he, like many elder authors, often used words imprecisely, and smeared their meanings across and beyond the categories we are now used to when analysing rights, such as for example the Hohfeldian incidents – the privilege, the claim, the power, and the immunity.[94] No wonder that, in his 1904 monograph *Stat och rätt*, Hägerström cautiously insisted on the ambiguity of "rights."[95] On the whole, we find an array of different suggestions: The subjective right is defined as (a) advantage[96] –

---

[90] A. Hägerström, *Socialfilosofiska uppsatser*, cit., p. 137: «fullkomligt realitetlösa föreställningar, som uppstå genom känslornas inflytande på vår uppfattning av verkligheten och sammanhänga med primitiva föreställningssätt.»

[91] H.L.A. Hart, *Legal Rights* (1973), now in *Essays on Bentham. Studies in Jurisprudence and Political Theory*, Clarendon Press, Oxford 1982, pp. 184–5 (italics added).

[92] A. Hägerström, *Socialfilosofiska uppsatser*, cit., pp. 126–127: «Rättigheten såsom moralisk är nu som sagt en av fysiska förhållanden oberoende *makt* eller *kraft* att kräva något av andra (...). *Kraft* är alltid något inre eller andligt (...). Kraften såsom något inre och andligt är given i en känsloupplevelse.»

[93] A. Hägerström, *Rätten och staten*, cit., pp. 221, 249: «en ren andens makt.»

[94] The American legal theorist Wesley Hohfeld (1879–1918) operated a classification of four basic elements: The privilege, the claim, the power, and the immunity. They each have a distinctive logical form and might constitute a right in themselves or be parts of a more complex structure. A is said to have a privilege to $\phi$ if and only if A has no duty not to $\phi$; and A has a claim that B $\phi$ if and only if B has a duty to A to $\phi$, where $\phi$ can also be a negative verb. A has a power if and only if A has the ability within a set of rules to alter her own or another's Hohfeldian incidents and B has an immunity if and only if A lacks the ability within a set of rules to alter B's Hohfeldian incidents. See W. Hohfeld, *Fundamental Legal Conceptions As Applied in Judicial Reasoning and Other Legal Essays*, W. Cook (ed.), Yale University Press, New Haven 1923. For an overview of the theory of rights, it is sufficient to mention J. Feinberg, *The Nature and Value of Rights*, in «Journal of Value Inquiry», 1970, 4, pp. 263–267; J. Raz, *On the Nature of Rights*, in «Mind», 1984, 93, pp. 194–214; J. Waldron (ed.), *Theories of Rights*, Oxford University Press, Oxford 1984; C. Wellman, *A Theory of Rights*, Roman & Allanheld, Totowa, NJ, 1985; C.S. Nino (ed.), *Rights*, New York University Press, NY 1992; and more recently, G. Rainbolt, *The Concept of Rights*, Springer, Dordrecht 2006.

[95] A. Hägerström, *Stat och rätt*, cit., p. 106.

[96] A. Hägerström, *Philosophy and Religion*, cit., p. 316. Hägerström explained that «the idea of rights in another sense than the advantages which the individual is granted through the system of rules, is an idea of super-sensible powers.» See also the manuscript *H 12:3* (from 1923), p. 3: *fördelar*.

(b) power[97] – (c) force[98] – (d) claim[99] – (e) requirement[100] – (f) interest[101] – (g) permission.[102] Strangely enough, "entitlement" is the only equivalent to right that he did not like to use.

Many of these definitions can be subject to criticism, but the issue is really another: The wide range of definitions suggests that Hägerström was not so concerned with the nature or *form* of rights. What aroused his interest was the question of the social and legal *function* of rights, that is the question of what rights do for those who hold them. So Hägerström's reading should be viewed against the background of the so-called choice- and interest theories,[103] the two main theories of the function of rights.

On one hand, according to choice-theorists, a promisee has a right because he or she has the power to waive the promisor's duty to keep the promise. In Hohfeldian terms, choice theorists assert that rights includes a Hohfeldian power over a claim. This is the sense of Hohfeld's assertion according to which in the strictest sense all rights are claims.[104] Whereas this reading of the function of rights can be traced back to Thomas Hobbes and Immanuel Kant, the modern debate on this issue is related to names such as H.L.A. Hart who famously argued that rights concern the proper distribution of freedom or choice rather than benefits:[105] «One who has a right has a choice respected by the law.»[106] This is a view that has been developed by

---

[97] A. Hägerström, *Naturrätt i straffrättsvetenskapen?*, in «Svensk Juristtidning», 1920:5, pp. 321–341. The Swedish word is *makt.*

[98] A. Hägerström, *Naturrätt i straffrättsvetenskapen?*, cit.; *Vergleich zwischen den Kraftvorstellungen der primitiven und modernen Kulturvölker*, in *Festskrift tillägnad professor emeritus Arvi Grotenfelt*, (ed.) E. Kaila, J.E. Saaloma, E. Ahlman, Ajatus, Porvoo 1933, pp. 63–84. The Swedish equivalent is *kraft.*

[99] A. Hägerström, *Social rättvisa*, in *Socialfilosofiska uppsatser*, cit., p. 123: *anspråk*. See also manuscript *H 111:1a*, p. 3 where he addressed Georg Jellinek's theory of "subjective public rights" in terms of claims.

[100] A. Hägerström, *Social rättvisa*, in *Socialfilosofiska uppsatser*, cit., p. 133: *krav.*

[101] A. Hägerström, *Om sociala vidskepelser*, in *Socialfilosofiska uppsatser*, cit., p. 116: *intresse.*

[102] A. Hägerström, *Stat och rätt*, cit., p. 106: *tillåtelse.*

[103] I prefer to speak of choice theory and not will theory in order to avoid confusion with what Hägerström himself called *will theory*, i.e. the idea that the binding force of law derives from it being the will of the sovereign. Nevertheless, for a historical reconstruction of the opposition between choice/will theory and interest/benefit theory in English, see H.L.A. Hart, *Legal Rights* (1973), now in *Essays on Bentham*, cit.; M.H. Kramer, N.E. Simmonds, H. Steiner, *A Debate over Rights*, Clarendon Press, Oxford 1998, pp. 115–145; and in Italian, and the excellent comparison in B. Celano, *I diritti nella* Jurisprudence *anglosassone contemporanea. Da Hart a Raz*, in «Analisi e diritto 2001», P. Comanducci, R. Guastini (eds.), Giappichelli, Torino 2002.

[104] W. Hohfeld, *Fundamental Legal Conceptions*, cit., p. 36.

[105] H.L.A. Hart, *Are There Any Natural Rights?*, in «Philosophical Review», 1955, 64, pp. 177–191, reprinted in *Theories of Rights*, ed. Jeremy Waldron, Oxford University Press, Oxford 1984, pp. 77–90.

[106] H.L.A. Hart, *Essays on Bentham*, cit., p. 188.

scholars such as Joel Feinberg,[107] Carl Wellman,[108] and N.E. Simmonds[109] among others.

On the other hand, according to interest-theorists, a promisee has a right because he or she has some interest in the performance of the promise, so the function of a right is to further the right-holder's interests. The pedigree of interest theory includes philosophers like Jeremy Bentham and John Stuart Mill, jurists like Rudolf von Jhering and John Salmond. Among contemporaries, Joseph Raz,[110] Neil MacCormick,[111] David Lyons[112] and Matthew Kramer are usually mentioned. Hägerström's view of rights clearly belongs to this second theory.

Just like Salmond believed that «a legal right (...) is an interest recognized and protected by a rule of legal justice,»[113] Hägerström was explicit when stating, in 1907, that a right (*rättighet*) is a form of «social protection» (*samhällskydd*) and a duty is a form of «social constraint.»[114] Rights are thus said to stand in «inextricable connection to interests»[115] and to be a «superstructure of our interests.»[116]

Hägerström nonetheless had a broad notion of interest which reflected the etymological sense of the term as equivalent to «general human aspirations»[117] or "ambition" as in some older writers, like in Niccolò Machiavelli, Adam Ferguson and Adam Smith.[118] Therefore Hägerström spoke of private, national and public interests, but also of social and human interests.[119] To this he added the Marxian

---

[107] J. Feinberg, *Rights, Justice and the Bounds of Liberty*, Princeton University Press, Princeton, NJ, 1980, pp. 148–150, 157–158, 232–238.

[108] C. Wellman, *A Theory of Rights*, cit., pp. 64–66.

[109] See Simmonds' contribution to M.H. Kramer, N.E. Simmonds, H. Steiner, *A Debate over Rights*, cit.

[110] J. Raz, *The Morality of Freedom*, Clarendon, Oxford 1986, p. 166: «'X has a right' if and only if X can have rights, and, other things being equal, an aspect of X's well-being (his interest) is a sufficient reason for holding some other person(s) to be under a duty.» See also Id., *Practical Reason and Norms*, Hutchinson, London 1975.

[111] N. MacCormick, *Children's Rights: A Test-Case for Theories of Rights*, in «Archiv für Rechts- und Sozialphilosophie», 1976, 62, p. 311: «The essential feature of rules which confer rights is that they have as a specific aim the protection or advancement of individual interests or goods.»

[112] D. Lyons, *Rights, Claimants and Beneficiaries* (1969), now in *Rights, Welfare and Mill's Moral Theory*, Oxford University Press, Oxford 1994.

[113] J. Salmond, *Jurisprudence*, 6th ed., Sweet and Maxwell, London 1920, p. 182.

[114] A. Hägerström, *I moralpsykologiska frågor*, in «Psyke», II, 5, p. 286.

[115] A. Hägerström, *Om sociala vidskepelser*, in *Socialfilosofiska uppsatser*, cit., p. 101.

[116] A. Hägerström, *Om sociala vidskepelser*, in *Socialfilosofiska uppsatser*, cit., p. 116: «en överbyggnad på våra intressen.» Here Hägerström explicitly refers to the Marxian conception of rights.

[117] See A.O. Hirschman, *The Passions and the Interests. Political Arguments for Capitalism before Its Triumph*, Princeton University Press, Princeton, NJ, 1977, pp. 32–37.

[118] See J.A. Bernstein, *Adam Ferguson and the Idea of Progress*, in «Studies in Burke and His Time», 1978, XIX, n. 2, pp. 99–118, especially pp. 105 ff.

[119] A. Hägerström, *Om sociala vidskepelser*, in *Socialfilosofiska uppsatser*, cit., pp. 102–104. See also the manuscript *H 119:5*, p. 7: *samhällsintresset*.

idea that private or "selfish" interests are already socially determined interests[120] which implies that the question "what is my interest?" cannot be addressed without answering the question "who am I?"

So, for Hägerström, a right is grounded in an interest protected by a duty-imposing rule. A right is said to be «the advantages which the individual is granted through the system of rules.»[121] This means that duties have priority over rights in the sense that there can be no rights without reflection in someone else's obligation. Theorists are usually divided between those who think that rights are the "reflex" of the duty and those who think that rights have a priority over it, i.e., rights ground duties. On this issue, Hägerström seems to agree with Bentham, Austin, and Hohfeld for instance.[122] It should be noted, however, that contemporary interest theorists tend to move away from this assumption, developing instead the idea of the priority of rights.[123]

But if rights are reflections of obligations as a system of protected interests in society, why do we talk about rights in terms of force, power and claims? And if rights refer to interests what is so "mystical" about them? Hägerström held rights to refer to superstructures of interest, but he also realised that lawyers usually define rights in very different ways. So, Hägerström criticised jurists for holding that rights are "powers" and "claims" while they are actually much more complex attitudes involving interest and cognitive elements like belief.[124] What is worth emphasizing is that Hägerström hence developed a view of what lawyers usually mean by "rights" which seems rather similar to Hohfeld's. The latter considered "rights" to be somewhat chameleonic because of a certain looseness of language: «The term "right" tends to be used indiscriminately to cover what in a given case may be a privilege, a power, or an immunity, rather than a right in the strictest sense.»[125] This need for disambiguation was later stressed by Alf Ross as well.[126] For Hägerström, a major concern for theorists trying to sort out what legal scholars mean by rights is that "rights" are often taken to be "legal advantages."[127]

---

[120]This idea was elaborated by K. Marx in *Grundrisse der Kritik der politischen Ökonomie* in 1859.

[121]A. Hägerström, *Philosophy and Religion*, cit., p. 316.

[122]On Hägerström's relation to Rudolf von Jhering's interest theory, see Chapter 4, § 4.2.

[123]See for example N. MacCormick, *Rights in Legislation*, in P.M.S. Hacker, J. Raz (eds.), *Law, Morality and Society*, Clarendon, Oxford 1977, pp. 200–201.

[124]See in particular A. Hägerström, *Naturrätt i straffrättsvetenskapen?*, in «Svensk Juristtidning», 1920:5, pp. 321–341.

[125]W. Hohfeld, *Some Fundamental Legal Conceptions As Applied in Judicial Reasoning*, in «Yale Law Journal», 1913, 23, pp. 16–59, quote on p. 36.

[126]A. Ross, *On Law and Justice*, Stevens & Sons, London 1958, p. 168: «The right-duty division is too superficial. The term "right" includes such heterogeneous concepts as claim, liberty, power (competence) and immunity, and "duty" is not differentiated from the rest of the passive modalities.»

[127]Cf. A. Hägerström, *Philosophy and Religion*, cit., p. 316 and W. Hohfeld, *Some Fundamental Legal Conceptions*, cit., p. 58. However, a significant difference between Hohfeld and Hägerström was that the latter did not really concentrate on the analysis of the *form*, but rather on the *function*

Overall, it seems that the rights Hägerström was interested in were first and foremost those of the individual. Moreover, he was essentially puzzled by their *social function in a polity* and therefore he did not direct much attention to the question of the logical structure or form of these "subjective rights" within the legal system. In a historical perspective, this circumstance is interesting since it puts Hägerström in the front row in the development of the interest theory of rights, which has increasingly enjoyed the spotlight of late twentieth century philosophy of law.

### 6.4.4 Conceptions of Right as Ideology

A second observation we should make concerns the relation between Hägerström's non-cognitivist theory and his theory of rights. In Hägerström, there seems to be a difference between rights and conceptions of right, in the sense that the former are a component of the latter but the latter encompasses more than just the former element. It is striking that Hägerström appears to have understood *conceptions of right*, like private property for instance,[128] as having a complex internal structure which often involves several of the Hohfeldian incidents. Such *conceptions of right* are ordered arrangements of several basic components, much in the same way that most molecules are ordered arrangements of several chemical elements.[129]

Furthermore, Hägerström held conceptions of right to incorporate not only different logical elements, but also several psychological ones. The fundamental elements that, if combined, engender a conception of right are (ideas about) values, interests and traditional beliefs.[130]

In the 1913 essay on *Social superstition*, Hägerström discussed four examples of *conceptions of right* that he deemed to be false. The four examples are the belief in the sanctity of the constitution, the idea of sovereignty, the right to private property

---

of rights. Bruno Celano elaborated a quadripartite scheme of theories of right in which Hägerström would be ordered, together with several other eighteenth century philosophers, in the category "anti-Hohfeldian interest theories." (see B. Celano, *I diritti nella* jurisprudence, cit., p. 50).

[128] A. Hägerström, *Stat och rätt*, cit., p. 174; *I moralpsykologiska frågor*, in «Psyke», 1907, III, vols. 1–2, pp. 90–91.

[129] This comparison was made by Hoheld's editor W. Cook, *Hohfeld's Contributions to the Science of Law*, in W. Hohfeld, *Fundamental Legal Conceptions*, cit., p. 15. See also L. Wenar, *The Nature of Rights*, in «Philosophy and Public Affairs», 2005, 33, n. 3, pp. 223–252. The atomic/molecule model was later criticised by Neil MacCormick, *Rights, Claims and Remedies*, in «Law and Philosophy», 1982, 1, p. 349: «Not all rights are either instances of the simple Hohfeldian categories, or reducible to aggregations thereof.» Such an interpretation is worthy of further assessment.

[130] It is not clear what specific role tradition plays in the reification process at hand in the psychological interiorisation process at the basis of the conception of right. Hägerström would probably have recognized that the "conception of right" advocated by, say, the monarchomachs was construed against tradition, not on its basis. Generally, however, Hägerström seems to have viewed the beliefs involved in the conception of right as deposited in tradition, since tradition is one of the stronger elements providing interiorisation of norms through the suggestive effect.

and human or natural rights. It is thus clear that conceptions of right involve *emotion* at some stage of its genesis. «Conceptions of right (...) all have a common characteristic in the fact that they refer to representations and emotions with an ideological content (...). Every ideology in this sense is illusionary since it is only a way in which the external nature, the economic conditions and interests are mirrored in the human consciousness.»[131] Now, the emotional attitude is neither true, nor false, but it is connected to beliefs that can be said to be true or false. It is this latter cognitive element which is ideological in nature and that makes the *conception of right* false. This explains why Hägerström departed from his axiological nihilism in his description of rights as a special category of norms. The conative impulse of duty in relation to a certain action (that I can only have from a first person perspective, since, in the third person perspective, the impartial observer fails to notice the emotional urge), i.e., this fundamental experience for ethical reasoning that Hägerström studied closely on many occasions (see Chapter 5), is a very different experience from upholding that the right to private property as inalienable or, with Hägerström's lexis, *sacrosanct*;[132] in other words, upholding or affirming something *as if* it were a purely alethic and theoretic assertion that an impartial observer might confirm. We may render the difference between ideas concerning values and conceptions of right with the following scheme.

**Conceptions of Right** (false)

| **Value-ideas** | **Interests** | **Elements of (false) Consciousness** |
|---|---|---|
| (neither true, nor false)<br>⇗ ⇘<br>**Emotion** and Mental Image of an Action | (neither true, nor false)<br>• on a personal, national and global *level*<br>• of a natural, social, economic *nature*<br>engender **rights** («advantages granted through rules») | Mental images turned into beliefs or travesties of cognitive elements based on Supranaturalism and usually sedimented in tradition |

To sum up, from Hägerström's perspective, «it is unconceivable that these fictitious ideas about rights and duties that belong or rest on individuals in some mysterious fashion can be kept alive. Then, the constricting force caused by this

[131] A. Hägerström, *Social teleologi*, cit., p. 57: «Rättsliga idéer (...) ha alla till gemensamt kännetecken att hänföra sig till föreställningar och känslor med ideellt innehåll (...). Hvarje ideologi i denna bemarkelse är illusorisk, så tillvida som den blott är ett sätt, hvarpå den yttre naturen, de ekonomiska förhållandena och intressena afspegla sig i människornas medvetande.»

[132] A. Hägerström, *Socialfilosofiska uppsatser*, cit., pp. 98–109.

idea, [the state as God], can be substituted with everybody's consensual understanding of the importance of maintaining the legal system.»[133] The false consciousness of jurists and citizens claiming that there are power-rights is really nothing more than an image of man as a superstitious being, destined to fade away.

The fictive ideas about rights and duties, once a source of vigour for us, have now become a font of tribulation. Yet we still have to explain how this change occurred by highlighting Hägerström's view of history that grounds his considerations.

## 6.5 The Philosophy of History

Against the background of Hägerström's thought it is possible to delineate a philosophy of history. Some interpreters have reduced his conception of history to some form of sheer positivism[134] or social Darwinism: «There is in Hägerström a pseudo-Darwinian explanation of history's development and it is this explanation that makes it possible for him to affirm that society is evolving towards consensus, which is the goal that he believes is set. (. . .) Hägerström means that it would be abnormal if the individual tried to resist this societal evolution since it rests on the interests of the majority.»[135] Indeed, he insisted on many occasions that *only what is useful for the continuation of society survives in the struggle for life.*[136] So the overall impression that Hägerström's philosophy of history leaves is that «it is a rationalistic and consensus-focused vision (. . .) that comes through.»[137]

There is also a more Hegelian touch to Hägerström's view of history. This is particularly clear from his personal correspondence where he spoke of "the Tribunal

---

[133] A. Hägerström, *Rätten och staten*, cit., p. 252: «ty det är otänkbart att dessa fiktiva idéer om rättigheter och skyldigheter, som på något mystiskt sätt skulle tillhöra eller påvila individerna, i längden kunna upprätthållas. Då kan den nedtryckande (. . .) kraft som vållats av denna idé [staten som Gud] blott ersättas av allas samfällda insikt i betydelsen av rättsordningens bestånd.»

[134] See the recent thesis in J. Bjarup, *Scepticism and Scandinavian Legal Realists*, cit., p. 58: «Hägerström subscribes to Auguste Comte's philosophy, holding that humanity is progressing from the theological state, characterized by superstitious beliefs in the existence of God as a source of values, through the metaphysical stage, characterized by the magical belief that human beings have natural rights related to their selfish interests, to the positive stage of scientific knowledge, based on facts and the cultivation of benevolent, or altruistic, feelings among people.»

[135] O. Sigurdson, *Den lyckliga filosofin*, cit., p. 77: «det finns hos Hägerström, en pseudodarwinistisk förklaring av historiens utveckling, och det är denna som möjliggör för Hägerström att hävda att samhället håller på att utveckla sig mot konsensus, vilket är det mål som Hägerström ser som givet. (. . .) Hägerström menar även att det vore abnormt av individen att sätta sig upp mot denna samhällsutveckling, eftersom den ligger i de flestas intresse.»

[136] A. Hägerström, *Om sociala vidskepelser*, cit., p. 95: «endast det (. . .) för samhällets bestånd nyttiga består i kampen om tillvaron.»

[137] O. Sigurdson, *Den lyckliga filosofin*, cit., p. 71: «Den är en rationalistisk och konsensusbetonad vison (. . .) som tonar fram.»

of history"[138] and echoed the understanding of the *Weltgeist*.[139] The ultimate scope of human existence in relation to world history must hence be to become a "link in the chain of culture" (*länk i kulturkedjan*). This is a topic he came back to often. In September 1898 he first declared that he must «carry on (...) towards the great goal to become a *link in the chain of culture* that connects departed generations to the future generations and that in turn constitutes the human element in the great world process, whose sense no one has grasped and probably never will.»[140] However, contrarily to Hegel, it is not liberty that sets history in motion but the striving towards peace and consensus. «The development of culture brings on the necessity to move (...) to a focus on joint effort for harmonic teamwork.»[141]

The link between Hägerström's conception of history and evolution and the call for tolerance, and a generally humanistic approach to practical and political issues, was stated as early as 1907.[142] With the "overturning of values" that occurred with the rise of Christianity, from the ethics of war to the morals of individual dignity, a conflict-reticent and solidarity-focused set of norms is not just valued but it is necessary.[143] The next step in this process towards consensus is the understanding that our ideological conceptions rest on our own needs. «There is only one way that can free mankind from the religious need: The insight into the chain of causes in nature.»[144] There are clear elements of nineteenth century positivism in this outlook.[145] However, there are also many elements coming from Enlightenment. To Hélène Apéria-Meurling, who interviewed him in April 1939, «Hägerström's whole

---

[138]Letter to Esther Nyander April 12th 1899, now in M. Waller, *Människan som få kände*, cit., p. 153.

[139]Letter to Esther Nyander, April 5th 1897, now in M. Waller, *Människan som få kände*, cit., p. 119. Moreover, in *De socialistiska idéernas historia*, cit., p. 265, he also speaks of the «sublation of the Greco-Roman culture in the German culture» which sounds as if it had been taken directly from Hegel's *History of Philosophy*.

[140]Letter to Esther Nyander, from September 1898, now in M. Waller, *Människan som få kände*, cit., p. 122: «därför framåt (...) mot det stora målet att bliva en länk i den kulturkedja, som binder förgångna släkten tillsammans med tillkommande och som utgör i sin ordning den insats, som mänskligheten gör i den stora världsprocessen, vars innebörd ännu ingen genomskådat och väl aldrig heller skall genomskåda.»

[141]A. Hägerström, *De socialistiska idéernas historia*, cit., p. 266: «kulturutvecklingen själv för med sig nödvändigheten att övergå (...) till ett inriktande av alla krafter på harmonisk samverkan.»

[142]It should however be noted that during the spring term 1904, Hägerström held a course on "evolutionary ethics."

[143]A. Hägerström, *Jesus. En karaktärsanalys*, ed. by M. Fries, Natur & Kultur, Stockholm 1968, p. 80: «När nu rättsordningen är sådan den är (...), så är personlig barmhärtighet mot dem som komma på livets skuggsidor nödvändig.»

[144]A. Hägerström, *Socialistiska idéernas historia*, cit., p. 55: «Det finns endast ett medel, som relativt befriar människan från det religiösa behovet, och det är insikten i natursammanhanget.»

[145]As Thomas Mautner stressed, Hägerström had a favourable opinion about Auguste Comte's tripartite scheme of evolution: *Hägerströms lära* i *moral. Hägerströms värdefrihetstes*, in «Insikt och handling. Hans Larsson samfundet», 2000, vol. 20, p. 43.

philosophy is an accusation of the era of religious wars in which we live.»[146] But let us look a little closer at the *political side* of what Hägerström believed to be the *Musik der Zukunft*.

## 6.6 Evolving Towards the *Weltrepublik*

«The assumption of eternal values is baroque. Man has, in superb folly, considered those ends and values, that are consistent with social relations and unsurpassable for us, as if they were given a cosmic meaning (...). A crazier thought cannot be imagined.»[147] Hägerström continuously insisted on the historical development of values, and corresponding legal constructions, norms and institutions. This emphasis has a specific political scope which should not be underestimated. In the political life of the early twentieth century – without universal and female suffrage, when the working class lacked voice and peaceful exit in most matters, institutional reforms lagged behind and royalist tendencies were still countering parliamentary rule and constitutionalism – the mere suggestion that rights and duties were shaped by historical struggles and hence subject to evolution should perhaps be considered an idea belonging to the progressive camp in politics.

The belief in *immutable* moral principles deriving from some form of *Volksgeist* or "essence" of legal institutions, or generally the idealist faith of Pandectists like Puchta, Windscheid and others provided motives for reactionary tendencies, directed foremost against the extension of franchise. From this perspective, there is a link between Hägerström and the so-called Swedish model that Gunnar Fredriksson, for one, highlighted: «Many came to see Hägerström as the philosopher behind the building of the welfare society. Hägerström probably also meant that the majority of people had an interest in unveiling conservative myths and substituting these with more rational ideas.»[148]

Hägerström maintained that belief in eternal values, although illusionary, had been a source of strength in human history but had developed into a source of suffering and tribulation in the present day.[149] In the spring lectures from 1917, he insisted on this aspect: «In the now raging war, the statesmen (...) of single countries put the welfare of their own state above all. For national welfare, it is not only

[146] H. Apéria en Meurling, *Samtal med en svensk tänkare*, in «Ord och bild», 1939, 48, p. 422: «hela den hägerströmska filosofien utgör en anklagelse mot den religionskrigens era, i vilken vi leva.»

[147] H. Apéria en Meurling, *Samtal med en svensk tänkare*, cit., p. 422: «Antagandet om eviga värden är barockt. Människan har i sin högfärdstokighet betraktat sådana ändamål och värden, som gjort sig gällande i den sociala umgängelsen och som tett sig som ofrånkomliga för henne, såsom ägnade kosmisk betydelse (...). Något galnare låter sig ej tänkas.»

[148] G. Fredriksson, *20 filosofer*, cit., p. 209: «därmed kom många att se Hägerström som filosofen bakom välfärdssamhällets uppbyggnad. Hägerström menade nog också, att folkmajoriteten hade intresse av att konservativa myter avslöjades och ersattes av mer rationella idéer.»

[149] Particularly clear is the account in A. Hägerström, *Om social rättvisa*, in «Spectrum», 1932, vol. 1, pp. 1–14.

considered fair to sacrifice individual members, but also to abandon the rules of *ius gentium*. (...) This interest (...) has to be carried through *without consideration* of the happiness of the individual.»[150]

Hägerström, who usually developed his philosophy of history through the history of philosophy, described a *signum prognosticum* in his 1909 lectures, *Socialistiska idéers historia*. He pointed to a tendency of development towards major freedom and greater social cohesion through the emancipation of the individual's beliefs from the convictions prevailing in society: «The development of society goes in waves, up and down. Again, the Platonic and medieval spirit would raise its ugly head (...). There is, in my opinion, a shift in the conception of the world. It consists in distancing ourselves from the idea that we live for intangible ends (...). It has also become clear that our goal is our own happiness in the material world and that we are not means for purposes that transcends our sensitive existence.»[151]

The three steps in this political development are the *old world* (that connected Platonism, via the Middle Ages, to the *Ancien régime*); *liberalism* in the eighteenth and nineteenth century version that created modern individualism and formal rights and liberties; and *socialism*, which launched the idea that social cohesion depends on the substantial autonomy for individuals being guaranteed.

According to Hägerström's argumentation, this third step will therefore alleviate the conflicts between social groups, allowing for more consensus and less violence. «In liberalism there is still a residual element from the past. There is an intangible element, i.e., the eternal justice in equality and liberty that liberalism sets as its goal (...). The key to understanding modern socialism is hereby given. It is, at the same time, a reaction against liberalism and Platonic tendencies. It still happens that socialism lives on liberal ideas of justice. But these ideas are then fashioned as equal right to happiness (...). But the sound and strong version of socialism does not have this nature. For this [version], society does not have any insubstantial ends.

---

[150] A. Hägerström, *Moralpsykologi*, Natur & Kultur, Stockholm 1952, p. 29: «I nu pågående krig är det så att de särskilda staternas statsmän (...) sätta den egna statens välfärd över allt annat. För denna välfärd anses det ej blott riktigt att de enskilda medlemmarna uppoffras (...), utan man anser även att bestående folkrättsliga regler måste vika (...). Detta intresse (...) är till för att ovillkorligt realiseras *utan hänsyn* till individens lycka.»

[151] A. Hägerström, *De socialistiska idéernas historia*, cit., pp. 29–30: «samhällsutvecklingen går som en böljegång från vågberg till vågdalar. Ännu en gång skulle den platonskt-medeltida anden resa sitt huvud (...). Det är enligt min mening en förskjutning i hela världsåskådningen. Den ligger däri, att vi kommit allt längre bort från den tanken, att vi leva för översinnliga mål (...). Det står också klart, att vårt mål är vår egen lycka i sinnevärlden och att vi icke äro medel för över vår sinnliga tillvaro stående mål.»

(...) Social cohesion (...) is important only in so far as it brings happiness to the individual.»[152]

Hägerström thus viewed modern social democracy as an "evolutionistic" outcome: «It is now clear that modern socialism has to be democratic (...). People are the natural leaders of social activity. But it is also clear that this democracy cannot have a liberal nature. In that case, the individuals would only promote particularistic interests in their economic activity (...). The individual has to operate for the whole (...). This presupposes solidarity of interest (...). Democracy therefore has to become a social democracy.»[153]

The future society that he named "social democracy" is an important step towards a *higher form of society* that is capable of addressing the friction between social groups and where consensus, not fear or superstition, drives social cohesion. However, some caution in interpretation is necessary because Hägerström wrote this down when Sweden had no universal suffrage and was decades away from welfare. So it is not always easy to specify what kind of "higher form of societal organisation" Hägerström had in mind.

From a general perspective, we can nevertheless say that this higher form of society is characterised by a predominant rational factor,[154] and promotes – through proper education – individual free thinking.[155] In more political terms, a few elements suggest that Hägerström foresaw a "future society" based on a federalist and trans-national conception of the political community. In *Socialistiska idéers historia*, for example, Hägerström drew a brief account of the political evolution of the West, where he explicitly mentioned the passage from medieval closed societies to "consolidated nation states," leading up to the contemporary *globalisation* of the *belle époque*: «The third [step...] belongs to the present day, when civilised Europe has become one single cultural system because of various circumstances. We also

---

[152] A. Hägerström, *De socialistiska idéernas historia*, cit., p. 32: «I liberalismen finns ännu kvar liksom en spillra från förgångna tider. Där finns ett osinnligt element, den s.k. eviga rättfärdigheten i jämlikheten och friheten, som liberalismen på sitt sätt gör till mål (...). Nu är emellertid på detta sätt nyckeln given till en förståelse av den moderna socialismens kynne. Det är på en gång en reaktion mot liberalismen och mot platoniserande tendenser. Visserligen händer det, att den ännu understundom lever på liberala rättsidéer. Dessa ha då den formen, att var och en har lika rätt till lycka (...). Men den sunda, livskraftiga socialismen har icke denna karaktär. För den har samhället överhuvud inga som helst osinnliga mål (...). Samhällsenheten (...) har sin betydelse blott såsom bringade de enskilda människorna lycka.»

[153] A. Hägerström, *De socialistiska idéernas historia*, cit., pp. 32–33: «Det är nu klart, att den moderna socialismen måste vara demokratisk (...). Därför är den naturliga ledaren för samhällsverksamheten folket självt. Men det är också klart, att denna demokrati ej kan ha liberalistisk karaktär. Då skulle individen i sin ekonomiska verksamhet verka blott för sina särintressen (...). Den enskilde måste även (...) verka för det hela (...). Detta förutsätter en intressesolidaritet (...). Demokratien måste sålunda bli en social demokrati.»

[154] See the manuscript *H 119:5* entitled *On the Victory of Reason* where Hägerström described reason and science as the major forces that defeat the antisocial tendencies in mankind.

[155] This is the central thesis in *Verkligt autonom moral* (1930), now in *Moralpsykologi*, cit. See also *I moralpsykologiska frågor*, cit., p. 273; and the letter to Esther Nyander from October 1898, now in M. Waller, *Människan som få kände*, cit., p. 123.

have good reason to presume that this cultural system, in order to gain solidity and order, will assume more advanced political forms in the course of evolution.»[156]

This conception of the political community should be put in relation with the European federalist tradition. The latter counts political thinkers and activists like Hägerström's favourite author, Kant, with his *Zum ewigen Frieden*, but also Henri de Saint-Simon, Victor Hugo, Carlo Cattaneo, Giuseppe Mazzini and one of Hägerström's contemporaries, Richard Coudenhove-Kalergi (1894–1972). In 1926, some 15 years after the aforementioned *Socialistiska idéers historia*, Coudenhove-Kalergi founded, the pan European movement in Vienna,[157] of which Aristide Briand was to be elected honorary president the following year and whose members counted Albert Einstein, Thomas Mann, Sigmund Freud, Rainer Maria Rilke, Miguel de Unamuno, Salvador de Madariaga, José Ortega y Gasset and one of the founding fathers of the modern European Union, Konrad Adenauer.

So, in Hägerström's reading of the "tendencies of development in modern society" (*det moderna samhällets utvecklingstendenser*), the *belle époque* corresponded to a first step in the direction of what we now call globalisation and what Hägerström saw in the following terms: «If we think of the newer social conditions (...) we are struck by the strong cultural relations between the societies of culture and that makes them to a certain extent the *same* culture (...). The cultural purpose of society has become so much wider and complex that it would be unintelligible according to the ancient view.»[158]

Moreover Hägerström believed that a federal structure of the constitution would not be enough to ensure world peace. Such a political structure needs to be combined with a federal economic policy. This is why Hägerström expressed criticism over the League of Nations and its so-called "Locarno spirit" since the economic situation in Germany, at the end of World War I, with the famous *Diktat* of the Versailles peace treaty, would only have led to new catastrophes. On February 14th 1933, he wrote: «It is clear to me that the now prevailing *mass psychosis* of the doctrine that holds states to have obligations to one another *independently of their life-upholding interests*, lacks reality and it is fruit of imagination. Only when the economic difficulties would induce a world organisation of production and distribution (...) would

---

[156] A. Hägerström, *De socialistiska idéernas historia*, cit., p. 265: «Den tredje [etappen...] hör till nutiden, då hela det kultiverade Europa kommit att på grund av olika omständigheter utgöra ett enda kultursystem. Man har också all anledning till att antaga, att detta kultursystem, för att vinna fasthet och ordning, under utvecklingens gång skall antaga även mer utpräglade politiska former.»

[157] Richard Coudenhove-Kalergi first composed his manifesto *Paneuropa* in 1923.

[158] A. Hägerström, *De socialistiska idéernas historia*, cit., p. 59: «Tänker man på de nyare samhällsförhållandena (...) så frapperas man av de starka kulturella förbindelser, som äga rum mellan kultursamhällena och som göra att de i vissa hänseenden bilda *ett* kultursamhälle (...). Det kulturella samhällsändamålet har vidgat sig till en omfattning och en komplicering som för ett antikt betraktelsesätt skulle te sig som alldeles obegripliga.» In his terminology, "societies of culture" (*kultursamhällena*) are opposed to "societies of nature" (*natursamhällena*), i.e. undeveloped countries or the pre-modern era. Hägerström did not dwell on the topic but some remarks can be found in *I moralpsykologiska frågor*, cit., pp. 91 ff.

the unconditional obligations of *ius gentium* become more than mist.»[159] Somehow, for Hägerström, the «beastly instincts»[160] ruling over international relations would be overcome, and the rationalisation within the history of *ius gentium* can be seen as a form of adaptation of our moral systems to evolution, making them more open.[161] Indeed, he often insisted on the fact that morals are a "phenomenon of fitting in."[162]

This political aspect of Hägerström has usually been neglected, but in a time of colonialism, widespread imperialism, nationalistic tendencies and xenophobic politics, it must be considered innovative. He appeared to be an avant-garde cosmopolitan. «As far as I am concerned, I hold the national sentiment to be important only as a preparatory step for the education of a sentiment for the *human being* (...) as, on one hand, a product of the *cultivated* man and, on the other, as what *cultivates* man. The national sentiment becomes bad if it goes beyond being preparatory and if it replaces what is *really humane* in the heart.»[163] Unsurprisingly, when his grandson John-Axel Waller was born in the autumn of 1935, he welcomed him as a "citizen of the world.[164]"

---

[159] A. Hägerström, *Marx och filosofin*, in «Tiden», 1933, 25, p. 148: «därför står det för mig klart att den som en folkpsykos verksamma nu aktuella läran om staternas skyldigheter mot varandra, *oberoende av deras livsintressen*, icke har något realitetsunderlag alls, utan är ett inbillningsfoster. Först om de ekonomiska svårigheterna skulle framtvinga en världsorganisation av produktionen och fördelningen (...) kunde föreställningen om ovillkorliga folkrättsliga skyldigheter bliva mer än dunst.» As known, Lundstedt continued this line of thought in *Superstition or Rationality in Action for Peace? Arguments against Founding a World Peace on the Common Sense of Justice*, Longmans, London 1925.

[160] A. Hägerström, *Socialfilosofiska uppsatser*, cit., p. 217.

[161] A. Hägerström, *Rätten och staten*, cit., p. 12. It should be noted that Henri Bergson developed the distinction between open and closed societies in *Les deux sources de la morale et de la religion*: This is one of Hägerström's sources. See A. Hägerström, *Moralfilosofins grundläggning*, Almqvist & Wiksell International, Stockholm 1987, p. 16. He dedicated one of his last seminars to this work by Bergson (autumn 1932).

[162] O. Sigurdson, *Den lyckliga filosofin*, cit., p. 54: *anpassningsfenomen*.

[163] M. Waller, *Människan som få kände*, cit., p. 134: «för min del anser jag att nationalkänslan har sin betydelse blott såsom förberedelse till fostrandet av vad jag vill kalla känslan för människan (...) såsom å ena sidan produkt av den *förädlade* människan, å anda sidan såsom självt förädlande människan. Nationalkänslan blir ett ont, om den går längre än att vara förberedande och tager upp *platsen* i hjärtat, så att intet finnes kvar för känslan av det *sant mänskliga*.»

[164] M. Waller, *Människan som få kände*, cit., p. 212.

# Chapter 7
# The Final Studies

*Whatever lives long is gradually so saturated with reason that its irrational origins become improbable.*
*Does not almost every accurate history of the origin of something sound paradoxical and sacrilegious to our feelings?*[1]

In time for his 55th birthday, on September 6th 1923, Hägerström and his wife Esther moved for their last time, settling in *Floragatan*, on the outskirts of town. This small house hosted the smoky studio and library room where he spent most of his remaining days, working on two immense tasks that only death could keep him from finishing. The first task was his overwhelming study on Roman law, and more specifically on the genesis of judicial notions such as obligation, duties, rights, and property.[2] The second task Hägerström dealt with during the last 15 years of his life was even more arduous and demanding: It involved both a criticism of Albert Einstein's theory of relativity and some fundamental concepts of contemporary science.

On the personal side of life, he received some bad news: His brother David died in 1926, and a few years later his admired teacher Burman passed away,[3] as well as his colleague Phalén. In 1933, as he retired from his chair, his mother passed away too. Conversely, he also had reason to be pleased: At the age of 57, he was elected "inspector" of his region's academic association, where he would take up many discussions with the students and keep the debates alive until late at night. Admired among scholars and students, and feared by colleagues, he held a key role in the academic world of Uppsala as long as he lived.

---

[1] F. Nietzsche, *Morgenröte. Gedanken über die moralischen Vorurteile* (1881); Eng. trans. by J.M. Kennedy, *The Dawn*, Book 1, § 1.

[2] This effort resulted foremost in what we may rightly call his opus magnum, *Der römische Obligationsbegriff* (see infra).

[3] See A. Hägerström, *E.O. Burman. Minnesord*, in «Upsala Nya Tidning», 15/06/1929.

P. Mindus, *A Real Mind*, Law and Philosophy Library 87,
DOI 10.1007/978-90-481-2895-2_7, © Springer Science+Business Media B.V. 2009

## 7.1 The Magic of Words: The Study of Roman Law

« It is understood that, in reality, obedience is determined by highly robust motives of fear and hope – fear of the vengeance of magical powers or of the power-holder, hope for reward in this world or in the next – and besides all this, by interests of the most varied sort.» This "magical" formulation fits perfectly in Hägerström's mouth, who, as early as 1920, stated clearly that his attention for archaic conceptions derived from his astonishment before the commonly shared idea that one could have a "power to someone else's obedience."[4] In this quote, however, it is not Hägerström speaking, but Max Weber in his lecture in Munich during the revolutionary winter of 1918–1919: *Politics as a Vocation.*[5] This overlapping of views shows, nevertheless, that Hägerström's interest for magic in law was not as eccentric as it might seem at a first glance.[6]

The dates are of some importance here to reconstruct Hägerström's final years and to clarify why he was no loner. Far too often he has been depicted as «an obscure visionary pioneer (...) a north-European oracle.»[7] On the contrary, he was rather entrenched in the great discussions of his day. As Carla Faralli correctly emphasised,[8] Hägerström was well-acquainted with the work of authors such as Fustel de Coulanges, Sumner Maine, and the Anglo-Saxon evolutionary school, of which he quoted Tylor's work on animism and James Frazer's *The Golden Bough.*[9] The common inspiration was clearly stated by Émile Durkheim in the introduction to the first issue of *Année sociologique*, where he glossed on Fustel de Coulanges' statement that *true sociology is history*, by claiming that «rien n'est plus incontestable pourvu que l'histoire soit faite sociologiquement.»[10]

---

[4] A. Hägerström, *Naturrätt i straffrättsvetenskapen?*, in «Svensk Juristtidning», 1920:5, pp. 321–341 (*makt till andras lydnad*).

[5] M. Weber, *Politik als Beruf* (1918/19), now in *Gesammelte Politische Schriften*, J. Winkelmann (ed.), Mohr, Tübingen 1988, p. 505.

[6] Another interesting coincidence is that Gurvitch would come to develop interests close to those of Hägerström: It shall suffice to recall *La magie et le droit* (1938, reed. Dalloz, Paris 2004); not to mention, of course, George Dumézil's work from the same period. The French linguist was active in Uppsala in the early 30s.

[7] H. Ruin, *Hägerström, Nietzsche och den svenska nihilismen*, in «Tidskrift för politisk filosofi», 2000:1, p. 5: «en dunkel visionär föregångare (...) ett nordeuropeiskt orakel.»

[8] C. Faralli, *Diritto e magia. Saggio su Axel Hägerström*, Giuffrè, Milano 1982. See also F. Cordero, *Riti e sapienza del diritto*, Laterza, Bari 1981.

[9] J. Frazer, *The Golden Bough. A Study in Comparative Religion* (1890), Oxford University Press, New York 1998 (abridged version); See A. Hägerström, *Das magistratische Ius in seinem Zusammenhang mit dem römischen Sakralrechte*, in *Minnesskrift utgiven av Juridiska fakulteten i Uppsala 1929 till hågkomst av dess första doktorspromotion 1629*, Lundequistska bokh., Uppsala 1929, pp. 27–28; Id., *Religionsfilosofi*, Natur & Kultur, Stockholm 1949, pp. 56 and 183.

[10] E. Durkheim, *Préface*, in «Année Sociologique», 1898, anno I, p. 1. Hägerström referred to the work of Durkheim and to his followers. In particular, Paul Huvelin who studied the relationship between law and sacral conceptions.

With this sociological, but also anthropological and ethnological outlook, Hägerström entered into one of the most significant debates of the time: The one regarding the origins of religion and magic. The schools of thought that studied animistic beliefs had discovered forms of emotional and irrational experiences at the root of magic and religious phenomena, just as Hägerström had emphasised the emotional element present in normative evaluations that we experience as associations between representations and feelings (see Chapter 3).

As early as 1865, in his studies on witchcraft, Edward Burnett Tylor (1832–1917) stressed that the overlapping of subject and object in magic occurs because of an unwarranted psychological association, from which religion would have sprung.[11] In 1892, John H. King, in *The Supernatural: Its Origin, Nature and Evolution* (1892), claimed that religion stems from magic since, in our reaction to exceptional or incomprehensible phenomena, we experienced *impersonal powers* provoking fear and hope long before any personal powers were discovered. Robert Ranulph Marett (1866–1943), influenced by Wilhelm Wundt's theory of animation, later held that the idea of *mana*, which underpins the entire construction of sacredness,[12] was the origin of religious practice, and that the notions of force and taboo were linked, and essential, in magic and religious phenomena alike. To the studies on animism, Marcel Mauss and Henri Hubert added the social dimension of magic when they argued, in *Ésquisse d'une théorie générale de la magie* from 1902, that it is essentially a social phenomenon, therefore related to religion but also to science and technology. As known, the social dimension of magic was later studied by Bronislaw Kaspar Malinowski (1884–1942).

It is against this background that Hägerström's final studies on the ancient world should be viewed. However, not only anthropologists and other social scientists were involved in this research programme. The philosophical agenda was influenced as well. From this viewpoint, it suffices to mention that these were years of mutual influence: In 1922, the same year Max Weber's *Wirtschaft und Gesellschaft* was edited, Lucien Lévy-Bruhl published his study on primitive mentality.[13] Meanwhile, Hägerström lectured on *Magical Elements in Roman Law*.[14] In 1923, when Cassirer's *Philosophy of Symbolic Forms* saw the light, Hägerström studied the so-called "symbolic principle" and applied it to the history of law and in particular to the *bona fide*-principle.[15] So, he entered a period when he dug deep into

---

[11] E.B. Tylor, *Researches into the Early History of Mankind and the Development of Civilisation* (1865), University of Chicago Press, Chicago 1964.

[12] R. Marett, *Mana, ad vocem*, in J. Hastings, J. Selbie (eds.), *Encyclopedia of Religion and Ethics*, T.&T. Clark, Edinburgh 1915. The notion of *mana* was studied by Edwin Sidney Hartland as well.

[13] L. Lévy-Bruhl, *La mentalité primitive*, Alcan, Paris 1922. Hägerström quoted Durkheim's *Les formes élémentaires de la vie religieuse. Le système totémique en Australie*, published a decade earlier (Puf, Paris 1912).

[14] Information taken from T. Mautner, *Vägledning till Hägerströmstudiet*, Almqvist & Wiksell, Stockholm 1994, p. 75 (list of lectures and seminars).

[15] During the academic year 1922–1923, the topic of Hägerström's courses was history of law and the spring term was dedicated to the bona fide-principle. This theme dominated the 1924 spring

the "magical roots"[16] of religious and moral beliefs: In 1924, he lectured on religion and morals; in 1926, on "spiritual religiosity" and, in 1929, on religion and magic. He always combined this attention for spirituality with his interest for the ancient world.[17] After years of tireless mapping of the genesis of legal concepts, in 1927, the same year Heidegger published *Sein und Zeit*, Hägerström finished the first volume of the monumental *Der römische Obligationsbegriff im Lichte der allgemeinen römischen Rechtsanschauung*.[18]

### *7.1.1 Obligationsbegriff*

Originally written in Swedish and later translated with the help of Konrad Flex,[19] this voluminous work is, on one hand, a criticism of the contemporary Romanist studies in law[20] and, on the other, a critique of the very cornerstones of Roman law. Its object is Roman private law. Or rather, a very narrow part of it. In fact, this convoluted reconstruction of ancient institutes examines archaic forms of contract, transaction agreements and other sorts of settlements in pre-classical Rome, in great detail and with philological meticulousness (that sometimes reaches Byzantine heights in its tortuous accuracy).[21]

The field of research is «obligation as a mystical bond on persons by means of another person.»[22] Therefore, the first aspect taken into consideration is the

term as well. Among the other commentaries Hägerström made in this period we should mention that on Roscoe Pound's *An Introduction to the Philosophy of Law* (spring 1926), Léon Duguit's *L'État and Hans Kelsen's Allgemeine Staatslehre* (spring 1927), Rudolf Smend's *Verfassung und Verfassungslehre* (autumn 1928) and Vinding Kruse's *Ejendomsrettens overgang* (autumn 1929).

[16] Hägerström first lectured on the *Religious Grounds for Ancient Greek and Roman Law* during the autumn of 1918.

[17] Hägerström had, during the first decade of the century, planned to write a monograph on ancient Greek law. See T. Mautner, *Vägledning till Hägerströmstudiet*, cit., p. 5.

[18] Hägerström never finished the follow-up: The ever more voluminous *Obligationsbegriff* II that was published posthumously by Karl Olivecrona in 1941 in an edited version transforming the extremely long footnotes into endnotes. It did not receive the attention the author would have hoped for: It was not reviewed, except by the editor.

[19] See the manuscript *H 32*, but generally *H 21–37*, vol. II was translated by, or with the help of, a student in Uppsala, Meissner. See manuscript *H 24*.

[20] Among the scholars Hägerström criticised in *Obligationsbegriff* we find Karlowa (pp. 37 ff.); Riccobono (pp. 199 ff.), Savigny and Jhering (pp. 221 ff.), Sokolowski (pp. 244 ff.), Haymann (pp. 21 ff.), Beseler (pp. 309 ff.), Girard (pp. 503 ff.), Paul Huvelin (p. 599) and Emilio Betti (p. 605). For a contextualisation of the criticisms, see C. Faralli, *Diritto e magia*, cit., pp. 97–142.

[21] The footnotes are famed because of their length, and can sometimes reach up to twenty seven pages.

[22] This is the generic title of *Obligationsbegriff*, vol. I, that might be considered as a subtitle to the entire work «Die Obligation als mystische Gebundenheit einer Person durch eine andere.»

difference between the «dingliches Recht» (*ius in re*) and the respective legal claims in relation to both contract and property law (*fordingsrätt/Forderungsrecht*). *Dingliches Recht* (or more commonly in contemporary German, *Sachenrecht*) corresponds roughly to property law. Its object is a thing (*res*) and it consists of powers that the entitled party can employ on the object, personal property and real estate alike, following the classic formulation by Justinian (Code 4, 35, 21) *ius utendi et abutendi in re sua. Ius in re* includes property as key component, but it also deals with institutes such as usufruct, leasehold, easement, hypothec, lien and so forth.

On the contrary, *fordringsrätt* is the Swedish name for the legal sphere concerned with claims correlated to what traditional civil law calls the law of obligation, involving situations where someone has incurred a personal liability. The claims of the *fordringsrätt* are claims between individuals, typically a debtor and a creditor making the claim (*borgenär*). This area of law is strictly related to the law of obligations, the core of private law in civil law systems, which originated in Roman law where – according to the *Institutes* of Justinian – obligation (from *ob-ligatus*) is defined as a "legal tie" or "legal bond." The grounds for the claim need not be contractual (e.g. extra-contractual obligations). They can also be related to (quasi-) delict law, addressing unintentional or wilful wrong, i.e., the civil law variant of the law of torts, and what common lawyers would consider negligence related issues.

The parts of the law of obligations that mostly interested Hägerström are obligations under contract, both innominate and nominate such as, for example, sales, gift, lease, carriage, mandate, association, deposit, loan, arbitration, and management of another party's property (*negotiorum gestio*).[23] In the second volume of *Obligationsbegriff*, which presents among other things some re-editions of previously published material, Hägerström's focus switched to contracts as enforceable agreements. Following Gaius' classification of contracts in consensual contracts, verbal contracts, contracts *re*, and contracts *litteris*, the second volume essentially concerns the second category.

Therefore, in order to shed light on the connection between procedural law and substantial law, i.e., between form and substance, Hägerström analysed archaic forms of contracts. The three principal forms are those of *gesta per aes et libram*, *in iure cessio*, and *sponsio*. The agreements through *gesta per aes et libram* were a form of settlement used before the introduction of money. In this form of agreement, a person obtains an advantage by giving a quantity of bronze (*aes*) that has to be weighted on a scale (*libra*) held by the *libripens* in the presence of five witnesses (*testes*). This form of agreement is examined at the core of the opening chapters in *Obligationsbegriff*.[24] The reason why these settlements aroused Hägerström's

[23]On Hägerström's view of various forms of *negotium*, see E. Pattaro, *Non si fanno cose con le parole. Il negozio giuridico nella prospettiva di Axel Hägerström*, in «Sociologia del diritto», 1981:3, pp. 25–42.

[24]A. Hägerström, *Obligationsbegriff*, cit., pp. 25–47.

primary interest was due to the fact that, in the archaic age (around the sixth century B.C.), these forms of *negotium*, later identified through the pontifical jurisprudence, were characterised by their solemn form, a stylised ritual of symbolic significance, based both on certain gestures being performed and certain words pronounced. To Hägerström these very ancient procedures of contract law clearly showed the ritualised culture of the Romans, and hence their "magical character."

In other words, we might say that Hägerström argued that rituality is essential to the efficacy of the law. In the realm of contracts, these covenants would only be papers with scrabbled words if they were deprived of the ritual and its significance. Therefore, the correct pronunciation of the *verba* is fundamental in order to confer validity to the contract. In fact, these words create psychological responses in the citizens but also in the "organs of the state" – from sheriffs to judges. The obligation hereby created originates nonetheless in "magic" and not in any "naturalistic" duty to fulfil the contractual obligation.

According to their function, three types of *gesta per aes et libram* can be distinguished: The *mancipatio* that originally served as a way to transfer ownership of a *res mancipi* after weighting the prize in bronze;[25] the *nexum* which created an obligatory bond following a loan of the respective bronze; and, finally, the *solutio per aes et libram* (*nexi liberatio*) that extinguished the *vinculum iuris* created by the *nexum*, through the repayment of the borrowed piece of bronze which had to be weighed again.

With the evolution of such a system and the introduction of money, the ritual survived in a symbolic form: The bronze became just a small piece (*raudusculum*), the *mancipatio* enabled the economic transaction according to an *imaginaria venditio* and the disbanding of the *nexum* became an *imaginaria solutio*. Hägerström particularly stressed how a «certain symbolic action» was actually "performed" through these *verba sollemnia*.[26] It is precisely this ritualisation of *gesta per aes et libram* that Hägerström deemed to be "magic."[27]

"Mystical" is, indeed, for Hägerström, something that is *realitätsfremde*, i.e., hostile towards and unreceptive of reality, whereas "magical" can be said of something that is conceptually explained on the grounds of the two major laws studied by James Frazer: The law of contact and the law of similitude (homeopathic magic). In fact, at the heart of all sorts of magic we find a correlation between things that are similar and things that have been in contact with each other. The "law of contact" explains why an animal can allegedly be suppressed by erasing its tracks, and the

[25] For a detailed reconstruction of Hägerström's analysis of *mancipatio*, see C. Faralli, *Diritto e magia*, cit., p. 128. In Roman civil law, *mancipatio* is the institute whereby if a slave was purchased, the purchaser of the slave would hold the slave with one hand and throw a copper coin onto a scale while reciting words to show that he had ownership of that slave from that point on.

[26] A. Hägerström, *Obligationsbegriff*, cit., p. 35: «gewissen symbolischen Handlung.»

[27] A. Hägerström, *Obligationsbegriff*, cit., pp. 36 ff.

law of similitude lies behind the idea of hurting someone by burning his or her effigy. In virtue of such a symbolic principle, divine forces were represented as powerful sovereigns; and words such as the *verba sollemnia*, pronounced in specific rituals, were believed to actually perform their inner meaning on the outer world.[28]

The crucial argument concerning *gesta per aes et libram* is that the *damnare* in which the debtor would incur if he did not manage to perform the *solutio* of the *nexum*, had the meaning of sentencing and inflicting punishment in origin. It was hence an institute related to criminal law.[29] This argument, which Hägerström developed at the end of *Obligationsbegriff*, implies that *obligatio* should not be confused with duty. Indeed, «the idea of duty is in any case not the essential part of the Roman concept of obligation.»[30] Whenever *obligatio* implied a duty to perform an action it was only secondary. Duty is, therefore, only «an expression of a psychological compulsion» which is linked to the awareness of the consequence, i.e., the punishment inflicted on the *Schuldner*.[31]

In order to reconstruct the difference between *obligatio* and duty, Hägerström analysed the institute of *pignoris capio*, which was a procedure of *legis actiones* that took place outside the court, without a magistrate and often *in absentia*. This procedure consisted of taking possession of the other party's belongings while pronouncing *certa verba*. This procedure applied not only to private law, but also to some public law sectors such as *aes militare*, through which the soldier could reclaim his *stipendium* or the *aes equestre* that enabled the knight to reclaim money to buy a horse. The *pignoris capio* interested Hägerström because it consisted essentially of psychological means of pressuring the other party – creating «an abstract, not practical necessity»[32] – and, furthermore, it did not proffer full ownership of what had been subjected to the procedure.[33]

The focus of *Obligationsbegriff* switches from section five onwards to the classical topic of detention, possession and property in Roman law. Hägerström examined how someone's right to property (*Eigentumsrecht*) can be limited by possession (*Besitzrecht*)[34] and he discovered hereby that the entire construction of *possessio* – whether *iustus* and thus defendable, or *iniustus* because obtained *vi clam*, out

[28] A. Hägerström, *Obligationsbegriff*, vol. I, cit., p. 21. Such an analysis is applied to *fiat lux*: See p. 36. Later these ideas were used by Olivecrona who applied Austin's performatives directly on the Roman experience. On these aspects, see C. Faralli, *Diritto e magia*, cit., pp. 128–131.

[29] A. Hägerström, *Obligationsbegriff*, cit., pp. 430 and 445: «Damnare (condemnare) als verurteilen hatte ursprünglich strafrechtliche Bedeutung.»

[30] A. Hägerström, *Obligationsbegriff*, vol. I, cit., p. 531: «die Pflichtidee jedenfalls nicht das Wesentliche in römischen Obligationsbegriff ist.»

[31] A. Hägerström, *Obligationsbegriff*, vol. I, cit., p. 531: «ein Ausdruck für den psychischen Zwang.»

[32] A. Hägerström, *Obligationsbegriff*, vol. I, cit., p. 537: «eine theoretische, keine praktische Notwendigkeit.»

[33] A. Hägerström, *Obligationsbegriff*, vol. I, cit., pp. 42–82 on *Pfandobligation*.

[34] A. Hägerström, *Obligationsbegriff*, vol. I, cit., p. 83.

of force, or *precario*, as a revocable bequest – is «dependent on its presupposed mysterious use of the force of the *dominus* on the body of the possessor.»[35]

By *possessio*, the Romans meant the power of a person upon a thing (*res facti*) as distinguished from legitimate property, with relevance both in *ius civile* and *ius honorarium*. Within the realm of *ius civile*, classical jurisprudence distinguished between, on one hand, *possessio civilis* (*ex iusta causa*) which could be recognised as *traditio*, *occupatio*, *usucapio*, etc., and, on the other hand, *possessio naturalis* as the merely physical (*corporalis*) detention lacking the *animus possedendi*, i.e., the intention of keeping the object as one's own. The difference depends on the reason behind the maxim *nemo sibi ipse causam possessionis mutare potest*. It is specifically this notion of *animus possedendi* that interested Hägerström.[36]

Since *animo possedendi* is not equivalent to the mere detention of the object, Hägerström spotted in the very distinction between *possessio civilis* and *possessio naturalis* yet another source of "mystical power." Thus he examined the Roman idea according to which *anima possedendi* could be transferred to other persons.[37] Moreover, it should be mentioned that no judicial protection is given to those possessors who have the item at their disposal, but lack *animo possedendi*, like the person with whom someone has deposited, the renter or the occupant. This idea was the outcome of the jurisprudential evolution and was not originally present in archaic times. However, in the classical age, only physical objects could be subject to *possessio*, whereas – earlier – all things or persons that could be the object of *vindicatio*, could also be the object of *possessio*. This explains why the possessor with *animo possedendi* has, ultimately, a (physical) power over the debtor's very body:[38] Through the *vindicatio* and the collection of debt (*skuldfodran/schuldforderung*), the divine order of things that had been shaken with the illegitimate detention of someone else's belongings could be re-established. «To sum up, we can now say that *ius* as a Roman legal system means an order of the immanent divine forces in humans and *iura* means an order of the forces of the Gods themselves.»[39]

Indeed, for Hägerström, Roman law is ultimately based on the link between the secular order, *ius*, and the sacred order, *fas*.[40] This is also the reason why this legal order cannot be the fruit of any will. *Ius* «cannot possibly be identical to the will

[35] A. Hägerström, *Obligationsbegriff*, cit., vol. I, p. 105: «abhängig von dessen vorausgesetzter mystischer Anwendung der Kraft des Oberhaupts bei dem eigenen körperlichen Besitz.»

[36] A. Hägerström, *Obligationsbegriff*, cit., pp. 141–276.

[37] A. Hägerström, *Obligationsbegriff*, cit., pp. 221–235.

[38] A. Hägerström, *Obligationsbegriff*, cit., p. 348.

[39] A. Hägerström, *Obligationsbegriff*, cit., p. 585: «Wir können nun zusammenfassend sagen, dass das Ius als eine römische Rechtsordnung eine Ordnung für in den Menschen immanente göttliche Kräfte und für die Kräfte der Götter selbst: *iura* bedeutet.»

[40] A. Hägerström, *Obligationsbegriff*, cit., p. 557, where he discusses the concept of *iussum* of the people.

of the people.»[41] At most, «we might say that the people, by their immanent divine forces, creates the law that is *ius*.»[42]

In *Obligationsbegriff*, Hägerström highlighted in particular the relation of both the doctrine of *possessio* and of *species* with animism[43] by identifying the origin of this "animistic belief" in «Platonic, Aristotelian and stoic doctrine of an inner being in things.»[44] Behind the "scientific" constructions of the Roman *iure consulti*, we ultimately find the Platonic theory of ideas as well as Aristotle's conception of *eídos*.[45] The very notion of *animus*, as what ultimately imprints the *telos* of its own being onto a thing, is rooted in even older forms of popular animism, and hence the Roman doctrine of *possessio* suffered from the same ontological dualism that affected Plato's metaphysics. Hägerström concluded in a scornfully ironic tone: «Here was the scientific conception of the nature of things!»[46] Yet the reason why these pseudo-scientific constructions were maintained was that they relied on the consciousness of law of the Roman people, and the Romans were influenced by animism and similar beliefs.

According to Hägerström's analysis, the meaning of fundamental legal categories in modern jurisprudence is thus erroneous and false because these concepts stem from a long history of misconstrued ideas about their original sense. In his view, modern Romanist jurisprudence – foremost the Pandect movement – committed the mistake of falling back on hereditary forms of legal reifications, elaborating abstract constructions alien to the Roman spirit.

Indeed, the genealogical perspective Hägerström adopted, which relies heavily on the conservatism of the Romans in particular, and of jurisprudence in general, shapes the general framework of his studies. The reason why he engaged in this very meticulous study of Roman law was his intention to investigate the genesis of legal ideology: «Modern science in general, and therefore modern legal science seeks to use only such notions that correspond to facts»[47] but, in Roman Law, «we may expect to find the concepts presenting themselves in a more naïve form. But we may also expect to find them free from that confusion of thought which inevitably arises, when, encouraged by the general critical tendency of modern science, jurists

---

41 A. Hägerström, *Obligationsbegriff*, cit., p. 557: «unmöglich mit dem Willen des Volkes identisch sein kann.»

42 A. Hägerström, *Obligationsbegriff*, cit., p. 557: «Das Volk, kann man sagen, schafft durch die ihm immanente göttliche Kraft die Ordnung, die das gesetzte Ius ist.»

43 A. Hägerström, *Obligationsbegriff*, cit., pp. 277–293.

44 A. Hägerström, *Obligationsbegriff*, cit., vol. I, p. 278: «die platonisch-aristotelische und stoische Lehre von einem inneren Wesen der Dinge.»

45 Hägerström specifically referred to the exposition of the doctrine of *nous* in *Phaido*, and the theory of ideas in *Sophist*. See A. Hägerström, *Obligationsbegriff*, cit., p. 289.

46 A. Hägerström, *Obligationsbegriff*, cit., vol. I, p. 281: «Hier hatte man ja die wissenschaftliche Auffassung von der Natur des Dinges!»

47 A. Hägerström, *Einleitung*, in *Obligationsbegriff*, cit., p. V; Eng. trans. in *Inquiries into the Nature of Law and Morals*, Almqvist & Wiksell, Uppsala 1953, p. 1.

attempt to reduce to actual facts the content of the mystical concepts which they employ.»[48]

This voluminous first volume of *Obligationsbegriff* was received in very different ways.[49] Most scholars ignored it, but some – like the Italian Emilio Betti, the target of some severe criticism at the end of Hägerström's book – hated it, and accused Hägerström of being nothing but a connoisseur of witchcraft, and null as a jurist. Others, conversely, received the important work with interest. Carla Faralli's study on how the volume was reviewed shows this well.[50] To confirm this viewpoint we should add that Hägerström was invited to an international congress in Rome in the early thirties, as his daughter recalls in her memoirs.[51]

I have not been able to determine with certainty who might have invited Hägerström to that congress in Rome. However, it seems plausible that the idea, if not the invitation, came from the prominent Italian legal scholar Pietro Bonfante (Poggio Mirteto 1864 – Roma 1932), who held the chair in Roman Law at *La Sapienza* University from 1917 until his death.[52] One of the main themes that he developed through his so-called "naturalistic method" in his monumental work on the institutions of Roman law,[53] was the idea that beneath the socio-economic function of an institute in the historical age lay an even older function of a different kind. For instance, the institution of the family would originally have had a political function. Bonfante also withheld a profound interest in Oriental studies, and taught Oriental law from 1919. The Italian scholar springs to mind because it seems likely that he would have been receptive to Hägerström's main thesis on the "magical" origin of Roman law, whilst it is clear that this thesis was hardly of the popular kind in the eyes of the majority of legal scholars, even though, as we shall see, Hägerström's genealogical perspective enjoyed a revival decades afterwards.

### *7.1.2 Later Work*

Whereas the 1927 *Obligationsbegriff* focused on the private sphere of law, in 1929 Hägerström extended his analysis to Roman public law in *Das magistratische Ius in seinem Zusammenhang mit dem römischen Sakralrechte*. During the autumn of that year, while lecturing on the topic of magic and religion, his starting point was the same: «But the introduction of moral elements into the ideal power upon things and persons – i.e., a "right" – is alien to Roman legal ideology. Since the Roman Gods influenced the natural world – and were in no way forms of hypostatised moral

[48] A. Hägerström, *Obligationsbegriff*, cit., vol. I, p. 18; Eng. trans. in *Inquiries*, cit., p. 16.

[49] For the reviews of *Obligationsbegriff*, see C. Faralli, *Diritto e magia*, cit., pp. 57–58, 64, 74, 76.

[50] C. Faralli, *Diritto e magia*, cit., pp. 57 ff.

[51] See n. 3 in Chapter 1.

[52] Another option might be Bonfante's pupil, Edoardo Volterra.

[53] P. Bonfante, *Istituzioni di diritto romano* (1896), *Storia del diritto romano* (1902), and the four volumes of *Corso di diritto romano* (1923).

principles exceeding natural causality or human functions – a person's "right" was experienced as a secret force over things and persons, connected to the physical forces. This force was immediately binding, regardless of bodily strength, without any supplementary "ought to" (...). Here we shall elucidate the factual meaning of the magistrate's *ius* in the light of Roman public law.»[54]

So as to illustrate the strong connection between the religious and magical aspects of the Roman *Weltanschauung* and the basic categories of law, Hägerström examined the religious nature of the magistrate's power, by insisting on the fact that, in archaic Roman customary law, it was not enough for the magistrate to be elected in order to receive the *auspices*, reflecting legitimate political power. Once *magistratus*, the person elected had to be subjected to a popular approbation act which implied a second election by the *comitia curiata*, making the magistrate *iustus*.[55] The power of *ius magistratus* hence derived from the auspices under whom the magistrate was elected. In addition, these auspices determined the power that the individual was to enjoy, according to the sector and level of competence the elected magistrate occupied in the public system.[56] As late as the end of the republican age, this secondary confirmation was deemed necessary although it had been reduced to a mere ceremony. This complicated system was grounded ultimately in religion.[57]

Moreover, in this period, Hägerström had the opportunity to present the major discoveries he had made in Roman law. On the 12th of October 1928 approximately two hundred people came to the Association for Philology to attend Hägerström's lecture on *The Concepts of* Dike, Ius, Lex, Iudicatus *and* Debere.[58] On May 2nd

---

[54] A. Hägerström, *Das magistratische Ius*, cit., pp. 4–5: «Dagegen ist diese Hineintragung moralischer Elemente in die ideale Macht über Dinge und Personen, die ein "Recht" bedeutet, der römischen Rechtsideologie fremd. Wie die römischen Götter keineswegs Hypostasierungen moralischer Prinzipien, sondern natürliche Verläufe oder menschliche Funktionen, als Wesen für sich gedacht, waren, die Einfluss auf die natürliche Welt übten, wurde das „Recht" einer Person in einer den physischen Kräften verwandten geheimnisvollen Macht über Dinge und Personen erblickt, die sich unabhängig von der natürlichen Macht unmittelbar, ohne Einmischung eines vermittelnden Sollens, geltend machte (...). Hier soll die Sachlage durch eine Untersuchung des öffentlichen römischen Rechtes hinsichtlich der Bedeutung des *magistratischen Ius* beleuchtet werden.» The first pages of this study is a summary of the thesis in the introduction to *Obligationsbegriff* and some earlier ideas formulated in *Till frågan om den objektiva rättens begrepp*. In particular, Hägerström brought up to discussion the "Rechtsideologie" in notions such as the will of the monarch, *Volkrepresentation* and the organs of the state.

[55] A. Hägerström, *Das magistratische Ius*, cit., p. 18: «der niedere magistratus, wenn er auch unmittelbar durch die erste Wahl *magistratus* ist, erst durch die nachfolgende Wahl – *lex curiata – iustus* magistratus wird.»

[56] A. Hägerström, *Das magistratische Ius*, cit., p. 9.

[57] A. Hägerström, *Das magistratische Ius*, cit., p. 19: «Er war vielmehr aus religiösen Gründen: *Zwecks Übertragung der Auspizien* anden *Gewählten*, erfoderlich.»

[58] This lecture corresponds to the manuscript *H 115:12*. By criticising some theses in Theodor Mommsen's *Römisches Strafrecht* from 1894 (p. 3), as well as Haymann and Biondi (*Le* actiones noxales *nel diritto romano classico*), Hägerström affirmed «one should become doubtful concerning the meaning that was accredited in ancient times to the words that seem to cover our concepts» («man skall bli misstänksam i frågan om den betydelse som man verkligen i äldre tider tilldelat de

1930 he held a talk on *Animistic Thinking in Old and New Times* at the Royal Academy of Science in Uppsala, and in December the same year he delivered a speech at the Association for History of Religion on *The Psychology of Magic*.

In 1932, as Uppsala conferred the *honoris causa* upon one of Hägerström's main sources, the Finnish scholar Edward Westermarck, Hägerström not only dedicated a lengthy seminar – from March 11th to May 10th – to Westermark's *Ursprung und Entwicklung der Moralbegriffe*: He also published a philological comment to Gellius N.A. 15, 13, 11 (Caecilius) where he developed some views from *Obligationsbegriff*[59] denying that the *lex Ursonensis* had direct *zivilrechtliche Kraft*.[60] Furthermore, in 1933, he wrote *Excerpts from Greek Authors*, *Ancient Greek Jurisprudence and Religion* and lectured on *Hellenic Thought*.[61] In 1934, he published the essay *Nehrman-Ehrenstråle's Conception of the Ground of the Binding Power of the Promise, Illustrated from the Standpoint of Both Roman Law and Natural Law*.[62]

In his analysis of the work of the Swedish legal scholar David Nehrman-Ehrenstråle, published for the 200th commemoration of Sweden's Statutory Code, Hägerström developed a section of *Obligationsbegriff* concerning the idea of duty as correlated to obligation in private law. The focus is on one of the basic categories in private law, *Rechtspflicht*, through which «the interested party obtains (...) a power to create a duty. He can claim the behaviour that the state prescribes as a duty (...). The state creates the duty but does so by offering the interested party a subjective right: An ideal power to create a duty.»[63] Hägerström consequently discussed the definition of "subjective rights" as legitimate interests in Jhering. From

ord som synas täcka våra begrepp» p. 5). «On the contrary *iustus* does not mean the same thing as *dikaiós* until Cicero the Stoic (...). Before the influence of stoicism, *iustus* meant righteous in the modern meaning and *ius* justice in the modern sense. But *iniuria* as impurity might correspond to *adikía* as what does not follow *díke*» («Däremot [betyder] *iustus* icke förrän hos den stoicerande Cicero det samma som *dikaiós* (...). Ännu mindre före stoicismens inflytande [betydde] *iustus* rätttrådig i nyare mening och *ius* rättvisa i nyare mening. Men *iniuria* såsom orenhet kan ha en betydelse som motsvarar *adikía* såsom oöverenstämmande med *díke*», p. 14).

59 See A. Hägerström, *Obligationsbegriff*, cit., vol. I, pp. 432 ff.

60 A. Hägerström, *Tab. III, 1–3 des Zwölftafelgesetzes*, in *Symbolae philologicae. O.A. Danielson octogenario dicatae*, (ed.) A. Nelson, Lundequistska Bokhandeln, Uppsala 1932, pp. 113–121. It was later reedited in the second volume of *Obligationsbegriff*.

61 There are many more manuscripts concerning ancient Greece at the *Carolina Rediviva* library in Uppsala.

62 A. Hägerström, *Nehrman-Ehrenstråles uppfattning av grunden för ett löftes juridiskt bindande kraft, belyst genom å ena sidan romersk, å andra sidan naturrättslig åskådning*, in *Minnesskrift ägnad 1734 års lag av jurister i Sverige och Finland*, Marcus, Stockholm 1934, vol. II, pp. 571–630; German translation by K. Wührer, edited by K. Olivecrona in *Recht, Plicht und bindende Kraft des Vertrages nach römischer und naturrechtlicher Anschauung*, SKHVSU Almqvist & Wiksell, Stockholm 1965.

63 A. Hägerström, *Nehrman-Ehrenstråles uppfattning*, cit., p. 573; *Recht, Plicht und bindende Kraft*, cit., p. 13: «den intresserade parten erhåller (...) en kraft att förplikta. Han kan själv kräva det handlingssätt, som genom lagen är plikt. (...) Staten förpliktar, men den gör det på det sättet att den skänker den intresserade en subjektiv rätt: en ideell makt att själv förplikta.»

this standpoint, there seems to be an overlapping between the Roman archetype and the modern notions of legal rights and duties. According to the latter, «a private subjective right always consists of an ideal power over a thing or a person, understood analogously as an outer, natural power over them.»[64]

Following the argumentation developed in *Obligationsbegriff*, the nature of the "ideal power" depends on whether the claim is over a *res* or a person. Besides the case of *dominio*, we should mention his argumentation in the case of *obligatio*: The plaintiff was considered to rule over the debtor through a *vinculum iuris*, ultimately conferring what we would now call a bio-political claim over the "naked life" (*zoe*), or in Hägerström's terms, a «right to the body of the debtor.»[65] In order to dissolve this *vinculum*, the debtor had to perform the equivalent service, delivering what was due to the plaintiff. Otherwise, the debtor became *alieni iuris*, and eventually reduced to the status of *res*, therefore becoming part of the property (*dominio*) of the creditor, i.e., his slave. In modern jurisprudence, the logic of this apparatus or *dispositif*, based on a claim to power over someone else's duty, survived. But it was transformed because of an over-interpretation of the actual Roman maxims (that Hägerström usually ascribes to poor attachment to the literal sources) giving rise to the modern idea of having a (subjective) right to another party's duty.[66]

In 1938, a year before passing away, Hägerström published the last essay printed in his lifetime: *On the Original Meaning of Shaking Hands*. Originally written for a homonymous lecture held at the Royal Academy of Science in Uppsala on April the 1st 1938, in this essay he analysed, in particular, the Roman institute of *promissio*, from which, according to his reconstruction, the modern promise derives.[67] The magical origin of *promissio* is the primitive notion of power (or force) as a sort of fluid,[68] namely the idea that power can be transmitted by contact, as the custom of wearing animal skins proves.[69] In the case of *promissio*, the force passed through the right hand with which the promisor held that of the promisee, while pronouncing the ritual formula *promittis? Promitto*. The Romans gave the name *fides* to this symbolic communion of the forces passed through the right hand. *Fides* hence became

---

[64] A. Hägerström, *Nehrman-Ehrenstråles uppfattning*, cit., p. 615; German trans., cit., p. 67: «besteht ein privates subjektives Recht *immer* in einer ideelen Macht über eine Sache oder eine Person, gedacht in Analogie mit äußerer natürlicher macht über diese.»

[65] A. Hägerström, *Obligationsbegriff*, cit., p. 349: «Recht über den Körper des Schuldners mit sich brachte.»

[66] A. Hägerström, *Nehrman-Ehrenstråles uppfattning*, cit., pp. 583–585; German trans., cit., pp. 27–29.

[67] The notion of the promise as a verbal contract is at the heart of the second volume of *Obligationsbegriff*, *Über die Verbalobligation*, ed. K. Olivecrona, SKHVSU Almqvist & Wiksell, Uppsala 1941. The article *On the Original Meaning of Shaking Hands* presents these ideas in a popular version. See T. Mautner, *Some Notes on Willing and Promising*, in E. Carlson & R. Sliwinski (eds), *Omnium-gatherum. Philosophical essays dedicated to Jan Österberg*, Uppsala Philosophical Studies 50, Uppsala 2001, p. 227 n. 30.

[68] A. Hägerström, *Socialfilosofiska uppsatser*, Bonniers, Stockholm 1939, p. 179.

[69] A. Hägerström, *Socialfilosofiska uppsatser*, cit., p. 180.

a divinity to whom the right hand was dedicated.[70] As the actual shaking of hands became redundant to guarantee the judicial value of the promise, the pronouncement of the verbal formulas was maintained as a symbol of the actual shaking of hands. Hägerström concluded his analysis of this practice, which has survived in Western culture until the present day even though it has lost its original magical connotations, by underlining how the term *ius* is closely related to the magical and religious vocabulary.[71]

«The union of people – made in this way [by shaking of hands] and in other ways – is sacred. This means that its fulfilment brings good fortune and the omission of performance entails the seed of misfortune: curses. As a fortune bringer, it is sometimes called *ius*. This word means, in archaic religious formulas as well as in the primitive use of Roman language, a power that brings fortune. *Ius est*, applied to an action that somehow concerns the sphere of the divine, actually means the power to attract the benevolence of the gods. The opposite is *religio est*: Then the action brings on curses, "sullies" or causes the anger of the gods. *Iustus* originally meant the same thing as *purus* (pure).»[72]

In essence, «his Roman Law studies yielded the conclusion that the Romans believed their legal system to be composed of magical powers which could be utilised and made to produce results in the world of fact if the appropriate acts were performed (...). The primitive Roman belief in magical powers survived into the modern age, though in a disguised form.»[73] Hägerström's work on ancient law – from the public law of the Greek city states, to Roman law, to medieval natural law – aimed relentlessly to show «that these notions in question cannot be reduced to anything in reality. The reason is that, in point of fact, they have their roots in traditional ideas of mystical forces and bounds.»[74] This stringent and harsh criticism of the very basic elements of Western legal tradition – from *ius* to *lex*, from property to liberty, from rights to duties – should not only be considered one of the first, if not the very first, attempt to perform a philosophical deconstruction of the cornerstones of law. Such attempts did not become current in philosophy until the end of

---

[70] A. Hägerström, *Socialfilosofiska uppsatser*, cit., p. 184.

[71] This is an issue he had stressed in *Obligationsbegriff*, cit., p. 555.

[72] A. Hägerström, *Socialfilosofiska uppsatser*, cit., p. 181: «Den på detta sätt frambragta, liksom den ur andra grunder bestående övernaturliga gemenskapen mellan personer är helig, vilket innesluter på en gång, att dess respekterande bringar lycka och att dess brytande för med sig frön till olycka – förbannelser. Såsom lyckobringande betecknas den understundom som *ius*. Detta ord betyder i urgamla religiösa formler och därmed också efter det äldsta romerska språkbruket en lyckobringande kraft. *Ius est*, utsagt som ett handlande, som på något sätt berör det gudomligas sfär, betecknar dess förmåga att draga till personen gudarnas välvilja. Motsatsen är *religio est*: handlingen för med sig förbannelser, "befläckar", eller den vållar gudarnas vrede. *Iustus* betyder ursprungligen det samma som *purus* (ren).»

[73] G. Mac Cormack, *Scandinavian Realism*, in «The Juridical Review», 1970, p. 53. See also Id., *Hägerström's Magical Interpretation of Roman Law*, in «The Irish Jurist», 1969, pp. 153–167, Id., *Formalism, Symbolism and Magic in Early Roman Law*, in «Tijdschrift voor Rechtgeschiedenis», 1969, pp. 439–468.

[74] A. Hägerström, *Obligationsbegriff*, cit., vol. I, p. 18; Eng. trans. in *Inquiries*, cit., p. 16.

the twentieth century with, for example, the famous deconstruction of sovereignty, justice and the like by Jacques Derrida (1930–2004).[75] Independently of later philosophical inquiries that seem akin to Hägerström's, what should be stressed about the studies in Roman law is, more specifically, the methodological outlook from which theses studies can be assessed: The genealogical perspective.

## 7.2 The Genealogical Perspective

In his 1909 lecture on *Philosophy as Science*, Hägerström had already endorsed the genealogical outlook as one of philosophy's best practices. Following his general evolutionary approach, he considered research on genesis to be deeply philosophical, since the true task of the research is to overtly indicate its own preconditions (see Chapter 2): «Philosophy has usually meant two things. On one hand, the task of philosophy has been to search for the ultimate ground. But such a task is by its own nature anthropocentric; it reflects the established belief in something independent that, naturally, is found in mankind. All sorts of metaphysics have such a character, even the one cloaked in the mantle of science (...). On the other hand, philosophy would consist only in a summary of the results of the special sciences (...). Both of these ways to conceive philosophy are based on a sort of faith and do not inquire deep enough into their own presuppositions.»[76]

One of the few scholars who noticed the importance of the genealogical perspective in Hägerström was Ernst Cassirer, who also criticised this methodological choice. «Yet again we have to ask whether this view on the genesis of culture at its very beginnings can help us to deepen the meaning of the different cultural functions» of phenomena such as the metaphor, for instance, within the legal realm.[77] Cassirer pointed his finger at the fact that the development of a notion is not *a priori* present in origin. Genealogy assumes unwarrantedly that the evolution of a notion is present *in nuce* in its source, therefore simply reverting the constructivist approach to human history. This is a very strong epistemological point that Cassirer made

---

[75] J. Derrida, *Force de loi. Le fondement mystique de l'autorité*, Galilée, Paris 1994.

[76] A. Hägerström, *Filosofi och vetenskap*, Ehlin, Stockholm 1957, p. 8: «Med filosofi har man vanligen menat två saker. Antigen har man tillagt den den uppgiften att söka den yttersta grunden. En sådan uppgift är emellertid till sin natur antropocentrisk, hvilar på en redan fastställd tro på något självständigt, som då naturenligt blir människan. All slags metafysik, äfen den i naturvetenskaplig kappa, har en sådan karaktär (...). Eller också skall filosofien bestå i en sammanfattning af fackvetenskapernas resultater och blott i detta (...). Båda dessa sätt att filosofera hvila därför på en viss slags tro och går icke till djupet, till en undersökning af sina egna förutsättningar.»

[77] E. Cassirer, *Axel Hägerström. Eine Studie zur schwedischen Philosophie der Gegenwart*, Göteborgs högskolas årskrift, Göteborg 1939; now in *Gesammelte Werke. Nachgelassene Manuskripte und Texte* (eds. K. Ch. Köhnke, J.M. Krois, O. Schwemmer), Bd. 21, Meiner, Hamburg 2005, p. 86: «auch hier erhebt sich die Frage, ob der Einblick in die genetischen Anfänge der Kultur uns auch den Einblick in die Bedeutung der verschiedenen Kulturfunktionen verschaffen kann.»

against Hägerströmian hermeneutics. In other words, just like ancient Greek philosophy is a transformation of mythical thought, «the very fact that, for the Roman lawyers of the classical age, the awareness of the mystical origin of some of their fundamental concepts has disappeared should not be considered in a purely negative way, but also in a positive way. Clearly, there is not just "oblivion" here; rather, it is a transformation that replaces the ancient standard.»[78]

Besides some historical simplifications that seem to follow from Hägerström's methodological choice of genealogy, he was aware of the problem stressed by Cassirer. In *Moralpsykologi*, he insisted on the fact that the genealogical method only allows historical *explanation*, but it cannot bring on any *justification* or any *ground* according to which we should continue in the path set out in the past.[79]

In any case, Hägerström's interest for genesis has re-emerged lately for scholarly attention. A recent debate concerning Hägerström opposed Hans Ruin and Sven Danielsson on the issue of genealogy. In effect, it seems that Hägerström's whole production cannot be fully comprehended, and hence assessed, if not from such a perspective. It is very puzzling that Hägerström spent almost two decades working on Roman law and archaic judicial, political and religious matters if the reconstruction of their genesis was not his aim. Ruin is correct to stress that Nietzsche's legacy in Hägerström essentially consists of the genealogical perspective that emphasizes the historically constructed character of moral concepts, as these result from a struggle between powers that continue to live in our present use of moral concepts.[80] In Hägerström, «the consciousness of duty which has an aprioristic nature in Kant, is subjected to the same genealogical criticism as the concepts of goodness and justice.»[81] According to Ruin, this legacy renders Hägerström particularly up-to-date, as the use of genealogy in Michel Foucault and Gilles Deleuze demonstrates.

I am not sure whether contemporary French deconstructivism of this latter kind is the aftermath Hägerström would have thought of. It seems more likely that the genealogical outlook, which he inherited from a fine-tuned philologist like Nietzsche, should be related to the kind of *Begriffsgeschichte* that was later

[78] E. Cassirer, *Axel Hägerström*, cit., p. 88: «Die Tatsache, daß schon den klassischen römischen Juristen der mystische Ursprung einzelner ihrer fundamentalen Begriffe nicht mehr bewusst oder daß er für sie verdunkelt war. Darf ja nicht rein negativ, sondern sie muß zugleich positiv gewertet werden. Hier liegt offenbar kein bloßes „Vergesse", sondern eine Umformung vor, die einen neuen Gehalt an Stelle des alten setzt.» A similar objection was formulated by D.D. Raphael, in his review of Hägerström's *Inquiries into Law and Morals* in «The Philosophical Quarterly», 1954, vol. 4, p. 347.

[79] A. Hägerström, *Moralpsykologi*, Natur & Kultur, Stockholm 1952, p. 64.

[80] H. Ruin, *Hägerström, Nietzsche och den svenska nihilismen*, cit., pp. 18–20. See also on Nietzsche's legacy, M. Jalava, *Lidelse och bragd*, in S. Nygård, J. Strang, *Mellan idealism och analytisk filosofi: den moderna filosofin i Finland och Sverige 1880–1950*, Atlantis, Stockholm 2006, pp. 51–78.

[81] H. Ruin, *Hägerström, Nietzsche och den svenska nihilismen*, cit., p. 20: «det pliktmedvetande som i Kants moralfilosofi har status av aprioristisk princip underkastas samma genealogiska kritik som det rätta och det goda.»

developed from the sixties onward by Reinhart Koselleck (1923–2006).[82] Such a "history of concepts" – conceived as a methodology of historical studies that focuses on the invention and development of the fundamental concepts underlying and informing a distinctively historical manner of being in the world – has significant implications for contemporary cultural studies that extend far beyond discussions on the practical problems of historical method.

Another author to whom Hägerström's genealogical perspective seems closely related is Karl Löwith (1897–1973). In *From Hegel to Nietzsche*, and particularly in *Meaning in History*,[83] he insisted on the fact that history lacks immanent logic and hence visions of history orientated in a teleological way require a vaster inquiry into the culture that produced it. By opposing the traditional Christian philosophy of history, and calling for a humanist form of philosophy of history, this sceptical attitude intended to stimulate freedom of thought and it was, just like Hägerström's, based on the idea that understanding our role in society presupposes a retrospective inquiry on the historical stratifications of concepts within which our most fundamental notions evolve.

Another name with whom Hägerström should perhaps be associated is the German *Kultursoziologe*, Norbert Elias (1897–1990), whose work focused on the relationship between power, behaviour, emotion and knowledge. In *Über den Prozess der Zivilisation*,[84] the founder of so-called figurational sociology examined the evolution of our second nature, that is cultural *habitus*, in terms of particular individual psychic structures moulded by social attitudes. By looking at how post-medieval European social standards were gradually transformed by increasing perceptions of shame and repugnance, Elias discovered the social function of internalised self-restraint as an element for rule-abiding behaviour, in a way that would certainly have aroused Hägerström's admiration since his own philosophy of law strongly insisted on the "internalisation" of rules in consciousness of law as a precondition for a well-functioning legal system in increasingly complex social interaction. Finally, Elias' view of "progress" as a metaphor for a social process fits Hägerström's philosophy of history well.

To sum up, we might say, by using the distinction elaborated by Adolf Phalén in 1914 between different types of philosophical approaches, that Hägerström's philosophy is at the same time inspired by methods of analytical, critical, and genealogical

[82] R. Koselleck, *Einleitung*, in *Geschichtliche Grundbegriffe*, Klett-Cotta, Stuttgart 1972, vol. I, pp. XIII–XXVIII; and Id., *Kritik und Krise: eine Studie zur Pathogenese der bürgerlichen Welt*, Karl Alber Freiburg, München 1959/Suhrkamp, Frankfurt 1992.

[83] K. Löwith, *Weltgeschichte und Heilsgeschehen* (1952), now in *Sämtliche Schriften*, Metzler Verlag, 1983, vol. II; Eng. trans. *Meaning in History: The Theological Implications of the Philosophy of History*, University of Chicago Press, Chicago 1957.

[84] N. Elias, *Über den Prozeß der Zivilisation. Soziogenetische und psychogenetische Untersuchungen. Erster Band. Wandlungen des Verhaltens in den weltlichen Oberschichten des Abendlandes* and *Zweiter Band. Wandlungen der Gesellschaft. Entwurf einer Theorie der Zivilisation*, Verlag Haus zum Falken, Basel 1939; English trans. *The Civilizing Process. Sociogenetic and Psychogenetic Investigations*, revised edition, Blackwell, Oxford 2000.

thinking.[85] This makes it a noteworthy effort to update and renew the philosophical methodology then prevailing. In fact, Hägerström's outlook is closer to late twentieth century philosophy that one might think. By abandoning clear-cut nineteenth century metaphysics and early twentieth century vitalism, and taking a step towards what would later become phenomenology, existentialism, meta-ethics, critical studies, and *Begriffsgeschichte,* Hägerström is a pioneer in the field of the complex method that was to become a landmark in twentieth century philosophy and *Kulturkritik.* He thus forged an integrated method that had its feet on both sides of the analytic and continental divide.

## 7.3 The Unpublished Study on Einstein

In the preface of *Filosofi och vetenskap* from 1957, Martin Fries explained that Hägerström had mentioned to him that «it was his intention, as soon as he had published the great work on the Roman concept of obligation, to complete the final edition of all his mathematical, logical, epistemological and psychological inquiries related to the theory of relativity, and to collect them in a volume for publishing.»[86] He never did finish this task.

In 1934 – two years before Alan Turing developed the mathematical proof of a universal computing machine and the same year that Karl Popper's *Logik der Forschung* saw the light, Hägerström wrote an analysis of the special theory of relativity. Part of this manuscript (*H 2:7*) was translated by Manfred Moritz in 1946 and later edited by Fries in *Filosofi och vetenskap.*[87] While still alive, however, Hägerström found the time to publish *Über die Gleichungen der speziellen Relativitätstheorie*, in the *liber amicorum* for the premature death of Adolf Phalén. This text was translated into Swedish only partially – leaving out many of the more elaborate mathematical formulas.[88] Some other work he published late in life were also related to his critical assessment of the fundamental notions in contemporary science, like the concepts of force and motion for instance, as well as more general

---

[85] A. Hägerström, *Moralfilosofins grundläggning*, Almqvist & Wiksell International, Stockholm 1987, p. 17.

[86] M. Fries, *Förord*, in A. Hägerström, *Filosofi och vetenskap*, cit., p. 12: «det var (...) hans avsikt att omedelbart efter publicerandet av detta arbete [*Obligationsbegriff*, vol. II] slutredigera samtliga sina matematiska, logiska, kunskapsteoretiska och psykologiska undersökningar i anslutning till relativitetsteorien, samt att utgiva dem i en samlad volym.» This statement can also be found in M. Fries, *Förord*, in A. Hägerström, *Religionsfilosofi*, cit., p. 9: «till undertecknad nämnde han dock en gång att det var hans avsikt att, sedan han avslutat de stora arbetena om det romerska obligationsbegreppet samt om Einsteins relativitetsteori, utgiva en skrift om religionsfilosofi.»

[87] A. Hägerström, *Erkenntnistheoretische Voraussetzungen der speziellen Relativitätstheorie Einsteins*, in «Theoria», 1946, XII, pp. 1–68. Manfred Moritz's lengthy yet partial translation into German was edited by Martin Fries in *Filosofi och vetenskap*, Ehlin, Stockholm 1957, pp. 190–241.

[88] A. Hägerström, *Relativitetsteori och kunskapsfilosofi*, in *Filosofi och vetenskap*, cit., pp. 190–241.

research related to what he called depreciatively the "emotive thinking" in modern *Weltanschauung*.[89]

Regardless of the then raging debates over Einstein's theory of relativity and despite the importance of epistemological investigations in Hägerström's philosophy in general, very little attention has been paid to this work on fundamental concepts in science, which only constitutes a piecemeal of the key study that he announced to Martin Fries. Nonetheless, Hägerström left abundant material concerning this unpublished study on Einstein: In his *Nachlaß* a significant part of his manuscripts is dedicated to *The Theory of Relativity and Epistemology*.[90] Moreover, the Uppsala university library keeps several of his writing books with mathematic formulas that have yet not been the object of any research.[91] Probably, the reason behind this state of affairs is that these materials, in order to be adequately assessed, require specific mathematical skills in combination with a philosophical reading of his extensive work on the concepts of force, motion, space, and time, as elaborated in his study on Einstein, but also, as we have seen, elsewhere. In other words, an in-depth reading would require a form of proficiency hard to come across nowadays.

Without hazarding into any systematic and methodical assessment,[92] what can be established, nonetheless, is that Hägerström, before passing away, had made considerable progress with his work. For example, we know that the Belgian mathematician Andries Mac Leod (1891–1977), with an interest in both physics and philosophy, had looked over and commented on the Einstein study.[93]

---

[89] In 1930, after taking some time off from university, he lectured during the spring term on *Truly Autonomous Morals*, and he wrote *On Emotive Thinking*: The original text entitled *Primitiv och modern kraftföreställning* was never found. Hägerström usually wrote in Swedish and had the text translated into German. The Swedish version, bearing the original title that is part of Martin Fries' edition of *Religionsfilosofi* (pp. 15–38), was translated by Birgit Olivecrona from the German transcript *Vergleich zwischen den Kraftvorstellungen der primitiven und modernen Kulturvölker* that had been published in *Festskrift tillägnad professor emeritus Arvi Grotenfelt*, (ed.) E. Kaila, J.E. Saaloma, E. Ahlman, Ajatus, Porvoo 1933, pp. 63–84. Moreover, Hägerström published the essay *On Primitive Rudiments in Modern Way of Thinking* (my trans.) in «Presens», 1935, 2, pp. 167–191.

[90] See the list in T. Mautner, *Vägledning till Hägerströmstudiet*, cit., pp. 19–57.

[91] See the manuscripts at Uppsala University library under signum *H 3:2, H 3:3Aa, H 3:4Ba, H 3:5Ab, H 3:5Ad, H 3:5B, H 3:6B, H 3:7B, H 3:8B, H 3:9B, H 3:10B, H 3:11B, H 3:15B, H 3:16A, H 3:17Aa, H 3:Ac, H 3:17B*.

[92] I thank the Argentinean-American mathematician Gregory Chaitin to whom I showed some of the mathematical formulas and who kindly offered his interpretation of them. This enabled me to confirm that the equations are in effect related to Einstein's theory of relativity. It should be noted that Hägerström never wandered off into the general theory of relativity and commented only on the 1905 special theory of relativity.

[93] See in particular the manuscripts *H 2:7, H 4:9*, and *H 20:18*. Hägerström had once put Mac Leod in contact with Phalén when the Belgian came to Sweden after having published *Introduction à la géométrie non-euclidienne* in Paris in 1922. In Sweden he became the secretary of the famous Swedish mathematician Gösta Mittag-Leffler in the twenties. In his Flemish thesis (he taught in Gent in the thirties) entitled *Eerste beginselen der speciale relativiteitstheorie, opgebouwd door middle van de newtoniaansche voorstellingen van ruimte en tijd* (later translated in the essay collection *Tre uppsatser om Hägerström, Zenon från Elea och relativitetsteorin*, Filosofiska föreningen

In 1928 – just as John von Neumann elaborated game theory – Hägerström was, furthermore, dedicated the traditional *Festschrift* for his 60th birthday, in which contemporary scientists collaborated: The chemist Harald Nordenson (1886–1980), for instance, participated with the contribution *Über Geometrie und Raumvorstellung*, where he exposed David Hilbert's view on indeterminacy.[94] Moreover, mention has to be made of Hägerström's correspondence with the theoretical physicist Oskar Klein (1894–1977).[95]

This unpublished material constitutes what may rightly be considered yet another enigma in the philosophy of this very grave Scandinavian thinker. So why so much silence around the Einstein study? It is usually not mentioned even in the more detailed accounts on Hägerström. The most elaborate attempt to fill this void is, as far as I have been able to find out, Thord Silverbark's PhD thesis on the *Philosophy of Physics*, which dedicated a section to the discussion of Hägerström's contribution to the contemporary discourse on physics.[96] One should not be under the impression that, after having abandoned epistemological research in the late twenties (*Selbstdarstellung* was published in 1929), Hägerström left this material unpublished simply because the *Obligationsbegriff* offered many more practical concerns. In fact, Hägerström's love for mathematics was an old passion of his that he had kept alive since his high-school years. Besides, he had examined thoroughly some of the central issues in the Einstein- and relativity-related debates that developed when Hägerström was active. Uppsala happened to be a very dynamic centre concerned with the contemporary revolution in science.

Additionally, we may ask what we should make of all the mathematical manuscripts at the Uppsala university library. Do they represent an epistemological crux or just a dead-end? Why did Hägerström spend so much energy on his Einstein study to the point where he was no longer able to conclude the second volume of *Obligationsbegriff*, his major worry in his last days? Last but not least, what annoyed him so much in Einstein's discoveries?

---

vid Uppsala universitet, Uppsala 1973), Mac Leod included a grateful thanking of Hägerström for letting him see the manuscript of the Einstein study. Hägerström sent Mac Leod a copy of it in December 1934 (see the letters in *H 4:9*, 15/12/34 and 22/1/35) and Mac Leod answered with a 37-page commentary (*Anmärkningar till Prof. Hägerströms manuskript om den speciella relativitetsteorin, H 4:9*).

[94]H. Nordenson, *Über Geometrie und Raumvorstellung*, in *Festskrift tillägnad Axel Hägerström den 6 september 1928*, Filosofiska och juridiska föreningarna i Uppsala, Almqvist & Wiksell, Uppsala 1928, p. 254: «Man muss in der tat Russell recht geben, dass die moderne Mathematik – wenigstens die moderne Geometrie – diejenige Wissenschaft ist, die weder weiss, wovon sie redet, noch ob was sie sagt wahr ist oder nicht.»

[95]For this correspondence see *H 4:10* and *H 20:18*. Published abstracts can be found in T. Silverbark, *Fysikens filosofi. Diskussioner om Einstein, relativitetsteorin och kvantfysiken i Sverige*, Östlings bokförl. Symposion, Stockholm/Eslöv 1999, pp. 170–173; pp. 315–320. Klein worked as a student for the Nobel institute of Arrehenius, he furthered his research in the United States and at the famed Niels Bohr institute for theoretical physics in Copenhagen.

[96]T. Silverbark, *Fysikens filosofi*, cit., especially pp. 165–187 dedicated to Hägerström.

### 7.3.1 Why Was Einstein so Annoying?

When James Clerk Maxwell achieved the unification of electricity and electromagnetism in the 1860s, as he realised that the waves passing through the electric and magnetic fields are light (from here followed the discovery of radio, infrared and ultraviolet light, etc.), an inconsistency in Newton's physics emerged: Maxwell's achievement was at odds with classical physics since, in doing various experiments, including measuring the speed of light, observers of the magnetic field claimed they could tell if they were themselves moving or not.

The problem in answer to which Einstein elaborated his theories was, as known, this discrepancy between classical mechanics (Galileo's unification of rest and motion through the principle of inertia) and electro-dynamics (Maxwell's unification of electricity and electromagnetism). It seemed implausible, from a physical standpoint, that matter which is moving in space would behave differently, according to the framework chosen. The world of physics, in other words, could not possibly depend on the system of coordinates through which it was observed. For classical physics, the world is one and independent of the subject observing it. In Hägerström's vocabulary, the world of classical physics was not "subjectivistic."

Einstein realised that the distinction between electrical and magnetic effects depends on the motion of the observer, and different observers would draw the distinction differently. From here followed the famous unification of space and time, according to which two observers in motion with respect to one another would disagree about whether two events at different places occur simultaneously.[97]

This was a first admonition in Hägerström's view. He was, of course, fully aware of the fact that rest is just motion at zero speed, according to the principle of inertia: A body at rest or in uniform motion remains in that state of rest or uniform motion unless it is disturbed by forces. To him, it was clear that whether a body is moving or not has no absolute meaning. Motion is defined only with respect to an observer. From this viewpoint, generically accepting relativity would not seem so difficult. Moreover, following Galileo and Newton, it was evident to Hägerström that the observer cannot tell whether he is moving, contrarily to what Aristotle believed. Over and again, in his work on Einstein, Hägerström came back to the "old" principle of relativity which enabled Galileo and later Newton to achieve a subtle victory over the "force"-focused Aristotelian and Ptolemaic worldview: «For Aristotle, if anything moved, there must be a force acting on it. For Newton, if the motion is uniform, it will persist forever.»[98] What appealed to Hägerström in classical physics was that no *force* was needed to explain motion and therefore "primitive rudimentary thinking" could be set aside.

---

[97] See, for example, the well-written *Einsteins Schleier. Die neue Welt der Quantenphysik*, by Anton Zeilinger, Verlag C.H. Beck, München 2003, Chapters IV and V.

[98] L. Smolin, *The Trouble with Physics. The Rise of String Theory, the Fall of a Science and What Comes Next*, Mariner Houghton Mifflin Company, Boston-New York 2007, p. 22.

In the first decade of the new century, Einstein also established the principle of equivalence, i.e., the effects of acceleration are indistinguishable from those of gravity, which eventually led to the discovery that gravity bends light rays.[99] This is the second caveat for Hägerström. Before Einstein, a sharp distinction was made between things in space and space itself. This distinction was never overcome by Hägerström. If one follows this line of thought, it is not hard to understand why it was impossible for Hägerström as for many others, to understand that if light rays, that move in straight lines, bend in the presence of a gravitational field, say, a star, then «Euclidean geometry is not true in the real world. Moreover, geometry is constantly changing, because matter is constantly moving.»[100] This, of course, is connected to the criticism of non-Euclidean geometry, of Riemann and Lobachevsky, that were current at the time.

Consequently, Hägerström attacked Einstein's concept of spacetime, the four-dimensional entity introduced in special relativity theory so as to unify space and time following a geometry analogous to Euclidean geometry, in that it makes it possible to distinguish a particle moving along a straight line at a constant speed from another accelerating (and which hence describes the gravitational field).

When Arthur Eddington photographed the total solar eclipse off the West coast of Africa, which confirmed the bent light rays of stars behind the sun, Einstein's theory gained momentum, and it triumphed over the concurrent thesis of Gunnar Nordström.[101] This was another aspect that Hägerström had trouble accepting. In the light of his epistemological outlook, as we have seen in Chapter 2, "observation" or "experimentation" cannot by itself tell us whether one theory is to be preferred over another. Theoretical reasons are required, such as consistency. And Nordström's theory was simple, beautiful and consistent. The same year, in 1919, Theodor Kaluza revived Nordström's idea by applying Einstein's general theory of relativity from 1915 to Nordström's five-dimensional world and realised it was coherent with electromagnetism. Later, in the 1920s, the Swedish physicist Oskar Klein developed this idea in what became the Kaluza-Klein theory, about which many, including Einstein, were enthusiastic until it was understood that it required a condition that could not be maintained.[102]

«In the midst of a scientific revolution there does not need to be a rational reason to choose one [proposal] over the others. At such times, even very smart people who chose between competing views too soon will often be wrong.»[103] Hägerström

---

[99] A. Zeilinger, *Einsteins Schleier. Die neue Welt der Quantenphysik*, cit., Chapter 5; R. Laughlin, *A Different Universe. Reinventing Physics From the Bottom Down*, Basic Books, New York 2003, Chapter 10.

[100] L. Smolin, *The Trouble with Physics*, cit., p. 41.

[101] In 1914, the Finn Gunnar Nordström wrote the equation that describes electromagnetism in a world of four dimensions of space (plus one of time) and thus made electromagnetism consistent with gravity by adding one extra dimension to space.

[102] The condition regarded the extra-dimension curled up into a circle whose radius was too small to see and frozen. See L. Smolin, *The Trouble with Physics*, cit., pp. 47–48.

[103] L. Smolin, *The Trouble with Physics*, cit., p. 27.

did wait however. Yet things in physics did not really calm down. In times of paradigmatic shifts, consensus is the exception, not the rule.

So, in 1923, Einstein visited Sweden, firing off the already intense debate on relativity.[104] What is more is that the Nobel Prize was even disputed![105] Even though Einstein had been thought of for the Nobel Prize as soon as 1909 (he was recommended by Wilhelm Ostwald), the Royal Swedish Academy of Science – the prize-awarding institution for the physics and chemistry prizes – did not confer the award until November 9th, 1922.

When Einstein finally did receive the world-famous recognition, he was on a journey to Japan: He thus broke not only with time-honoured principles of physics, but also with the Nobel Foundation Code of Statutes, according to which he should have collected his prize in Stockholm "within six months of the Founder's day" and, principally, his Nobel lecture should have touched upon "the subject treated in the work which the prize has been awarded."[106] In fact, when he later addressed the Nordic Assembly of Naturalists at Gothenburg on July 11th, 1923, he spoke of the theory of relativity, whilst the Academy members in Stockholm had voted to give Einstein the prize for «his discovery of the law of photoelectric effect» with the explicit reservation that his theories of relativity should not be included.[107]

If the Nobel committee had a hard time agreeing on the issue, it is comprehensible that the extra-professional debate became even more controversial. In this climate, it shall therefore not come as a surprise that an authoritative philosopher like Hägerström would contribute to the philosophical discussion on relativity.

### *7.3.2 Outline of a Book that Never Was*

For the curious scholar, the material Hägerström left behind is a riddle too many. In the attempt to establish a chronological outline, we need to ask when Hägerström engaged in this debate. The seemingly oldest version of the manuscript on Einstein (*H I:I*) bears no date. So it is hard to give any exact information, but some clues are at hand: In spring 1911, Hägerström was convinced that it was of primary importance

---

[104] Just to name a few of the internationally better known figures who participated in the debate: Rudolf Carnap visited the Philosophical Association in Uppsala in November 1932; Otto Neurath went on a missionary trip around Scandinavia in 1934, promoting the Vienna views on physics and Bertrand Russell held a lecture in Sweden in 1935 on the topic *Determinism in Physics*.

[105] It must be said that it had already been controversial to nominate Hendrik Antoon Lorentz for the Nobel prize (he was nominated by Gösta Mittag-Leffler) in physics since he – and his famed transformations – were held to be too "theoretical" compared to, for example, the first Nobel laureate in the field; Wilhelm Röntgen, and his "applied" X-rays. The same problem afflicted Henri Poincaré's nomination a few years later.

[106] My source is Anders Bárány, *Introduction*, in A. Einstein, *Fundamental Ideas and Problems of the Theory of Relativity. Lecture delivered to the Nordic Assembly of Naturalists at Göteborg on July 11, 1923*, Nobel Foundation, Stockholm 2006, p. 3.

[107] See A. Elzinga, *Einstein's Nobel Prize – A Glimpse Behind Closed Doors*, Science History Publ., Sagamore beach (USA) 2006.

to (re)assert the absolute character of space and time: «The reality of the fact that time has this or that determination cannot in turn fall within a timeframe, because the reality of time, being determined, *is* naturally the very condition [*betingningen*] that enables something to be said to be set in time. Caesar's passage over the Rubicon occurs at one point in time, but the reality of this, or in other words, the truthfulness of this judgement does not occur in time, given that, to a certain extent, in this judgement, time itself, with its content, is determined as real.»[108] The same thing can be said about space: «Naturally, determinacy is situated in space. But the reality of it as such, the reality of space, being determined, is not in itself located in space.»[109]

As we have seen in Chapter 2, it was an essential task in his philosophy of knowledge to confute the fundamental assumption of subjectivism (consciousness is the only self-evident datum), since the knowledge that we think we have concerning our own consciousness presupposes time and space. If consciousness were not inserted into the all-encompassing spatio-temporal world of experience, knowledge would be impossible. We also know that on November 8th, 1912, Hägerström held a talk on *Time and Space* at the Philosophical Association, and in 1921, a year before Einstein was given the Nobel Prize, Hägerström had been studying "the metaphysical perspective" at the root of the idea of the indeterminate character of space and time.[110] Hence, he would have discovered metaphysical aspects in the so-called special sciences.[111]

These are, nevertheless, rather general theoretical terms and they are mainly related to Hägerström's critique of empiricism (see Chapter 2). If we look more specifically for themes connected to the debate on contemporary physics, perhaps the first occurrence is in *Selbstdarstellung* from 1929, where he discussed «the use of concepts in physics»[112] without, however, ever mentioning Einstein. According to Silverbark's reconstruction, this text should be considered a "hidden Einstein

108 A. Hägerström, *Moralfilosofins grundläggning*, cit., p. 104: «Verkligheten av att tiden själv har den eller den bestämdheten kan icke i sin ordning *själv* falla i någon tid. Ty verkligheten av tiden med dess bestämdhet *är* naturligtvis själv betingningen för att något skall kunna sägas falla i tiden. Ceasars övergång över Rubicon faller i en viss tidpunkt, men verkligheten av just detta eller som vi också kunna säga, sanningen av detta omdöme faller icke själv i tiden, emedan i detta omdöme tiden själv med dess innehåll i ett visst avseende bestämmes såsom verklig.»

109 A. Hägerström, *Moralfilosofins grundläggning*, cit., p. 105: «Bestämdheten själv faller naturligtvis i rummet. Men verkligheten av den i denna sin karaktär, verkligheten av rummet i sin bestämdhet, faller själv alls icke i rummet.»

110 A. Hägerström, *Moralpsykologi*, cit., pp. 129 ff.: Here he stressed that Spinoza and Plato were both liable to "fantasy thinking" (*fantasitänkande*) on this issue.

111 See the manuscript *H 104:1*.

112 A. Hägerström, *Filosofi och vetenskap*, cit., pp. 143–182.

criticism."[113] Anyhow, this dating seems much more plausible that the one established by Martin Fries who claimed that Hägerström spent "two decades" working on Einstein.[114] It was hence not until he retired in 1933 that he found the time to convey more seriously into the matter.[115]

As far as the structure of the missing book is concerned, it is possible to draw a plausible sketch of the mysterious Einstein study on the basis of the unpublished material. The following arrangement can, in fact, be distinguished from the 138-page typed version of it (manuscript *H 2:7*): pp. 1–36 are missing, pp. 37–76 were never published, pp. 76–122 were edited in *Filosofi och vetenskap*, and pp. 83–138 were translated and printed posthumously, under the name *Erkenntnistheoretische Voraussetzungen der speziellen Relativitätstheorie Einsteins*, in the oldest Swedish philosophy review, *Theoria*. The review then harboured a debate between the Uppsala school and the Vienna circle, represented by Philipp Frank, who happened to be Einstein's close friend and successor in Prague (see Chapter 2).

There are good reasons for asserting that the missing pages correspond to *Über die Gleichungen der speziellen Relativitätstheorie*, published in 1937 in Adolf Phalén's *Festschrift*: «This is, in all likelihood, the first chapter of the Einstein study, perhaps even its introduction (...). That it is the first chapter of the inquiry is a hypothesis that is strengthened by the fact that the first chapter of the manuscript is missing – it might have ended up somewhere else in connection with the translation and never returned. Moreover, the start of the second section of the four published is identical to the first chapter in earlier versions of the manuscript of the study. Last but not least, the published text can be identified as the first chapter of the study through Mac Leod's commentary.»[116] In effect, according to Andries Mac Leod's 1935 commentary on the Einstein study, the now missing first part dealt with the same issues as the 1937 essay on the *Equations in the Theory of Special Relativity*.

We are now able to indicate more precisely the table of contents of the "missing" book: In the introduction, corresponding to the first section in the 1937 essay on Einstein's equations, Hägerström asserted that his interest in the topic depended on the contradictions that would arise in the theory of relativity in connection with the notion of motion, conceived as objectively given, and not as a mere change in

---

[113]The argumentation in *Selbstdarstellung* seems to be based on the lecture series from spring 1927 of which we have an anonymous student transcript (Hägerström P 97C, Uppsala University Library) where Newton and Einstein are explicitly discussed: T. Silverbark, *Fysikens filosofi*, cit., pp. 167–169.

[114]M. Fries, *Förord*, in *Filosofi och vetenskap*, cit., p. 11. On the same occasion, Fries called the Einstein study Hägerström's «spiritual testament.»

[115]A precise date that can be singled out is the end of the manuscript *H 2:7* that comments on Russell, and two essays, by Oséen and Kaila. The latter two essays were published first 1932, which means that the Einstein study cannot have been written earlier than that date.

[116]T. Silverbark, *Fysikens filosofi*, cit., p. 185: «Det är också med stor sannolikhet Einstein avhandlingens första kapitel, möjligen även dess inledning (...). Att det skulle röra sig om avhandlingens första kapitel är en hypotes som stärks av att manuskriptets första kapitel saknas – det kan ha hamnat på annat håll i samband med översättningen och sedan aldrig återbördats. Dessutom visar det sig att av den publicerade uppsatsens fyra delar inleds ordagrant på samma sätt som det första kapitlet i tidigare versioner av avhandlingsmanuskriptet. Och sist men inte minst kan den tryckta texten identifieras som avhandlingens första kapitel genom Mac Leods anmärkningar.»

position relative to the observer. The introduction then offers a brief synopsis of the rest of the work.

In the first chapter, corresponding to section two in the 1937 essay (i.e., pp. 161 ff.), Hägerström presented the strict mathematical features of his work: This chapter concerns the implications of the equations that appear in the first appendix to Einstein's *Über die spezielle Relativitätstheorie* from 1905,[117] the very equations that made Hägerström ascribe to Einstein "an extraordinary mathematical intuition."[118]

The second chapter was entitled *On the Special Theory of Relativity as Concerned with Realities beyond Knowledge, i.e., as Metaphysics, not Physics.*[119] Here, Hägerström argued that a "metaphysical" element can be detected in the philosophical implications or consequences of Einstein's argumentation in his theory of special relativity. This element is identified in the fact that, in order to show the relativity of time, an "immeasurable" time is presupposed – time *in se*, or a form of duration (*varaktighet*) that somehow recalls Bergson's *durée*[120] – in making the actual time measurement and in rendering two relative systems comparable: «When it [the theory of special relativity] attempts to confer meaning to the relative magnitude of the disparate seconds, it introduces covertly the method of physical measurement.»[121] In other words, the alleged inconsistency is that there seems to be implicit presuppositions, based on traditional Newtonian physics, behind the idea of rendering commensurable the two relative systems in Hägerström's view, whilst the theory would withhold a strict incommensurability between the systems.[122] He deepened his view by discussing the famous example of the principle of relativity with the two observers; one on the train and the other on the track.[123]

The third chapter dealt with the idea of a four-dimensional space-time as elaborated by Einstein and one of his teachers, Hermann Minkowski.[124] More specifically, Hägerström discussed the philosophical implications that he saw in the use of the "imaginary entity" $\sqrt{-1}$, in the time coordinate of the equations.[125] At the end of the study, the focus switches from the theory of relativity to more

---

[117] A. Hägerström, *Über die Gleichungen der speziellen Relativitätstheorie*, cit., p. 186.

[118] Letter from A. Hägerström to O. Klein, 19/10/1938 in *H 4:10.*

[119] See beginning of the manuscript *H 2:7*, pp. 37 ff. Cf. T. Silverbark, *Fysikens filosofi*, cit., p. 175.

[120] H. Bergson, *Durée et simultanéité. À propos de la théorie d'Einstein*, Alcan, Paris 1922; Eng. trans. *Duration and Simultaneity*, Robin Durie (ed.), Clinamen Press, Manchester 1999.

[121] A. Hägerström, *H 2:7*, p. 42; quote from T. Silverbark, *Fysikens filosofi*, cit., p. 175: «då den [den speciella relativitetsteorin] söker göra de disparata sekundernas relativa storhet begriplig, sker det genom en insmygning av den fysikaliska tidmätningens metod.»

[122] See *H 2:7*, p. 42.

[123] See *H 2:7*, p. 47. See R. Laughlin, *A Different Universe*, cit., Chapter 10.

[124] *H 2:7*, pp. 161 ff.

[125] On the "imaginary entity" $\sqrt{-1}$, P.J. Nahin, *An Imaginary Tale. The Story of* $\sqrt{-1}$, Princeton University Press, Princeton, NJ, 2007, pp. 105 ff. See also *H 2:7*, pp. 68–75. In this chapter he also discussed the recent essay in the review *Cosmos* by one of his scientific colleagues, C.W. Oséen *On the Construction of Space in Physics.*

traditional epistemological issues, such as Hägerström's criticism of "sensualism" which basically follows his argumentations in earlier writings (see Chapter 2). The study ends with two commentaries on Bertrand Russell and the Finnish logician Eino Kaila.

It is not of crucial importance to give a further detailed account of Hägerström's argumentations.[126] Most of his discussion revolves around (the generally sane) ideas that what is graced with mathematical beauty is not necessarily real and no observation can by itself confer the ring of truth. However, the intricate elaborations also include less flattering traits: Some of his basic arguments concern the illusionary nature of the notion of motion, the impossibility to perceive it, his drastic refusal of the notion of diachronical identity, the spatial analogy used in time-measurement, and the subjectivistic basis and immeasurableness of duration (this latter being precisely the issue that made the atheist Einstein declare, after a public dialogue with Henri Bergson at the *Société philosophique* in Paris in 1922, "may God forgive him for he knows not"). Then again, it is always a little too easy to rejoice in hindsight over misconstrued interpretations.

What is more interesting is, nonetheless, that Hägerström was well-inserted into the debate of the time. Within the contemporary and often extra-academic discussions in Scandinavia, «the ideas about relativity and quantum physics must be understood not only as expressions of some individuals' more or less adequate knowledge, but also as expressions of different styles of thought. One such thought-style was formed in Uppsala, where some philosophers strongly opposed both the relativity of the new physical space and time concepts and the "uncertainty" of quantum mechanics.»[127] Secondly, it should be remembered that he was taken (sufficiently) seriously so as to maintain the discussion with Oskar Klein.

But most of all, Hägerström belonged to the few contemporaries who realised the profound philosophical implications of the fact that Einstein had formulated a *background independent theory*. «Before Einstein, space and time were thought to have properties that were fixed for all eternity. The geometry of space is, was, and always would be as Euclid described (. . .). For Newton, space and time constituted an absolute background (. . .). Einstein's general theory of relativity is completely different. There is no fixed background. The geometry of space and time changes and evolves, as does everything else in nature. Different geometries of spacetime describe the histories of different universes. (. . .) We have a bunch of fields all interacting with one another, all dynamic, all influencing one another, one of which is the geometry of spacetime. We call such a theory a *background independent theory*.»[128] It was this dynamical aspect and highly complex interaction that disturbed Hägerström. If everything was moving, how could the *criterium veri* be fixed? That he tried to confute Einstein's revolutionary insights must be considered physiological for someone

[126] Summaries of the major arguments can be found in Silverbark's aforementioned book.

[127] T. Silverbark, *Fysikens filosofi*, cit., quote from the English abstract.

[128] L. Smolin, *The Trouble with Physics*, cit., p. 44.

who had dedicated his whole career to developing the epistemological necessity of creating *background dependent theories*.

All in all, Hägerström seems to have understood that the very basic tenets of his own epistemological theory, i.e., the ontological monism that was grounded in determinate reality, were roughly shaken by this bold new form of physics. As we have seen in Chapter 2, reality as *Selbstidentität* or "determinateness" guaranteed the cognitive interdependence between Consciousness (the subject) and what is externally the focus of knowledge (traditionally, the object). This implies that, for Hägerström, reality is, so to say, *embedded* in all (meaningful) judgments. This is connected to the fact that his "Copernican revolution" was grounded in the ultimate context, the all-encompassing spatio-temporal world of experience. However, he seems to have conceived this spatially and timely determinate world as based on certain *a priori* assumptions that were essentially those that grounded the axioms in Newton's mechanics and that construed absolute time and Euclidean space.

But then again, Ernst Mach did not believe in atoms, James Clerk Maxwell believed in aether, and Albert Einstein rejected the outcome of quantum mechanics. Axel Hägerström belonged to that generation who had seen a revolution too many to believe in them all. In the end, it should perhaps be added that he seemed to have abandoned the plan of publishing the Einstein study: If true, it does not excuse his scientific shortcomings, but it is definitely a credit for intellectual honesty.[129]

## 7.4 Nine Weeks Later

In the summer of 2008, I went back to Uppsala and visited the small house in *Floragatan* as well as some of the places where Hägerström used to work. The surroundings of the university still breathe calm pleasance, and much has been left untouched in this town that he never left, apart from some rare journeys southward; quick academic trips to other cities like Lund, and a few visits to Stockholm where his daughter brought up his grandson, John-Axel, who later in life became a civil engineer. The most original and outstanding philosophical thought that this part of the world has single-handedly developed came from this far-off little township. Notwithstanding its remoteness, Hägerström spent an intellectually vivid life, and his imagination and genius gave him a vibrantly colourful existence that his biography does not betray. As mentioned, he turned down an invitation to the eternal city in the early thirties. Yet he kept dreaming of the marble dust that the Mediterranean winds grind off the Roman monuments in the city where I first became acquainted with his work.

In spite of this apparent isolationism, he was *mysteriously* tuned in to the *Zeitgeist*. Perhaps his grandmother first encouraged this attention for what goes on in the world in his early youth. What is beyond doubt, however, is that Hägerström put his finger on some of the most significant problems that were soon to become the great issues of the day, that made us change our comprehension of world history

[129]This is withheld by Silverbark, *Fysikens filosofi*, cit., p. 174.

and our role within it. So, admiration for the perspicacious insights of a real mind can be confirmed by marking his legacy in the following four points:

1. His political views inspired by cosmopolitanism, tolerance and advocacy for an open society
2. His ferocious deconstruction of nineteenth century legal dogmatism and its organic and holistic preconditions, such as the will, *Volksgeist* and so on
3. His unrelenting insistence on clarity in the concepts used for social analysis
4. His deep scepticism towards entanglements and overlappings of descriptive and normative discourse that inaugurated modern non-cognitivism

While deepening the analysis of Roman law and the critical assessment of modern physics, he had the opportunity, in his last years, to show how an important philosophical scholarship is, by virtue of its own nature, a work in progress. In these chapters, I have highlighted how and why Hägerström's key problem was *reality as such* and its impact on our lives. He addressed this issue by delving into the maze of ancient history, and back again to the breaking news of science in his day. The inexorable effort to apply critical reason to our most inveterate convictions, so as to question prejudice and detect what we can change from what we cannot, was upheld by humane compassion and sincere curiosity, true to the spirit of *philo-sophia*. The correspondence and the manuscripts that have been published here for the first time offer an unexceptionable testimony of his inquisitiveness and the very real quest that Axel Hägerström pursued, until passing away, after 3 weeks of agony, on a warm Friday, July 7th 1939. The world he lived in came to an abrupt end, as Germany invaded Poland nine weeks later.

# Appendix: Hägerström's Life and Work in Brief

## Bibliography and Chronology

Axel Hägerström was a prolific writer and an inexhaustible lecturer. He left a significant amount of manuscripts after his death. No critical or complete edition of his work has been published and some of his writings are quite hard to come across. This is why a lengthy bibliography serves the purpose of a map.

The complete bibliography of Hägerström's writings can be found in T. Mautner, *Moralfilosofins grundläggning*, Almqvist & Wiksell International, Stockholm 1987, which also includes listings of lectures, seminars, papers and correspondence. It does not make for easy reading, besides using Swedish as its reference language. This bibliography aims to give scholars an unchallenging overview of Hägerström's work by sorting out various kinds of literature and providing extra information in footnotes. Hägerström's *Nachlaß* was first catalogued by Martin Fries, and then by Thomas Mautner. It can be found at the Uppsala University Library, *Carolina Rediviva*. Manuscripts are classified under the code (UUB signum) *Hägerström*(H) *decimal: number*; typed manuscripts under the code *H centimal: number*. A selected bibliography of secondary literature has also been added.

As far as his biographical data is concerned, the most detailed description can be found in the memoirs written by his daughter Margit Waller, *Människan som få kände*, which also includes family portraits and pictures. An English account, based on this book, can be found in Jes Bjarup's PhD thesis *Reason, Emotion and the Law. Studies in the Philosophy of Axel Hägerström*, Press of the Faculty of Law, Aarhus 1982. Another source in English is C.D. Broad's *Memoir of Axel Hägerström* in R.T. Sandin (ed.), *Philosophy and Religion*, Allen & Unwin, London 1964, pp. 15–29. No critical biography has been published and most sources of secondary literature repeat information found in the aforementioned titles and do not follow a chronological progression. This chronology offers a brief synopsis of the major events in his life, both private and intellectual.

P. Mindus, *A Real Mind*, Law and Philosophy Library 87,
DOI 10.1007/978-90-481-2895-2_BM2,  

# Organised Overview of Hägerström's Bibliography

## Monographs*

1- *Aristoteles etiska grundtankar och deras teoretiska förutsättningar* (The Principles of Aristotle's Ethical Thought and Its Theoretical Premises), Berling, Uppsala 1893
2- *Undersökning af den empiriska etikens möjlighet med särskild hänsyn till dess moderna hufvudformer* (Inquiry into the Possibility of Empirical Ethics with Special Reference to the Main Modern Forms), Berling, Uppsala 1895
3- *Om den moraliska känslan och driften såsom förnuftiga i den moderna rationalismens hufvudformer*, vol. I: *Den moderna rationalismens hufvudformer* (On Feeling and Thrust in Morals as a Rational Phenomenon in the Main Forms of Modern Rationalism), Berling, Uppsala 1895
4- *Om "Den empiriska etiken" och "Den moraliska känslan". Svar på kritik* (On "Empirical Ethics" and "Moral Sense." A Reply), Berling, Uppsala 1897[1]
5- *Kants Ethik im Verhältnis zu seinen erkenntnistheoretischen Grundgedanken. Systematisch dargestellt*, Almqvist & Wiksell/Harrassowitz, Uppsala-Leipzig 1902
6- *Stat och Rätt. En rättsfilosofisk undersökning* (State and Law. An Inquiry in Philosophy of Law), vol. I, Almqvist & Wiksell, Uppsala 1904
7- *Das Prinzip der Wissenschaft. Eine logisch-erkenntnistheoretische Untersuchung*, SKHVSU Almqvist & Wiksell, Uppsala 1908

---

* Hägerström's work was often edited by *Kungliga humanistiska vetenskapssamfundet i Uppsala* (i.e., *Acta Societatis litterarum humaniorum regiae Upsaliensis*). I therefore use Thomas Mautner's abbreviation: SKHVSU. Since these *Acta* were usually printed by the firm Almqvist & Wiksell, I use this reference as the publishing house. It should also be mentioned that Berling was the Academic publisher, serving the University of Uppsala ("Akademiska Boktryckeriet").

[1] This monograph on Hägerström's "declaration of incompetence" was written the year before with the title *Om den af de sakkunnige vid tillsättandet af professuren i praktisk filosofi Uppsala 1896 företagna granskningen af mina avhandlingar*. The difference between the two essays only concerns the foreword (See T. Mautner, *Moralfilosofins grundläggning*, Almqvist & Wiksell International, Stockholm 1987, p. 202).

8- *Social teleologi i marxismen* (Social Teleology in Marxism), in *Uppsala universitets årsskrift*, Almqvist & Wiksell, Uppsala 1909[2]
9- *Botanisten och filosofen. Om kunskapsfilosofiens nödvändighet*, (The Botanist and the Philosopher. On the Necessity of Philosophy of Knowledge), Bonniers, Stockholm 1910[3]
10- *Till analysen av det empiriska självmedvetandet. En psykologisk och filosofisk undersökning* (Contribution to the Analysis of Empirical Self-Consciousness. A Psychological and Philosophical Inquiry), Berling, Uppsala, edited 1910, distributed 1945[4]
11- *Om moraliska föreställningars sanning* (On the Truth of Moral Ideas), Bonniers, Stockholm 1911[5]
12- *Till frågan om den objektiva rättens begrepp*, vol. I: *Viljeteorien* (On the Concept of Objective Law. Vol. I: The Will-Theory), SKHVSU Almqvist & Wiksell, Uppsala 1917[6]
13- *Der römische Obligationsbegriff im Lichte der allgemeinen römischen Rechtsanschauung,*vol. I, SKHVSU Almqvist & Wiksell, Uppsala-Leipzig 1927[7]
14- *Der römische Obligationsbegriff im Lichte der allgemeinen römischen Rechtsanschauung*, vol. II, *Über die Verbalobligation*, ed. K. Olivecrona, SKHVSU Almqvist & Wiksell, Uppsala 1941

---

[2]The volume includes a written version of the lectures held in 1907 entitled *Den sociala rörelsens drivkrafter* (The Driving Forces of the Social Movement).

[3]Since the first edition only counted around a thousand copies it was reedited by Martin Fries in *Filosofi och vetenskap*, Ehlin, Stockholm 1957, pp. 15–110. The new edition however presents a somewhat longer text. In the preface (p. 10), Fries claims to use the unpublished "clean version" with the title *Är filosofisk kunskapslära överfödig?* (first written in 1908). In his bibliography in *Moralfilosofins grundläggning* from 1987, Thomas Mautner offers a precise scheme over the variations between the two texts (p. 204).

[4]This essay was never distributed because Hägerström considered it to have been composed too hastily (see M. Waller, *Axel Hägerström. Människan som få kände*, Natur & Kultur, Stockholm 1961, p. 186). Martin Fries edited it in 1945, after the death of Hägerström.

[5]Hägerström's inaugural lecture was reedited in the first edition *Socialfilosofiska uppsatser*, Bonniers, Stockholm 1939, pp. 37–65 as well as in the second edition, Bonniers, Stockholm 1961, pp. 35–57 and, its last reediting can be found in *Moralfilosofins grundläggning*, Thomas Mautner (ed.), Almqvist & Wiksell International, Stockholm 1987, pp. 27–50. Eng. trans. by R. Sandin, *On the Truth of Moral Propositions* in *Philosophy and Religion*, Allen & Unwin, London 1964 by T. Mautner, *On the Truth of Moral Ideas*, ANU, Canberra 1971; German trans. by D. Lang, *Über die Wahrheit moralischer Vorstellungen* in «Perspektiven der Philosophie», 1979, pp. 219–242.

[6]Translated by C.D. Broad under the title *On the Question of the Notion of Law*, in *Inquiries into the Nature of Law and Morals*, Almqvist & Wiksell, Stockholm 1953, pp. 56–256. The pages 116–201 of the translation were reedited by R.T. Sandin in *Philosophy and Religion*, Allen & Unwin, London 1964, pp. 97–172 with the title *On the Idea of Duty*.

[7]There is an English translation of the introduction with the title *General View*, by C.D. Broad in *Inquiries into the Nature of Law and Morals*, Almqvist & Wiksell, Stockholm 1953, pp. 1–16; and an Italian translation in S. Castignone (ed.), *Il realismo giuridico scandinavo e americano: antologia di scritti giuridici*, Mulino, Bologna 1981.

15- *Jesus. En karaktärsanalys* (Jesus. An Analysis of his Character), M. Fries (ed.), Natur & Kultur, Stockholm 1968[8]

## Essays

16- *Om filosofins betydelse för människan* (On the Importance of Philosophy for Man), in *I vår tids lifsfrågor. Skrifter utgivna af Sydney Alrutz*, Skoglund, Stockholm 1898, pp. 5–47

17- *Kritiska punkter i värdepsykologien* (Critical Aspects in Psychology of Value), in *Festskrift tillägnad E.O. Burman*, Appelgrens boktr., Uppsala 1910, pp. 17–75

18- *Om sociala vidskepelser* (On Social Superstition), in «Tiden. Socialdemokratisk idé- och debattidskrift», 1913, vol. 5, pp. 321–332[9]

19- *Är gällande rätt uttryck att vilja?* (Is Law in Force a Matter of Will?), in *Festskrift tillägnad prof. Vitalis Norström på 60-årsdagen den 29 januari 1916*, Elanders Boktryckeri, Göteborg 1916, pp. 171–210[10]

20- *Naturrätt i straffrättsvetenskapen?* (Natural Law in Legal Science Concerned with Criminal Law?), in «Svensk Juristtidning», 1920, vol. 5, pp. 321–341

21- *Hägerström Axel, ad vocem*, in *Filosofiskt lexikon*, A. Alhberg (ed.), Natur & Kultur, Stockholm 1925, pp. 89–92[11]

22- *Axel Hägerström, ad vocem*, in R. Schmidt (ed.), *Die Philosophie der Gegenwart in Selbstdarstellungen*, Meiner, Leipzig 1929, vol. VII, pp. 111–159[12]

23- *Das magistratische Ius in seinem Zusammenhang mit dem römischen Sakralrechte*, in *Minnesskrift utgiven av Juridiska fakulteten i Uppsala 1929 till hågkomst av dess första doktorspromotion 1629*, Lundequistska bokh., Uppsala 1929

---

[8]It contains the manuscript *Hägerström 106:2*, edited in 1968 for the commemoration of the 100th anniversary of his birth.

[9]Reedited in *Socialfilosofiska uppsatser*, Bonniers, Stockholm 1939, pp. 93–120, and 1966[2], pp. 77–96.

[10]Second edition in *Rätten och viljan. Två uppsatser av Axel Hägerström*, (ed. Karl Olivecrona), Gleerup, Lund 1961, pp. 59–95; Eng. trans. by C.D. Broad, *Is Positive Law an Expression of Will?*, in *Inquiries into the Nature of Law and Morals*, Almqvist & Wiksell, Stockholm 1953, pp. 17–55.

[11]The Swedish version of this entry was reedited in 1931, 1951 and 1963. There is an English translation with the title *The Philosophy of Axel Hägerström, Appendix B*, in *Philosophy and Religion*, ed. R. Sandin, Allen & Unwin, London 1964, pp. 313–316.

[12]Translated into Swedish, with subtitles and subsection added, in M. Fries (ed.), *Filosofi och vetenskap*, Ehlin, Stockholm 1957, pp. 112–180. Partially translated into English by R. Sandin with the title *A Summary of My Philosophy* in *Philosophy and Religion*, Allen & Unwin, London 1964, pp. 33–74.

24- *Tab. III, 1-3 des Zwölftafelgesetzes*, in *Symbolae philologicae. O.A. Danielson octogenario dicatae*, A. Nelson (ed.), Lundequistska Bokhandeln, Uppsala 1932, pp. 113–121[13]

25- *Om social rättvisa* (On Social Justice), in «Spectrum», 1932, vol. 1, pp. 1–14[14]

26- *Marx och filosofin* (Marx and Philosophy), in «Tiden», 1933, vol. 25, pp. 147–148

27- *Vergleich zwischen den Kraftvorstellungen der primitiven und modernen Kulturvölker*, in *Festskrift tillägnad professor emeritus Arvi Grotenfelt*, eds. E. Kaila, J.E. Saaloma, E. Ahlman, Ajatus, Porvoo 1933, pp. 63–84[15]

28- *Nehrman-Ehrenstråles uppfattning av grunden för ett löftes juridiskt bindande kraft, belyst genom å ena sidan romersk, å andra sidan naturrättslig åskådning* (Nehrman-Ehrenstråle's Conception of the Ground of the Binding Power of the Promise, Illustrated from the Standpoint of Both Roman Law and Natural Law), in *Minnesskrift ägnad 1734 års lag av jurister i Sverige och Finland*, Marcus, Stockholm 1934, vol. II, pp. 571–630[16]

29- *Om Pliktmedvetandet* (On Consciousness of Duty), in «Presens»,1934, våren (spring), vol. I, pp. 55–68[17]

30- *Begreppet viljeförklaring på privaträttens område* (*The Conception of a Declaration of Intention in the Sphere of Private Law*), in «Theoria», 1935:1, pp. 32–57, and 1935:2, pp. 121–138[18]

31- *Om primitiva rudimenter i modernt föreställningssätt* (On Primitive Rudiments in Modern Way of Thinking), in «Presens», 1935, vol. 2, pp.167–191[19]

32- *Über die Gleichungen der speziellen Relativitätstheorie*, in *Adolf Phalén in memoriam. Philosophical Essays*, Almqvist & Wiksell, Uppsala 1937, pp. 144–200[20]

---

[13]Reedited in *Der römische Obligationsbegriff*, vol. II, SKHVSU Almqvist & Wiksell, Uppsala 1941, pp. 113–121.

[14]Reedited in *Socialfilosofiska uppsatser*, Bonniers, Stockholm 1939, pp. 121–140, and 1966$^2$, pp. 97–111.

[15]Translated into Swedish by Birgit Olivecrona with the title *Primitiv och modern kraftföreställning* in *Religionsfilosofi*, (ed. M. Fries), Natur & Kultur, Stockholm 1949, pp. 15–38.

[16]German translation by K. Wührer, edited by K. Olivecrona in *Recht, Plicht und bindende Kraft des Vertrages nach römischer und naturrechtlicher Anschauung*, SKHVSU Almqvist & Wiksell, Stockholm 1965. This translation includes a previous but partial translation entitled *Über den Grund der bindenden Kraft des Konsensualkontaktes nach römischer Rechtsanschauung*, signed "K. Olivecrona Lund, December 1941" published in «Zeitschrift der Savigny-Stiftung für Rechtsgeschichte. Romanistiche Abteilung», 1943, 63, pp. 268–300.

[17]Reed. in *Socialfilosofiska uppsatser*, Bonniers, Stockholm 1939, pp. 67–92 and 1966$^2$, pp. 58–76.

[18]Reed. in *Rätten och viljan*, Gleerup, Lund 1961, pp. 99–154. Eng. trans. by C.D. Broad in *Inquiries into the Nature of Law and Morals*, Almqvist & Wiksell, Stockholm 1953, with the title *The Conception of a Declaration of Intention in the Sphere of Private Law*, pp. 299–357.

[19]Reed. in *Socialfilosofiska uppsatser*, Bonniers, Stockholm 1939, pp. 143–18 and 1966$^2$, pp. 112–132.

[20]Partially translated into Swedish in *Filosofi och vetenskap* (ed. M. Fries), Ehlin, Stockholm 1957 with the title *Relativitetsteori och kunskapsfilosofi* (pp. 190–241).

33- *Om handslagets ursprungliga innebörd* (On the Original Sense of Shaking Hands), in «Presens», 1938, vol. 5, pp. 53–72[21]
34- *En straffrättslig principundersökning* (An Inquiry on the Principles of Criminal Law), in «Svensk Juristtidning», 1939, vol. 24, pp. 209–225[22]
35- *Om svikligt förtigande såsom straffbart efter 22:1 S.L.* (On Fraudulent Non-Disclosure as Liable to Punishment According to the Swedish Law 22:1), in «Svensk Juristtidning», 1939, vol. 24, pp. 311–335[23]

## Reviews and Shorter Publications

36- *Selbstanzeige*, in «Kant-Studien», 1902, vol. 7, pp. 467–469
37- *I moralpsykologiska frågor* (On Issues of Moral Psychology) [review of K. Birch-Reichenwald Aars, *Gut und Böse. Zur Psychologie der Moralgefühle*, Christiania 1907], in «Psyke. Tidskrift för psykologisk forskning», 1907, anno II, vol. 5, pp. 273–287 and 1908, anno III, vols. 1–2, pp. 85–99
38- *Sven Helander, Marx och Hegel: en kritisk studie över socialdemokratisk världsåskådning* (Sven Helander, Marx and Hegel: A Critical Study on the Worldview of Socialdemocracy) [Fahlbeckska stiftelsen, Lund 1920], in «Statsvetenskaplig tidskrift», 1922:25, pp. 245–258
39- *Edvard Petrini in memoriam*, in «Arkiv för psykologi och pedagogik», 1922, vol. 1, pp. 225–256
40- *Öppet brev till O. Lagercrantz* (Open letter), in «Upsala Nya Tidning» 8/12/1922
41- *Öppet brev till O. Lagercrantz* (Open letter), in «Upsala Nya Tidning» 22/12/1922
42- *Andreas Bjerre, ad vocem*, in *Svenskt biografiskt lexikon*, 1923, vol. 4, pp. 508–510
43- *Kriminalpsykologiska reflexioner* (Thoughts on Criminal Psychology) [review of A. Bjerre, *Bidrag till mordets psykologi*, Norstedts, Stockholm 1925], in «Svensk Juristtidning»,1925:10, pp. 329–353[24]
44- *Sydney Alrutz in memoriam*, in «Ergo. Tidning för Uppsala studenter», 1925, vol. 2, p. 21

---

[21] Reed. in *Socialfilosofiska uppsatser*, Bonniers, Stockholm 1939, pp. 171–190 and 1966$^2$, pp. 133–149.

[22] Reed. in *Socialfilosofiska uppsatser*, Bonniers, Stockholm 1939, pp. 231–255 and 1966$^2$, pp. 179–198; Eng. trans. by C.D. Broad in *Inquiries into the Nature of Law and Morals*, Almqvist & Wiksell, Stockholm 1953, with the title *On Fundamental Problems of Law* (pp. 348–366).

[23] This is the continuation of the article *Straffrättslig principundersökning* from 1939. It was never translated by Broad in *Inquiries* and never reedited in *Socialfilosofiska uppsatser*.

[24] There are two later editions of this review: in *Socialfilosofiska uppsatser*, Bonniers, Stockholm 1939, pp. 191–228 and 1966$^2$, pp. 150–178.

45- *Hans Kelsen. Allgemeine Staatslehre* (Springer, Berlin 1925), in «Litteris. An International Critical Review of the Humanities», 1928, vol. 5, pp. 81–99[25]
46- *E.O. Burman. Minnesord*, in «Upsala Nya Tidning» 15/06/1929
47- *Docent Nymans "Erinringar". Ett genmäle*, Uppsala 1929
48- *Per Persson. En Biografi*, in *Kungliga Svenska Vetenskapsakademiens årsbok för år 1931*, Almqvist and Wiksell, Uppsala 1931, pp. 350–352
49- *Till frågan om begreppet gällande rätt* (On the Concept of Valid Law) [review of A. Ross, *Theorie der Rechtsquellen*, Deuticke, Leipzig/Wien 1929], in «Tidskrift for retsvidenskab», 1931, pp. 48–91
50- *Brev till Lundstedt*, in «Fönstret», 1934:4 (Letter on Bohman's thesis to Lundstedt)
51- *Brev till S. Bohman* (Letter to Bohman), in «Upsala Nya Tidning» 3/11/1934
52- *Ein Stein, ihr Herren, ist ein schlechtes Argument*, in «Fönstret», 1934:6–7, p. 3

There is some published correspondence as well. It is usually excerpts. Chiefly, these letters are addressed to family members (see M. Waller, *Människan som få kände*, Natur & Kultur, Stockholm 1961 and, for the correspondence with his half-brother Gustaf, P.-Å. Walton (ed.) in «Sophia», 1997:2, pp. 14–17; *Brev 26/3/1893* in «Insikt och handling», 2000:20, pp. 101–102); to Andres Karitz (in S. Nordin, *Från Hägerström till Hedenius. Den moderna svenska filosofien*, Doxa, Lund 1983, pp. 41–42); to Arnold Solvén: See *Ett Hägerström brev* (A letter from Hägerström), dated 4/1/1931 in «Tiden», 1940, vol. 32, pp. 85–93; and to Oscar Klein (in T. Silverbark, *Fysikens filosofi. Diskussioner om Einstein, relativitetsteorin och kvantfysiken i Sverige*, Östlings bokförlag Symposion, Stockholm/Eslöv 1999, pp. 170–173).

## Posthumously Collected Work and Translations

53- *Socialfilosofiska uppsatser* (Essays on Social Philosophy), Bonniers, Stockholm 1939, 1966[2]
54- *Über den Grund der bindenden Kraft des Konsensualkontraktes nach römischer Rechtsanschauung*, in «Zeitschrift der Savigny-Stiftung für Rechtsgeschichte. Romanistische Abteilung», 1943, vol. 63, pp. 268–300[26]

[25]English translation by C.D. Broad, entitled *Kelsen's Theory of Law and the State*, in *Inquiries into the Nature of Law and Morals*, Almqvist & Wiksell, Stockholm 1953, pp. 257–298.

[26]Partial translation into German by K. Olivecrona of the 1934 essay *Nehrman-Ehrenstråles uppfattning av grunden för ett löftes juridiskt bindande kraft*, reedited 1965 in *Recht, Plicht und bindenden Kraft des Vertrages* SKHVSU Almqvist & Wiksell, Stockholm-Upsala 1965 (pp. 16–43). According to Pattaro, this essay on the binding force of contracts was conceived as the basis for the third, uncompleted volume of *Der römische Obligationsbegriff* (see E. Pattaro, *Il realismo giuridico scandinavo. Vol. I Axel Hägerström*, Clueb, Bologna 1974, p. 12).

55- *De socialistiska idéernas historia* (History of Socialistic Ideas), ed. M. Fries, Natur & Kultur, Stockholm 1946[27]

56- *Erkenntnistheoretische Voraussetzungen der speziellen Relativitätstheorie Einsteins*, in «Theoria», 1946, vol. XII, pp. 1–68[28]

57- *Lectures on so-called Spiritual Religion*, in «Theoria», 1948, vol. XIV, pp. 28–67[29]

58- *Religionsfilosofi* (Philosophy of Religion), ed. M. Fries, Natur & Kultur, Stockholm 1949[30]

59- *Moralpsykologi* (Moral Psychology), ed. M. Fries, Natur & Kultur, Stockholm 1952[31]

60- *Inquiries into the Nature of Law and Morals*, Almqvist & Wiksell, Uppsala 1953[32]

61- *Filosofi och vetenskap* (Philosophy and Science), ed. M. Fries, Ehlin, Stockholm 1957[33]

---

[27] Edited by Martin Fries, this volume contains the transcription of the manuscripts *Hägerström 108:1* and *Hägerström 110:2*, which correspond to the preparatory notes for the spring semester 1909.

[28] It is the lengthy but partial translation into German by Manfred Moritz of the Swedish manuscript *Hägerström 2:7* from 1934, conserved at the university library in Uppsala and edited in *Filosofi och vetenskap*, by Martin Fries, Ehlin, Stockholm 1957, pp. 190–242.

[29] English translation by C.D. Broad of the manuscript *Hägerström 118:2*, entitled *Andlig religion*, which corresponds to the preparatory notes for the courses of the spring semester 1926, edited by Martin Fries in *Religionsfilosofi*, Natur & Kultur, Stockholm 1949, pp. 41–79. There is a second translation by Robert T. Sandin in *Philosophy and Religion*, Allen & Unwin, London 1964, pp. 224–259.

[30] This collected work includes the Swedish translation by Birgit Olivecrona of the essay *Vergleich zwischen den Kraftvorstellungen der primitiven und modernen Kulturvölker* from 1933 (pp. 15–38); the aforementioned manuscripts *Hägerström 118:2* on spiritual religion (pp. 41–79); *Hägerström 118:1* (pp. 83–134) corresponding to the lecture notes from the spring semester 1923, translated by R. Sandin in *Philosophy and Religion*, Allen & Unwin, London 1964, with the title *Metaphysical Religiosity*, pp. 175–223; *Hägerström 118:4* (pp. 137–250) corresponding to the lecture notes from autumn 1920, partially translated into English by R.T. Sandin 1964 with the title *The Truth-value of Christian Dogmatics* (Mautner accounts for the discrepancy between the texts, in *Vägledning till Hägerströmstudiet*, Almqvist & Wiksell, Stockholm 1994, p. 218).

[31] This collection contains three previously unpublished manuscripts: *Hägerström 112:4* (spring lectures 1917, pp. 15–110); *Hägerström 111:4* (spring lectures 1921, pp. 111–147) and *Hägerström 111:1* (spring lectures 1930, pp. 149–204).

[32] This collection, edited by K. Olivecrona, contains the English translations by C.D. Broad of the introduction to the first volume of *Der römische Obligationsbegriff* (pp. 1–16), *Är gällande rätt uttryck av vilja?* from 1916 (pp. 17–55), *Till frågan om den objektiva rätten begrepp* (pp. 56–256); the review of Hans Kelsen dating from 1928 (pp. 257–298), *Begreppet viljeförklaring på privaträttens område* from 1935 (pp. 299–347); and *Straffrättslig principundersökning* from 1939 (pp. 348–366).

[33] It collects the reediting of *Botanisten och filosofen* from 1910; the Swedish edition of *Erkenntnistheoretische Voraussetzungen der speziellen Relativitätstheorie Einsteins* from 1946 to which the first chapter, based on the manuscript *Hägerström 2:7* from 1934 has been added (pp. 183–190); the Swedish translation of *Selbstdarstellung* from 1929 entitled *Framställning av den egna filosofien*.

62- *Rätten och viljan. Två uppsatser av Axel Hägerström* (Law and Will. Two Essays of Axel Hägerström), ed. Karl Olivecrona, Gleerup, Lund 1961[34]
63- *Rätten och staten. Tre föreläsningar om rätts- och statsfilosofi* (The Law and the State. Three Lectures on Philosophy of Law and State), ed. M. Fries, Natur & Kultur, Stockholm 1963[35]
64- *Philosophy and Religion*, translated and edited by R.T. Sandin, Allen & Unwin, London 1964[36]
65- *Recht, Pflicht und bindenden Kraft des Vertrags: nach römischer und naturrechtlicher Anschauung* (ed.) Karl Olivecrona, German trans. by Karl Wührer, apart from pp. 16–43 translated by the editor, SKHVSU Almqvist & Wiksell, Stockholm-Uppsala 1965[37]
66- *Filosofien som vetenskap* (Philosophy as Science) in «Filosofisk tidskrift», 1980:2, pp. 1–13 and 1981:3, pp. 45–47, ed. Thomas Mautner[38]
67- *Moralfilosofins grundläggning* (The Foundation of Moral Philosophy), ed. Thomas Mautner, Almqvist & Wiksell International, Stockholm 1987[39]

[34]It contains two essays previously published, respectively in 1916 (*Är gällande rätt uttryck av vilja?*) and 1935 (*Begreppet viljeförklaring på privaträttens område*).

[35]It contains the manuscripts *Hägerström 116:3, 115:7, 115:8*, respectively entitled *Del I: Rättsidéers uppkomst* (*The Genesis of Judicial Ideas*) from 1917; *Del II: Stat och statsformer* (*The State and Its Forms*) from 1921; *Del III: Förhållandet mellan staten och rätten* (*On the Relation between the State and the Law*) from 1924.

[36]It contains *Memoirs of Axel Hägerström* by C.D. Broad (pp. 15–29); a partial translation of *Selbstdarstellung* (pp. 33–74); Eng. trans. of the inaugural lecture from 1911; Eng. trans. of the section of the 1917-essay *Till frågan om den objektiva rättens begrepp* on the sense of duty (pp. 97–172); Eng. trans. of the manuscript *Hägerström 118:1*, published in Swedish in 1949; Eng. trans. of the manuscript *Hägerström 118:2* on spiritual religion; a partial translation of the manuscript *Hägerström 118:4* (winter courses 1920); Eng. trans. of pp. 40–45 in *Hägerström 104:1* (dating from the a.y. 1925/1926) entitled *Appendix A. Metaphysics in the Special Sciences*; Eng. trans. of the second edition of the entry *Axel Hägerström* from 1925 in *Filosofiskt lexikon*, ed. A. Ahlberg (pp. 313–316) entitled *Appendix B. The Philosophy of Axel Hägerström*.

[37]It is the German translation of *Nehrman-Ehrenstråles uppfattning av grunden för ett löftes juridiskt bindande kraft* from 1934. The pages 16–43 present a reedition of the partial translation carried out by Olivecrona in 1941.

[38]It is the first edition of the manuscript *Hägerström 104:3*, which is a talk held at the Verdandi association April 21st, 1909.

[39]It contains the famous inaugural lecture from 1911 (with explanatory remarks by the editor) and the manuscript *Hägerström 105:6* (spring courses 1911) with student notes.

# Secondary Literature on Hägerström


Ahlberg, A., *Hans Larsson, Ernst Cassirer och Axel Hägerström*, in «Insikt och handling. Hans Larsson Samfundet», 1955, vol. 1, pp. 5–15

Apéria-Meurling, H., *Axel Hägerström. Samtal med en svensk tänkare*, in «Ord och bild», 1939, anno 48, pp. 419–422

Bjarup, J., *Skandinavischer Realismus: Hägerström, Lundstedt, Olivecrona, Ross*, Kolleg Rechtstheorie, 3:1, Alber, Freiburg 1978

Bjarup, J., *Reason, Emotion and the Law. Studies in the Philosophy of Axel Hägerström*, Press of the Faculty of Law, Aarhus 1982

Bjarup, J., *Epistemology and Law according to Axel Hägerström*, in «Scandinavian Studies in Law», vol. 29, Almqvist & Wiksell, Stockholm 1985, pp. 13–47 now available at http://www.cenneth.com/sisl/pdf/29-1.pdf

Bjarup, J., *Legal Realism or Kelsen versus Hägerström*, in E. Kamenka, R.L. Summers, W. Twining (eds.), *Soziologische Jurisprudenz und realistische Theorien des Rechts*, Rechtstheorie Beiheft 9, Duncker und Humblot, Berlin 1986, pp. 243–257

Bjarup, J., *Scandinavian Legal Realism*, in C.B. Gray (ed.), *The Philosophy of Law: An Encyclopedia*, Garland, New York 1999

Bjarup, J., *Ought and Reality. Hägerström's Inaugural Lecture Re-considered*, in P. Wahlgren (ed.), «Scandinavian Studies in Law», vol. 40, Almqvist & Wiksell, Stockholm 2000, pp. 11–72

Bjarup J., *Axel Hägerströms filosofi, värdenihilism och rättspositivism*, in «Juridisk Tidskrift», 2004/05, anno 16, n. 1, pp. 25–41

Bjarup J., *The Philosophy of Scandinavian Legal Realism*, in «Ratio Juris», 2005, vol. 18, n. 1, pp. 1–15

Bjarup, J., *Scepticism and Scandinavian Legal Realists*, in T. Endicott, J. Getzler, E. Peel (eds.), *Properties of Law. Essays in Honour of Jim Harris*, Oxford University Press, Oxford 2006, pp. 52–68

Blinder, J., (*Review of*) *Axel Hägerström, Der römische Obligationsbegriff*, in «Kritische Vierteljahreschrift für Gesetzgebung und Rechtswissenschaft», 1931/1932, pp. 269–315

Broad, C.D., *Hägerström's Account of Sense of Duty and Certain Allied Experiences*, in «Philosophy», 1951, 26, pp. 99–113

Broad, C.D., *Memoir of Axel Hägerström*, in R.T. Sandin (ed.), *Philosophy and Religion*, Allen & Unwin, London 1964, pp. 15–29

Campbell, A.H., *Review of Axel Hägerström, Inquiries into the Nature of Law and Morals*, in «Modern Law Review», 1954, pp. 174–178

Carlsson, J., *Statsabsolutismens rättsfilosofi: en studie av Boströms och Hägerströms rättsfilosofi med avseende på deras bakgrund, innehåll och konsekvenser för juridiken*, Juridiska Fakulteten, Lund 2001; http://www.jur.lu.se/Internet/Biblioteket/Examensarbeten.nsf/0/F7C0DCF9A3EB3E98C1256AE60047A1A9/$File/xsmall.pdf?OpenElement

Cassirer, E., *Axel Hägerström. Eine Studie zur schwedischen Philosophie der Gegenwart*, Göteborgs högskolas årskrift, Göteborg 1939; now in *Gesammelte Werke. Nachgelassene Manuskripte und Texte* (eds. K. Ch. Köhnke, J. M. Krois, O. Schwemmer), Bd. 21, Meiner, Hamburg 2005; Swedish trans. *Axel Hägerström. En studie i samtida svensk filosofi*, Thales, Stockholm 2005; French trans. *Éloge de la métaphysique. Axel Hägerström. Une étude de la philosophie suédoise contemporaine*, Cerf, Paris 1996; Italian trans. *Axel Hägerström. Uno studio sulla filosofia svedese contemporanea*, G. Saponaro (ed.), Dispense Universitarie, Roma 1998

Castberg, F., *Philosophy of Law in the Scandinavian Countries*, in «The American Journal of Comparative Law», 1955, pp. 388–400

Castberg, F., *Problems of Legal Philosophy*, Oslo University Press, Oslo 1957², pp. 27–37

Castignone, S., *Axel Hägerström e la nozione del dovere*, in «Annali della facoltà di giurisprudenza dell'università di Genova», Giuffrè, Milano 1966

Castignone, S., *Axel Hägerström. Alle origini del realismo giuridico scandinavo*, in G. Tarello (ed.), *Materiali per una storia della cultura giuridica*, vol. I, Il Mulino, Bologna 1971, pp. 251–328

Castignone, S., *La macchina del diritto. Il realismo giuridico in Svezia*, Edizioni di Comunità, Milano 1974

Castignone, S., *Il realismo giuridico scandinavo: principi teorici e proposte operative*, in AA.VV., *La formazione storica del diritto moderno in Europa. Atti del terzo congresso internazionale della società italiana di storia del diritto*, II, Olschki, Firenze 1977, pp. 1473–1485

Castignone, S., *L'irrealismo scandinavo*, in «Materiali per una storia della cultura giuridica», 1984, vol. XIV, pp. 171–189

Castignone, S., *Hägerström e il dispotismo*, in «Materiali per una storia della cultura giuridica», 1984, vol. XVI, pp. 277–283

Castignone, S., *Diritto, linguaggio, realtà. Saggi sul realismo giuridico*, Giappichelli, Torino 1995

Danielsson, S., *Hägerströms huvudargument*, in «Filosofisk Tidskrift», 1990, anno 11, n. 2, pp. 16–22

Danielsson, S., *Värdenihilismen i praktiken*, in *Forskningsprofiler, Uppsala Universitet: Installationsföreläsningar 1989/1990*, Uppsala University Press, Uppsala 1990, pp. 12–19

Danielsson, S., *Några värdenihilismer*, in Å. Andersson, N.-E. Sahlin, *Huvudinnehåll*, Nya Doxa, Nora 1993, pp. 33–45

Danielsson, S., *Hägerström, Nietzsche och Hans Ruin*, in «Tidskrift för politisk filosofi», 2000, n. 2, pp. 45–52 (Ruin's rejoinder pp. 53–56)

Eliaeson, S., *Axel Hägerström and Modern Social Thought*, in «Nordeuropaforum», 2000, vol. 1, pp. 19–30

Faralli, C., *Diritto e magia. Saggio su Axel Hägerström*, Giuffrè, Milano 1982

Fredriksson, G., *20 filosofer*, Norstedt, Stockholm 1994, pp. 201–222

Fries, M., *Grunddragen i Hägerströms filosofi*, in A. Hägerström, *Socialfilosofiska uppsatser*, Bonniers, Stockholm 1939, pp. 9–34

Fries, M., *Verklighetsbegreppet enligt Hägerström. En systematisk framställning av grundtankarna i Hägerströms kunskapsteori med särskild hänsyn till hans lära om verklighetsbegreppet*, Lundquistska Bokhandeln, Uppsala 1944 (orginally in «Uppsala Universitets Årskrift», 1944, vol. 3, pp. XXV–XXVI)

Fries, M., *Förord*, in A. Hägerström, *Religionsfilosofi*, Natur & Kultur, Stockholm 1949, pp. 9–12

Fries, M., *Zur Interpretation einiger Gedanken in der Philosophie Hägerströms*, in «Theoria», 1951, vol. XVII, pp. 39–45

Fries, M., *Förord*, in A. Hägerström, *Filosofi och vetenskap*, Ehlin, Stockholm 1957, pp. 7–12

Frändberg, Å., *Die skandinavische Reaktion auf Hans Kelsens Reine Rechtslehre*, in *Einfluß der Reinen Rechtslehre auf die Rechtstheorie in verschiedenen Ländern*, Bd 2, Manz, Wien 1978, pp. 69–97

Fröström, L., *Hägerströms analys av värdeupplevelsen*, in S. Halldén, G. Hermerén, L. Stille (eds.), *Logik, rätt och moral. Filosofiska studier tillägnade Manfred Moritz*, Studentlitt., Lund 1969, pp. 49–60

Garlan, E.N., *(Review of) Axel Hägerström Inquiries into the Nature of Law and Morals*, in «The Journal of Philosophy», 1955, vol. 52, pp. 24–25

Harris, J.W., *Legal Philosophies* (1980), Butterworth London 1997², pp. 98–102

Hart, H.L.A., *Axel Hägerström – Inquiries into the Nature of Law and Morals (review)*, in «Philosophy», 1955, vol. 30, pp. 369–73

Hart, H.L.A., *Scandinavian Realism*, in «The Cambridge Law Journal», 1959, November, pp. 233–240; now in *Essays in Jurisprudence and Philosophy*, Clarendon Press, Oxford 1983, pp. 161–169

Hartnack, J., *Scandinavian Philosophy*, in Paul Edwards (ed.), *The Encyclopedia of Philosophy*, vol. 7, Macmillan, New York 1967, pp. 294–302

Hedén, E., *Recension av Axel Hägerström, Botanisten och filosofen*, in «Tiden», 1910, vol. 2, pp. 222–224

Hedenius, I., *Ueber den alogische Charakter der sog. Werturteil. Bemerkungen zu Ernst Cassirer: Axel Hägerström*, in «Theoria», 1939, vol. V, n. 4, pp. 314–329

Hedenius, I., *Om Hägerströms filosofi*, in «Tiden», 1940, vol. 32, pp. 35–44

Heidegren, C.-G., *Den nya Uppsala-filosofin och brytningen med trascendentalismen* [*The New Uppsala Philosophy and the Break with Transcendentalim*], in «Lychnos. Årsbok för idé- och lärdomshistoria», 2001, vol. LXV, pp. 71–102

Hemberg, J., *Religion och metafysik. Axel Hägerström och Anders Nygrens religionsteorier och deras inflytande i svensk religionsdebatt*, Diakonistyr., Stockholm 1966

Hierro, L.L., *El realismo jurídico escandinavo. Una teoría empirista del derecho*, Torres, Valencia 1981; Iustel, Madrid 2009²

Hjalmar, A., Lindroth, J., *Verkligheten och vetenskapen. En inblick i Axel Hägerströms filosofi*, Lindblad, Uppsala 1929

Horosz, W., *Axel Hägerström – Philosophy and Religion (review)*, in «Philosophy and Phenomenological Research», 1967/1968, vol. 28, pp. 296–97

Horvath, B., *Neuere Richtungen der Rechtsphilosophie in Den Vereinigten Staaten und Skandinavien*, in «Österreichische Zeitschrift für öffentliches Recht», 1955, vol. 6, pp. 65–93

Klingberg, W., *Den intellektuella spärren: trons svårigheter i belysning av Axel Hägerströms filosofi*, Natur & Kultur, Stockholm 1966

Kübler, B., *(Review of) Axel Hägerström, Der römische Obligationsbegriff*, in «Philologische Wochenschrift», 1929, pp. 209–17

Kunkel, W., *(Review of) Axel Hägerström, Der römische Obligationsbegriff*, in «Zeitschrift der Savigny-Stiftung für Rechtsgeschichte. Romanistische Abteilung», 1929, vol. 62, pp. 479–490

Källström, S., *Värdenihilism och vetenskap. Uppsalafilosofin i forskning och samhällsdebatt under 1920- och 1930-talen*, Acta Universitatis Gothoburgenis, Göteborg 1984

Källström, S., *Den gode nihilisten. Axel Hägerström och striderna kring Uppsalafilosofin*, Rabén & Sjögren, Stockholm 1986

Källström, S., *Filosofi och politik. Axel Hägerström och samhällsdebatten*, in G. Bexell, H. Stenius (eds.), *Värdetraditioner i nordiskt perspektiv*, Lund University Press, Lund 1997, pp. 143–158

Lang, D., *Axel Hägerström über der Wahrheit moralischen Vorstellung*, in «Perspektiven der Philosophie», Rodopi, Amsterdam 1979, Bd. 5, pp. 207–217

Lang, D., *Wertung und Erkenntnis. Untersuchungen zu Axel Hägerströms Moraltheologie*, Rodopi, Amsterdam 1981

Lévy-Bruhl, H., *Axel Hägerström, Der römische Obligationsbegriff*, in «Année sociologique», 1940–1948, pp. 601–604

Logren, E., *Huvuddragen av Hägerströms filosofi*, Lundequistska bokhandeln, Uppsala 1944

Lunau, H., *(Review of) Axel Hägerström Inquiries into the Nature of Law and Morals*, in «Cornell Law Quarterly», 1954/1955, vol. 40, pp. 364–69

Lundahl, A., *Det filosofiska arvet från Uppsala*, Nya Doxa, Nora 1997

Lundstedt, V., *Det Hägerström-Lundstedtska misstaget. Sju föreläsningar samt efterskrift*, Geber, Stockholm 1942

Lyles, M., *Uppsalaskolans kritik av den ologiska, overkliga och metafysiska rättsvetenskapen*, in E. Trolle Önnerfors, P. Reslow (eds.), *Rättslig integration och pluralism*, Rönnells, Stockholm 2001, pp. 117–127

Lyles, M., *"Scire leges non hoc est, verba earum tenere, sed vim ac postestatem"*, in P. Wahlgren (ed.), *Perspectives on Jurisprudence*, «Scandinavian Studies in Law», vol. 48, Jure, Stockholm 2005, pp. 177–202

Lyles, M., *A Call for Scientific Purity. Axel Hägerström's Critique of Legal Science*, Rönnells, Stockholm 2006

Mac Cormack, G., *Hägerström's Magical Interpretation of Roman Law*, in «The Irish Jurist», 1969, pp. 153–167

Mac Cormack, G., *Formalism, Symbolism and Magic in Early Roman Law*, in «Tijdschrift voor Rechtgeschiedenis», 1969, pp. 439–468

Mac Cormack, G., *Scandinavian Realism*, in «The Juridical Review», 1970, pp. 33–55

Mac Cormack, G., *Hägerström on Rights and Duties*, in «The Juridical Review», 1971, pp. 59–78

Mac Leod, A., *Anmärkningar till Prof. Hägerströms manuskript om den speciella relativitetsteorin*, (manuskript H 4:9)

Mac Leod, A., *Om ett värdeobjektivistiskt inslag i Hägerströms moralfilosofiska teorier*, (manuskript), Uppsala 1972

Mac Leod, A., *Tre uppsatser om Hägerström, Zenon från Elea och relativitetsteorin*, Filosofiska föreningen vid Uppsala universitet, Uppsala 1973

Marc-Wogau, K., *Studier till Axel Hägerströms filosofi*, Prisma, Falköping 1968

Marc-Wogau, K., *Axel Hägerström's Ontology*, in R.E Olson, A.M. Parel (eds.), *Contemporary Philosophy in Scandinavia*, John Hopkins Press, Baltimore 1972, pp. 479–490

Marc-Wogau, K., *Die Ontologi Hägerströms*, in R. Haller (ed.), *Jenseits von Sein und Nichtsein. Beiträge zur Meinong-Forschung*, Akademische Druck, Graz 1972, pp. 47–54

Mautner, T., *Axel Hägerström, Philosophy and Religion (review)*, in «Australasian Journal of Philosophy», 1965, pp. 232–39

Mautner, T., *A Summary in English [of Hägerström's manuscript 105:6 from 1911]*, in A. Hägerström, *Moralfilosofins grundläggning*, T. Mautner (ed.), Almqvist & Wiksell International, Stockholm 1987, pp. 201–233

Mautner, T., *Vägledning till Hägerströmstudiet*, Almqvist & Wiksell, Stockholm 1994

Mautner, T., *Hägerströms lära* i *moral. Hägerströms värdefrihetstes*, in «Insikt och handling. Hans Larsson samfundet», 2000, vol. 20, pp. 27–48

Mautner, T., *Some Notes on Willing and Promising*, in E. Carlson, R. Sliwinski (eds.), *Omnium-gatherum. Philosophical Essays dedicated to Jan Österberg*, Uppsala Philosophical Studies 50, Uppsala 2001

Mindus, P., *À l'origine du non-cognitivisme moderne: Axel Hägerström*, in eds. P. Comanducci, R. Guastini, *Analisi & diritto 2008*, Marcial Pons, Madrid 2009

Moritz, M., *Philosophy of Law in Sweden*, in R. Klibansky, *Contemporary Philosophy*, vol. IV, La Nuova Italia, Firenze 1968, pp. 135–143

Nordin, S., *Från Hägerström till Hedenius. Den moderna svenska filosofin*, Doxa, Lund 1984, pp. 25–51

Nordin, S., *Axel Hägerström, Hans Larsson och värdeteorin*, in «Insikt och handling. Hans Larsson Samfundet», 2000, vol. 20, pp. 63–72

Nygren, G., *Religion och sanning: studier i Axel Hägerströms religionsfilosofi med särskild hänsyn till hans kritik av dogmatiken*, Acta Academiae Aboensis Nr 30:2, Åbo 1968

Olivecrona, K., *Axel Hägerström in memoriam*, in «Svensk Juristtidning», 1939, vol. 25, pp. 513–515

Olivecrona, K., *Axel Hägerström*, in «Zeitschrift der Savigny-Stiftung für Rechtsgeschichte. Romanistische Abteilung», 1940, vol. 74, pp. 347–349

Olivecrona, K., *The Legal Theories of Axel Hägerström and Vilhelm Lundstedt*, in «Scandinavian studies in law», vol. 3, Almqvist & Wiksell, Stockholm 1959, pp. 128–149

Olivecrona, K., *Inledning*, in A. Hägerström, *Rätten och viljan. Två uppsatser av Axel Hägerström*, Gleerup, Lund 1961, pp. 7–56

Olivecrona, K., *Grundtankar hos Hägerström och Lundstedt. Tre uppsatser*, Studentlitt., Lund 1962

Passmore, J., *Hägerström's Philosophy of Law*, in «Philosophy», 1961, vol. 36, n. 137 (April–July), pp. 143–160

Passmore, J., *Axel Hagerstrom and his Disciples*, in G. Sawer (ed.), *Studies in the Sociology of Law*, Australian National University, Canberra 1961, pp. 111–136

Pattaro, E., *Il realismo giuridico come alternativa al positivismo giuridico*, in «Rivista Internazionale di Filosofia del Diritto», 1971, vol. 1, pp. 61–126, now in K. Olivecrona, *La struttura dell'ordinamento giuridico*, Etas, Milano 1972

Pattaro, E., *Il realismo giuridico scandinavo*, vol. I, *Axel Hägerström*, Cooperativa libraria universitaria editrice, Bologna 1974

Pattaro, E., *Non si fanno cose con le parole. Il negozio giuridico nella prospettiva di Axel Hägerström*, in «Sociologia del diritto», 1981, vol. 3, pp. 25–42

Pattaro, E., *A Treatise of Legal Philosophy and General Jurisprudence*, vol. 1, *The Law and the Right*, Springer, Dordrecht 2005 (and the forthcoming volume 15)

Peterson, C., *Die Uppsala Schule und die Politisierung der Rechtswissenschaft*, in K. Modéer, H. Mohnhaupt (eds.), *Europäische Rechtsgeschichte und europäische Integration*, Rönnells, Stockholm 2002, pp. 141–166

Peterson, C., *Uppsalaskolan och politiseringen av rättsvetenskapen*, in «Juridisk Tidskrift», 2003–2004, n. 3, pp. 571–585

Peterson, C., *Låt oss fixera begreppen! Ett genmäle*, in «Juridisk Tidskrift», 2004–2005, vol. 16, n. 3–4, pp. 977–980

Petersson, B., *Axel Hägerströms värdeteori*, Filosofiska föreningen vid Uppsala universitet, Uppsala 1973

Petersson, B., *The Substitution Argument*, in *ThD 60. Philosophical Essays dedicated to Thorild Dahlqvist on his Sixtieth Birthday*, Philosophical Society and the Department of philosophy/University Uppsala Press, Uppsala 1980, pp. 118–128

Petersson, B., *Tolkningen av Hägerströms huvudargument*, in «Filosofisk Tidskrift», 1990, anno 11, n. 3, pp. 16–24

Phillips, D.Z., *Axel Hägerström, Philosophy and Religion (review)*, in «Philosophy», 1965, vol. 40, pp. 257–58

Raphael, D.D., *Law and Morals*, in «The Philosophical Quarterly», 1954, vol. 4, pp. 340–350

Rawls, J., *Review of Axel Hägerström Inquiries into the Nature of Law and Morals*, in «Mind», 1955, vol. 64, pp. 421–422

Regnéll, H., *Axel Hägerström, Hans Larsson och Ernst Cassirer*, in «Insikt och handling. Hans Larsson Samfundet», 2000, vol. 20, pp. 73–96

Rowe, W.L., *(Review of) Philosophy and Religion – Axel Hägerström*, in «The Philosophical Review», 1968, vol. 77, pp. 248–250

Rudberg, G., *Axel Anders Theodor Hägerström: Biografi*, in «Kungliga Svenska vetenskapsakademiens årsbok», Almqvist-Wiksell/Geber Stockholm 1940, pp. 303–310

Ruin, H., *Hägerström, Nietzsche och den svenska nihilismen*, in «Tidskrift för politisk filosofi», 2000, vol. 1, pp. 5–30

Sandin, R., *Axel Hägerström's Philosophy of Religion, with Special Reference to his Philosophy of Knowledge and his Concept of Reality*, Ann Arbor University Microfilm, Michigan 1959

Sandin, R., *The Founding of the Uppsala School*, in «Journal of the History of Ideas», 1962, vol. 23, pp. 496–512

Sandin, R., *The Concept of Reality and the Elimination of Metaphysics*, in «The Monist», 1966, vol. 50, n. 1 (January), pp. 87–97

Sandin, R., *Axel Hägerström, Philosophy and Religion (review)*, in «International Philosophical Quarterly», 1966, pp. 323–25

Sandström, M., *Axel Hägerström och realismen*, in «Juridisk tidskrift», 2001–2002, vol. 4, pp. 847–857
Sandström, M., *Axel Hägerström und der Realismus. Ein Beitrag zur Geschichte der Irrtümer*, in K. Modéer, H. Mohnhaupt (eds.), *Europäische Rechtsgeschichte und europäische Integration*, Rönnells, Stockholm 2002, pp. 169–193
Sandström, M., *Law – Fact, Fiction or In Between? Axel Hägerström's Quest for Legal Realism*, in «Scandinavian Studies in Law. Perspectives on Jurisprudence. Essays in Honour of Jes Bjarup», vol. 48, Jure, Stockholm 2005, pp. 329–340
Sato, S., *A Biographical Sketch of A. Hägerström*, in «The Aoyama Law Review», 1959, vol. 32, n. 3–4, pp. 329–366
Schmidt, F., *The Uppsala School of Legal Thinking*, «Scandinavian Studies in Law», vol. 22, Almqvist & Wiksell International, Stockholm 1978
Sigurdson, O., *Den lyckliga filosofin: etik och politik hos Hägerström, Tingsten, makarna Myrdal och Hedenius*, Östlings bokförl. Symposion, Eslöv 2000
Silverbark, T., *Fysikens filosofi. Diskussioner om Einstein, relativitetsteorin och kvantfysiken i Sverige*, Östlings bokförl. Symposion, Stockholm/Eslöv 1999, pp. 165–187
Simmonds, N.E., *The Legal Philosophy of Axel Hägerström*, in «The Juridical Review», 1976, pp. 210–228
Sundberg, J., *The Swedish Philosopher Axel Haegerstroem and his Relationship to Finland's Struggle to Preserve her Legal Order 1899–1917*, Rothman, Littleton, CO 1983
Sundberg, J., *Uppsalaskolan och den nationella inkapslingen*, in « Tidskrift utgiven av Juridiska föreningen i Finland», 1999, pp. 170–180
Sundberg, J., *A Chair in Jurisprudence*, in «Scandinavian Studies in Law. Perspectives on Jurisprudence. Essays in Honour of Jes Bjarup», vol. 48, Jure, Stockholm 2005, pp. 432–464
Strang, J., *Axel Hägerström och Gunnar Myrdal. Om den svenska värdenihilistiska traditionen*, in «Historisk Tidskrift för Finland», 2003, vol. 1, pp. 43–61
Strang, J., *Two Generations of Scandinavian Legal Realists*, in «Retfaerd», 2009: 1
Strömberg, H., *Är Uppsalafilosofin död?*, in «Tidsskrift for Rettsvitenskap», 1986, vol. 99, pp. 209–214
Strömholm, S., *Hauptströmungen der schwedischen Rechtsphilosophie und Rechtstheorie in der Nachkriegszeit*, in «Rechtstheorie: Zeitschrift für Logik, Methodenlehre, Kybernetik und Soziologie des Rechts», III, 1972, pp. 35–61
Strömholm, S., Vogel, H.-H., *Le « réalisme scandinave » dans la philosophie du droit*, LGDJ, Paris 1975
Strömholm, S. (ed.), *Uppsalaskolan och efteråt*, Almqvist & Wiksell, Stockholm 1978
Strömholm, S., *La teoria del diritto in Svezia*, in E Pattaro (ed.), *Legal Philosophical Library. Sweden*, CLUEB, Bologna 1980, pp. 39–49
Tammelo, I., *Review of Axel Hägerström Inquiries into the Nature of Law and Morals*, in «The Sidney Law Review», 1957, pp. 387–389
Tegen, E., *Nya riktlinjer inom rättsfilosofi och straffrätt* (1921), now in *I filosofiska frågor*, Almqvist & Wiksell, Uppsala-Stockholm 1927, pp. 109–145
Tegen, E., *Axel Hägerström*, in «Theoria», 1939, vol. V, no. 3, pp. 229–232
Tegen, E., *The Basic Problem in the Theory of Value*, in «Theoria», 1944, vol. X, pp. 28–52
Trentman, J., *The Uppsala School and the New Logic*, in «Journal of the History of Ideas», 1967, vol. 28, pp. 445–450
Vannérus, A., *Hägerströmstudier*, Bonniers, Stockholm 1930
Waller, M., Axel Hägerström. *Människan som få kände*, Natur & Kultur, Stockholm 1961
Wedberg, A., *Hägerström, Axel Anders Theodor*, in *Svenska män och kvinnor*, vol. III, Bonniers, Stockholm 1946, pp. 586–588
Wedberg, A., *Metaphysica est delenda. Axel Hägerström och Uppsalaskolan*, in *Filosofins historia*, vol. III, Thales, Stockholm 1966, pp. 366–396
Wedberg, A., *Axel Hägerström, ad vocem*, in *Encyclopedia of Philosophy*, III, Macmillian, New York 1967, pp. 402–404

Wedberg, A., *Axel Hägerström. Några minnesbilder och intryck*, in L. Bergström (ed.) *Ditt och datt. Festskrift till Harald Ofstad*, SthlmUnivers./OBE, Stockholm 1970, nr. 23, pp. 1–12; reprint in Wedberg, A., *Axel Hägerström. Några minnesbilder och intryck*, in «Svensk litteraturtidskrift», 1971, vol. 34, 1, pp. 27–31

Wedberg, A., *Hägerström, Axel Anders Theodor*, in *Svenskt biografiskt lexikon*, vol. XIX, SBL, Stockholm 1971–1973, pp. 607–611

Villey, M., *Axel Hägerström, Inquiries into the Nature of Law and Morals (Review)*, in «Année sociologique», 1952, pp. 445–446 and in «Revue historique de droit français et étranger», 1956, pp. 120–121

Vogel, H.H., *Der Skandinavische Rechtsrealismus*, Alfred Metzner Verlag, Frankfurt a.M. 1972

Ziegert, K.A., *Rechtssoziologie in Skandinavien – Der Skandinavische Rechtsrealismus mit anderen Mitteln (Ein Beitrag zur vergleichenden Rechtssoziologie mit Bibliographie)*, in «Informationsbrief für Rechtssoziologie», 1978, vol. 14, pp. 27–73

# Chronology of the Life and Work of Hägerström

1868, on September, 6th: Birth of Hägerström
1873: The boy starts to read
1879: He moves to Jönköping for nine years (*realskola* & *gymnasium*).
1880: Hägerström's family moves to Örberga (Vadstena)
1882: Birth of Lundstedt (1882–1955)
1886, on May 27th: Hägerström graduates in Jönköping, learns English and teaches at Sjuenda. In autumn, he moves to Uppsala.
1887: Student at Uppsala University
He passes the examination in theology and philosophy (*teologicofilen*), but announces that he will be a philosopher.
1888: First university degree; he holds a lecture on the Trinity doctrine in Plato at the philosophical association ("Filosofiska föreningen").
1889: While making a living from teaching, he joins the philosophical association. The following year he holds talks on *Stoic Ethics* and *The Doctrine of Logos in Philo Judaeus*
1892: With his newly conquered title (fil. lic.), he suffers poverty. In the summer, he meets Esther Nyander, his future wife. He reads Georg Brandes.
1893: He reads Nietzsche with enthusiasm. He is increasingly active at the philosophical association: he lectures on *Dogmatism in Philosophy*.
He publishes *Aristoteles etiska grundtankar och deras teoretiska förutsättningar*
On September, 1st: he becomes doctor in philosophy, and starts his academic career in October.
1894: Burman publishes *Schleiermachers kritik av Kants och Fichtes sedeläror*. Hägerström teaches at high school.
1895: He continues to study Nietzsche.
He publishes *Undersökning av den empiriska etikens möjlighet med särskild hänsyn till dess moderna huvudformer* and *Om den moraliska känslan och den moraliska driften såsom förnuftiga i den moderna rationalismens huvudformer*.
On November, 1st: He lectures on *The General Bad Use of Ethical Ideas and Formal Concepts* at the philosophical association.
1896: Hägerström is advised to retire from the competition for the Chair in practical philosophy. Burman obtains the chair and Hägerström is declared incompetent. He replies in *Om den af de sakkunnige vid tillsättandet af professuren i praktisk filosofi Uppsala 1896 företagna granskningen af mina avhandlingar*, but never publishes it.
June: Engagement with Esther Nyander.
1897: Birth of Karl Olivecrona (1897–1980)
Hägerström wins the award "Filénska legatet", thanks to Burman.
He starts to write on Kant's ethics and plans to write on Nietzsche. He sets up his first philosophical outline and writes *Om "Den empiriska etiken" och "Den moraliska känslan." Svar på kritik*, regarding the declaration of incompetence.

On October, 26th: He holds a talk at the philosophical association entitled *A Philosophical Method for the Study of the History of Philosophy*.

1898: He reads Kierkegaard and Ibsen and writes *Filosofins betydelse för människan*.

1899, on June 28th: He marries Esther.

1902: He publishes *Kants Ethik*

1903–1910: He teaches practical philosophy in Burman's place.

1904: He publishes *Stat och rätt*. He lectures on socialism before numerous students.

1906: He wins the Oscar II-award on Geijer's proposal.

1907: He reads and reviews *Gut und Böse*. In autumn, he lectures on *History of Christian Ethics* (published 1968).

1908: *Das Prinzip der Wissenschaften* is published. He continues to lecture on socialism (lectures edited 1946)
He writes *Är filosofisk kunskapslära överflödig?*, basis for the 1910-popular essay *Botanisten och filosofen*.

1909: He lectures on socialism and *Philosophy as Science*.

1910: *Botanisten och filosofen* is published. In order to obtain the chair in practical philosophy, he writes *Kritiska punkter in värdepsykologien* and *Till analysen av det empiriska självmedvetandet*
He publicly attacks the physicist Oséen on the topic "free will"

1911: Once Professor, he holds his notorious opening lecture: *On the Truth of Moral Propositions*.

1912: He holds a lecture on *Time and Space*.

1914: He visits the Dalecardia region and encounters Lundstedt.

1916: *Är gällande rätt uttryck av vilja?* is published.
Adolf Phalén becomes Professor in theoretical philosophy.

1917: He is honored with the *laurea honoris causa* in October. He lectures on *The Genesis of Judicial Ideas*.

1918: In spring, he holds the course *Doctrines on Value and Psychology of Value*.

1920: He reads and reviews *Marx and Hegel*, while teaching on *Religion and Truth*.

1921: He holds the course *The State and Its Form*, while offering hospitality to a Viennese student.

1923: Einstein visits Sweden: It is the beginning of the debate on physics.

1924: In spring, he teaches on *Religion and Morals*. The future Secretary General of the UN, Dag Hammarskjöld is among the students of the autumn course on *The Relation between the State and the Law*.

1925: He works on *Metaphysics in the Special Sciences*.

1927: He publishes the first volume of *Der römische Obligationsbegriff*.

1928: He continues his work on emotions and religion. A *liber amicorum* is published in his honour.

1929: Burman dies. Hägerström publishes *Das magistratische Ius*, on public Roman law. The debates are raging. He starts having more students from law school than philosophy.

1930: In spring, he lectures on *Truly Autonomous Morals* and writes *On Emotive Thinking*, which was later lost (there is however a German translation in *Kraftvorstellungen*).

1932: Phalén dies of cancer only 47 years old. Hägerström lectures on *Comparison between Stoic and Kantian Philosophy of Religion*. He travels to Motala in August.

1933: He retires in June. Later that summer, his mother dies.
He commemorates the 50th anniversary of Marx's death in *Marx och filosofin*. He lectures on *Natural Law in Criminal Law* and *Hellenistic Philosophy*. He writes *Excerpter ur grekiska författare*, *Forngrekisk rätt och religion* and *Hellenistisk filosofi*. In September, he is introduced to Hans Kelsen in Uppsala.

1934: The debate on Bohman's thesis is frenzy: Hägerström writes *Ein Stein, ihr Herren, ist ein schlechtes Argument*. He writes on Einstein's theory of relativity and develops the argument of substitution in *Om pliktmedvetandet*.

1938: Hägglund dies. Hägerström publishes his last essay: *Om handslagets ursprungliga innebörd*.

1939, on July 7th: Hägerström dies after three weeks of agony.

# References


Aall, A., *Filosofien i Norden*, Videnskapsselskapetsskrifter, Kristiania 1919

Abegg, J.F., *Die verschiedenen Strafrechtstheorien in ihrem Verhältnisse zu einander und zu dem positiven Rechte und dessen Geschichte* (1835), reprint Neudruck, Frankfurt 1969

Aczel, A.D., *Entanglement: The Greatest Mystery in Physics*, Four Walls Eight Windows, New York 2001

Adachi, H., *Die Radbruchsche Formel. Eine Untersuchung der Rechtsphilosophie*, Nomos, Baden-Baden 2006

Adler, M., *Kausalität und Teleologie in Streite um der Wissenschaft*, Brand, Wien 1904

Agersnap, T., *Theodor Geiger. Pioneer of Sociology in Denmark*, in «Acta Sociologica», 2000, vol. 43, n. 4, pp. 325–330

Ahlberg, A., *Maktfilosofi och värdenihilism*, in (ed.), *Varför svenska folket reagerar*, Natur & Kultur, Stockholm 1941, pp. 7–30

Alexander, G.S., *Comparing the Two Legal Realisms – American and Scandinavian*, in «The American Journal of Comparative Law», 2002, winter, vol. 50, n. 1, pp. 131–174

Allen, C.K., *Law in the Making*, Clarendon Press, Oxford 1930[2]

Andrew, G., *Conscience and Its Critics: Protestant Conscience, Enlightenment Reason and Modern Subjectivity*, Toronto University Press, Toronto 2001

Arendt, H., *On Revolution*, Viking Press, New York 1963

Arnholm, C.J., *Some Basic Problems in Jurisprudence*, in «Scandinavian Studies in Law», Almqvist & Wiksell, Stockholm 1957, pp. 9–50

Arnholm, C.J., *Olivecrona on Legal Rights. Reflections on the Concept of Rights*, in «Scandinavian Studies in Law», Almqvist & Wiksell, Stockholm 1962, pp. 9–31

Austin, J., *Lectures on Jurisprudence, or The Philosophy of Positive Law*, R. Campbell (ed.), vol. 2, 4th ed. rev., John Murray, London 1879, now reprint Thoemmes Press, Bristol 2002

Ayer, A.J., *Language, Truth and Logic* (1936), Dover Publication, New York 1952

Ayer, A.J., *Logical Positivism*, Free Press, New York 1959

Bárány, A., *Introduction*, in A. Einstein, *Fundamental Ideas and Problems of the Theory of Relativity. Lectured delivered to the Nordic Assembly of Naturalists at Göteborg on July 11, 1923*, Nobel Foundation, Stockholm 2006, pp. 3–4

Battail, J.-F., *Le mouvement des idées en Suède à l'âge du bergsonisme*, Lettres Modernes, Paris 1979

Bengtsson, J., *Den fenomenologiska rörelsen i Sverige: mottagande och inflytande 1900–1968*, Daidalos, Göteborg 1991

Berendt, M., *Tilfaeldet Sverige*, Chr. Erichsen, Copenhagen 1983

Berggren, N., *Rättspositivism och äganderätt*, in N. Berggren, N. Karlson (eds.), *Äganderättens konsekvenser och grunder*, Ratio, Stockholm 2005, pp. 180–215

Bergson, H., *Durée et simultanéité. A propos de la théorie d'Einstein*, Alcan, Paris 1922; Eng. trans. *Duration and Simultaneity*, Robin Durie (ed.), Clinamen Press, Manchester 1999

Bergson, H., *Les deux sources de la morale et de la religion* (1932), in *Œuvres*, Puf, Paris 1963; Eng. trans. by R. Ashley Audra, C. Brereton, *The Two Sources of Morality and Religion*, University of Notre Dame Press, Notre Dame, IN 1977

Bergström, L., *Värdenihilism och argumentation i värdefrågor*, in «Filosofisk tidskrift», 1980, vol. I, n. 1, pp. 35–56

Berkeley, G., *A Treatise Concerning the Principles of Human Knowledge* (1710), ed. J. Dancy, Oxford University Press, Oxford 1998

Bernstein, J.A., *Adam Ferguson and the Idea of Progress*, in «Studies in Burke and His Time», 1978, vol. XIX, n. 2, pp. 99–118

Beyers, H., *Nietzsche og Norden*, vols. I–II, Universitetsförlaget, Bergen 1957–1959

Binding, K., *Grundriss des deutschen Strafrechts* (1879), Engelmann, Leipzig 1902

Bix, B., *Ross and Olivecrona on Rights*, in «Minnesota Legal Studies Research Paper no 06-14» available at SSRN: http://ssrn.com/abtract=892788

Blandhol, S., *Juridisk ideologi – Alf Ross' kritik av naturretten*, Jurist- og Økonomforbundet Universitetsforlaget, Copenhagen 1999

Blandhol, S., *The Rhetorical Foundations of Nordic Jurisprudence*, in «Ideas in History. The Nordic Society for the History of Ideas», 2006, vol. 1, n. 1–2, pp. 33–56

Bloch, M., *Les rois thaumaturges* (1924), Gallimard, Paris 1997

Blomberg, O., *Disentangling the Thick Concept Argument*, in «Sats. Nordic Journal of Philosophy», 2007, vol. 8, n. 2, pp. 63–78

Bobbio, N., *Diritto e forza*, in «Rivista di diritto civile», 1966, pp. 537–48

Bobbio, N., *La politica* (1987), now in M. Bovero (ed.), *Teoria generale della politica*, Einaudi, Torino 1999, pp. 161–183

Bondeson, U.V., *Nordic Moral Climates: Value Continuities and Discontinuities in Denmark, Finland, Norway and Sweden*, Transaction Publishers, London 2003

Bonfante, P., *Istituzioni di diritto romano*, Barbera, Firenze 1896

Bonfante, P., *Storia del diritto romano*, SEL, Milano 1902

Boström, C.J., *Satser om lag och lagstiftning med tillägg och anmärkningar*, Schultz, Uppsala 1871

Boström, C.J., *Grundlinier till philosophiska statsläran*, Victor Roos, Uppsala 1882

Boström, C.J., *Grundlinier till philosophiska statslärans propaedeutik*, Adolph Johnsons förlag, Stockholm 1901

Boström, C.J., *Filosofiska sentenser*, Hilaritas, Johanneshov 1998

Boström, C.J., *Den förnuftiga viljans etik*, J. Siöcrona (ed.), Hilaritas, Johanneshov 2002

Boye, K., *Studentska på 20-talet*, in S. Thulin (ed.), *Bland professorer och studenter. Hågkomster och livsintryck XIX*, Lindblad, Uppsala 1938

Brandt, R., *Ethical Theory*, Prentice-Hall, Englewood Cliffs 1959

Brunet, P., *Le "positivisme" français dans la lumière du Nord. Le réalisme juridique scandinave et la doctrine française*, available at: http://halshs.archives-ouvertes.fr/index.php?halsid=qgos79p7r7vb6jmk3bntb702j1&view_this_doc=halshs-00009770&version=1

Bultmann, R., *Die liberale Theologie und die jüngste theologische Bewegung*, Mohr, Tübingen 1924

Böckenförde, E., *Die deutsche verfassungsgeschichtliche Forschung im 19. Jahrhundert. Zeitbundene Fragestellungen und Leitbilden*, Dunker & Humblot, Berlin 1961

Carcaterra, G., *Il problema della fallacia naturalistica. La derivazione del dover essere dall'essere*, Giuffrè, Milano 1969

Carnap, R., *Logische Syntax der Sprache*, Springer, Wien 1934

Carty, A., *Scandinavian Realism and Phenomenological Approaches to Statehood and General Custom in International Law*, «European Journal of International Law», 2003, vol. 14, n. 4, pp. 817–841

Cassirer, E., *Nachgelassene Manuskripte und Texte*, K. Ch. Köhnke, J.M. Krois, O. Schwemmer (eds.), 20 vols, Meiner, Hamburg 1995 ff.

Cassirer, E., *Gesammelte Werke. Aufsätze und kleine Schriften (1936–1940)*, Bd. 22, Meiner, Hamburg 2006

Celano, B., *I diritti nella* jurisprudence *anglosassone contemporanea.* in *Da Hart a Raz*, «Analisi e diritto 2001», P. Comanducci, R. Guastini (eds.), Giappichelli, Torino 2001, pp. 1–58

Clark, E.C., *History of Roman Private Law*, Cambridge University Press, Cambridge 1914

Colla, P., *La Värdenihilism comme « idéologie suédoise »? Une lecture de la pédagogie des valeurs dans la réforme suédoise*, in Ph. Bouquet, P. Voilley, *Droit et littérature dans le contexte suédois*, Flies France, Paris 2000, pp. 53–81

Comanducci, P., *Assaggi di metaetica*, Giappichelli, Torino 1992

Comanducci, P., *Assaggi di metaetica due*, Giappichelli, Torino 1998

Cordero, F., *Riti e sapienza del diritto*, Laterza, Bari 1981

Coudenhove-Kalergi, R., *Paneuropa*, Paneuropa Verlag, Wien 1923

Croce, B., *Ciò che è vivo e ciò che è morto della filosofia di Hegel* (1906); Eng. trans. *What is Alive and What is Dead in the Philosophy of Hegel*, Macmillan, London 1915

Deligiorgi, K., *Hegel. New Directions*, Acumen, Chesham 2006

Derrida, J., *Force de loi. Le fondement mystique de l'autorité*, Galilée, Paris 1994

Durkheim, E., *De la division du travail social* (1893), Puf, Paris 1968

Durkheim, E., *Jugements de valeur et jugements de réalité*, in *Atti del congresso internazionale di filosofia* (Bologna), Formiggini, Genova 1911, vol. I, pp. 99–114

Durkheim, E., *Les formes élémentaires de la vie religieuse. Le système totémique en Australie*, Puf, Paris 1912

Eckhoff, T., *Rettvesen og rettsvitenskap i USA*, Gleerup, Lund 1953

Ehrenfels, Ch. von, *System der Werttheorie*, Reisland, Leipzig 1897–1898

Einstein, A., *Fundamental Ideas and Problems of the Theory of Relativity. Lectured delivered to the Nordic Assembly of Naturalists at Göteborg on July 11, 1923*, Nobel Foundation, Stockholm 2006

Ekelöf, P.O., *The Expression "Valid Rule": A Study in Legal Terminology*, «Scandinavian Studies in Law», vol. 15, Almqvist & Wiksell, Stockholm 1971, pp. 57–74

Elias, N., *Über den Prozeß der Zivilisation. Soziogenetische und psychogenetische Untersuchungen*, Verlag Haus zum Falken, Basel 1939; Eng. trans. *The Civilizing Process. Sociogenetic and Psychogenetic Investigations*, Blackwell, Oxford 2000

Eliaeson, S., *Geiger, the Uppsala-school of Value Nihilism – and Weber*, in U. Fazis, C.N. Jachen (eds.), *Gesellschaftstheorie und Normentheorie. Theodor Geiger Symposium*, Social Strategies, Basel 1993, pp. 225–34

Elvander, N., *Rudolf Kjellén och nationalsocialismen*, in «Statsvetenskaplig Tidskrift», 1956, vol. 59, n. 1, pp. 1–41

Elzinga, A., *Einstein's Nobel Prize – A Glimpse Behind Closed Doors*, Science History Publication, Sagamore beach (USA) 2006

Faralli, C., *The Reception of Scandinavian Legal Realism*, paper presented at the IVR-meeting in Lund 2003, abstract in C. Wong (ed.) *Law and Politics – In Search of Balance*, Media-Tryck, Lund 2003, pp. 61–62

Faralli, C., *The Legacy of American Legal Realism*, in P. Wahlgren (ed.), «Scandinavian Studies in Law. Perspectives on Jurisprudence» n. 48, Jure, Stockholm 2005, pp. 75–82

Feinberg, J., *The Nature and Value of Rights*, in «Journal of Value Inquiry», 1970, vol. 4, pp. 263–267

Feinberg, J., *Rights, Justice and the Bounds of Liberty*, Princeton University Press, Princeton, NJ 1980

Feuerbach, P.J.A., *Anti-Hobbes oder über die Grenzen der höchsten Gewalt und das Zwangsrecht der Bürger gegen den Oberherrn*, Erfurt, Henning 1798

Feuerbach, P.J.A., *Revision der Grundsätze und Grundbegriffe des positiven peinlichen Rechts*, I, (1799), Scientia Verlag, Aalen 1966

Ferrari, M., *Ernst Cassirer – Stationen einer philosophischen Biographie: Von der Marburger Schule zur Kulturphilosophie*, Cassirer-Forschung, vol. 11, Meiner, Hamburg 2003

Fester, R., *Die Säkularisation der Historie*, in «Historische Vierteljahrsschrift», 1908, vol. 11, pp. 441–459
Fleischmann, E., *La science universelle ou la logique de Hegel*, Plon, Paris 1968
Fogelqvist, T., *Filosofie kandidaten*, in S. Thulin (ed.), *Bland professorer och studenter. Hågkomster och livsintryck*, Lindblad, Uppsala 1938
Frazer, J., *The Golden Bough. A Study in Comparative Religion* (1890), Oxford University Press, New York 1998 (abridged version)
Friedmann, W., *Legal Theory*, Columbia University Press, New York 1967
Frängsmyr, T., *Svensk idéhistoria: bildning och vetenskap under tusen år*, vol. 2, Natur & Kultur, Stockholm 2000
Føllesdal, A., *Er normativ politisk teori død i Norden? Diagnose og prognose*, in «Distinktion», 7, 2003, pp. 129–138
Garner, R., Rosen, B., *A Systematic Introduction to Normative Ethics and Meta-Ethics*, Macmillan, New York 1967
Gaubert, J., *Présentation et avertissement des traducteurs*, in E. Cassirer, *Éloge de la métaphysique. Axel Hägerström. Une étude de la philosophie suédoise contemporaine*, Cerf, Paris 1996, pp. 7–34
Gaubert, J., *Le réalisme pratique en débat: la réception de la pensée d'Axel Hägerström par Ernst Cassirer*, in Ph. Bouquet, P. Voilley, *Droit et littérature dans le contexte suédois*, Flies France, Paris 2000, pp. 31–48
Geiger, Th., *Debat med Uppsala om moral och ret*, Carl Bloms tryckeri, Lund 1946
Geiger, Th., *Ideologie und Wahrheit. Eine soziologische Kritik des Denkens*, Humblot, Stuttgart 1953
Gilmore, G., *Legal Realism: Its Cause and Cure*, in «Yale Law Journal», 1961, vol. LXX, n. 7, pp. 1037–1048
Gomard, B., *Civil Law, Common Law and Scandinavian Law*, in «Scandinavian Studies in Law», vol. 5, Almqvist & Wiksell, Stockholm 1961, pp. 27–38
Grue-Sørensen, K., *Vor tids moral skepticisme. Om muligheden af en objektiv etik* (1937); Swed. trans. *Vår tids moralnihilism: Om möjligheten av en objektiv moral*, Natur & Kultur, Stockholm 1937
Gurvitch, G., *Le temps présent et l'idée du droit social*, Vrin, Paris 1932
Gurvitch, G., *La magie et le droit* (1938), Dalloz, Paris 2004
Hahr, A., *I Vasaslottets skugga*, Nyblom, Uppsala 1943
Hansen, M.H., *The Democracy in the Age of Demosthenes. Structures, Principles and Ideology*, Blackwell, London 1991
Hansson, J., *Idealistisk vändning i svensk filosofi. Hans Larsson och Badenskolan*, in «Insikt och handling. Hans Larsson Samfundet», 2000, vol. 20, pp. 9–26
Hansson, J., *Ernst Cassirer. The Swedish Years*, Peter Lang, Berlin 2006
Hare, R.M., *Sorting Out Ethics*, Clarendon, Oxford 1997
Harman, G., *Change in View*, MIT Press, Cambridge, MA 1988
Harris, J.W., *Olivecrona on Law and Language – The Search for Legal Culture*, in «Tidskrift for Rettsvitenskap», 1981, vol. 94, pp. 625–646
Hart, H.L.A., *Are There Any Natural Rights?*, in «Philosophical Review», 1955, vol. 64, pp. 177–191, reprinted in *Theories of Rights*, ed. J. Waldron, Oxford University Press, Oxford 1984, pp. 77–90
Hart, H.L.A., *Legal Rights* (1973), now in *Essays on Bentham. Studies in Jurisprudence and Political Theory*, Clarendon Press, Oxford 1982, pp. 171–201
Hebeisen, M.W., *Pragmatismus, Pluralismus, Realismus: Essayistische Abhandlungen zu den wissenschaftsphilosophischen Grundlagen für eine integrale Jurisprudenz sowie ergänzende rechtsphilosophische Anhänge*, Bd. 1, Schweizerischer Wissenschafts- und Universitätsverlag (BoD), Biel/Bienne 2005
Hedenius, I., *Sensationalism and Theology in Berkeley's Philosophy*, Uppsala University (Diss.), Uppsala 1936

Hedenius, I., *Begriffsanalyse und kritischer Idealismus* (I), in «Theoria», 1939, vol. V, n. 3, pp. 281–313
Hedenius, I., *Uppsalafilosofin och diktaturstaternas framfart*, i «Tiden», 1940, vol. 3, pp. 174–178
Hedenius, I., *Om rätt och moral*, Wahlström & Widstrand, Stockholm 1941, 1963²
Hedenius, I., *Axiological Nihilism: Some Theses*, in «Inquiry», 1961, vol. 4, pp. 274–280
Hedenius, I., *I Egen Sak – och andras*, Rabén och Sjögren, Stockholm 1976
Hedenius, I., *Om stora män och små*, Rabén och Sjögren, Stockholm 1980
Hedvall, K., *Öppna bref till professorerna Hans Larsson och Harald Höffding*, Almqvist & Wiksell, Uppsala 1905
Hegel, G.W.F., *Wissenschaft der Logik* (1812–1816), Theorie Werkausgabe, Bd 5, Suhrkamp Verlag, Frankfurt a.M. 1969; Eng. trans. by A.V. Miller, *Science of Logic*, Allen & Unwin, London 1969
Hegel, G.W.F., *Grundlinien der Philosophie des Rechts* (1820), Eng. trans. by H.B. Nisbet *Elements of the Philosophy of Right*, ed. A.W. Wood, Cambridge University Press, Cambridge 1991
Heidegren, C.-G., *Idealistisk systemfilosofi kontra den positiva andan i finsk och svensk universitetsfilosofi*, in S. Nygård, J. Strang, *Mellan idealism och analytisk filosofi: den moderna filosofin i Finland och Sverige 1880–1950*, Atlantis, Stockholm 2006, pp. 43–45
Hirschman, A.O., *The Passions and the Interests. Political Arguments for Capitalism before Its Triumph*, Princeton University Press, Princeton, NJ 1977
Hohfeld, W., *Fundamental Legal Conceptions as Applied in Judicial Reasoning and Other Legal Essays*, W. Cook (ed.), Yale University Press, New Haven 1923
Holland, T.E., *The Elements of Jurisprudence* (1900), reprint from 1924 ed. Scientia Verlag, Aalen 1979
Holt, E.B. (ed.), *The New Realism: Cooperative Studies in Philosophy*, Macmillan, New York 1912
Horwitz, M.J., *The Transformation of American Law. 1870–1960. The Crisis of Legal Orthodoxy*, Oxford University Press, Oxford 1992
Hudson, W.D. (ed.), *The Is-Ought Question. A Collection of Papers on the Central Problem in Moral Philosophy*, Macmillan, London 1969
Hume, D., *A Treatise on the Human Nature* (1739–1740), ed. by D.F. Norton, M.J. Norton, Oxford University Press, Oxford 2000
Hume, D., *Enquiry Concerning the Principles of Morals* (1751), Oxford University Press, Oxford 1998
Husserl, E., *Logische Untersuchungen* (1900); Eng. trans. by J.N. Findlay, *Logical Investigations*, Routledge, London/New York 2001
Høffding, H., *Filosofiske Problemer* (1902); Eng. trans. *The Problems of Philosophy*, Macmillan, New York 1905
Höög, V., *The Philosophers on the Market Square. Philosophical Modernism from Vienna to Uppsala*, in T. Rønnow-Rasmussen, B. Petersson, J. Josefsson, D. Egonsson (eds.), *Hommage à Wlodek. Philosophical Papers Dedicated to Wlodek Rabinowicz* at www.fil.lu.se/hommageawlodek, pp. 1–15
Inwood, M., *A Hegel Dictionnary*, Blackwell, Oxford 1992
Jakob, L.H., *Philosophische Rechtslehre oder Naturrecht* (1795), reprint, Culture et Civilisation, Bruxelles 1981
Jalava, M., *Lidelse och bragd*, in S. Nygård, J. Strang, *Mellan idealism och analytisk filosofi: den moderna filosofin i Finland och Sverige 1880–1950*, Atlantis, Stockholm 2006, pp. 51–78
Jarvad, I.M., *The Scandinavian Realism. A Critique. A Defense. A Restatement*, Institut for samfundsøkonomi, Roskilde 1984
Joyce, R., *Myth of Morality*, Cambridge University Press, Cambridge 2001
Joyce, R., Kirchin, S., (eds.), *A World Without Values. Essays on John Mackie's Moral Error Theory*, Springer, Dordrecht-New York 2009
Kainz, H., *Notes to the Glossary*, in Hegel's *The Encyclopedia Logic* (ed. T. Geraets et al.), Hackett, Indianapolis 1991

Kainz, H., *Introduction*, in G.W.F. Hegel, *Phenomenology of Spirit: Selections*, Penn State Press, State College, PA 1994

Kantorowicz, E.H., *The King's Two Bodies: A Study in Mediaeval Political Theology*, Princeton University Press, Princeton, NJ 1957

Kato, M., *Techne und Philosophie bei Platon*, P. Lang, Frankfurt-New York 1986

Kaufmann, W., *Hegel: Texts and Commentary*, Doubleday, New York 1965

Kelly, J.M., *A Short History of Western Legal Theory*, Oxford University Press, Oxford 1992

Kelsen, H., *Reine Rechtslehre, Einleitung in die rechtswissenschaftliche Problematik* (1934), Swedish trans. *Den rena rättsläran. Dess metod och grundbegrepp*, in «Statsvetenskaplig tidskrift», 1933, vol. 36, pp. 193–244

Kelsen, H., *General Theory of Law and State*, Harvard University Press, Cambridge, MA 1945

Kelsen, H., *Eine "Realistische" und die Reine Rechtslehre. Bemerkungen zu Alf Ross: On Law and Justice*, in «Österreichische Zeitschrift für öffentliches Recht», 1959, X, pp. 1–25

Kilander, S., *Den nya staten och den gamla. En studie i ideologisk förändring*, Studia historica upsaliensia 164, Acta universitatis upsaliensis, Uppsala 1991

Kjellén, R., *Staten som lifsform*, Hugo Gerbers förlag, Stockholm 1916

Kojève, A., *Esquisse d'une phénoménologie du droit* (1943), Gallimard, Paris 1981; Eng. trans. *Outline of a Phenomenology of Right*, Rowman & Littlefield, Lanham 2000

Korsgaard, Ch., *The Sources of Normativity*, Cambridge University Press, Cambridge, MA 1996

Koselleck, R., *Kritik und Krise: eine Studie zur Pathogenese der bürgerlichen Welt*, Karl Alber Freiburg, München 1959/Suhrkamp, Frankfurt 1992

Koselleck, R., *Einleitung*, in *Geschichtliche Grundbegriffe*, Klett-Cotta, Stuttgart 1972, vol. I, pp. XIII–XXVIII

Kramer, M.H., Simmonds, N.E., Steiner, H., *A Debate over Rights*, Clarendon Press, Oxford 1998

Kusch, M., *Psychologism. A Case Study in the Sociology of Philosophical Knowledge*, Routledge, London-NY 1995

Lagerroth, F., *Boström och Kelsen. En jämförelse*, in «Statsvetenskaplig tidsskrift», 1925, anno 28, pp. 1–37

Laughlin, R., *A Different Universe. Reinventing Physics from the Bottom Down*, Basic Books, New York 2003

Leiter, B., *Legal Realism and Legal Positivism Reconsidered*, in «Ethics», 2001, vol. 111, n. 2 (Jan.), pp. 278–301

Leiter, B., *Naturalism in Legal Philosophy*, in *Stanford Encyclopedia of Philosophy* (Fall 2002 Edition), available at: http://plato.stanford.edu/entries/lawphil-naturalism/

Leiter, B., *Naturalizing Jurisprudence: Essays on American Legal Realism and Naturalism in Legal Philosophy*, Oxford University Press, Oxford 2007

Lévy-Bruhl, L., *La mentalité primitive*, Alcan, Paris 1922

Liebmann, O., *Kant und die Epigonen. Eine kritische Abhandlung*, Schober, Stuttgart 1865

Liljeqvist, E., *Efraim Liljeqvist. Die Philosophie der Gegenwart in Selbstdarstellungen*, Bd. VI, Meiner, Leipzig 1927

Liljeqvist, E. *et al.*, *Festskrift tillägnad Axel Hägerström den 6 september 1928 av filosofiska och juridiska föreningarna i Uppsala*, Almqvist & Wiksell, Uppsala 1928

Lloyd, D., *Introduction to Jurisprudence*, Stevens & Sons, London 1965

Lundstedt, V., *Föreläsningar över valda delar av obligationsrätten*, Norblad, Uppsala 1920–1953

Lundstedt, V., *Superstition and Rationality in Action for Peace? Arguments against Founding a World Peace on the Common Sense of Justice. A Criticism of Jurisprudence*, Longmans, London 1925

Lundstedt, V., *Die Unwissenschaftlichkeit der Rechtswissenschaft*, Rothschild, Berlin 1932–1936

Lundstedt, V., *Europas demokratier – förenen eder!*, Natur & Kultur, Stockholm 1949

Lundstedt, V., *Law and Justice* [1950, originally presented at the 3rd international conference of comparative law], Almqvist & Wiksell, ed. Å. Malmström, Stockholm/Uppsala 1952

Lundstedt, V., *Legal Thinking Revised: My Views on Law*, Almqvist & Wiksell, Stockholm 1956

Lyons, D., *Rights, Claimants and Beneficiaries* (1969), now in *Rights, Welfare and Mill's Moral Theory*, Oxford University Press, Oxford 1994

Lönnqvist, C., *Hägerström och Hitler*, in «Göteborgs Handels- och sjöfartstidning», 03/07/1940

Löwith, K., *Weltgeschichte und Heilsgeschehen* (1952), now in *Sämtliche Schriften*, Metzler Verlag, 1983, vol. II; Eng. trans. *Meaning in History: The Theological Implications of the Philosophy of History*, University of Chicago Press, Chicago 1957

MacCormick, N., *Children's Rights: A Test-Case for Theories of Rights*, in «Archiv für Rechts- und Sozialphilosophie», 1976, vol. 62, pp. 305–317

MacCormick, N., *Rights in Legislation*, in P.M.S. Hacker, J. Raz (eds.), *Law, Morality and Society*, Clarendon, Oxford 1977, pp. 189–209

MacCormick, N., *Rights, Claims and Remedies*, in «Law and Philosophy», 1982, vol. 1, pp. 337–357

MacCormick, N., *Contemporary Legal Philosophy: The Rediscovery of Practical Reason*, in «Journal of Law and Society», 1983, vol. 10, n. 1 (Summer), pp. 1–18

Mackie, J.L., *Ethics: Inventing Right and Wrong*, Viking Press, London 1977

Mac Leod, A., *Introduction à la géométrie non-euclidienne*, Hermann, Paris 1922

Maier, H., *Psychologie des emotionalen Denkens*, Mohr, Tübingen 1908

Malminen, T., *The Effect of Scandinavian Legal Realism on Finnish Legal Studies*, in V. Duss, N. Linder *et al.* (eds.), *Rechtstransfer in der Geschichte*, Martin Meidenbauer, München 2005, pp. 297–308

Marett, R.R., *Mana, ad vocem*, in J. Hastings, J. Selbie (eds.), *Encyclopedia of Religion and Ethics*, T.&T. Clark, Edinburgh 1915

Martin, M., *Legal Realism. American and Scandinavian*, Peter Lang, New York 1997

Marty, A., *Untersuchungen zur Grundlegung der allgemeinen Grammatik und Sprachphilosophie*, Niemeyer, Halle 1908

Marx, K., *Grundrisse der Kritik der politischen Ökonomie* (1859), Eng. trans. *Foundation of the Critique of Political Economy*, Penguin, London 1993

Mayr, O., *Authority, Liberty and Automatic Machinery*, John Hopkins Press, Baltimore 1986

McCoubrey, H., White, N.D., *Textbook on Jurisprudence*, Blackstone Press, London 1999[3]

McIlwain, Ch., *Constitutionalism. Ancient and Modern*, Cornell University Press, Ithaca 1940

McTaggart, J.M.E., *A Commentary on Hegel's Logic*, Cambridge University Press, Cambridge 1931

Messer, A., *Kants Ethik: Eine Einführung in ihre Hauptprobleme und Beiträge zu deren Lösung*, Veit & Comp, Leipzig 1904

Métall, R.A., *Hans Kelsen. Leben und Werk*, Franz Deuticke, Wien 1969

Michaut, F., *Réalisme*, in A.-J. Arnaud (ed.), *Dictionnaire encyclopédique de théorie et de sociologie du droit*, LGDJ, Paris 1993[2], pp. 509 ff.

Millard, E., Jouanjan, O. (ed.), *Les théories réalistes du droit*, Presses universitaire de Strasbourg, Strasbourg 2000

Millard, E. (ed.), *Special Issue of* «Droit & Société», *Une théorie empiriste du droit est-elle possible?* 2002, 50

Millard, E., *Le réalisme scandinave et la théorie des contraintes*, in M. Troper, V. Champeil-Desplats, C. Grzegorczuk (eds.), *Théories des contraintes juridiques*, LJDJ, Paris 2005, pp. 143–154

Millard, E., *Alf Ross*, in O. Cayla, J.L. Halpérin (eds.), *Dictionnaire des grandes oeuvres juridiques*, Dalloz, Paris 2008

Miller, W.I., *An Eye for an Eye*, Cambridge University Press, Cambridge 2006

Minda, G., *Postmodern Legal Movements: Law and Jurisprudence at Century's End*, New York University Press, New York 1995

Mindus, P., *Deliberare, negoziare e argomentare sulle incerte sorti della legge di Hume*, in «Teoria politica», 2008, vol. XXIII, no.1, pp. 145–155

Mommsen, T., *Römisches Strafrecht*, Duncker & Humblot, Leipzig 1894

Moore, G.E., *Principia Ethica* (1903), Cambridge University Press, Cambridge 1954

Moreso, J.J., *Teoría del derecho y neutralidad valorativa*, paper presented at XIII Congresso Italo-spagnolo di Teoria Analitica del Diritto "Teoría analítica y enfoques socio-jurídicos" (September 2007), available at http://www.iisj.net
Morin, E., *Le sfide della complessità*, in *La sfida della complessità*, G. Bocchi, M. Ceruti (eds.), Feltrinelli, Milano 1985
Moritz, M., *Inledning i värdeteori*, Studentlitteratur, Lund 1969[2]
Mortati, C., *La costituzione in senso materiale*, Giuffrè, Milano 1940
Münsterberg, H., *Philosophie der Werte. Grundzüge einer Weltanschauung*, Barth, Leipzig 1908
Myrdal, G., *Vetenskap och politik i nationalekonomin*, Rabén & Sjögren, Stockholm 1971
Nahin, P.J., *An Imaginary Tale. The Story of* $\sqrt{-1}$, Princeton University Press, Princeton, NJ 2007
Nelson, L., *Die kritische Methode und das Verhältnis der Psychologie zur Philosophie: Ein Kapitel aus der Methodenlehre*, in «Abhandlungen der Fries'schen Schule: Neue Folge», 1:1 [1904], Vanderhoeck & Ruprecht, Göttingen 1906
Nergelius, J., *Konstitutionellt rättighetsskydd: svensk rätt i ett komparativt perspektiv*, Fritzes, Stockholm 1996
Nergelius, J. (ed.), *Rättsfilosofi: samhälle och moral genom tiderna*, Studentlitteratur, Lund 2001
Nino, C.S. (ed.), *Rights*, New York University Press, New York 1992
Nordenson, H., *Über Geometrie und Raumvorstellung*, in *Festskrift tillägnad Axel Hägerström den 6 september 1928*, Filosofiska och juridiska föreningarna i Uppsala, Almqvist & Wiksell, Uppsala 1928, pp. 237–255
Nordin, S., *Den Boströmska skolan och den svenska idealismens fall*, Doxa, Lund 1981
Nordin, S., *Romantikens filosofi. Svensk idealism från Höijer till hegelianerna*, Doxa, Lund 1987
Nordin, S., *Den svenska liberalismens historia*, Timbro, Stockholm 1999
Nordin, S., *Vilhelm Moberg et l'école d'Uppsala dans* Det Gamla riket, in P. Bouquet, P. Voilley, *Droit et littérature dans le contexte suédois*, Flies France, Paris 2000, pp. 49–52
Nordin, S., *Ingmar Hedenius. En filosof och hans tid*, Natur & Kultur, Stockholm 2004
Nordin, S., *Filosofin historia: det västerländska förnuftets äventyr*, Studlitt., Lund 2005
Nyblaeus, A., *Den filosofiska forskningen i Sverige från slutet av adertonde århundradet*, vols. I–IV, Glerup, Lund 1879–1897
Nygård, S., Strang, J., *Mellan idealism och analytisk filosofi: den moderna filosofin i Finland och Sverige 1880–1950*, Atlantis, Stockholm 2006
Ogden, C.K., Richards, I.A., *The Meaning of Meaning* (1923), Kegan, London 1927[2]
Olivecrona, K., *Legal Language and Reality, in Essays in Jurisprudence in Honour of Roscoe Pound*, R.A. Newman (ed.), Bobbs-Merrill, Indianapolis-New York 1962, pp. 151–191
Olivecrona, K., *The Imperative Element in Law*, in «Rutgers Law Review», 1964, vol. 18, pp. 794–810
Olivecrona, K., *Law as Fact*, Steven & sons, London 1971[2]
Olivecrona, K., *Rättsordningen*, LiberLäromedel, Lund 1976
Orfield, L.B., *A Survey of Scandinavian Legal Philosophy*, in «Wisconsin Law Review», 1959, pp. 448–480
Orfield, L.B., *The Growth of Scandinavian Law*, Temple University Publications, Pennsylvania 1953, 2002[2]
Örne, A., *Uppsalafilosofin – reflexioner av en lekman*, in «Tiden», 1940, vol. 3, pp. 167–173
Östlund, D., *A Knower and Friend of Human Beings, Not Machines*, in «Ideas in History», 2007, vol. 2, n. 2, available at http://www.ideasinhistory.org/cms/index.php?page=a-knower-and-friend-of-human-beings#main
Oxenstierna, G., *Sannolikhetens filosofi*, Studentföreningen Verdandis småskrifter, Stockholm-Uppsala 1937
Oxenstierna, G., *Vad är Uppsalafilosofien?*, Bonniers, Stockholm 1938 [ed. org. Studentföreningen Verdandis småskrifter No. 400, Uppsala 1938]
Pattaro, E., *Validità o verificabilità del diritto?*, in «Rivista trimestrale di diritto e procedura civile», 1966, vol. 3, pp. 1006–1056

Pattaro, E., *Diritto, morale e concezione realistica del diritto*, in «Rivista trimestrale di diritto e procedura civile», 1970, 3, pp. 986–999

Peczenik, A., *Den skandinaviska rättsrealismen*, in J. Nergelius (ed.), *Rättsfilosofi: samhälle och moral genom tiderna*, Studentlitteratur, Lund 2001

Petersson, B., *Värdegemenskap – vad är det?*, in G. Bexell (ed.), *Värdegemenskap i ett mångkulturellt samhälle*, Lund University Press, Lund 1998

Petersson, B., *Kritiken av värdenihilismen*, in *Värderingar och faktum. Studier i Hans Larssons moralfilosofi*, Centrum för tillämpad etik vid Linköpingsuniversitet, UniTryck, Linköping 2004, pp. 27–68

Phalén, A., *Kritik av subjektivismen i olika former med särskild hänsyn till transcendentalfilosofien*, Appelberg, Uppsala 1910

Phalén, A., *Om det kvantitativa betraktelsesättet i logiken*, Berling, Uppsala 1911

Phalén, A., *Das Erkenntnisproblem in Hegels Philosophie. Der Erkenntniskritik als Metaphysik*, Berling – Akademiska bokhandeln, Uppsala 1912

Phalén, A., *Beitrag zur Klärung des Begriffs der inneren Erfahrung*, in Uppsala universitets årsskrift, Uppsala 1913

Phalén, A., *Zur Bestimmung des Begriffs des Psychischen*, Berling – Akademiska bokhandeln, Uppsala 1914

Phalén, A., *Ueber die Relativität der Raum - und Zeitbestimmungen*, SKHVSU/Berling, Uppsala 1922

Phalén, A. *et al.*, *Die Philosophie der Gegenwart in Selbstdarstellungen*, Meiner, Leipzig, vol. V, 1924

Poincaré, H., *Dernières pensées*, Flammarion, Paris 1913

Portinaro, P.P., *Il terzo. Una figura del politico*, FrancoAngeli, Milano 2006

Pound, R., *An Introduction to the Philosophy of Law*, Yale University Press, New Haven 1926

Pound, R., *The Call for a Realistic Jurisprudence*, in «Harvard Law Review», 1931, vol. XLIV, pp. 697–711

Putnam, H., *The Collapse of the Fact/Value Dichotomy*, Harvard University Press, Cambridge, MA 2003

Radbruch, G., *Einführung in die Rechtswissenschaft* (1910), Quelle & Meyer, Leipzig 1913

Radbruch, G., *Der Geist des englischen Rechts und die anglo-amerikanische Jurisprudenz: Aufsätze* (1946), H. Scholler (ed.), Lit, Berlin 2006

Rainbolt, G., *The Concept of Rights*, Springer, Dordrecht 2006

Rawls, J., *Review of A. Vilhelm Lundstedt, Legal Thinking Revised*, in «Cornell Law Quarterly», 1958–59, vol. 44, pp. 169–171

Raz, J., *Practical Reason and Norms*, Hutchinson, London 1975

Raz, J., *On the Nature of Rights*, in «Mind», 1984, vol. 93, pp. 194–214

Raz, J., *The Morality of Freedom*, Clarendon, Oxford 1986

Rehm, H., *Allgemeine Staatslehre*, Mohr, Freiburg 1899

Reischle, M., *Werturteile und Glaubensurteile*, Niemeyer, Halle 1900

Rickert, H., *Die Grenzen der naturwissenschaftlichen Begriffsbildung. Eine logische Einleitung in die historischen Wissenschaften*, Mohr, Tübingen 1921

Roochnik, H.L., *Socrates' Use of the Techne-Analogy*, in H.H. Benson (ed.), *Essays on the Philosophy of Socrates*, Oxford University Press, Oxford 1992

Ross, A., *Kritik der sogenannten praktischen Erkenntnis: zugleich Prolegomena zu einer Kritik der Rechtswissenchaft*, Munksgaard, Copenhagen 1933

Ross, A., *Virkelighed og gyldighed i retslaeren: en kritik af den teoretiske retsvidenskabs grundbegreber*, Munksgaard, Copenhagen 1934

Ross, A., *Hvorfor Demokrati?*, Munksgaard, København 1946; Eng. trans. in J.A. Lauwerys (ed.), *Scandinavian Democracy*, Danish Institute/Norwegian Office of Cultural Relations/The Swedish Institute, Copenhagen 1958

Ross, A., *Towards a Realistic Jurisprudence. A Criticism of the Dualism in Law*, Munkgaard, Copenhagen 1946

Ross, A., Koch, H. (eds.), *Nordisk demokrati*, Halvorsen & Larsen, Copenhagen 1949
Ross, A., *On Law and Justice*, Stevens & Sons, London 1958
Ross, A., *Directives and Norms*, Routledge, London 1968
Ross, A., *Skyld, ansvar og straf* (1970), Eng. trans. *On Guilt, Responsibility and Punishment*, Berkeley University Press, Los Angeles 1975
Ryding, E., *Den svenska filosofiens historia*, Natur & Kultur, Stockholm 1959
Salmond, J., *Jurisprudence*, 6th ed., Sweet and Maxwell, London 1920
Saltman, M., *Legal Realism in Cross-cultural Context*, in «International Journal for the Semiotics of Law», 1989, vol. 2, n. 2, pp. 113–128
Satris, S., *The Theory of Value and the Rise of Ethical Emotivism*, in «Journal of the History of Ideas», 1982, vol. 43, n. 1, pp. 109–128
Satris, S., *Ethical Emotivism*, Martinus Nijhoff/Kluwer, Dordrecht 1987
Schauer, F., Wise, V.J., *Legal Positivism as Legal Information*, in «Cornell Law Review», 1996/1997, pp. 1080–1110
Schlick, M., *Positivism and Realism* (Eng. trans. by D. Rynin), in A.J. Ayer (ed.) *Logical Positivism*, Free Press, New York 1959
Schmitt, C., *Politische Theologie. Vier Kapitel zur Lehre der Souveränität* (1922), Eng. trans. *Political Theology*, MIT Press, Cambridge, MA 1985
Schurz, G., *The Is-Ought Problem: An Investigation in Philosophical Logic*, Kluwer, Dordrecht 1997
Searle, J., *How to Derive Ought from Is*, in «Philosophical Review», 1964, vol. 73, pp. 43–58
Segerstedt, T., *Boströms betydelse i svenskt kulturliv*, in «Ord och bild», 1947, anno 56, pp. 425–435
Segerstedt, T., *Den Boströmska filosofin och det svenska samhället*, in «Lychnos», 1977/1978, pp. 1–9
Sjöberg, B., *Den underminerade nihilisten. Sivar Arnér, fransk existentialism och svensk kulturdebatt*, Lund University Press, Lund 1993
Skarin, C., *Björkqvistarne: dikter*, förf:s förlag, Jönköping 1897
Smend, R., *Verfassung und Verfassungslehre*, Duncker-Humblot, München 1928
Smolin, L., *The Trouble with Physics. The Rise of String Theory, the Fall of a Science and What Comes Next*, Mariner, Doughton Mifflin Company Boston-New York 2007
Solomon, R., *In the Spirit of Hegel*, Oxford University Press, Oxford 1983
Spaak, T., *(Review of) Legal Theory (Peter Wahlgren ed. 2000)*, in «Archiv für Rechts- und Sozialphilosophie», 2002, vol. 88, n. 2, pp. 298–304
Spaak, T., *Naturalism in Scandinavian and American Realism: Similarities and Differences*, 25-year Anniversary Uppsala-Minnesota Conference 2008, available at SSRN: http://ssrn.com/abstract=1354154
Stammler, R., *Wirtschaft und Recht nach der Materialistischen Geschichtsauffassung: Eine sozialphilosophische Untersuchung*, Von Veit, Leipzig 1896
Stevenson, Ch.L., *Facts and Values*, Yale University Press, New Haven-London 1963
Strang, J., *Why Nordic Democracy?*, Paper presented at the research seminar at the department of philosophy, Helsinki, October 2006, available at: http://www.helsinki.fi/filosofia/tutkijaseminaari/whynordicdemocracy.pdf
Strang, J., *Theoria and Logical Empiricism*, in Vienna Circle Institute Yearbook 15, Springer, Dordrecht (forthcoming)
Sundell, J.-O., *Vilhelm Lundstedt – A Biographical Sketch*, in «Scandinavian Studies in Law. Perspectives on Jurisprudence. Essays in Honour of Jes Bjarup», n. 48, Jure, Stockholm 2005, pp. 465–478
Tegen, E., *Der antimetaphysische Objektivismus in Uppsala*, in *Actes du congrès international de philosophie scientifique*, VIII, 1936, pp. 38–47; Swedish ed. *Kritisk objektivism*, in «Theoria», 1936, II, pp. 27–57
Timmons, M., *Morality without Foundations: A Defense of Ethical Contextualism*, Oxford University Press, Oxford 1999

Tingsten, H., *Idékritik*, Bonniers, Stockholm 1941

Troeltsch, E., *Die Bedeutung des Protestantismus für die Entstehung der modernen Welt*, Oldenbourg, München-Berlin 1911; Eng. trans. *Protestantism and Progress: A Historical Study of the Relation of Protestantism to the Modern World*, Kessinger Publishing Company, Whitefish, MT 1912

Twining, W., *Talk about Realism*, in «New York University Law Review», 1985, vol. 60, no. 3, pp. 329–384

Tylor, E.B., *Researches into the Early History of Mankind and the Development of Civilisation* (1865), University of Chicago Press, Chicago 1964

Urmson, J., *The Emotive Theory of Ethics*, Hutchinson University Library, London 1968

Vegetti, M., *Techne*, in Plato, *Rep.* (trans. by M. Vegetti), Bibliopolis, Napoli 1998, pp. 193–208

Verdross, A., *Abenländische Rechtsphilosophie; ihre Grundlagen und Hauptprobleme in geschichtlicher Schau*, Springer Verlag, Wien 1958

Villa, V., *Relativismo: un'analisi concettuale*, in «Ragion Pratica», 2007, vol. 1, pp. 55–76

Waldron, J. (ed.), *Theories of Rights*, Oxford University Press, Oxford 1984

Weber, M., *Politik als Beruf* (1918/1919), now in *Gesammelte Politische Schriften*, Johannes Winkelmann (ed.), Mohr, Tübingen 1988

Wedberg, A., *Den logiska strukturen i Boströms filosofi. En studie i klassisk metafysik*, Almqvist & Wiksell, Uppsala 1937

Wedberg, A., *Bertrand Russell's Empiricism*, in *Adolf Phalén. In memoriam*, I. Hedenius (ed.), Almqvist & Wiksell, Stockholm-Uppsala 1937, pp. 345–387

Wellman, C., *A Theory of Rights*, Roman & Allanheld, Totowa, NJ 1985

Wenar, L., *The Nature of Rights*, in «Philosophy and Public Affairs», 2005, vol. 33, no. 3, pp. 223–252

Westermarck, E., *The Origin and Development of Moral Ideas*, Macmillan, London 1906

White, M.G., *Social Thought in America: The Revolt against Formalism*, Viking Press, New York 1949

Wittgenstein, L., *Tractatus logico-philosophicus*, Routledge & Kegan Paul, London 2001

Wright, G.H. von, *Norm and Action. A Logical Enquiry*, Routledge, London 1963

Wright, G.H. von, *Intellectual Autobiography*, in P.A. Schlipp, *The Philosophy of Georg Henrik von Wright*, Open court, La Salle (Ill.) 1989, pp. 1–55

Zamboni, M., *Legal Realisms and the Dilemma of the Relationship of Contemporary Law and Politics*, in P. Wahlgren (eds.), «Scandinavian Studies in Law. Perspectives on Jurisprudence. Essays in Honor of Jes Bjarup», n. 48, Jure, Stockholm 2005, pp. 583–606

Zamboni, M., *Legal Realisms: On Law and Politics*, in «Res Publica: A Journal of Social and Legal Philosophy», 2006, vol. 12, n. 3, pp. 295–317

Zamboni, M, *The Policy of Law. A Legal-Theoretical Framework*, Hart, Oxford 2007

Zeilinger, A., *Einsteins Schleier. Die neue Welt der Quantenphysik*, Verlag C.H. Beck, München 2003.

# Index

Breinigsville, PA USA
08 October 2009
225468BV00005B/23/P

9 789048 128945